Emotional Expression and Health

Emotional Expression and Health covers the major themes that are important for gaining insight into the role emotional expression and inhibition may play in staying healthy or falling ill. Written by leading experts in the field, chapters rely on thorough theory building and empirical research. They focus on:

- How we can measure emotional expression or inhibition and how we can distinguish between their various facets.
- The role of attachment and development of emotional information processing.
- Alexithymia, emotional suppression, deception, emotional disclosure, defensiveness, repression, psychological mindedness, and emotional intelligence and self-efficacy.

This unique approach will be of interest to all those in the fields of health and medical psychology, psychiatry, and behavioral medicine, as well as professionals working with patients in whom emotional expression or inhibition may play a role in a disease's etiology, course, or prognosis.

Ivan Nyklíček is Assistant Professor in the Department of Psychology and Health, Tilburg University, Tilburg, The Netherlands.

Lydia Temoshok is Director of the Behavioral Medicine Program in the Institute of Human Virology, University of Maryland, Baltimore, MD, USA.

Ad Vingerhoets is Professor of Clinical Health Psychology in the Department of Psychology and Health, Tilburg University, Tilburg, The Netherlands.

Emotional Expression and Health

Advances in theory, assessment and clinical applications

Edited by
Ivan Nyklíček, Lydia Temoshok
and Ad Vingerhoets

Brunner-Routledge
Taylor & Francis Group

HOVE AND NEW YORK

First published 2004
by Brunner-Routledge
27 Church Road, Hove, East Sussex BN3 2FA

Simultaneously published in the USA and Canada
by Brunner-Routledge
29 West 35th Street, New York NY 10001

Brunner-Routledge is an imprint of the Taylor & Francis Group

Typeset in Times by Keystroke, Jacaranda Lodge, Wolverhampton
Printed and bound in Great Britain by TJ International Ltd, Padstow, Cornwall
Cover design by Hybert Design

This publication has been produced with paper manufactured to
strict environmental standards with pulp derived from sustainable
forests.

British Library Cataloguing in Publication Data
A catalogue record for this book is available from the British Library

Library of Congress Cataloging-in-Publication Data
Emotional expression and health / edited by Ivan Nyklíček,
Lydia Temoshok, and Ad Vingerhoets.
   p. ; cm.
Includes bibliographical references.
  ISBN 1-58391-843-4 (hbk)
   1. Medicine and psychology. 2. Emotions—Health aspects. 3. Mind and
body. I. Nyklíček, Ivan. II. Temoshok, Lydia. III. Vingerhoets, A. J. J. M.
   [DNLM: 1. Emotions—physiology. 2. Psychophysiology—methods.
3. Affective Symptoms—physiopathology. 4. Psychosomatic
Medicine—methods. WL 103 E535 2004]
  R726.5.E435 2004
   616.08--dc22
                                            2003017408

ISBN 1-58391-843-4 (hbk)

Contents

List of figures

List of tables

List of contributors

Francine Albach, Psychotherapeutic Center The Pionier, Amsterdam, The Netherlands.

Marleen C. Becht, Tilburg University, Tilburg, The Netherlands.

Marrie H.J. Bekker, Tilburg University, Tilburg, The Netherlands.

Bob Bermond, University of Amsterdam, The Netherlands.

Jos F. Brosschot, University of Leiden, The Netherlands.

Lisa D. Butler, Stanford University School of Medicine, Stanford, USA.

Catherine Classen, Stanford University School of Medicine, Stanford, USA.

Randolph R. Cornelius, Vassar College, Poughkeepsie, USA.

Susanna Corsini, University of Louvain at Louvain-la-Neuve, Belgium.

Johan Denollet, Tilburg University, Tilburg, The Netherlands.

Nazanin Derakshan, University of Leeds, UK.

Agneta H. Fischer, University of Amsterdam, The Netherlands.

Charles V. Ford, UAB Neoropsychiatry Clinic, University of Alabama and Birmingham, USA.

Bert Garssen, Helen Dowling Institute, Utrecht, The Netherlands.

Janine Giese-Davis, Stanford University School of Medicine, Stanford, USA.

Melanie A. Greenberg, Alliant University, San Diego, USA.

James J. Gross, Stanford University, Stanford, USA.

Gwénola Herbette, University of Louvain at Louvain-la-Neuve, Belgium.

Jennifer Joss, Stanford University School of Medicine, Stanford, USA.

Elly A. Konijn, Vrije University, Amsterdam, The Netherlands.

Cheryl Koopman, Stanford University School of Medicine, Stanford, USA.

Willem Koops, Utrecht University, Utrecht, The Netherlands.

Stephen J. Lepore, Brooklyn College and The Graduate Center, City University of New York, USA.

Antony S. R. Manstead, University of Amsterdam, The Netherlands.

Iris B. Mauss, Stanford University, Stanford, USA.

Peter Paul Moormann, Leiden University, The Netherlands.

Lynn B. Myers, University College London, UK.

Gary R. Morrow, University of Rochester CC, USA.

Ivan Nyklíček, Tilburg University, Tilburg, The Netherlands.

Bram Orobio de Castro, Utrecht University, Utrecht, The Netherlands.

James W. Pennebaker, The University of Texas at Austin, USA.

Margot Remie, Helen Dowling Institute, Utrecht, The Netherlands.

Albert Reijntjes, Vrije Universiteit, Amsterdam, The Netherlands.

Bernard Rimé, University of Louvain at Louvain-la-Neuve, Belgium.

John Roberts, MCV MBCCOP of Virginia, USA.

Richard Rosenbluth, Northern New Jersey CCOP, USA.

Peter Salovey, Yale University, USA.

Carl Eduard Scheidt, University Clinic Freiburg, Freiburg, Germany.

Janel D. Sexton, California State University at San Bernardino, USA.

David Spiegel, Stanford University School of Medicine, Stanford, USA.

Hedy Stegge, Vrije Universiteit, Amsterdam, The Netherlands.

Suzanne Stougie, Tilburg University, Tilburg, The Netherlands.

Graeme J. Taylor, University of Toronto and Mount Sinai Hospital, Toronto, Canada.

Lydia Temoshok, University of Maryland, Baltimore, USA.

Mark Meerum Terwogt, Vrije Universiteit, Amsterdam and Utrecht University, Utrecht, The Netherlands.

Julian F. Thayer, National Institute on Aging, Baltimore, USA.

Nathalie van Tijen, Vrije Universiteit, Amsterdam, The Netherlands.

Ad Vingerhoets, Tilburg University, Tilburg, The Netherlands.

Elisabeth Waller, University Clinic Freiburg, Freiburg, Germany.

Alison Woolery, University of California, Los Angeles, USA.

Acknowledgments

We would like to gratefully acknowledge the financial support of the Second International Conference on the (Non)Expression of Emotions in Health and Disease, held in October 1999, on the basis of which this volume has been realized. Support was obtained from the Faculty of Social and Behavioral Sciences of Tilburg University, the Dutch Research Institute Psychology and Health, the Dutch Organization for Scientific Research (NOW), and the Royal Dutch Academy of Science (KNAW).

Introduction

*Ivan Nyklíček, Lydia Temoshok
and Ad Vingerhoets*

In popular lay beliefs and western folk psychology the expression of emotions, including crying, is often considered to be beneficial for one's health. Accordingly, inhibition and repression of emotions are believed to result in maladaptive chronic activation of the body and, consequently, ill health. In addition, people are generally convinced that talking about emotional experiences with others is beneficial and facilitates emotional recovery. Freud encouraged patients to remember traumatic events and to re-experience the negative emotions as vividly as possible (Freud, 1915/1957). Although he already had some doubts concerning the efficacy of cathartic therapy and abandoned it, many others in the medical community did not. In the 1940s, there were several examples of publications in which the positive effects of this approach were described. Symonds (1954), for example, concluded in his review of the literature that catharsis was the most frequent cause of success in psychotherapy.

The past decade has witnessed renewed interest in the role of emotional expression and non-expression in health (e.g. Kennedy-Moore & Watson, 1999). An increasing number of studies have been conducted on this theme, both in the tradition of (quasi-)experimental research on general mechanisms (including intervention studies) and in research into individual differences in emotional expression. For instance, a Medline search on "emotional expression" revealed 1,782 hits, of which 1,176 were from the past ten years. For PsycInfo the corresponding figures were 1,419 and 782, respectively, suggesting an even greater increase in interest from the medical community.

Studies on emotional disclosure in relation to health, as developed by the social psychologist James Pennebaker (Pennebaker & Beall, 1986; see also reviews by Pennebaker, 1997; Smyth, 1998), have stimulated research employing the (quasi-)experimental approach. This author introduced a paradigm in which individuals write for some days about traumatic or emotional experiences. The effects of this written self-expression on psychological and physiological functioning, and health, are then examined. In addition, psychophysiologists started studying the immediate effects of expressing or holding back emotions on physiological, in particular cardiovascular, processes (e.g. Brosschot & Thayer, 1998; Gross & Levenson, 1993, 1997; Labott et al., 1990). This research has advanced theoretical thinking in the field of emotional expression rapidly. In Part I of the present volume, some of the central theoretical perspectives related to emotional expression that may be beneficial or detrimental to one's health are discussed.

Part I opens with a chapter by Ford on lying and self-deception. Deceit usually includes either emotional non-expression or expression that is not in agreement with one's inner feelings with the purpose to mislead the other or oneself. It is argued that many forms of deception are actually adaptive and a prerequisite for successful living, in particular for maintaining social relations and one's own psychological and maybe even physical health.

Rimé et al. discuss emotional expression as a part of the larger concept of social sharing. They have conducted several studies on the potential beneficial effects of social sharing on emotional recovery. Contrary to expectations, spontaneously occurring social sharing after traumatic events as well as experimentally induced sharing did not have clear impacts on emotional recovery. However, individual differences in emotional expression did affect emotional recovery in the expected direction. The authors argue that social sharing, including emotional expression, is more important for cognitive restructuring of the traumatic events that took place and for receiving social support than for direct emotional relief.

Greenberg and Lepore discuss the potential mechanisms which may be involved in the beneficial effects of disclosure. They suggest that disclosure helps to tolerate and regulate one's negative emotions by means of emotional habituation, cognitive reappraisal, and validation of emotions. In addition, adjusting one's cognitive schemata to the experienced negative events is claimed to be crucial to well-being and health. In this process, maintaining a positive self-image may play an important mediating role.

The suppression of emotion as a potential etiologic factor relevant for cardiovascular disease is discussed by Mauss and Gross. Based on literature findings, mainly epidemiological studies on long-term health consequences, and on results of their own laboratory experiments on short-term effects of emotional suppression, it is concluded that suppression of negative emotion seems to explain an additional portion of the variance regarding cardiovascular abnormalities, over and above the variance explained by the experience or expression of negative emotion. Additionally, psychophysiological and psychosocial mechanisms are proposed that may be responsible for the putative elevated risk of cardiovascular disease related to emotional suppression.

A discussion of the mechanisms potentially involved in the development of alexithymia and related dysfunctions is the contribution by Moormann et al. They differentiate between two subtypes of alexithymia, which have different relations with other psychiatric conditions, such as conversion, anesthesia, and hysteria. In their Reality Escape Model, it is proposed that all these conditions are different expressions of the same underlying non-feeling state, which may result from traumatic experiences.

Brosschot and Thayer emphasize the potentially important role of worrying, or perseverative thinking, in both mental and physical health. Not only may perseverative thinking, in which negative emotions play an important role, be at the core of many psychopathologies, but it may also be related to physiological dysfunctions, possibly resulting in ill health. In addition to the often hypothesized major role of past or current stressors in the disease process, these authors emphasize the importance of distress resulting from worrying about all possible future stressors. Because perseverative thinking may prolong psychophysiological arousal beyond the experience of a stressor, it may be important for the development of pathophysiological states, such as cardiovascular disease.

In addition to experimental research, a second major tradition within the emotional expression field has been the individual differences approach. There has been a growing interest of psychologists to examine the relationship between individual differences in emotional expression – considering it as a stable personality trait – and health. Non-expression of emotions seems to be a crucial element of many personality features which have been related to health, such as alexithymia (Sifneos, 1973) and defensiveness/ repression (Weinberger *et al.*, 1979). Some of the central individual differences constructs that may be important to health are discussed in Part II.

The first chapter of Part II is by Garssen and Remie. They discuss the conceptual similarities and differences of the various constructs connected with individual differences related to non-expression of emotions, such as repression, defensiveness, self-restraint, and the Type C response pattern. They argue for a division of the emotional non-expression space along the dimensions of social defensiveness and personal defensiveness, which is related to the division into impression management and self-deception. In addition, the Type C coping pattern is described as a multidimensional construct encompassing other elements besides its core of emotional non-expression. Finally, they discuss briefly constructs beyond their definition of emotional non-expression as a habitual tendency, such as self-disclosure, repressed memories, but also alexithymia.

Alexithymia is discussed extensively by Taylor. The emphasis is on the history of the concept, including its conceptual and psychometric development. Nowadays, alexithymia is usually conceptualized as referring to an inability to understand and express verbally one's emotions, together with a cognitive emphasis on external details instead of one's emotions. Alexithymia seems to be independent of other non-expression of emotions concepts, in that it reflects a reduced cognitive *ability* to process emotions, rather than a cognitive *tendency* to inhibit emotions or their expression. Research from the field of cognitive neuroscience, as well as studies regarding its links with both psychiatric and medical disorders, are discussed.

Woolery and Salovey focus on the possible association between emotional intelligence and physical health. Emotional intelligence is a set of competencies including emotional expression, but also the ability to identify, analyze, understand, and regulate one's own and other people's emotions. It is argued that some of the emotional expression related concepts, which have been shown to be associated with better physical health, in fact reflect aspects of emotional intelligence. For instance, emotional intelligence is claimed to be a prerequisite for appropriate emotional disclosure, which has been demonstrated to have beneficial effects on both mental and physical health. Conversely, emotional disclosure will probably enhance self-perceived emotional intelligence. Finally, the authors plead for the use of an ability-based approach for measuring ability concepts such as emotional intelligence, instead of self-report measures, which often may be biased.

Myers and Derakshan provide an overview of the literature and their own experiments regarding the concept of repression, as defined by Weinberger et al. (1979). They present evidence for a discrepancy between the low self-reported distress, on the one hand, and both behavioral signs and elevated physiological arousal indicative of high distress, on the other hand. In addition, methodological issues are considered regarding the problems associated with self-reports of distress and well-being in repressors, since they have a tendency to avoid negative affect. Finally, studies finding links between repression and adverse physical health are discussed.

An old concept from the psychodynamic literature, psychological mindedness, is broadened and its relevance for contemporary health psychology and behavioral medicine is advocated by Denollet and Nyklíček. These authors propose that psychological mindedness, defined as "the intrinsic motivation to be in touch with one's inner feelings and thoughts by monitoring and analyzing them in an adaptive way", may be relevant for one's health. A short measure of the construct is presented, including some preliminary evidence for its validity (being unrelated to a measure of repression). The extent to which this construct overlaps with related constructs, such as emotional intelligence and especially (inversely) the externally oriented thinking facet of alexithymia, should be considered in future research.

Part II concludes with a chapter on the psychometric properties of a new measure of emotional self-efficacy for cancer patients: the Stanford Emotional Self-efficacy Scale – Cancer (SESES-C; by Giesse-Davis and Spiegel). This scale consists of three facets: (i) communicating emotions, (ii) remaining focused in the moment, and (iii) confronting death and dying issues. Results indicate adequate values of psychometric indices of reliability and validity of the scale.

Emotional expression researchers have generally neglected developmental issues, which nevertheless may be crucial determinants of emotional expression later in life. Part III is devoted to the developmental perspective on the expression of emotions. Specifically, the roles of attachment representation, the development of children's conceptions of emotional regulation, and emotional information processing in children showing problem behaviors are discussed.

Part III starts with a contribution by Scheidt and Waller, who emphasize the role of attachment representation in adequate affect regulation. Evidence is presented for the link between insecure attachment types and a narrowed spectrum of affect regulation, especially regarding the expression of negative emotions. In addition, findings are discussed regarding the high prevalence of insecure attachment styles in patients with psychopathology and the association between insecure attachment styles and elevated physiological reactivity to stressors, which is considered a risk factor for systemic disease.

Children's conceptions of the emotion process are the focus of the chapter by Stegge *et al*. In a number of studies, these authors have examined the development of ideas children have concerning strategies used for and strategies thought to be effective in emotion regulation, especially improving one's mood. These strategies include behavioral and mental avoidance, behavioral and mental confrontation, and the use of reappraisals. Results indicate that these conceptions normally develop along a certain path, which may be important for acquiring an effective and healthy emotion regulation repertoire while growing up.

Orobio de Castro *et al*.'s chapter is devoted to the role of emotional information processing in disruptive behavior in children. Empirical findings are presented, which show that boys with disruptive behavior problems have deviant representations of one's own and other people's emotions, and possess less adaptive emotion regulation strategies. A model is presented incorporating the various information processing factors relevant for emotion regulation at the various stages leading to expression or non-expression of emotion in children with disruptive behavior. These factors may play a causal role in disruptive behavior. Interventions aimed at changing emotional information processing may lead to less problem behavior in these children.

In the last part of the present volume (IV), a specific form of emotional expression (crying) is discussed, as well as issues related to emotional expression in specific groups. Current theoretical models of crying are described by Stougie *et al*. These authors further try to identify possible functions of crying. In addition, empirical findings addressing the extent to which crying enhances mood and health or is rather associated with more unfavorable outcomes are discussed extensively. It is attempted to reconcile the frequent discrepancies regarding the effects of crying on well-being, which have been found in research using different methodological approaches.

Fischer *et al*. discuss gender differences in crying behavior, including factors that may explain the larger crying proneness in women. These are mechanisms related to biological (endocrine), psychological (appraisal of the situation), social, and cultural factors. It is concluded that feelings of powerlessness, resulting from an interplay of these potentially relevant factors, may be key factors for the gender differences in crying. In addition, these authors briefly discuss whether these differences in crying are related to sex differences in health.

The use of actors in psychophysiological studies on emotion and emotional expression is challenged in the chapter by Konijn. In a series of studies, she has examined the extent to which professional actors from various acting traditions experience the emotions they portray. She found that even actors from the involvement tradition experience emotions that are related to their performance task rather than to the emotions of their characters. Also taking into account findings from other literature, it is concluded that results regarding psychophysiological differentiation of emotions obtained in studies using actors portraying certain emotions may not be valid regarding the assumption that the physiological concomitants found are indeed associated with the portrayal emotions.

In the final chapter, Sexton and Pennebaker discuss the effects of emotional non-expression and disclosure in socially stigmatized groups. While non-expression seems to have unfavorable effects on self-esteem and health outcomes, disclosure enhances one's personal narrative and identity, which may have a protective effect against the distress of being stigmatized.

From this overview of topics discussed in this volume, one may conclude that the question of the role of emotional expression and non-expression in health is addressed from diverse angles and research traditions, the combination of which in one volume is unique. In addition, it underscores the complex nature of emotional expression, in which many factors play a role. As argued by Kennedy-Moore and Watson (1999), emotional (non-)expression is the outcome of a complex cognitive–decisional process taking place as several subsequent stages. Internal (cognitive–affective) and external (the social environment) factors may influence this process at every stage, indicating that the end outcome of expression or non-expression may differ qualitatively, depending on the stage of the process and the factors that led to expression or non-expression. In addition, these qualitatively different ways of expression and non-expression may be associated with different effects on well-being and health. It is a challenge for future researchers and clinicians to get insight into these processes and the accompanying factors associated with each stage of the process leading to either expression or inhibition of emotion, as well as into the putatively different links with well-being and health.

References

Brosschot, J.F. & Thayer, J.F. (1998). Anger inhibition, cardiovascular recovery, and vagal function: a model of the links between hostility and cardiovascular disease. *Annals of Behavioral Medicine*, **20**, 326–332.

Freud, S. (1915/1957). Repression and the unconscious. In J. Strachney (ed. and transl.), *The standard edition of the complete psychological works of Sigmund Freud*, Vol. 14 (pp. 141–195). London: Hogarth Press.

Gross, J.J. & Levenson, R.W. (1993). Emotional suppression: physiology, self-report, and expressive behavior. *Journal of Personality and Social Psychology*, **64**, 970–986.

Gross, J.J. & Levenson, R.W. (1997). Hiding feelings: the acute effects of inhibiting negative and positive emotion. *Journal of Abnormal Psychology*, **106**, 95–103.

Kennedy-Moore, E. & Watson, J.C. (1999). *Expressing emotion. Myths, realities, and therapeutic strategies*. New York: Guilford Press.

Labott, S.M., Ahleman, S., Wolever, M.E., & Martin, R.B. (1990). The physiological and psychological effects of the expression and inhibition of emotion. *Behavioral Medicine*, **16**, 182–189.

Pennebaker, J.W. (1997). Health effects of the expression (and non-expression) of emotions through writing. In A.J.J.M. Vingerhoets, F.J. Van Bussel, & A.J.W. Boelhouwer (eds), *The (non)expression of emotions in health and disease* (pp. 267–278). Tilburg, Netherlands: Tilburg University Press.

Pennebaker, J.W. & Beall, S.K. (1986). Putting stress into words: health, linguistics, and therapeutic implications. *Journal of Abnormal Psychology*, **95**, 274–281.

Sifneos, P.E. (1973). The prevalence of "alexithymic" characteristics in psychosomatic patients. *Psychotherapy and Psychosomatics*, **22**, 255–262.

Smyth, J.M. (1998). Written emotional expression: effect sizes, outcome types, and moderating variables. *Journal of Clinical and Consulting Psychology*, **66**, 174–184.

Symonds, P.M. (1954). A comprehensive theory of psychotherapy. *American Journal of Orthopsychiatry*, **24**, 697–714.

Weinberger, D.A., Schwartz, G.E., & Davidson, R.J. (1979). Low-anxious, high-anxious, and repressive coping styles: psychometric patterns and behavioral and physiological responses to stress. *Journal of Abnormal Psychology*, **88**, 369–380.

Part I

Theoretical perspectives

Chapter 1

Lying and self-deception in health and disease

Charles V. Ford

Introduction

Deceit and the need to detect deception are prevalent in the animal kingdom, and reaches their highest evolutionary development in *Homo sapiens*. Deceit is an intricate part of human communication involving, via a dynamic process, self-deception and the deception of others. When used in "normal" ways, we are often unaware of our deceptive communications to others. Deceit serves to promote social support and helps to sustain mental and physical health. However, blatant (pathological) forms of deceit may, to the contrary, be destructive to the self and others. The sophisticated person uses deceit in a subtle manner while, in contrast, crude and pathologic deceit is frequently associated with neurocognitive dysfunction or distorted developmental processes.

The language of lying

"Man was given a tongue with which to speak and words to hide his thoughts." This Hungarian proverb indicates the ubiquity of deceptive communications. In fact, the development of different languages and symbolic communication has been hypothesized as being the result of the need for social groups to maintain cohesion and secrecy (Steiner, 1975). The ways in which man can deceive are almost endless. Included are the words we speak, or don't speak, as well as our non-verbal channels of communication. Further, colloquialisms, words, and non-verbal communication are often culture specific. That which may be considered a polite communication in one culture may be considered a lie in another. Saying "No" in some cultures is considered unacceptably rude and therefore "Yes" does not always necessarily mean yes.

The following brief descriptions of various forms of deceit will serve to lay a foundation for topics considered in this communication.

Definition

Lying, by definition (in American dictionaries), involves the deliberate mis-statement of information believed by the protagonist to be false and with the intent to deceive. This definition involves not only the content of a communication but also its intent. It is interesting and important to note that one can speak "the truth" with the intent to deceive, thereby leading the "target" to a false belief. This is commonly done by providing only half the truth, leading the intended target of the communication to a false assumption. For example, a person late to an appointment may say that there was an automobile accident that had tied up traffic. The statement itself may be factually true but "in truth" the automobile accident had nothing to do with the person's tardiness. The person who hears the proffered excuse may assume, however, that the tardiness was due to the accident and not the fault of the late person.

Euphemisms

Lies, lying and accusations about lying are highly charged emotional words. The statement "you are a liar" can be the basis of a feud or end a friendship forever. In an effort to avoid such highly emotionally charged words, the English language has evolved a number of euphemisms that serve to communicate the idea of deceit yet fall short of calling someone a "liar". It has been reported that the German language contains even more euphemisms than the English language (Shibles, 1985).

Non-verbal deceit

Words are only one channel of communication between persons. Other forms of communication include non-verbal messages that are both symbolic gestures (and often very culturally determined) and expressions of emotion (e.g. anger), skepticism, affection, or of one's somatic state (e.g. pain) (DePaulo, 1988). Non-verbal communications include gestures, posture, bodily movements and inflections of voice and other sounds (e.g. sighs, groans, and changes in pitch) (Ekman & Friesen, 1969; Johnson *et al.*, 1975).

Levels of deceit

In terms of the sophistication of the attempt to deceive another person, are at least four separate levels of deceit have been described (Leekam, 1992; Ford, 1996). Ordinarily as children mature they develop the capacity to deceive at the third level; highly skilled liars may achieve the fourth level. These levels are as follows.

1   A simple false statement without any capacity to determine what another person may know or divine about the situation. For example, a small child with cookie crumbs smeared all over his/her face may make a statement that he/she did not eat the cookies.
2   The liar takes into account that the target of a lie may have some information by which the veracity of the statement can be judged. Thus one will not say

something false when the target of the lie can readily detect that it is not true. For example, at level two a liar would not say that it is raining outside knowing that the recipient of the communication can quickly look outside to determine the weather.

3   This level of lying involves the capacity, while making a false statement, to read the non-verbal expressions of the recipient of the lie and, depending on the degree of credulity perceived, make alterations in the statements being presented. For example, a student who is making an excuse about why homework has not been completed may change the story mid-stream if the teacher appears to be non-convinced.

4   Lying at this level, the highest and most skillful form of deceit, involves the capacity of the liar to dissociate his or her non-verbal communications from the words being spoken in such a manner as to provide mixed messages. For example, a politician may praise another person while communicating non-verbally that in truth he has no respect for that individual. As a result, he can say "honestly" that he has said nothing except nice things when in truth the communications have been damning.

Self-deception

Terminology around the issue of self-deception has been the subject of philosophical treatises. In my opinion, and that of at least some philosophers, self-deception can be described in terms of the various "ego defense mechanisms" (Hamlyn, 1985). In labeling these forms of self-deception one is describing phenomology rather than providing explanations. We can speculate that many, if not all, of these defense mechanisms have neurophysiological mechanisms, which will ultimately be better understood. These mechanisms by which self-deception is initiated and/or maintained include, among others, denial, projection, rationalization, isolation, dissociation and repression.

Socio-biology of deceit

Prevalence in animal kingdom

Deceit is prevalent throughout the animal kingdom. In a world of eat-or-be-eaten, deceit may be the determining factor as to whether one has a meal in order to live another day, and whether one avoids being a meal in order to live another day. Camouflage is a passive form of deception. Active forms of deception include defensive behaviors such as piloerection in order to appear larger or more formidable, or the emission of false signals to attract would-be sexual partners of another species who instead become a meal (Lloyd, 1986; Lewin, 1987; Stowe et al., 1995). Deceitful behaviors that are apparently willful have been described in dogs, primates, and elephants (deWaal, 1986; Morris, 1986; Mills, 1997). From this we can see that the deceitfulness of man has a rich phylogenetic legacy.

Driving force in the evolution of the human brain

It has been hypothesized by Robert Trivers (1971) that the evolution of the human brain was propelled by an "arms race" influenced by the selective advantages of effective deception and, as the counterpoint, the capacity to detect deception by others. Trivers (1985) has also hypothesized that deception is most effective when the deceiver also believes the false message being delivered. Therefore, self-deception has evolved simultaneously with deception of others. One example is the infatuated person who makes statements of love to intended sexual partners. Deceit can be used to create power or to compete for sexual (reproductive) opportunities. Similarly, the capacity to detect such manipulative ploys is to the advantage of the would-be victim.

Irrespective of whether deceit was the driving force in the evolution of the human brain, there can be little question that it is the neo-cortex of the pre-frontal cerebral lobes that functions as the decoder and modulator of the subtleties of social interaction. Further, this wondrous piece of computing equipment requires an extensive period of time for development and maturation. Young humans require extensive parental investment and prolonged protection prior to the achievement of independence. We can postulate from this need for protection during maturation the development of families and extended families. Further, for groups to remain cohesive, there must be commitment; some individuals sacrifice for the whole (altruism) and loyalty one to another. I propose that the need to create and maintain group cohesion, in order to provide protection for the young and for effective collecting and conservation of food resources, is responsible for the codification of moral values. Accurate non-deceptive communications *within* the group are essential for the group to function effectively. Deceptive communications to *other* competing groups may also be effective ways of preserving and extending the power of a social group. Thus, in a hierarchy of moral values, loyalty ranks higher than truthfulness (in the abstract). One example of this principle is the sociological study of a gang in a large city, in which it was found that lying to fellow gang members was condemned, but lying to outsiders was praised (Miller *et al.*, 1961).

Research by DePaulo and Kashy (1998) can be interpreted in support of the above postulate. They found that "normal" persons lied frequently, but more often to persons with whom they did not have a close relationship (56–77 percent of all social interactions!) than to persons with whom they had very close relationships such as a spouse or lover (10 percent of social interactions). Moreover, lies to a close acquaintance were more likely to be altruistic (e.g. to protect the other's self-esteem) than lies to strangers, which were likely to serve self-enhancement. Subjects also reported more distress about lying to persons close to them.

Deceit as a normal developmental skill

Lying is often condemned as a "naughty" behavior in children and regarded as reflecting moral deficits in adults. "In truth", lying is a developmental skill, which is necessary for the preservation of the sense of self, the maintenance of individual autonomy, and the capacity to relate well with other persons. People whom we call "liars" or "pathological liars" are generally unsuccessful liars, while those who are more successful and skillful are not identified as such. To provide an analogy, the prisons are full of unsuccessful criminals; successful liars become chief executive officers of health insurance companies. The following discussion outlines the development of deceit and how it is incorporated as a healthy part of one's coping mechanisms and interpersonal skills.

Defensive lies

The first lies that children tell are of denial or defensive, in order to protect one from disapproval or punishment. They begin to appear at approximately age two and consist of statements such as "I didn't do it" or disclaimers of knowledge as to how something may have happened. These lies are fairly primitive and it does not require much skill to detect them as untruthful statements. In addition to possible incriminating evidence, the child has little control over the non-verbal expressions that give him away. Some children will also lie in a playful or humorous way to frustrate parents or to provide entertainment; for example, deliberately misnaming an animal.

Wish fulfillment lies

Young children have confusion as to wishes, fantasy, and reality. They may tell stories that represent that which they want, with perhaps the belief that what they say will become real. For example, the daughter of divorced parents told her father that she wanted to have a television set in her bedroom just as she had at her mother's house. When confronted gently with the idea that what she was saying was that she really wanted a television at her mother's house (which she did not have) and also one at her father's house, she acknowledged that indeed this was the situation. Other children may tell false stories of planned trips to Disneyland or having relatives who are famous football players or other tales that would increase their sense of self-importance or personal wishes for gratification. Such stories have a soothing function and have similarity to the daydreams of adolescents and adults.

Lies to establish autonomy

Victor Tausk (1933), a psychoanalytic pioneer, postulated that lying is an essential component of differentiating one's self from the mother. Young children have the universal belief that the parents, particularly the mother, can read their minds. It is only through successful lies that children can establish that they have minds of their own which are private and separate from those of the parents. Characteristically these lies start at age four to five. Lies of this type are also prominent during adolescence when the adolescent, in order to effect separation, must make the parents unaware of his/her behaviors, thoughts, and feelings (Goldberg, 1973). This need for autonomy occurs particularly in the sexual realm and other excursions into that which is regarded as adult behavior.

Pretense/impression management

The young child is unaware of how his or her demeanor and emotions are signaled to other persons. Such information can be used by others for manipulative purposes and the person who does not learn the skill of keeping one's emotions secret is often prey to the unscrupulous. Thus, as a social skill, and necessary defense mechanism, the child is progressively taught and learns to present a face to the world that is not necessarily accurate of the internal self (Saarni & von Salisch, 1993). This is called pretense (or impression management) and although this word is sometimes used derogatorily it is, in fact, a necessary developmental skill. One example of pretense is that of learning how to control one's emotions in order not to make another person uncomfortable, such as how to appear gracious and thankful for an unwanted gift or invitation. Small children, when given an inappropriate gift, will immediately voice their displeasure. Older children, normally beginning at about age eight to nine, are able to disguise their disappointment or unhappiness and feign pleasure and/or gratitude. An example is when a grandmother provides a gift that would be more appropriate for much younger children. Similarly, students and employees learn to disguise feelings of dislike, displeasure, or anger toward teachers and employers. Children learn how not to act hurt or vulnerable when teased by their classmates. Thus, healthy and effective functioning in society includes the ability to disguise one's true emotional state to others and to feign appropriate emotions and attitudes.

Lies of loyalty

Children are told, often beginning in early childhood, that there "is nothing worse than a liar". Simultaneously, and particularly as they start school, they are also told "there is nothing worse than a traitor" (or "fink" in the vernacular). These two edicts set up one of the first ethical dilemmas for children. Almost inevitably a child will be asked to identify which of his or her siblings and/or classmates was responsible for some type of misbehavior. One can respond by lying, "I don't know", or by betraying a friend. Students quickly learn that it is far better to be punished for lying than to be socially ostracized for disloyalty. This type of lying then extends throughout life and includes such behaviors as the provision of incomplete or false letters of recommendation, lies to cover absences or tardiness for fellow employees, and so forth.

Altruistic lies

With increasing maturity, the child learns that at times the truth can be hurtful, not only to oneself but to others (Goldberg, 1973). There is an increasing sensitivity to the feelings and sensibilities of others. To quote Vasek (1986), "The skills required in deception are also used in being compassionate and coordinating our actions with those of others and without them society might not exist." One may engage in "white lies", flattery, or outright deceit in efforts to make other people feel better (Satran, 1993). White lies have been called "the lubricants of polite society" and all of us are guilty of providing thanks and compliments for something we, in truth, did not enjoy; for example, a wretched meal at a friend's home. For example, we may superficially agree with another person's point of view rather than cause pain or confrontation. As reported by DePaulo and colleagues, we often say supportive things we do not believe in our attempts to make people feel better about themselves (DePaulo *et al.*, 1996; DePaulo & Bell, 1996).

Other altruistic lies may be to protect fellow human beings even at the risk of personal safety; for example, the Dutch people who helped hide Jews during the Second World War and who lied about knowledge of their whereabouts.

Altruistic lies are also exemplified by physicians' statements to sick/dying patients. Which one of us has not tried to provide unwarranted optimism or minimize complications for someone suffering from an agonizing terminal illness?

Lies to promote self-esteem

As each of us mature, we develop a sense of personal identity. A part of that identity is the "personal myth" (Green, 1991). This myth is composed of our views of ourselves as competent effective people (or sometimes as victims) who have persevered against adversity. We tend to minimize our faults, exaggerate our accomplishments, and see ourselves in a generally favorable light. This positive view helps sustain us through difficult times and provides an outside face to the world of competence and geniality. Paulhus (1998) found that self-enhancement and self-promotion are intrapsychically adaptive in regard to facilitating a positive view of oneself. Individuals with more of these characteristics make good first impressions, appearing to be agreeable, well adjusted and competent. With increased contact, however, the initial impression deteriorates and such persons are perceived more negatively.

Deception and self-deception in health and disease

Lying and self-deception, as detailed above, are pervasive throughout life. In fact, DePaulo *et al.* (1996) have found that college students lie at least twice a day and community subjects once a day. This constitutes a lie at a rate between 25 and 50 percent of all social interactions that last ten minutes or longer.

We should not be surprised then to find that lying is prevalent in medicine for both patients and physicians (Sobel, 1996).

Physicians

Physicians lie about their qualifications in attempts to compete for prestigious training positions, and/or their interest in such positions with the hope of being favorably ranked (Boudreaux, 1992; Sekas & Hutson, 1995; Young, 1997), medical students cheat on examinations (Anderson & Obenshain, 1994) and medical faculty may engage in research fraud (Miller & Hersen, 1992). Lying for the benefit of patients may occur in order to protect a patient's secret (e.g. a venereal disease) or to obtain additional insurance benefits for patients of limited financial means (Novack et al., 1989). They may also lie about treatments in an attempt to establish an accurate diagnosis – e.g. pseudo-seizures from genuine epilepsy (Howe, 1997).

In a possibly more positive light, physicians and nurses, in their efforts to make patients more comfortable, to sustain hope and promote optimism, may use deceitful tactics. This is done by "bending the truth" through the provision of incomplete information, silence, minimization of problems or prognosis or, at times, outright lies (Tuckett, 1998). The unmitigated truth may be brutal and sadistic (Lear, 1993). Further, the effective physician/nurse has learned to maintain the pretense (impression) of competence, confidence, and equanimity. Such a demeanor reassures patients, reduces anxiety, and facilitates positive placebo responses. A flustered, fumbling physician is not an effective healer irrespective of his/her extent of medical knowledge. The skillful provision of these types of deceit may be a component of good medical care in order to facilitate patient's beneficial use of self-deception and self-enhancement.

Patients

Patients deceive both through overt and conscious ways and via self-deception/self-enhancement to make things more positive than they really are. They may lie to avoid embarrassment or criticism or self-deceive in order to preserve optimism.

Overt lying is common in patients with substance abuse problems, smoking or high-risk sexual behavior (Ford, 1996). Lying is also a frequent occurrence with the non-compliant patient. For example, a group of asthmatics were given instructions to use their inhalers four times a day (Rand et al., 1992). A microchip installed into the inhaler, unbeknown to the patients, recorded actual use. The large majority of patients falsely reported that they used the inhaler more than they actually did. Some patients actually activated it repetitively before return visits in order that it would appear that they were using it per instructions. Similarly, many subjects of a group of diabetics who were instructed to keep log books of their blood glucose levels used meters that had a secretly installed microchip which recorded date, time, and blood glucose each time it was used. It was found that over-reporting, or the addition of phantom readings, occurred about 40 percent of the time and 26 percent of logbook readings did not correspond with the actual readings (Mazze *et al.*, 1984). In a study of obese subjects, it was determined that, as a group, they under-reported actual food intake by 47 percent and over-reported physical activity by 51 percent (Lichtman *et al.*, 1992).

Knowledge of false information by a patient may be very important in patient care management, but of even greater importance is the role of self-deception/self-enhancement. Most people have "positive illusions" by which they maintain a better view of themselves than would be supported by reality. We see ourselves as better than others, in more control of our lives than is true, and have optimistic views of our capabilities to weather adversity including physical disease (Russel, 1993; Taylor & Armor, 1996). These characteristics of self-deception are so prevalent, and have been confirmed so repetitively by various investigators, that we must regard them as normal. Self-deception (cognitive distortions) and self-enhancement (our deceptive presentations of ourselves to others) are closely tied to self-esteem and a sense of well-being (Taylor & Brown, 1988; Taylor & Armor, 1996; Hoorens, 1995). Further, it has been proposed by Lane and colleagues and others that self-deception may help protect against mental illness (Sackheim & Gur, 1979; Sackheim & Wegner, 1986; Lane *et al.*, 1990). Several investigators have found that depressed persons have a more realistic view of themselves and their control over life events than do normal people (Alloy & Abramson, 1979, 1982; Lewinsohn *et al.*, 1980). It appears that mental health is associated with the bias of seeing oneself with positive illusions, or put differently, viewing the world through rose-tinted glasses.

The relationship of self-deception and adjustment to physical disease has been investigated through numerous studies. In general, the term used to describe such self-deception has been "denial" and the following discussion will use this term in a generic manner that includes the use of various other related ego defense mechanisms. Varying research findings may largely reflect differing operational definitions of these psychological mechanisms (Goldbeck, 1997).

Most investigations have found that denial facilitates acute adjustment to severe illness and is often associated with lower morbidity/morality and increases psychological well-being (Goldbeck, 1997; Taylor & Armor, 1996). For example, high deniers with coronary heart disease hospitalized for cardiac surgery spend fewer days in intensive care, have fewer signs of cardiac dysfunction during hospitalization, and have better psychologic adjustment during the first few months of their convalescence (Levine *et al.*, 1987; Folks *et al.*, 1988). Findings at one year may be more ominous in that high deniers may do more poorly, presumably related to decreased compliance with medical treatment (Levine *et al.*, 1987). Related to this general concept of denial is that positive illusions about the capacity to control one's disease process are related to a sense of psychological well-being (Taylor & Armor, 1996). Such optimism may even influence the underlying disease process itself by modifying immune mechanisms in a positive direction (Segerstrom *et al.*, 1998).

The descriptions of self-deception (denial) provided above should be regarded as that which is characteristic of normality. Further, the use of such mechanisms may have both positive and negative aspects. Greater extremes of self-deception are maladaptive; for example, failing to acknowledge signs or symptoms of disease at stages at which it can be treated or to believe that one is immune from the ill effects of smoking or risky sexual behavior. For most people their degree of self-deception/self-enhancement is kept within acceptable limits by the capacity to respond to feedback from other persons and the environment. Further, there may be "time-outs" in which decision making is facilitated by reality-based considerations (Taylor & Armor, 1996).

It seems ironic that one of the principles of psychoanalysis is that mental health is associated with greater self-awareness and that the purpose of psychotherapy is to provide greater knowledge and understanding of the unconscious portions of our minds. The findings above suggest that the opposite may be more beneficial and increased introspection is not desirable. To function as a healthy mature adult involves the capacity to maintain self-esteem through effective defensive operations that can be best described as self-deceptive, and the presentation to the world of the pretense of optimism and confidence. Dysphoria, including depression, results when these forms of deceit break down.

Pathological forms of deceit

The preceding discussion of deceit has focused on variations of normal processes. Deceit can become so predominant in a person's life as to be the entire focus of being and destructive to the individual liar himself or herself. Included are various forms of impostureship and those who make a career out of simulated disease. Many other non-medical forms of deceit are also destructive to society, such as various forms of fraud and false and misleading advertising.

Among the various categories of pathological forms of deceit that become a focus of attention in psychiatric and medical settings are the following.

Habitual lying

Some persons lie repetitively even when the truth would serve them better. They lie about things that apparently make little difference to them in terms of personal gain, and often when the false information they provide to another person has little significance. Habitual (compulsive) liars differ from those with pseudologia fantastica (see below) in that the former lie repetitively but do not provide grandiose, fantastic or largely fabricated stories about themselves. They are not necessarily sociopathic although some antisocial behaviors may be mixed in among their various prevarications. As a general rule, compulsive liars are preoccupied with issues of autonomy and may also demonstrate oppositional behaviors. In their efforts to maintain their personal sense of self they withhold information about themselves for fear that any disclosures would represent intrusions upon their autonomy. For example, a husband when questioned as to why he was late coming home from work might say that he stopped at the drug store when in truth he stopped at the library. These persons frequently have troubled interpersonal relationships because of their inabilities to initiate or maintain genuine intimacy in the face of their pervasive deceit and their need to maintain rigid interpersonal boundaries. In clinical settings they are most frequently seen by marital therapists in response to complaints by troubled spouses. Because of its effect on interpersonal relationships, habitual lying becomes ultimately destructive to the individual himself or herself. Habitual liars were usually raised in families in which there was little warmth, affection and unconditional acceptance of the child. Instead these families were characterized by authoritarianism, performance-oriented approval, and rigid controls that prevented the development of a mature differentiated individual.

Pseudologia fantastica

Pseudologues engage in a fascinating phenomenon in which they not only prevaricate but tell stories that have a slightly fantastic quality to them. The stories are not so fantastic that they immediately create suspicion, but they do have the quality of making an individual special or unique. For example, an pseudologue may talk about graduating from a prestigious university, of athletic exploits, of knowing important persons, or of having unusual adventures. One patient, previously reported by me (Ford, 1973), told tales (which were originally believable) of being an official in the World Health Organization with involvement in rescuing orphaned children from war zone areas. She also talked of knowing a variety of nationally known people and receiving awards for her humanitarian efforts. In fact, she was a middle-class woman who had never been out of her neighborhood except to go to the hospital. Persons with pseudologia fantastica, at best, have marginal social adjustment. They may complete school and be employed, but at times of stress they tend to decompensate and display a variety of somatizing disorders. Of importance to note, most persons with pseudologia fantastica are the products of dysfunctional families of origin and/or demonstrate evidence of cerebral dysfunction (especially deficits in non-dominant hemispheric functioning) and/or learning disabilities (King & Ford, 1988; Pancratz & Lezak, 1987). Pseudologia fantastica is apparently the result of efforts to increase self-esteem but is also related to a failure in the ability to regulate thinking and separate fantasy from one's verbalizations.

Pathological denial

Persons with normal development, as noted above, have the capacity to selectively remember events that are positive and to minimize one's failings. However some persons use self-deception to an extreme and pathological extent. These persons may deny reality when it stares them in the face and they continue to fail to take appropriate action and/or persist with self-injurious behaviors. For example, I have seen physicians ignore their own symptoms of ischemic heart disease; the result of which was sudden death. Patients may continue to drink ethanol in the presence of hepatitis or smoke cigarettes while receiving oxygen for emphysema. One woman whom I saw in consultation had denied the presence of her orange-size breast tumor until it became ulcerated and its malodorous discharge necessitated her family seeking medical care for her. Persons with addictive problems are characterized by denial of the extent of their problems and also pervasive lying in their attempts to hide the addiction from self and others.

Somatizing disorders

Although most people do not generally consider the somatizing disorders to be forms of deception, in fact they are. They represent deceptive non-verbal behaviors that imply disease when there is no disease or it is grossly exaggerated. What differentiates the somatizing disorders from other forms of abnormal illness behavior (see below) is the degree of *self-deception* involved. Although there is considerable overlap among the somatoform disorders, each will be briefly and separately considered.

Conversion symptoms

Conversion symptoms are among the most ancient of all described medical conditions. The person with a conversion disorder demonstrates an apparent lack of function in a sensory or motor function that implies the presence of underlying and generally disabling neurologic disease. These pseudoneurologic symptoms have, in recent years, been considered to be forms of non-verbal communication that are utilized when more explicit verbal communication is blocked for any reason. Among the reasons that verbal communication may be impaired are: low intelligence, underlying central neurologic disease, poor education and lack of psychologic sophistication, and social situations in which a direct expression of distress is forbidden (e.g. ongoing sexual abuse of a teenage girl by a family member) (Ford & Folks, 1985). Although deception (e.g. the false appearance of disease) is involved, the conversion symptom can also be regarded as a coping mechanism that serves to rescue a person from an intolerable situation.

Somatization disorder

Somatization disorder describes people who demonstrate repetitive use of somatic symptoms, including pain and conversion symptoms, to obtain medical care and to seek the benefits of the sick role. Similar to conversion, there is no underlying organic disease or there is gross exaggeration of any disease process present. Symptoms communicate a deceptive message of disease to others and, similar to conversion, the patient is self-deceptive concerning the origin of symptoms. Most patients with somatization disorder are comorbid for another Axis I or Axis II psychiatric disorder and substance abuse is also common. Etiologic factors believed to be important in the development of somatization disorder include a dysfunctional family of origin, overwhelming social stressors (e.g. low socioeconomic status, poor education, single parent status, abusive relationships) and cerebral dysfunction (Ford, 1983). Somatization disorder can be viewed as a coping mechanism; using the sick role as a way to avoid or minimize that which is regarded as overwhelming life responsibilities.

Pain disorder

Pain disorder involves the experience and communication of the pain with the seeking of medical care. The pain cannot be explained by known physiological/ pathological processes and is sufficiently severe to cause impairment/disability. It is of importance to note that chronic and relatively severe pain is fairly prevalent among the general population and only a subset of these persons repetitively seek treatment for their pain and, in essence, make a career out of pain (Ford, 1995). The experience of pain can be self-deceptive and/or overtly deliberately deceitful. Chronic pain (e.g. low back pain) is one of the most common reasons given for disability and large numbers of persons receive disability benefits based on their supposed inability to work secondary to pain. A complaint of pain can be used to obtain analgesic medications including opiates and other controlled substances. The complaint of pain is a frequent excuse or rationalization for failure to assume a variety of adult activities including sexual behavior. Pain is a subjective symptom; no one knows exactly what another person is feeling and, therefore, it is easy to deceive about that which one is experiencing. Further, one can deceive by using non-verbal communications, including grimacing, awkward movements, and posturing to imply the presence of pain. In a study of pain clinic patients who were involved in litigation, covert surveillance determined that 20 percent of them were overt malingerers (Kay & Morris-Jones, 1998). Psychologic investigations of pain disorder patients discloses that many, but by no means all, have backgrounds of childhood abuse (Blumer & Heilbronn, 1981).

Malingering

Malingering is the deliberate production, feigning, or exaggeration of a physical symptom in order to obtain a discernible external incentive. Examples of malingering involve feigning of a physical illness to avoid military conscription, simulating psychiatric illness to avoid punishment for criminal activity, or the feigning or production of physical illness in an effort to obtain the award of money in a lawsuit and/or disability benefits. Because malingering is in essence an accusation of misbehavior, most physicians are loath to append this label to their patients. As a result, the true incidence of malingering is unknown, but is certainly much higher than would be recognized by a review of medical records. Physicians are not detectives and, therefore, the information necessary to detect the presence of malingering is often absent. Insurance companies may, as mentioned above, engage in covert surveillance with videotape recordings of unsuspecting patients. I have viewed some of these videotapes and it is remarkable how differently the "patient" behaves at home or on vacation as opposed to the medical office when they are not aware of being observed. An irony is that many of these individuals, who must work hard to prove their illness and disability, ultimately assume the sick role as part of their identity; through the process of pretending disability they become truly disabled.

Factitious disorders

Factitious disorders are similar to malingering in that they are consciously produced with the goal of fooling both physicians and acquaintances. However, unlike malingering, there is no discernible external incentive other than that of seeking the sick role. The capacity of some of these patients to simulate rare or dramatic illnesses is truly remarkable (Feldman & Ford, 1994; Feldman & Eisendrath, 1996). Many of the patients also engage in a variety of other types of prevarication, including pseudologia fantastica. Experience with a large number of these patients suggests that many start as factitious disorders, but because of secondary benefits from their illnesses, symptoms are perpetuated by external incentives; thus, factitious disorder evolves into malingering (Eisendrath, 1996). The pervasive deceit of these patients with factitious disorder makes it difficult to obtain accurate information about their personal histories. That information which is available suggests that the majority of these patients suffer from severe personality disorders and/or some form of cerebral dysfunction. Many of the patients come from clearly dysfunctional homes characterized by illness, abuse, or abandonment (Ford, 1983).

In summary, this brief review of persons for whom deceit has gone awry and become pathological suggests that many have some evidence of cerebral dysfunction and/or failed to achieve normal developmental tasks that facilitated their capacities for effective social interchange to obtain their needs. Instead of using sophisticated forms of (self-)deception, their crude employment of deceitful behaviors is maladaptive.

Summary/conclusions

Deceit, which is pervasive throughout the animal kingdom, reaches its highest evolutionary development in humans. Deception/self-deception is a fact of every-day life, so common as to be frequently out of our minute-to-minute conscious awareness. The skills of deception/self-deception represent developmental tasks that require both intact higher cortical functions and an extended period of normal socialization, including effective parenting. Self-deception in the forms of self-enhancement and positive illusions helps to protect us from depression (and other psychologic distress) and provides strength to cope with physical disease. Our skills at lying often serve to help maintain social support.

Obviously not all deceit is positive; in fact, it can be devastating to the self and others. Pathological lying involves lies to others and/or oneself that are injurious to the self. It is, as a general rule, associated with impaired higher cognitive functions and/or dysfunctional parenting/socialization. Thus, pathologic lying reflects deficits in basic ego functions as well as in the superego. However, for normal persons lying and self-deception provide mechanisms by which we maintain self-esteem and support others. To quote Nietzsche – "We need lies in order to live."

References

Alloy, L.B. & Abramson, L.Y. (1979). Judgment of contingency in depressed and nondepressed students: sadder but wiser? *Journal of Experimental Psychology: General*, **108**, 441–485.

Alloy, L.B. & Abramson, L.Y. (1982). Learned helplessness, depression, and the illusion of control. *Journal of Personality & Social Psychology*, **42**, 1114–1126.

Anderson, R.E. & Obenshain, S.S. (1994). Cheating by students: findings, reflections, and remedies. *Academic Medicine*, **69**, 323–331.

Blumer, D. & Heilbronn, M. (1981). The pain-prone disorder: a clinical and psychological profile. *Psychosomatics*, **22**, 395–402.

Boudreaux, A.M. (1992). Integrity in the National Resident Matching Program (letter). *JAMA*, **268**, 3315.

DePaulo, B.M. (1988). Nonverbal aspects of deception. *Journal of Nonverbal Behavior*, **12**, 153–161.

DePaulo, B.M. & Bell, K.L. (1996). Truth and investment: lies are told to those who care. *Journal of Personality & Social Psychology*, **71**, 703–716.

DePaulo, B.M. & Kashy, D.A. (1998). Everyday lies in close and casual relationships. *Journal of Personality & Social Psychology*, **74**, 63–79.

DePaulo, B.M., Kashy, D.A., Kirkendal, S.E., Wyer, M.M., & Epstein, J.A. (1996). Lying in everyday life. *Journal of Personality & Social Psychology*, **70**, 979–995.

deWaal, F. (1986). Deception in the natural communication of chimpanzees. In R.W. Mitchell & N.S. Thompson (eds), *Deception: Perspectives on human and nonhuman deceit* (pp. 221–244). Albany, NY: State University of New York Press.

Eisendrath, S.J. (1996). When Munchausen becomes malingering: factitious disorders that penetrate the legal system. *Bulletin of the American Academic Psychiatry and the Law*, **24**, 471–481.

Ekman, P. & Friesen, W.V. (1969). The repertoire of nonverbal behavior: categories, origins, usage, and coding. *Semiotica*, **1**, 49–98.

Feldman, M.D. & Eisendrath, S.J. (eds) (1996). *The spectrum of factitious disorders*. Washington, DC: American Psychiatric Press.

Feldman, M.D. & Ford, C.V. (1994). *Patient or pretender: Inside the strange world of factitious disorders*. New York: Wiley.

Folks, D.G., Freeman, A.M., Sokol, R.S., & Thurstin, A.H. (1988). Denial: predictor of outcome following coronary bypass surgery. *International Journal of Psychiatry in Medicine*, **18**, 57–66.

Ford, C.V. (1973). The Munchausen syndrome: a report of four new cases and a review of psychodynamic considerations. *Psychiatry in Medicine*, **4**, 31–45.

Ford, C.V. (1983). *The somatizing disorders: Illness as a way of life*. New York: Elsevier.

Ford, C.V. (1995). Dimensions of hypochondriasis and somatization. *Neurology Clinics of North America*, **13**, 241–253.

Ford, C.V. (1996). *Lies! Lies!! Lies!!!: The psychology of deceit*. Washington, DC: American Psychiatric Press.

Ford, C.V. & Folks, D.G. (1985). Conversion disorders: an overview. *Psychosomatics*, **26**, 371–383.

Goldbeck, R. (1997). Denial in physical illness. *Journal of Psychosomatic Research*, **46**, 575–593.

Goldberg, A. (1973). On telling the truth. In S.C. Feinstein & P.L. Giovacchini (eds), *Adolescent psychiatry: Developmental and clinical studies*, Vol. II (pp. 98–112). New York: Basic Books.

Green, A. (1991). On the constituents of the personal myth. In P. Hartocollis & I.D. Graham (eds), *The personal myth in psychoanalytic theory* (pp. 63–87). Madison, CT: International Universities Press.

Hamlyn, D.W. (1985). Self-deception. *Journal of Medical Ethics*, **11**, 210–211.

Hoorens, V. (1995) Self-favoring biases, self-presentation and the self-other asymmetry in social comparison. *Journal of Personality*, **63**, 793–817.

Howe, E.G. (1997). Deceiving patients for their own good. *Journal of Clinical Ethics*, **8**, 211–216.

Johnson, H.G., Ekman, P., & Friesen, W.V. (1975). Communicative body movements: American emblems. *Semiotica*, **15**, 335–353.

Kay, N. R. & Morris-Jones, H. (1998). Pain clinic management of medico-legal litigants. *Injury*, **29**, 305–308.

King, B.H. & Ford, C.V. (1988). Pseudologia fantastica. *Acta Psychiatrica Scandanavia*, **77**, 1–6.

Lane, R.D., Merikangas, K.R., Schwartz, G.E., Huang, S.S., & Prusoff, B.A. (1990) Inverse relationship between defensiveness and lifetime prevalence of psychiatric disorder. *American Journal of Psychiatry*, **147**, 573–578.

Lear, M.W. (1993). Should doctors tell the truth? The case against terminal candor. *The New York Times Magazine*, 24 Jan., 17.

Leekam, S.R. (1992). Believing and deceiving: steps to becoming a good liar. In S.J. Ceci, M.D. Leichtman, & M.E. Putnick (eds), *Cognitive and social factors in early deception* (pp. 47–62). Hillsdale, NJ: Erlbaum.

Levine, J., Warrenburg, S., Kerns, R., Schwartz, G., Delvaney, R., Fontana, A., Gradman, A., Smith, S., Allen, S., & Cascione, R. (1987). The role of denial in recovery from coronary heart disease. *Psychosomatic Medicine*, **49**, 109–117.

Lewin, R. (1987). Do animals read minds, tell lies? *Science*, **238**, 1350–1351.

Lewinsohn, P.M., Mischel, W., Chaplin, W., & Burton, R. (1980). Social competence and depression: the role of illusionary self-perceptions. *Journal of Abnormal Psychology*, **89**, 203–212.

Lichtman, S.W., Pisarska, K., Berman, E.R., Pestone, M., Dowling, H., Offenbacher, E., Weisel, H., Heshka, S., Matthews, D.E., & Heymsfield, S.B. (1992). Discrepancy between self-reported and actual caloric intake and exercise in obese subjects. *New England Journal of Medicine*, **327**, 1893–1898.

Lloyd, J.E. (1986). Firefly communication and deception: "oh what a tangled web". In

R.W. Mitchell & N.S. Thompson (eds), *Deception: Perspectives on human and nonhuman deceit* (pp 113–128). Albany, NY: State University of New York Press.

Mazze, R.S., Shamoon, H., Pasmantier, R., Lucido, D., Murphy, J., Hartmann, K., Kuykendall, V., & Lopatin, W. (1984). Reliability of blood glucose monitoring by patients with diabetes mellitus. *American Journal of Medicine*, 77, 211–217.

Miller, D.J. & Hersen, M. (1992). *Research fraud in the behavioral sciences*. New York: Wiley.

Miller, W.B., Geertz, H., & Cutter, H.S.G. (1961). Aggression in a boys' street corner group. *Psychiatry*, 24, 283–298.

Mills, C. (1997). Unusual suspects. *The Sciences*, 37(4), 32–36.

Morris, M.D. (1986). Large-scale deception: deceit by captive elephants? In R.W. Mitchell & N.S. Thompson (eds), *Deception: Perspectives on human and nonhuman deceit* (pp. 183–191). Albany, NY: State University of New York Press.

Novack, D.H., Detering, B.J., Arnold, R., Forrow, L., Ladinsky, M., & Pezzulo, J.C. (1989). Physician's attitudes toward using deception to resolve difficult ethical problems. *JAMA*, 261, 2980–2985.

Pancratz, L. & Lezak, M.D. (1987). Cerebral dysfunction in the Munchausen syndrome. *Hillside Journal of Clinical Psychiatry*, 9, 195–206.

Paulhus, D.L. (1998). Interpersonal and intrapsychic adaptativeness of trait self-enhancement: a mixed blessing. *Journal of Personality & Social Psychology*, 74, 1197–1208.

Rand, C.S., Wise, R.A., Nides, M., Simmons, M.S., Bleecker, E.R., Kusek, J.W., Li, V.C., & Tashkin, D.P. (1992). Metered-dose inhaler adherence in a clinical trial. *American Review of Respiratory Disease*, 146, 1559–1564.

Russel, G.C. (1993). The role of denial in clinical practice. *Journal of Advanced Nursing*, 18, 938–940.

Saarni, C. & von Salisch, M. (1993). The socialization of emotional dissemblance. In M. Lewis & C. Saarni (eds), *Lying and deception in everyday life* (pp. 106–125). New York: Guilford.

Sackheim, H.A. & Gur, R.C. (1979). Self-deception, other deception, and self-reported psychopathology. *Journal of Consulting and Clinical Psychology*, 47, 213–215.

Sackheim, H.A. & Wegner, A.Z. (1986). Attributional patterns in depression and euthymia. *Archives of General Psychiatry*, 4, 553–560.

Satran, P.R. (1993). The lies we tell for love. *Redbook*, Jan., 56–59.

Segerstrom, S.C., Taylor, S.E., Kemeny, M.E., & Fahey, J.L. (1998). Optimism is associated with mood, coping and immune change in response to stress. *Journal of Personality & Social Psychology*, 74, 1646–1655.

Sekas, G. & Hutson, W.R. (1995). Misrepresentation of academic accomplishments by applicants for gastroenterology fellowships. *Annals of Internal Medicine*, 123, 38–41.

Shibles, W. (1985). *Lying: a critical analysis*. Whitewater, WI: Language Press.

Sobel, R. (1996). Deception/trust. *Israel Journal of Medical Sciences*, 32, 256–259.

Steiner, G. (1975). *After Babel: Aspects of language and translation*. Oxford: Oxford University Press.

Stowe, M.K., Turlings, T.C., Loughrin, J.H., Lewis, W.J., & Tumlinson, J.H. (1995). The chemistry of eavesdropping, alarm and deceit. *Proceedings of the National Academy of Science*, 92, 23–28.

Tausk, V. (1933). On the origin of the "influencing machine" in schizophrenia. *Psychoanalytic Quarterly*, 2, 519–556.

Taylor, S.E. & Armor, D.A. (1996). Positive illusions and coping with adversity. *Journal of Personality*, **64**, 873–898.

Taylor, S.E. & Brown, J.D. (1988). Illusion and well-being: a social psychological perspective on mental health. *Psychological Bulletin*, **103**, 193–210.

Trivers, R.L. (1971). The evolution of reciprocal altruism. *Quarterly Review of Biology*, **46**, 35–57.

Trivers, R.L. (1985). *Social evolution*. Menlo Park, CA: Benjamin/Cummings.

Tuckett, A. (1998). "Bending the truth": professionals' narratives about lying and deception in nursing practice. *International Journal of Nursing Studies*, **35**, 292–302.

Vasek, M.E. (1986). Lying as a skill: the development of deception in children. In R.W. Mitchell & N.S. Thompson (eds), *Deception: Perspectives on human and nonhuman deceit* (pp. 271–292). Albany, NY: State University of New York Press.

Young, T.A. (1997). Teaching medical students to lie – the disturbing contradiction: medical ideals and the resident-selection process. *CMAJ*, **156**, 219–222.

Chapter 2

The social sharing of emotion

Illusory and real benefits of talking about emotional experiences

Bernard Rimé, Gwénola Herbette
and Susanna Corsini

Talking about emotional experiences

Talking about an emotional experience is a well-known and common consequence of exposure to very intense negative emotional conditions. As early as 1910, William James, after witnessing the San Francisco earthquake, wrote to Pierre Janet about the victims' apparent need to talk about their experiences. At night, he noted, it was impossible to sleep in the tents which served as temporary housing for the earthquake victims, due to the continuous verbal exchanges (Janet, 1926/1975, p. 326). This early anecdotal observation was confirmed in surveys conducted on San Francisco residents after the Loma Prieta Earthquake. Pennebaker and Harber (1993) recorded that one week after this earthquake, the average person still thought and talked about it nine times per day. Similarly, one week after the beginning of the Persian Gulf War, these authors observed that the average Dallas residents thought and talked about the war 12 times daily. According to Janoff-Bulman (1992, p. 108), people who are exposed to strong negative emotional circumstances experience a seemingly insatiable need to tell others about their experience, as if they felt coerced into talking. Data from numerous sources document the pervasiveness of this phenomenon. The need to talk about their experience was mentioned by 88 percent of rescuers operating in a North Sea oil platform disaster (Ersland *et al.*, 1989), by 88 percent of people who had recently lost a relative (Schoenberg *et al.*, 1975), and by 86 percent of patients with a recent diagnosis of cancer (Mitchell & Glickman, 1977). In sum, there is strong evidence that exposure to a major negative emotional event elicits a need to be with others and to talk about it.

The social sharing of emotion

Research conducted by our group at the University of Louvain in the past decade revealed that a comparable behavior develops after any emotional experience. It is not typical solely of trauma or of major negative life events. It develops after everyday emotional events of all kinds. This is what we found by investigating "the social sharing of emotion". The social sharing of emotion is a process that takes place during the hours, days, and even weeks and months following an emotional episode. It involves the evocation of an emotion in a socially shared language to some addressee by the person who experienced it (Rimé, 1989; Rimé et al., 1991a). Our empirical research showed that when people experience an emotion, they very generally – in 80 to 95 percent of cases – talk about it (Rimé et al., 1991a, 1991b; for reviews, see Rimé et al., 1992, 1998). The studies revealed that this propensity is not dependent upon people's level of education. It is evidenced whether the persons hold a university degree, or whether their education was limited to elementary school. It is also observed with approximately equal importance in cultures as diverse as Asian, North American and European ones. The type of primary emotion felt in the episode appears not to be a critical factor with regard to the need to talk about it. Episodes which involved fear, or anger, or sadness are reported to others as often as episodes which involved happiness or love. However, emotional episodes involving shame and guilt tend to be verbalized to a somewhat lesser degree.

These observations lead us to conclude that the process of talking after emotional experiences has a very high generality. In a majority of cases, it starts very early after the emotion – usually on the day it happened. It extends over weeks or even months when the episode involved a high intensity of emotion and it is typically a repetitive phenomenon, i.e. the emotions are generally shared often or very often, and with a variety of target persons.

The paradox of social sharing

Accessing the memory of an emotional episode generally has the effect of reactivating the various components (i.e. physiological, sensory, experiential) of the emotion involved (e.g. Bower, 1981; Lang, 1983; Leventhal, 1984). Does the same happen during the social sharing process? In order to answer that question, Rimé et al. (1991b) had participants recall and describe at length a past emotional experience. They were then asked questions about what they experienced while recalling and sharing. Nearly all of them reported experiencing vivid mental images of the event. Reports of feelings and bodily sensations were only slightly less frequent. The type of primary emotion involved (joy, anger, fear, or sadness) had no significant impact on these variables, although it influenced the pleasantness of the social sharing situation. Not surprisingly, reporting an experience of joy was rated as more pleasant than reporting an emotion of sadness, of fear, or of anger. More surprising was the fact that reporting fear, sadness or anger was rated by only a minority of the participants as painful or extremely painful. Notwithstanding the reactivation of vivid images, feelings, and bodily sensations of a negative emotional experience, the sharing did not appear as aversive as one could have expected. This was confirmed by participants' answers to the question of whether they would be willing to undertake the sharing of another emotional memory of the same type as the first one. Indeed, 93.7 percent of the participants gave a positive answer. The proportion was similar in all four emotion conditions. These data thus definitely reveal the paradoxical character of social sharing situations. On one hand, social sharing reactivates the various components of the emotion, which, in the case of negative emotion, should be experienced as aversive. On the other hand, sharing an emotion, whether positive or negative, does seem to be a situation in which people engage willingly. In fact, field experience reveals that being open to the sharing of people's emotions is one of the nicest gifts that can be offered to them.

Does socially sharing an emotion contribute to emotional recovery?

Why are people so willing to engage in a social process in which they re-experience negative affects? One would assume that some powerful incentive drives them to do so and that they find some important benefit in it. What could this profit be? Common sense offers a ready-made answer to this question. Indeed, we commonly assume that verbalizing an emotional memory can transform it and that after verbalization, this memory would lose a significant part of its emotional load. A study by Zech (2000) showed that more than 80 percent of the respondents in a large sample of adult laypersons endorsed such a view. If this layperson's belief was true, if data could confirm that verbalizing emotions brings "emotional recovery" or "relief", then the paradox would clear up. People would tolerate re-experiencing negative emotions because of this final profit. We thus examined this question in a large number of studies (for a review, see Rimé *et al.*, 1998; Zech, 2000). In all of them, participants rated the level of emotional distress felt when recalling a specific emotional episode. We examined how far this rating evolved as a function of the social sharing of the episode, i.e. to what extent sharing, which develops spontaneously after an emotional event, contributes to relieve people from its emotional impact.

Spontaneous social sharing and emotional recovery

In most of our studies on spontaneous social sharing, the research design generally involved the assessment of (1) the initial intensity of the emotion elicited by the episode, (2) the extent of social sharing that developed after the event, and (3) the residual intensity of the emotion elicited when the episode was recalled later. We tested the hypothesis of a positive association between the amount of social sharing developed spontaneously after the emotional event and the degree of emotional recovery, this latter variable being assessed by the difference between (1) and (3). We expected that the more people socially shared an emotional episode, the more they would feel relieved.

This hypothesized association was first considered in one of the recall studies conducted by Rimé *et al.* (1991a, Study 6), which demonstrated that neither the amount nor the delay of social sharing was related to emotional recovery. Equally, in two studies on emotional secrecy (Finkenauer & Rimé, 1998a), emotional recovery failed to discriminate between shared and non-shared emotional memories.

Assessments of stressfulness and traumatic impact also failed to support the prediction that secret events would be less recovered from than shared ones. Overall, our studies on emotional secrecy suggested that talking about an emotional experience does not contribute to emotional recovery. Additionally, in one of the diary studies mentioned above (Rimé *et al.*, 1994, Study 3), recovery was assessed by the difference between the impact each daily event had when it occurred and its residual impact as rated at follow-up several weeks later. Again, no significant relation was observed between this recovery index and extent of social sharing manifested when the event happened.

Similar analyses were conducted in many other correlational studies of social sharing. They all consistently yielded the same negative results, failing to support the prediction that verbalizing an emotional experience reduces the emotional load associated with the memory of this experience. Should we thus conclude from these diary data that the social sharing of emotion has no effect on emotional recovery?

Research conducted by Pennebaker and colleagues (for a review, see Pennebaker, 1989) suggested that certain qualitative aspects of sharing should be considered. For instance, Pennebaker and Beall (1986) had participants write essays on previously unrevealed traumas. Dependent on the condition they were assigned to, participants had to describe either the facts or the feelings elicited by the episode, or both facts and feelings. As compared to a control condition in which participants wrote on trivial topics, follow-up health assessments evidenced positive effects for people who described their feelings, or their feelings and the facts, but not for those who only gave a description of the facts. Emphasizing the feeling dimension may thus be critical for social sharing to have some impact. In such terms, the extent to which people express their emotions and feelings is expected to correlate with recovery. However, assessing qualitative aspects of spontaneous social sharing in survey research raises several difficulties. In general, respondents do not seem to be able to specify what they talked about in their previous social sharing, nor which aspect (facts or feelings) they shared most. Therefore, subsequent studies were conducted using an experimental induction of social sharing of emotion.

Induced sharing and emotional recovery

In several experimental studies, we systematically explored how feelings communicated through social sharing might affect emotional recovery, comparing several types of sharing. Rimé *et al.* (1996b) compared four different modes of sharing emotions for their effect upon emotional recovery. One hundred and thirty psychology students enrolled in an advanced class on emotion each interviewed one of their relatives who had agreed to contribute to the student's training in the practice of interviewing. Students first asked the volunteer to recall a recently experienced negative emotional event and then to indicate the emotional impact this memory still had. A one-hour social sharing interview centered around the negative emotional episode was then conducted by the interviewee according to one of four different modes to which s/he had been randomly assigned. The students were provided with detailed instructions on how to conduct the interview. In a first mode, the focus was on factual aspects. In the second, it was on feelings and emotions experienced during the episode. In the third one, the accent was on the meanings elicited by the episode, while in the fourth mode, the relative talked about the episode freely with no specific instructions.

Dependent measures included seven different indices of emotional recovery obtained from subtracting participants' ratings collected one week after the interview from those collected before the interview. In general, no significant effect of interviewing mode was found for any of these indices. Similarly, no effect of mode was found on extent of social sharing in the course of the week following the interview. Thus, the specific interviewing modes did not differ in their capacity to elicit emotional recovery or emotional relief.

Interviewers' ratings of the extent to which the participant had been emotionally expressive during the sharing situation, however, suggested that this individual difference variable was correlated with emotional recovery: the more participants were perceived as expressing their emotions, the greater was their recovery after the episode. Thus, more attention should be paid to the role of individual differences in emotional expression in this context. Finally, ratings collected before the interview on the impact the event still had significantly predicted the extent of social sharing reported by the person in the week following the interview. This result is clearly consistent with findings from previous studies showing that more intense emotions are more extensively shared than less intense ones. All in all, this study led to the conclusion that emotional recovery is better predicted by "natural" individual differences in sharing mode than by experimentally induced ones. Also, episode-related emotionality felt before the interview could predict the extent of social sharing developed after, whereas interviewing modes failed to impact significantly on this variable.

A replication in the laboratory

In the study just described, students acting in their natural environment conducted the social sharing interviews. We felt the need to conduct a similar study in the more controlled conditions of a laboratory environment. Zech (2000) assigned undergraduate volunteers to three conditions of verbally sharing an emotional memory, each conducted by the same interviewing person. In two conditions, participants were instructed to talk extensively about the most upsetting event of their life, with a focus either on felt emotions ("feeling condition") or on facts and circumstances ("fact condition"). In a third condition ("control"), participants simply mentioned the upsetting event and then had to talk extensively about a trivial topic. Dependent variables (distress when recalling the upsetting event, bodily symptoms, and emotional impact) were collected four times: (1) before the sharing situation, (2) immediately after, (3) at one week follow-up, and (4) at a follow-up session two months later.

Manipulation checks revealed marked differences between groups in the expected directions. Participants in the emotion condition rated their sharing as being more emotionally expressive than participants in the fact and control conditions. Emotion and fact participants rated their sharing as deeper, more personal and more important than control participants. Furthermore, compared with emotion and fact participants, control participants reported having talked in a more detailed manner about general facts and having been more descriptive.

It was predicted that participants in the two trauma-disclosure conditions would show less distress, bodily symptoms, and emotional impact than control participants, and that this effect would be even stronger for participants in the "emotion" condition than for those in the "fact" condition. Individual recovery scores ("time 1" minus "time 3"; "time 1" minus "time 4") were computed for each dependent variable. Contrary to expectations, no significant results were found. Thus, social sharing of emotions was not shown to affect long-term well-being or emotional recovery from the event, irrespective of an emphasis on the emotional aspect or on the factual aspect.

In a final questionnaire, participants rated to what extent they found the experiment meaningful and interesting, as well as the extent to which they thought the interview had influenced their view of the emotional event. Analyses of their answers yielded significant differences between conditions. Participants in the emotion condition rated the social sharing as more meaningful, more interesting, and higher in overall subjective impact than participants in the other two conditions. Thus, the emotional social sharing elicited the feeling that it makes sense to share events and that it may help to alleviate the emotional memory more than the other two conditions. Yet, in spite of this evidence collected retrospectively through overt declarative bases, indices of emotional recovery gathered in the study failed to provide data consistent with these declarations.

These negative results raise many questions. First, one may wonder whether the concept of emotional recovery makes any sense at all. Rimé et al. (1996a) addressed this question, when asking students to recall two recent unpleasant emotional experiences: one that they considered being recovered from and one that they had not yet recovered from and which was thus still considered as being a cause of distress. For each experience, participants rated initial (at the time of the event) and residual (at the time of the experiment) emotional impact, as well as initial and residual sharing. The results showed that both types of episodes elicited comparable initial emotional impact as well as comparable initial sharing. However, confirming that the notion of "recovery" makes sense, the two types of episodes differed markedly in their residual emotional impact and thus yielded marked differences on the recovery index. Consistent with former findings showing that more intense emotions are more extensively shared, data showed that episodes not recovered from elicited more residual sharing than recovered ones.

Mere sharing cannot change the memory of an emotion

Our data show that after experiencing an emotional episode, whether positive or negative, people feel compelled to talk about it. A widespread belief upholds the idea that socially sharing an emotion brings emotional relief. Both laypersons' naïve representation and some professional views often attach the old "cathartic notion" to the mere "putting of emotion into words". They expect that putting an emotion into words would have the effect of buffering or of eliminating the emotional memory. Our data clearly failed to support such a notion. They lead us to conclude that the cathartic notion is an illusion; the simple fact of socially sharing an emotion does not have the power to change the emotional memory. After all, this idea does make sense in terms of adaptation. An emotional memory carries important information regarding future situations that may be encountered. If we had the potential to alter the emotion-arousing capacities of such memories by merely talking about them, such a tool would deprive us of the vital fruits of our experience.

This conclusion should be considered very carefully. Let us stress that it regards the *mere verbalization of an emotional experience*, a response reflecting the strong urge to share generally manifested after an emotional episode. Our conclusion, however, does not imply that verbalizing and sharing of emotion would be devoid of effects when developed in a proper context in which appropriate cognitive and social factors would come in response, such as in counseling and psychotherapy. Specifying the precise conditions under which the sharing of an emotional experience can bring relief and recovery, however, is still a question largely open to investigation.

Some other benefits of socially sharing an emotion

If the sharing of emotions spontaneously developed after emotional exposure does not affect the recovery process, why does it accompany emotional experiences almost systematically? Should it be concluded that the urge to share generally elicited by exposure to emotional events is a useless manifestation? Alternative potential effects of socially sharing an emotion are probably numerous and may involve important health, cognitive and social functions. However, they may be masked to our eyes because we were focused on the idea that social sharing served emotional relief functions. In the following, we discuss some other possible benefits that have already been observed or are currently under investigation.

Subjective benefits of social sharing

Zech (2000) instructed a large number of psychology students to conduct an interview in which a relative would specify, rate, and then share an emotional episode, which this person had not yet recovered from. In control conditions, an emotional event of the same kind was also specified and rated, but the relative either shared a non-emotional episode, or did not share at all. Three days later, the emotional impact of the target event was assessed again. In addition, relatives were asked to rate their perceived benefits of the sharing session. Confirming previous findings, no differences between conditions occurred for emotional recovery. However, participants who had shared an emotional event reported much more other benefits than those in the two control conditions. The differences regarded: (i) general benefits (e.g. the session was meaningful); (ii) relief (e.g. the session made them feel better); (iii) cognitive benefits (e.g. the session helped them understand themselves better); and (iv) interpersonal benefits (e.g. they felt understood). These observations replicated those made in the laboratory study mentioned in the previous section. Altogether, these data show that, although social sharing does not bring emotional recovery, people experience the sharing of an emotion as clearly beneficial. In our current research, we try to specify which factors are instrumental in eliciting such feelings.

Self-disclosure and health

Pennebaker has been investigating the effects of expressing emotion on physical health. In his theory of inhibition, Pennebaker (e.g. 1985, 1989) proposed that the conscious efforts exerted in order to inhibit thoughts, feelings, or behavior require physiological work. When such efforts are exerted chronically, the probability of developing stress-related physical and psychological problems increases. The prediction that follows this theory is that putting stress or trauma into words reduces the physiological work and is thus beneficial to health. Various studies tested this idea and generally confirmed that expression of trauma-related feelings and thoughts impacts positively on health indicators (e.g. Esterling *et al.*, 1994; Pennebaker *et al.*, 1989; 1990; Pennebaker & Beall, 1986; Pennebaker & O'Heeron, 1984). To illustrate, as compared to students who merely reported facts, those who disclosed a past personal trauma in enhancing their deepest emotions and feelings showed less frequent visits to the campus health center and fewer self-reported illnesses in a six-month follow-up (Pennebaker & Beall, 1986). Thus, although the sharing of emotions does not relieve the *emotional load* of the event, it is associated with *physical health* improvement (for a discussion, see Pennebaker *et al.*, 2001).

This finding was replicated by Finkenauer and Rimé (1998a) in the context of a study on non-shared emotions and emotional secrecy. Anonymous participants indicated if they could recall an important emotional life event that they kept secret. In addition, they rated scales assessing health status, life satisfaction, and negative affectivity. The data revealed that participants with the memory of a non-shared emotion reported a higher number of health problems than those without such a memory. Also, they were overall less satisfied with their lives.

Consolidating the memory of the emotional episode

Because of its repetitive aspect, the social sharing of an emotion contributes to the consolidation of the memory of the emotional episode, leading to a vivid memory of those events that caught people by surprise. Finkenauer *et al.* (1998) investigated the memory of the unexpected death of Belgium's king Baudouin in a large sample of Belgian citizens. The data revealed that the news of the king's death had been widely socially shared. By talking about the event, people gradually construct a social narrative and a collective memory of the emotional event. At the same time, they consolidated their own memory of the personal circumstances in which the event took place. Though this information may not be critical to personal adaptation where the king's death is concerned, the information storage is probably of high survival value when personal emotional events are involved. The more an event is socially shared, the more it will be fixed in people's minds. Social sharing thus may help to counteract some defense mechanisms. Naturally, people should be driven to "forget" undesirable events. Thus, someone who just lost a close relative often inclines initially to deny the death. The repetitive social sharing of the loss powerfully contributes to realism.

Processing and constructing the emotional memory

Social sharing can also contribute to the construction of the memory of emotions. With their partner's aid, the person can add some of the meanings that were missing so that a partially rewritten interpretation can be stored in memory. Emotion challenges the beliefs that people hold in order to preserve a sense of coherence, predictability and control over themselves and the world (Janoff-Bulman, 1992; Parkes, 1972; Tait & Silver, 1989). Hence, emotion elicits a mental "working through" process aimed either at the restoration of beliefs or at finding meaning in the event (e.g. Silver & Wortman, 1980; Tait & Silver, 1989). Social sharing can be expected to play some role in completing the cognitive business elicited by the emotion. Consistent with this, Finkenauer and Rimé (1998b) observed that, as compared to shared emotional memories, non-shared memories were associated with (1) greater search for meaning, (2) greater efforts at understanding what had happened, and (3) greater attempts at "putting order in what happened". Similar items were later included in several studies in which the memory of an emotional experience was investigated some time after the occurrence of the event. In each of these studies, a significant positive correlation was obtained between need for completion and need for sharing. Future research should examine how far social sharing actually involves such a completion task. It should also explore to what extent the considered process could contribute to reinstate in the person a sense of coherence and predictability, as well as a sense of control and mastery.

Enhancing interpersonal relationships and social integration

Social sharing has the power to refresh and to strengthen social ties. Specific dynamics take place between the speaker and the listener. A typical response of the listener is the expression of interest in the emotional story (Christophe & Rimé, 1997), as people tend to be particularly attracted to this type of story. Another response of the listener is empathy. The more emotional a story is, the more the listener will experience emotion, and will consequently express support and warmth. A third response is attraction. The more the story requests his or her interest and support, the more the listener "likes" the speaker. And this is also true for the other way around. The more the speaker receives interest and support, the more he or she will "like" the listener. Christophe and Rimé observed that when intense emotions are shared, listeners reduce their use of verbal mediators in their responses. As a substitute, they display non-verbal comforting behaviors, like hugging, kissing, or touching. This suggests that sharing an intense emotional experience may decrease the physical distance between two persons, thus contributing to the maintenance and improvement of interpersonal relationships and social integration.

Construction and dissemination of social knowledge on emotion

Social sharing does not only have an impact on the individual memory. Through "secondary" and "tertiary" social sharing, the community surrounding the individual is informed about what happened to him or her. A high-intensity emotional experience is usually shared with more than six people in the following hours and days. Each of these people then has a high probability of engaging in secondary social sharing with an average of at least two other persons who, in turn, are inclined to share the emotional episode that they heard (Christophe, 1998). Thus, in a very short time span, any emotional event of some importance is spread across a broad social group. Recently, it was shown that people store a large amount of information about emotional events, emotional feelings, and emotional responses (e.g. Russell *et al.*, 1995). It was also shown that this knowledge is represented collectively in the form of emotion prototypes (Shaver *et al.*, 1987), or of social schemata (Rimé *et al.*, 1990). This social knowledge about emotion carries information that is critical to adaptation. The social sharing of emotion appears to be a major potential contributor to the continuous extension and updating of this knowledge.

Concluding comments

In conclusion, the research described in this chapter was consistently faced with three sets of facts. First, there is abundant evidence that people who experienced an emotional experience want to talk about it and want to share it socially despite the emotional reactivation that is aroused in the process. Second, our studies systematically failed to provide evidence that sharing an emotional experience has the effect of alleviating the emotional memory. Third, in the course of these studies, we very consistently observed that after having shared an emotion, participants expressed positive feelings and subjective benefits. This set of facts thus raises a number of questions. Why do people want to share their emotions? Why do they have positive feelings after having shared their emotions? To be able to answer this question, we need to reconsider what is going on exactly in an emotional experience.

We know that emotion arises from rapid and automatic meaning analyses of supervening events (e.g. Frijda, 1986; Scherer, 1984). For example, if meanings such as "danger", "no control", "no escape" are elicited in a situation one is faced with, a variety of emergency reactions will develop in one's body and one will experience fear. There is, however, a second wave of meanings in emotion that people are generally unaware of. Situation-specific meanings such as "danger", "no control", "no escape" spread to broader meanings such as "the world is unsafe", "I am vulnerable and helpless", and "life is unfair". Meanings of this kind affect how one views the world and how one views oneself. In other words, they pervade what we would like to refer to as "one's symbolic universe". What is meant by symbolic universe? In current life, people live and behave under a subjective canopy of apparent order and meaning – a symbolic universe. Thanks to it, they can face the world and manage it relatively peacefully. Thanks to it, they can act as if it was just normal that they stand here on this planet, somewhere between the Milky Way and Eternity. Emotional events often have the power to undermine this delicate architecture. They challenge the canopy. Traumatic situations have been shown to be particularly deleterious in this regard (Epstein, 1987; Janoff-Bulman, 1992; Parkes, 1972). But in principle, any emotion has an impact on this symbolic architecture because emotion precisely develops at its fissures – or where things go unpredicted, unexpected, out of control, etc. By making fissures apparent, emotion makes people feel the weakness of the construction. This is probably the source of this obscure need for cognitive clarification, for understanding, for finding meaning, abundantly reported by people who just went through some important emotional episode.

But why do people also feel the need to be with others and to talk with others after an emotion? It should be stressed that the symbolic universe is everything but a solitary construction. No one could make sense of the world alone. Sociologists showed that people enter a culturally shaped subjective universe early in life (Berger & Luckmann, 1967). The attachment process is the basic tool through which the construction is installed in the young human being. All along the development process, in everyday interactions, parents transmit to their children the view of the world that is shared in their culture. Later on, the construction is kept alive, strong and valid by the social consensus in which everyone takes part minute after minute throughout their life as members of our community. Consequently, a crack in this symbolic universe not only opens a breach in their meanings that will elicit cognitive needs. It also has the effect of making people feel insecure and lonely, eliciting a very strong urge to re-immerse themselves in the social consensus. These are probably the reasons why after an emotion people feel the need to be with their intimates and to share the emotion with them. Their intimates are those who keep the attachment process alive for them, providing them with social support and security. Their intimates are those with whom people share the social consensus, providing them with a coherent subjective universe.

Being with their intimates and sharing the emotional experience with them will probably not have the effect of altering the memory of the emotion and of bringing people emotional relief. However, being with them and sharing the emotion with them can result in enhancing people's experience of social support and in consolidating their symbolic universe. In other words, intimates will help people to make future life possible and meaningful in spite of what happened.

Acknowledgments

Research reported in this paper was supported by grants FRFC 8.4506.98 and 2.4546.97 from the Belgian National Fund for Scientific Research.

References

Berger, P. & Luckmann, T. (1967). *Social construction of reality*. Garden City, NY: Doubleday.

Bower, G.H. (1981). Mood and memory. *American Psychologist*, **36**, 129–148.

Christophe, V. (1998). *Le partage social des émotions du point de vue de l'auditeur [Social sharing of emotion on the side of the target]*. Unpublished doctoral dissertation, Université de Lille III, France.

Christophe, V. & Rimé, B. (1997). Exposure to the social sharing of emotion: emotional impact, listener responses and secondary social sharing. *European Journal of Social Psychology*, **27**, 37–54.

Epstein, S. (1987). Implications of cognitive self-theory for psychopathology and psychotherapy. In N. Cheshire & H. Thomae (eds), *Self, symptoms, and psychotherapy*. New York: Wiley.

Ersland, S., Weisoeth, L., & Sund, A. (1989). The stress upon rescuers involved in an oil rig disaster, "Alexander Kielland" 180. *Acta Psychiatrica Scandinavica*, **80**, 38–49.

Esterling, B.A., Antoni, M.H., Fletcher, M.A., Margulies, S., & Schneiderman, N. (1994). Emotional disclosure through writing or speaking modulates latent Epstein-Barr Virus antibody titers. *Journal of Consulting and Clinical Psychology*, **62**, 130–140.

Finkenauer, C., Luminet, O., Gisle, L., Van der Linden, M., El-Ahmadi, A., & Philippot, P. (1998). Flashbulb memories and the underlying mechanisms of their formation: towards an emotional–integrative model. *Memory and Cognition*, **26**, 516–31.

Finkenauer, C. & Rimé, B. (1998a). Socially shared emotional experiences vs. emotional experiences kept secret: differential characteristics and consequences. *Journal of Social and Clinical Psychology*, **17**, 295–318.

Finkenauer, C. & Rimé, B. (1998b). Keeping emotional memories secret: health and subjective well-being when emotions are not shared. *Journal of Health Psychology*, **3**, 47–58.

Frijda, N.H. (1986). *The emotions*. New York: Cambridge University Press.

Janet, P. (1975). *De l'angoisse à l'extase [From anxiety to ecstasy]*. Paris: Société Pierre Janet et Laboratoire de Psychologie Pathologique de la Sorbonne (Original work published 1926).

Janoff-Bulman, R. (1992). *Shattered assumptions: Towards a new psychology of trauma*. New York: Free Press.

Lang, P.J. (1983). Cognition in emotion: concept and action. In C. Izard, J. Kagan, & R. Zajonc (eds), *Emotion, cognition, and behavior*. New York: Cambridge University Press.

Leventhal, H. (1984). A perceptual-motor theory of emotion. In L. Berkowitz (ed.), *Advances in experimental social psychology*, Vol. 17 (pp. 117–182). New York: Academic Press.

Mitchell, G.W. & Glickman, A.S. (1977). Cancer patients: knowledge and attitude. *Cancer*, **40**, 61–66.

Parkes, C.M. (1972). *Bereavement: Studies of grief in adult life*. London: Tavistock Publications.

Pennebaker, J.W. (1985). Traumatic experience and psychosomatic disease: exploring the roles of behavioral inhibition, obsession, and confiding. *Canadian Psychology*, **26**, 82–95.

Pennebaker, J.W. (1989). Confession, inhibition, and disease. In L. Berkowitz (ed.), *Advances in experimental social psychology*, Vol. 22 (pp. 211–244). New York: Academic Press.

Pennebaker, J.W., Barger, S.D., & Tiebout, J. (1989). Disclosure of traumas and health among Holocaust survivors. *Psychosomatic Medicine*, **51**, 577–589.

Pennebaker, J.W. & Beall, S. (1986). Confronting a traumatic event: toward an understanding of inhibition and disease. *Journal of Abnormal Psychology*, **95**, 274–281.

Pennebaker, J.W., Colder, M., & Sharp, L.K. (1990). Accelerating the coping process. *Journal of Personality and Social Psychology*, **58**, 528–537.

Pennebaker, J.W. & Harber, K.D. (1993). A social stage model of collective coping: the Loma Prieta earthquake and the Persian Gulf war. *Journal of Social Issues*, **49**, 125–145.

Pennebaker, J.W. & O'Heeron, R.C. (1984). Confiding in others and illness rate among spouses of suicide and accidental-death victims. *Journal of Abnormal Psychology*, **93**, 473–476.

Pennebaker, J.W., Zech, E., & Rimé, B. (2001). Disclosing and sharing emotion: psychological, social and health consequences. In M. Stroebe, W. Stroebe, R.O. Hansson, & H. Schut (eds), *New handbook of bereavement: Consequences, coping, and care* (pp. 517–544). Washington, DC: American Psychological Association.

Rimé, B. (1989). Le partage social des émotions [The social sharing of emotions]. In B. Rimé & K.R. Scherer (eds), *Les émotions [The emotions]* (pp. 271–303). Neufchâtel: Delachaux et Niestlé.

Rimé, B., Finkenauer, C., Luminet, O., Zech, E., & Philippot, P. (1998). Social sharing of emotion: new evidence and new questions. In W. Stroebe & M. Hewstone (eds), *European review of social psychology*, Vol. 9 (pp. 145–189). Chichester: Wiley.

Rimé, B., Hayward, M.S., & Pennebaker, J.W. (1996a). *Characteristics of recovered vs. unrecovered emotional experiences*. Unpublished raw data.

Rimé, B., Mesquita, B., Philippot, P., & Boca, S. (1991a). Beyond the emotional event: six studies on the social sharing of emotion. *Cognition and Emotion*, **5**, 435–465.

Rimé, B., Noël, M.P., & Philippot, P. (1991b). Episode émotionnel, réminiscences mentales et réminiscences sociales [Emotional episodes, mental remembrances and social remembrances]. *Cahiers Internationaux de Psychologie Sociale*, **11**, 93–104.

Rimé, B., Philippot, P., Boca, S., & Mesquita, B. (1992). Long-lasting cognitive and social consequences of emotion: social sharing and rumination. In W. Stroebe & M. Hewstone (eds), *European review of social psychology*, Vol. 3 (pp. 225–258). Chichester: Wiley.

Rimé, B., Philippot, P., & Cisamolo, D. (1990). Social schemata of peripheral changes in emotion. *Journal of Personality and Social Psychology*, **59**, 38–49.

Rimé, B., Philippot, P., Finkenauer, C., Legast, S., Moorkens, P., & Tornqvist, J. (1994). *Mental rumination and social sharing in current life emotion.* Unpublished manuscript, University of Louvain at Louvain-la-Neuve, Belgium.

Rimé, B., Zech, E., Finkenauer, C., Luminet, O., & Dozier, S. (1996b). *Different modalities of sharing emotions and their impact on emotional recovery.* Poster session presented at the 11th General Meeting of the European Association for Experimental Social Psychology, Gmunden, Austria.

Russell, J.A., Fernandez-Dols, J.M., Manstead, A.S.R, & Wellenkamp, J.C. (1995). *Everyday conceptions of emotions. An introduction to the psychology, anthropology and linguistics of emotion.* Dordrecht, The Netherlands: Kluwer.

Scherer, K.R. (1984). Emotion as a multicomponent process: a model and some cross-cultural data. In P. Shaver (ed.), *Review of personality and social psychology*, Vol. 5 (pp. 37–63). Beverly Hills, CA: Sage.

Schoenberg, B., Carr, A.C., Peretz, D., Kutscher, A.H., & Cherico, D.J. (1975). Advice of the bereaved for the bereaved. In B. Schoenberg, I. Gerber, A. Wiener, A.H. Kutscher, D. Peretz, & A.C. Carr (eds), *Bereavement: Its psychological aspects* (pp. 362–367). New York: Columbia University Press.

Shaver, P., Schwartz, J., Kirson, D., & O'Connor, L. (1987). Emotion knowledge: further exploration of a prototype approach. *Journal of Personality and Social Psychology*, **52**, 1061–1086.

Silver, R. & Wortman, C. (1980). Coping with undesirable life events. In J. Garber & M.E.P. Seligman (eds), *Human helplessness* (pp. 279–340). New York: Academic Press.

Tait, R. & Silver, R.C. (1989). Coming to terms with major negative life events. In J.S. Uleman & J.A. Bargh (eds), *Unintended thought* (pp. 351–382). New York: Guilford Press.

Zech, E. (2000). *The effects of the communication of emotional experiences.* Unpublished doctoral dissertation, University of Louvain, Louvain-la-Neuve, Belgium.

Chapter 3

Theoretical mechanisms involved in disclosure

From inhibition to self-regulation

Melanie A. Greenberg and Stephen J. Lepore

Introduction

Individuals who freely express their thoughts and feelings about stressful life events can benefit both physically and psychologically (Smyth, 1998). Initially, emotional disclosure was thought to facilitate adjustment to previously unexpressed traumas. Then it was shown to help individuals deal with less severe and ongoing stressful events. Recent research suggests an even further broadening of the scope of disclosure. Health improvements occur in both healthy and medically ill populations. Writing about imaginary traumas and writing about life goals can also improve health. How do we make sense of these diverse findings? We argue that a self-regulation approach can explain many of the apparent contradictions.

This chapter begins with a brief review of the experimental disclosure literature. Next, we turn to disclosure theories. We describe the influential inhibition model (Pennebaker, 1989) and discuss research that addresses its utility. Next, we discuss findings suggesting that disclosure might enhance self-regulation of emotion. We then highlight research on disclosure, intrusive thoughts, and social constraints that is consistent with a self-regulation approach. Next, we consider how emotional disclosure might help people to regulate their emotions and consider the processes of emotional habituation and cognitive reappraisal of one's emotional reactions. Finally, we review studies that suggest disclosure can promote cognitive regulation of self-images and goals.

Pennebaker's disclosure paradigm: major findings

Numerous investigators have replicated and extended Pennebaker and Beall's original (1986) findings regarding the health benefits of disclosure. In controlled experimental studies with healthy individuals (mostly college students), disclosure decreased physician visits (Greenberg *et al.*, 1996; Pennebaker *et al.*, 1990), reduced reported physical symptoms (Greenberg & Stone, 1992; Lepore & Greenberg, 2002), enhanced immune outcomes (Pennebaker *et al.*, 1988; Petrie *et al.*, 1995), diminished psychological distress (Lepore, 1997a; Paez *et al.*, 1999) and facilitated adaptive behaviors (Lepore & Greenberg, 2002; Spera *et al.*, 1994). Disclosure can also benefit medical patients. Rheumatoid arthritis (RA) patients who disclosed thoughts and feelings about a stressor reported less affective disturbance and physical disability at three-month follow-up than controls. Asthma patients assigned to a written disclosure intervention improved in lung function and RA patients improved in disease activity, relative to controls (Smyth *et al.*, 1999).

In the following section, we will trace theories that explain why this relatively brief intervention produced such striking mental and physical health benefits.

Inhibition or emotional self-regulation?

In this section, we describe Pennebaker's (1989) inhibition model and empirical studies that support and challenge the model. We then introduce the concept of emotional self-regulation as an alternative explanatory mechanism to inhibition. Emotional self-regulation is part of the broader construct of self-regulation or self-control and refers specifically to control over the quality, frequency, intensity, or duration of responses in any of the three emotion channels – experience, physiology, and behavior. This process influences what types of emotions people have, how intensely they experience these emotions, and how they express them (see Lepore *et al.*, 2002, for a more comprehensive definition).

The inhibition model

In the original disclosure paradigm (Pennebaker & Beall, 1986) participants wrote mostly about undisclosed traumas. The rationale was that individuals typically inhibit traumas because of their emotional intensity and to avoid negative social responses. Inhibition was hypothesized to adversely affect physiological systems, including the central nervous and immune systems. Chronic physiological strain due to inhibition was thought to increase susceptibility to illness. Disclosure, on the other hand, was seen as reducing the negative physiological effects of chronic inhibition (Pennebaker, 1989). Consistent with this model, correlational studies have revealed negative effects on health of concealing one's gay identity (Cole *et al.*, 1996), not disclosing past traumas (Pennebaker & Susman, 1988), and not discussing one's feelings about a spouse's death with others (Pennebaker & O'Heeron, 1984).

Challenges to the inhibition model

Ironically, the success of some disclosure studies posed a challenge to the inhibition model. Writing about recent, ongoing, or upcoming events had similar or better psychosocial health benefits than writing about past traumas (Smyth, 1998). College students who wrote about adjusting to college reduced their physician visits and improved their grade point averages (Cameron & Nicholls, 1998; Pennebaker *et al.*, 1990). Students who wrote about their reactions to an upcoming examination reduced their depression, relative to controls (Lepore, 1997a). Unemployed professionals who wrote down their emotions about job loss found jobs more quickly than controls (Spera *et al.*, 1994). Students who wrote about a recent relationship breakup had fewer upper respiratory symptoms, less tension, and less fatigue than controls (Lepore & Greenberg, 2002). These studies suggested that release of chronic long-term inhibition may not be the most important component of disclosure interventions. When a stressful event is ongoing or anticipated, individuals may concurrently inhibit some of their emotional reactions, but inhibition would not cumulate over time and lead to physiological damage as described by the model.

Other findings also challenge the inhibition model (see review by Littrell, 1998). In a sample of bereaved spouses, emotional repressors and those who did not express grief at six months post-loss had especially good psychological outcomes at 14 months post-loss (Bonanno *et al.*, 1995). These results were consistent with an earlier extensive literature review (Wortman & Silver, 1989) that found very few instances of delayed grief reactions in those who did not express grief initially. These findings only indirectly challenge inhibition, however. Lack of grief expression might be due to consistently low emotional experience, rather than deliberate inhibition. Further, there may have been adverse physiological effects in these studies that were not assessed.

Some studies also suggest that venting previously suppressed feelings is not necessary or sufficient to achieve beneficial effects. Writing about both thoughts and feelings enhanced the benefits of disclosure beyond those achieved by simple ventilation of feelings (Pennebaker & Beall, 1986). In a sample of college students assigned to express their emotions through movement alone, movement plus writing, or to a non-expressive control (Krantz & Pennebaker's study as cited in Pennebaker, 1997), expressive movement without writing was of little benefit. A third study (Pennebaker *et al.*, 1990), found no evidence that participants who had inhibited their traumas more or were higher in self-concealment benefited more from emotional writing. Writing about positive aspects of past traumas produced the same health benefits as confronting negative feelings about these events (King & Miner, 2000).

The abovementioned studies call into question whether prior inhibition is necessary or sufficient for effective disclosure. In addition, some individuals feel the need to express painful feelings repeatedly, a phenomenon which the inhibition model cannot easily explain. Could written experimental disclosure be beneficial even if individuals had expressed their feelings before?

To address this issue, we randomly assigned participants to write about undisclosed past traumas, previously disclosed traumas, or to a neutral events control (Greenberg & Stone, 1992). Follow-up assessments two months later found no differential effects of writing about disclosed versus undisclosed traumas on either reported health or physician visits. Surprisingly, the disclosed trauma group also reported greater negative mood and physical symptom increases than the undisclosed trauma group at immediate post-test. Previous disclosure was therefore associated with more intense rather than attenuated emotional reactions to the traumas disclosed. These findings suggested that prior inhibition did not necessarily enhance the health effects of disclosure. Yet we could not rule out prior inhibition altogether, because even the disclosed trauma group reported previously holding back their feelings about these traumas to a moderate degree (mean of 3.91 on a 7-point scale).

Stimulus- and response-related emotional habituation

An early study in the clinical literature (Watson & Marks, 1972) raised additional questions about the necessity of confronting past personal experiences to reduce negative emotional reactions. In a sample of phobic clients, exposure to phobia-irrelevant stimuli (e.g. scenes of being eaten by tigers) reduced anxiety and avoidance as much as exposure to the stimuli involved in their phobias (e.g. scenes involving crowded places). The authors suggested that exposure to fearful stimuli promoted physiological and psychological habituation, leading to a reduction in the fear response over time. Two different types of habituation were hypothesized. First, being confronted with specific fear-related stimuli for long periods may decrease emotional reactivity to these cues (*stimulus-related habituation*). Second, exposure to phobia-irrelevant stimuli may promote *response-related habituation*, resulting in a better ability to tolerate the experience of fear, regardless of its context.

This study had potentially important implications for the emotional disclosure paradigm. Writing or talking about past traumas also involves exposure to emotionally-charged stimuli and also stimulates negative emotional experience. Perhaps emotional disclosure manipulations are beneficial because they facilitate emotional self-regulation via both stimulus-related and response-related habituation. The next set of studies addressed these issues.

Disclosing imaginary traumas and emotional self-regulation

If disclosure causes response-related habituation, it follows that the experience of negative emotion in a safe context is all that is necessary to produce health benefits. The specific content of writing does not necessarily have to be a past personal trauma. Writing about imaginary traumas should therefore improve health as much as writing about real traumas.

To address this issue, we (Greenberg et al., 1996) experimentally manipulated event-specific inhibition by randomly assigning participants to write about past personal traumas, imaginary traumas that they had not previously experienced, or non-emotional events. Imaginary events could not, by definition, have any inhibition attached to them. Imaginary trauma participants were yoked to their real trauma counterparts and wrote about the same topics. Results indicated that, as hypothesized, the topic written about made little difference to the efficacy of the disclosure intervention. As shown in Figure 3.1, both real and imaginary trauma groups visited the student health center for illness less often at one-month follow-up, relative to controls. The health effects in the imaginary group could not be explained by inhibition alone. Findings were, however, consistent with response-related habituation. Participants in the imaginary group could accommodate to negative emotional experience in a safe context. Perhaps this increased their self-regulation and tolerance of negative emotion in other areas of their lives.

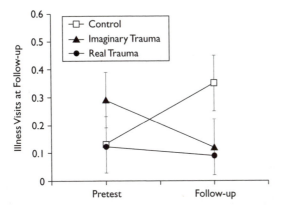

Figure 3.1 Group means for illness visits at pretest and follow-up. © 1996, American Psychological Association. Reprinted with modifications by permission of the publisher and author from Greenberg *et al.* (1996).

Whereas the previous study examined habituation to the experience of negative emotion in general, the next set of studies focused on how opportunities for disclosure and social constraints surrounding disclosure might affect individuals' emotional responses to intrusive stress-related thoughts and stimuli.

Disclosure and reactions to stress-related thoughts and stimuli

One implication of the self-regulation perspective is that emotional expression in a safe context should attenuate negative affective and physiological responses to stress-related stimuli. By "safe" context, we mean one in which there are comforting social cues, encouragement of open emotional expression, or an absence of critical evaluation. A safe context can help individuals to prolong their exposure to painful stimuli, thereby enabling them to positively revise their views and feelings about the stimuli (see related discussions by Foa & Kozak, 1986; Lepore, 2001; Lepore *et al.*, 1996). By extension, we would expect that expression of trauma-related thoughts and feelings in an unsafe context would undermine the benefits of emotional expression. In fact, emotional expression in an unsafe context might exacerbate negative emotional and physiological responses to stressors by stirring up additional negative emotions and reinforcing feelings of helplessness.

In recent years, a number of findings have emerged that are directly relevant to these predictions. These studies all focus on how emotional expression influences individuals' responses to stress-related intrusive thoughts, which are unbidden thoughts, memories, and images of stressors. If emotional expression in a safe context facilitates self-regulation of negative responses to reminders of stressors, then the association between intrusive thoughts and mental and physical health outcomes should be attenuated in individuals who express their emotions in a safe context. Expression in an unsafe context might even exacerbate negative responses.

Two experimental studies have examined how written emotional expression modulates responses to intrusive thoughts. Written emotional expression provides a feeling of present safety, because emotional expression is encouraged, there is no social evaluation of the expression, and there is a certain degree of anonymity. In the first study (Lepore, 1997a), expressive writing attenuated the association between intrusive thoughts and depressive symptoms among individuals who were anticipating graduate-school entrance examinations. As shown in Figure 3.2, intrusive thoughts measured one month prior to the exam were positively related to depressive symptoms three days prior to the exam in the control-writing group, but not in the expressive-writing group. In the second study (Lepore & Greenberg, 2002), expressive writing attenuated the association between a composite measure of intrusive/avoidant thoughts and upper respiratory illness (URI) symptoms among individuals who had a relationship breakup. As shown in Figure 3.3, a higher level of intrusive/avoidant reactions was related to short-term increases in URI symptoms in participants who wrote about a control topic, but was unrelated to URI symptoms in participants who wrote expressively about their breakup.

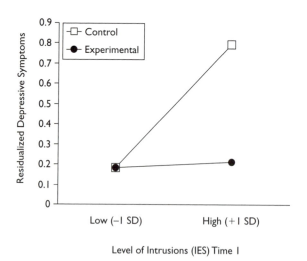

Figure 3.2 Relation between intrusive thoughts and changes in depression from Time 1 to Time 2 (residualized) as a function of writing condition. © 1997, American Psychological Association. Reprinted from Lepore (1997a).

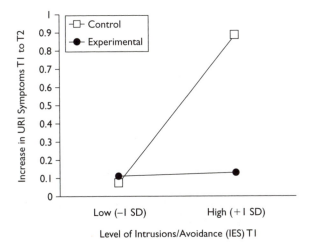

Figure 3.3 Relation between level of intrusions/avoidance at Time 1 and changes in upper respiratory illness (URI) symptoms from Time 1 to Time 2 (T2 – T1) as a function of writing condition. Reprinted from Lepore, S.J. & Greenberg, M.A. (2002).

While most of the data presented above focus on nonsocial disclosure, disclosure seldom occurs in a social vacuum. Indeed, as we discuss in the next section, the responses of others can be critical to the efficacy of disclosure in modulating negative thoughts and emotions.

Negative social responses impede emotional regulation

A growing number of quasi-experimental field studies have investigated how the social context of disclosure moderates the relation between intrusive thoughts and various emotional, physical, and mental health outcomes. Two studies involved cancer patients. One study found that a subset of men reported social constraints in talking with significant others about their prostate cancer (Lepore & Helgeson, 1998). These men, when compared with their peers who had fewer constraints, reported more cancer-related intrusive thoughts and were more likely to avoid thinking and talking about their cancer. Moreover, constraints potentiated the association between intrusive thoughts and poor mental health. There was a stronger negative association between intrusive thoughts and mental health in men who had high social constraints than in men who had relatively few constraints. A more rigorous test of the model was provided in a longitudinal study on the emotional adaptation of women who had been treated for localized breast or colon cancer (Lepore, 1997b). Data were collected from women three months (T1) and 11 months (T2) after their diagnosis. Regression analyses revealed that T1 social constraints moderated the association between T1 intrusive thoughts about cancer and T2 negative affect, after statistically controlling for T1 negative affect: a higher level of intrusive thoughts was associated with an increase in negative affect in women who had high social constraints, but was unrelated to negative affect in women with relatively few social constraints.

Studies involving other trauma populations reveal a similar pattern of results. In a study of bereaved mothers, intrusive thoughts at three weeks post-loss were associated with increases in depressive symptoms if mothers felt constrained in talking about the loss but not if they felt relatively unconstrained (Lepore et al., 1996). In children exposed to inner-city violence, violence exposure was associated with higher levels of internalizing symptoms (Kliewer et al., 1998). The highest risk group for internalizing symptoms consisted of children with a high level of violence-related intrusive thoughts combined with a low level of social support or a high level of social constraints.

The findings from these studies are quite robust: they have emerged in people of many different ages (children, college students, adults), in people experiencing very diverse stressors (cancer, violence, examinations, relationship breakups), in both experimental and quasi-experimental studies, and for many different outcomes (e.g. depressive symptoms, upper-respiratory symptoms). In addition to our studies reported above, other investigators have found that the social context moderates the effects of intrusive thoughts on psychological adjustment to stressors (e.g. Lutgendorf et al., 1999; Major & Gramzow, 1999; Manne, 1999). It appears that emotional expression in a safe context does indeed increase regulation of negative responses to intrusive thoughts whereas an unsafe social context exacerbates negative affective reactions to intrusive thoughts. What is not known is whether this negative affective exacerbation is actually the result of preexisting low social support or negative social responses or whether certain types of people are ineffective at expressing emotions to others and inadvertently drive away support and provoke negative reactions.

Emotional self-regulation mechanisms

The previous studies suggest that effective disclosure helps people to tolerate and regulate negative emotional responses. Drawing on both the disclosure and broader clinical literatures, we highlight two emotional self-regulation processes: *emotional habituation* and *cognitive reappraisal of emotion*.

Emotional habituation

One mechanism by which emotional disclosure might facilitate adjustment is habituation. "The writing assignment may produce extinction of negative emotional associations through repetition and exposure" (Bootzin, 1997, p. 167). When individuals actively confront memories of past traumas or ongoing aversive situations, their physiological and subjective emotional responses should gradually diminish as they accommodate to these events. As described above, a more general habituation process may also occur in which people learn to tolerate the experience of negative emotions, regardless of context, so that the emotions themselves become less aversive.

Foa and colleagues (Foa & Kozak, 1986) theorized that habituation affects cognitive structures underlying fear. They proposed that these cognitive structures provide information about situations that evoke fear (e.g. past traumas or predators), the nature of fear responses (e.g. physiological arousal or feelings of terror), and the subjective meaning of these situations and responses (e.g. this situation is dangerous, my response is bad). To decrease fear, one should first activate the fear structure and then provide incompatible information. When a person experiences habituation following prolonged exposure, this reduction in the fear response contradicts response elements of the structure. This should also change meaning elements so that the situation is viewed as less dangerous and less negative and the self as more competent.

In successful habituation, individuals should experience strong negative emotions initially, with gradual decreases in negative emotion within and across exposure sessions (Foa, 1997). Two recent studies of post-traumatic stress disorder (PTSD) patients support these hypotheses. Rape survivors who showed the most intense facial expressions of fear during the first session of exposure benefited the most from treatment (Foa et al., 1995). Assault victims who reported high initial anxiety during exposure and gradual habituation of anxiety across sessions had lower levels of PTSD symptoms at follow-up (Jaycox et al., 1998). Contrary to expectations, however, within-session habituation was unrelated to treatment outcome. Clients whose fear remained high across an entire session did not necessarily benefit any less from treatment than those whose anxiety gradually diminished during the session.

The emotional disclosure paradigm is similar to exposure therapy in that it also involves confrontation with negative stimuli and emotions. Is there any evidence that emotional engagement and habituation occur following disclosure?

Some studies support the role of emotional engagement. Disclosure participants rated by judges as revealing the most emotion in their voices had lower skin conductance levels during disclosure than those who expressed less emotion (Pennebaker et al., 1987). Participants with a higher proportion of emotion-focused words in their essays had lower levels of antibody to Epstein-Barr virus (EBV) immediately after writing, indicating better immune functioning, than those who wrote fewer words (Esterling et al., 1990). Participants who demonstrated the highest emotional involvement in disclosure had the greatest decreases in antibody titers to EBV from pre-test to four-week post-test (Lutgendorf et al., 1994).

Studies using pre–post mood measures have, however, provided only mixed support for emotional engagement. In arthritis patients, more negative mood increases during disclosure were associated with less objectively-assessed joint swelling at follow-up (Kelley et al., 1997). A meta-analysis, however, found no association between changes in negative affect during essay-writing and the outcome of disclosure (Smyth, 1998). Average mood change may not, however, be a good measure of habituation, because participants with high initial negative mood who habituated across sessions could have the same average score as those with moderate initial mood who did not habituate.

Does habituation occur during disclosure sessions? In one study (Petrie *et al.*, 1998), college students who wrote about emotional topics showed decreases in self-reported tension across the three writing days. Another study (Segal & Murray, 1994) did not, however, find changes in reported negative affect across four days of verbal disclosure. Other evidence comes from studies using physiological measures. College students who wrote about stressful events showed greater decreases in skin conductance across the four writing days than non-emotional event controls (Petrie *et al.*, 1995), suggesting that habituation occurred between sessions. Participants who viewed an emotional film and then talked about their responses were more autonomically aroused initially when viewing the film again (Mendolia & Kleck, 1993). However, when the second viewing was 48 hours later, emotion condition participants had lower autonomic arousal than controls. This is consistent with clinical literature suggesting that habituation decreases emotional arousal between sessions, rather than within-session.

In summary, emotional engagement and habituation mechanisms are involved in emotional disclosure interventions. When individuals confront their negative feelings about stressful events, the physiological and perhaps subjective intensity of these feelings is diminished over time.

Cognitive reappraisal of emotion

We now turn to the second mechanism whereby emotional disclosure interventions might enhance emotional regulation. Disclosure might lead to cognitive changes in how people view their emotional reactions. Actively confronting negative emotions could enhance perceptions of self-efficacy and control over emotion. Tuning in to one's own feelings in a safe context may also promote deeper understanding, validation and acceptance of these reactions. We will discuss each of these processes.

Disclosure might provide mastery experiences in which individuals observe themselves tolerating and diminishing negative emotions. As a result, they might start to see themselves as people who can handle negative emotions. In other words, their self-efficacy for emotional regulation should increase. In explaining why writing about imaginary traumas produces health benefits, Greenberg and colleagues wrote, "the benefits of disclosure may extend beyond revision of specific past events to include more general perceptions of control and mastery over one's emotional reactions, regardless of how these are triggered" (Greenberg *et al.*, 1996, p. 589). When people feel more control over their emotional experiences, negative moods should be less prolonged and intense, resulting in less chronic subjective stress.

There is some empirical support for this proposition. Stronger mood regulation expectancies were associated with lower distress and physical symptoms in college students and caregivers of Alzheimer's patients (Brashares & Catanzaro, 1994;

Kirsch *et al.*, 1990). But does disclosure change people's cognitive appraisals of their own emotional reactions? A recent study (Paez *et al.*, 1999) supports this idea. College students who wrote about emotional reactions to undisclosed traumas reported decreases in the negative affective valence induced by remembering at two-month follow-up, relative to controls. Thus, disclosure helped them to view their emotional engagement as less negative and more beneficial. This is consistent with the emotional blunting to intrusive thoughts observed in previous studies (Lepore, 1997a; Lepore & Greenberg, 2002). Further, in the study by Paez and colleagues, experimental participants also perceived their traumatic experiences as more controllable at follow-up.

The idea that disclosing emotions can promote emotional self-efficacy was examined in a sample of patients with metastatic breast cancer attending supportive–expressive group psychotherapy (Giese-Davis *et al.*, 2000). Disclosing emotions associated with cancer and fears of death during group therapy enhanced perceived self-efficacy to tolerate these emotions, relative to controls. Support group participants tended to maintain their self-efficacy to confront cancer-related feelings over time, whereas controls evidenced a decrease. Support group partici-pants also decreased their emotional suppression over time, relative to controls. Perhaps increased emotional self-efficacy was associated with fuller emotional experience in these patients. Because supportive– expressive therapy can increase survival time with cancer (Spiegel *et al.*, 1989), it is possible that increased emotional self-efficacy might play a part in the health benefits. Perhaps increased perceived control over emotion reduces subjective stress and chronic autonomic arousal, with subsequent immune benefits.

Disclosure may also enhance emotional self-regulation by providing the oppor-tunity to understand, explore, and accept one's own emotional experiences. This mechanism may be particularly applicable to trauma victims because trauma can impair people's ability to experience and regulate emotion. Clinical observations suggest that "among the direct effects of severe trauma in adults is a lifelong dread of the return of the traumatic state and an expectation of it. Emotions are frequently experienced as trauma screens; hence, there is a fear of one's emotion and an impairment of affect tolerance" (Krystal, 1988, p. 147). One study (Van der Kolk & Ducey, 1989) found that trauma survivors responded to ambiguous affect-arousing stimuli in an all-or-none manner. They were unable to modulate emotion and therefore either did not experience their feelings at all or were flooded with intense and overwhelming affect.

Theoretical models of psychological adaptation to trauma (McCann *et al.*, 1988) explain this lack of emotion-regulation in trauma survivors as due to disrupted self-schemata in the areas of trust and intimacy. Disruption of self-trust schemata means that people no longer trust their own perceptions, reactions, and judgments. Because they were unable to protect themselves from victimization, they may not consider their own reactions to be valid indicators of external reality. This leaves them vulnerable to invalidation by powerful others. If somebody else tells them they should not feel a certain way, they are likely to put aside their own feelings.

Even if not invalidated by others, they question and doubt the legitimacy of the feelings they experience. Disruption of self-intimacy schemata means that people no longer feel connected with their own selves. Lacking a stable sense of self (Kohut, 1977), they are unable to calm, soothe, or nurture themselves so as to modulate negative affective states.

Expressive writing manipulations can help people to feel more connected with their own selves and to experience and accept their own emotional reactions. The typical instructions encourage people to explore their deepest thoughts and feelings and implicitly suggest that such feelings are valid, and that it is permissible and even potentially beneficial to experience them. Delving deeply into one's own feelings without having to monitor one's self-presentation, include other people's perspectives, or make the story easier for others to hear may enhance feelings of connection with one's self. People may come to see their feelings as an integral part of themselves, rather than pushing them away. Integrating feelings with thoughts and memories during disclosure may enhance the subjective validity of these reactions. People may begin to understand the roots of these feelings in specific past or ongoing events. Emotional disclosure manipulations, like certain types of psychotherapy, may therefore set the stage for "allowing into awareness an organization of one's experience previously regarded as unacceptable and accepting it" (Greenberg & Safran, 1987, p. 193).

Empirical studies provide some support for these theories. In one study (Greenberg et al., 1996), some participants wrote poignantly in their essays about doubting their own feelings and trying to suppress them. In another study (Paez et al., 1999), participants with more alexithymic deficits in the ability to differentiate and describe their feelings had larger reductions in negative mood than those with fewer deficits, suggesting that disclosure may enhance emotional experiencing. A recent dissertation study in the first author's laboratory found that gay men who wrote about their deepest thoughts and feelings about being gay tended to report increased clarity of gay-related feelings and were less likely to avoid these feelings at two-month follow-up, relative to trivial event controls. The experimental group also reported fewer psychosomatic symptoms at follow-up, and decreases in avoidance were associated with concomitant decreases in symptoms (Swanbon, 1999).

A recent experimental study (Lepore et al., 2000) also supports the emotional regulation hypothesis. Undergraduates who watched a highly distressing film were assigned to either a no-talk control condition or to talk alone, to a validating confederate, or to an invalidating confederate. Talking about one's emotional reactions to the film alone or to a validating confederate reduced intrusive thoughts and perceived stress on reexposure to the stressor, relative to not talking. Those in the invalidate condition did not, however, report the same reductions in intrusion or stress as participants in the other disclosure conditions. These findings suggest that disclosure has an implicit emotionally validating function. Talking alone had the same psychological benefits as receiving social validation. Invalidation diminished disclosure's beneficial impact.

Emotional disclosure and cognitive regulation of self-images

A recent disclosure study (King, 2001) extends the self-regulation paradigm to cognitive rather than emotional regulation. Participants were randomly assigned to write narrative descriptions of their best possible future selves, their thoughts and feelings about past traumas, both future selves and past traumas, or to a non-emotional event control. In the future selves condition, participants imagined a future in which all of their life goals had been realized. Writing about future selves, past traumas, or both, decreased health center visits over the next five months, relative to control writing.

The authors argued that writing about future selves was a form of self-regulation in that it could promote awareness and clarity about one's goals and values and lead to a reorganization of priorities. Writing about positive life goals does not, however, involve emotional confrontation and cannot fit within an emotion regulation framework. This suggests that disclosure may facilitate a different type of self-regulation. Perhaps disclosure allows people to cognitively regulate their views of self so as to promote positive self-images and motivate adaptive behavior. A qualitative study that examined drug addicts' narratives of recovery (McIntosh & McKeganey, 2000) found that recovering addicts used narratives to reinterpret their drug-using lifestyle, describe turning points which led to their recovery, and reconstruct new non-addict identities. In their narratives, individuals differentiated who they were "at heart" and their "future self" from their "self on drugs." This allowed them to forgive themselves for past mistakes and maintain hope.

This perspective is consistent with McAdams's (1990) life-story theory of adult identity which suggests that "the process of identity development … is the gradual construction and reconstruction of a personal myth integrating one's perceived past, present, and anticipated future, while specifying ways in which the individual fits into and distinguishes him- or herself in the social world" (McAdams & de St Aubin, 1992, p. 1007). Writing expressive narratives may help people to construct a stable sense of identity that gives meaning and purpose to their lives. It can also help them to integrate their past experiences, including traumas, with their current values and goals, perhaps leading to a deeper understanding of how their lives have been shaped by these events. Constructing narratives may also help people adjust to an ongoing stressor by helping them to frame this event within the overall context and direction of their lives.

Expressive narratives may promote self-regulation of identity in helping people to make sense of their lives overall and to incorporate specific discrepant events into their self-views. Two correlational studies highlight particular types of narratives that are associated with optimal psychosocial adjustment. In one study, adults rated as highly generative could be distinguished from their less generative counterparts by life narratives that expressed a clear, temporally stable personal ideology, transformed bad experiences into good outcomes, and set goals for the future to benefit society (McAdams et al., 1997). In the other study (Wong & Watt,

1991), adults judged to be aging successfully and unsuccessfully recounted critical past incidents that had significantly influenced their lives. Unsuccessful agers were less able to reconcile, integrate, and accept past problematic experiences in their narratives. In contrast, successful agers described more cohesive narratives that accepted and integrated the past and more instrumental narratives that recounted past achievements and successful coping.

Future disclosure interventions might be enhanced by using instructions that promote integration of past experiences with current self-views and future goals or encourage to tell stories which emphasize their past history of competence and problem-solving abilities.

Summary

This chapter reviewed recent developments in the disclosure literature and proposed a self-regulation theory. Initially, the benefits of disclosure were thought due to expressing suppressed emotions about traumas. However, disclosure also enhances adjustment to ongoing or forthcoming events. Disclosure also diminishes the psychic toxicity of intrusive thoughts, reducing their associations with depression and illness. Writing about imaginary traumas or future possible selves also benefits health. We argue that disclosure interventions enhance emotional self-regulation by promoting habituation, emotional self-efficacy, and emotional validation, and they enhance cognitive self-regulation by helping people to integrate stressful events with goals and values so as to maintain positive self-images and motivate adaptive behavior.

Acknowledgments

Contributions to this chapter were partly supported by NIMH grants 1-54217, 1-49432, CA-68354, and CA-61303, and by a grant from The City University of New York PSC-CUNY Research Award Program. We are grateful to Megan Holmes for assisting with the library research for this chapter.

References

Bonanno, G.A., Keltner, D., Holen, A., & Horowitz, M.J. (1995). When avoiding unpleasant emotions might not be such a bad thing: verbal–autonomic response dissociation and midlife conjugal bereavement. *Journal of Personality and Social Psychology*, **69**, 975–989.

Bootzin, R.R. (1997). Examining the theory and clinical utility of writing about emotional experiences. *Psychological Science*, **8**, 167–169.

Brashares, H.J. & Catanzaro, S.J. (1994). Mood regulation expectancies, coping responses, depression, and sense of burden in female caregivers of Alzheimer's patients. *Journal of Nervous and Mental Disease*, **182**, 437–442.

Cameron, L.D. & Nicholls, G. (1998). Expression of stressful experiences through writing: effects of a self-regulation manipulation for pessimists and optimists. *Health Psychology*, **17**, 84–92.

Cole, S.W., Kemeny, M.W., Taylor, S.E., & Visscher, B.R. (1996). Elevated health risk among men who conceal their homosexuality. *Health Psychology*, **15**, 243–251.

Esterling, B.A., Antoni, M.H., Kumar, M., & Schneiderman, N. (1990). Emotional repression, stress disclosure responses, and Epstein-Barr viral capsid antigen titers. *Psychosomatic Medicine*, **52**, 397–410.

Foa, E.B. (1997). Psychological processes related to recovery from a trauma and an effective treatment for PTSD. *Annals of the New York Academy of Sciences*, **21**, 410–424.

Foa, E.B. & Kozak, M.J. (1986). Emotional processing of fear: exposure to corrective information. *Psychological Bulletin*, **99**, 20–35.

Foa, E.B., Riggs, D.S., Massie, E.D., & Yarczower, M. (1995). The impact of fear activation and anger on the efficacy of exposure treatment for PTSD. *Behavior Therapy*, **26**, 487–499.

Giese-Davis, J., Koopman, C., Butler, D., Classen, C., Cordova, M., Fobair, P., Benson, J., Carlson, R.W., & Spiegel, D. (2000). Change over time in emotional control in supportive–expressive group therapy for metastatic breast cancer patients. Paper presented at the Society of Behavioral Medicine, Nashville, TN.

Greenberg, L.S. & Safran, J.D. (1987). *Emotion in psychotherapy*. New York: Guilford Press.

Greenberg, M.A. & Stone, A.A. (1992). Emotional disclosure about traumas and its relation to health: effects of previous disclosure and trauma severity. *Journal of Personality and Social Psychology*, **63**, 75–84.

Greenberg, M.A., Wortman, C.B., & Stone, A.A. (1996). Emotional expression and physical health: revising traumatic memories or fostering self-regulation? *Journal of Personality and Social Psychology*, **71**, 588–602.

Jaycox, L.H., Foa, E.B., & Morral, A.R. (1998). Influence of emotional engagement and habituation on exposure therapy for PTSD. *Journal of Consulting and Clinical Psychology*, **66**, 185–192.

Kelley, J.E., Lumley, M.A., & Leisen, J.C.C. (1997). Health effects of emotional disclosure in rheumatoid arthritis patients. *Health Psychology*, **16**, 331–340.

Kliewer, W.L., Lepore, S.J., Oskin, D., & Johnson, P.D. (1998). The role of social and cognitive processes in children's adjustment to community violence. *Journal of Consulting and Clinical Psychology*, **66**, 199–209.

King, L.A. (2001). The health benefits of writing about life goals. *Personality and Social Psychology Bulletin*, **27**, 778–807.

King, L.A. & Miner, K.N. (2000). Writing about the perceived benefits of traumatic events: implications for physical health. *Personality and Social Psychology Bulletin*, **26**, 220–230.

Kirsch, I., Mearns, J., & Catanzaro, S.J. (1990). Mood-regulation expectancies as determinants of dysphoria in college students. *Journal of Counseling Psychology*, **37**, 306–312.

Kohut, H. (1977). *The restoration of self*. New York: International Universities Press.

Krystal, H. (1988). *Integration and self-healing: Affect, trauma, alexithymia*. Hillsdale, NJ: The Analytic Press.

Lepore, S.J. (1997a). Expressive writing moderates the relation between intrusive thoughts and depressive symptoms. *Journal of Personality and Social Psychology*, **73**, 1030–1037.

Lepore, S.J. (1997b). Social constraints, intrusive thoughts, and negative affect in women with cancer. Paper presented at the Society of Behavioral Medicine, San Francisco, CA.

Lepore, S.J. (2001). A social–cognitive processing model of emotional adjustment to cancer. In A. Baum & B.L Andersen (eds), *Psychosocial interventions for cancer* (pp. 94–116). Washington, DC: American Psychological Association.

Lepore, S.J. & Greenberg, M.A. (2002). Mending broken hearts: effects of expressive writing on mood, cognitive processing, social adjustment, and health following a relationship breakup. *Psychology and Health*, **17**, 547–560.

Lepore, S.J., Greenberg, M.A., Bruno, M., & Smyth, J.M. (2002). Expressive writing and health: self-regulation of emotion-related experience, physiology and behavior. In S.J. Lepore & J.M. Smyth (eds). *The writing cure: How expressive writing influences health and well-being.* Washington, DC: American Psychological Association.

Lepore, S.J. & Helgeson, V. (1998). Social constraints moderate the relation between intrusive thoughts and mental health in prostate cancer survivors. *Journal of Social and Clinical Psychology*, **17**, 89–106.

Lepore, S.J., Ragan, J.D., & Jones, S. (2000). Talking facilitates cognitive–emotional processes of adaptation to an acute stressor. *Journal of Personality and Social Psychology*, **78**, 499–508.

Lepore, S.J., Silver, R.C., Wortman, C.B., & Wayment, H.A. (1996). Social constraints, intrusive thoughts, and depressive symptoms among bereaved mothers. *Journal of Personality and Social Psychology*, **70**, 271–282.

Littrell, J. (1998). Is the reexperience of painful emotion therapeutic? *Clinical Psychology Review*, **18**, 71–102.

Lutgendorf, S., Anderson, B., Larsen, K., Buller, R.E., & Sorosky, J.I. (1999). Cognitive processing, social support coping, and distress in gynecological cancer patients. *Cancer Research, Therapy, and Control*, **8**, 9–19.

Lutgendorf, S.K., Antoni, M.H., Kumar, M., & Schneiderman, N. (1994). Changes in cognitive coping strategies predict EBV-antibody titer change following a stressor disclosure induction. *Journal of Psychosomatic Research*, **38**, 63–78.

McAdams, D.P. (1990). Unity and purpose in human lives: the emergence of identity as a life story. In A.I. Rabin, R.A. Zucker, R.A. Emmons, & S. Frank (eds), *Studying persons and lives* (pp. 148–200). New York: Springer.

McAdams, D.P. & de St Aubin, E. (1992). A theory of generativity and its assessment through self-report, behavioral acts, and narrative themes in autobiography. *Journal of Personality and Social Psychology*, **62**, 1003–1015.

McAdams, D.P., Diamond, A., de St Aubin, E., & Mansfield, E. (1997). Stories of commitment: the psychosocial construction of generative lives. *Journal of Personality and Social Psychology*, **72**, 678–694.

McCann, I.L., Sakheim, D.K., & Abrahamson, D.J. (1988). Trauma and victimization: a model of psychological adaptation. *The Counseling Psychologist*, **16**, 531–594.

McIntosh, J. & McKeganey, N. (2000). Addicts' narratives of recovery from drug use: constructing a non-addict identity. *Social Science and Medicine*, **50**, 1501–1510.

Major, B. & Gramzow, R.H. (1999). Abortion as stigma: cognitive and emotional implications of concealment. *Journal of Personality and Social Psychology*, **77**, 735–745.

Manne, S.L. (1999). Intrusive thoughts and psychological distress among cancer patients: the role of spouse avoidance and criticism. *Journal of Consulting and Clinical Psychology*, **67**, 539–546.

Mendolia, M. & Kleck, R.E. (1993). Effects of talking about a stressful event on arousal: does what we talk about make a difference? *Journal of Personality and Social Psychology*, **64**, 283–292.

Paez, D., Velasco, C., & Gonzalez, J.L. (1999). Expressive writing and the role of alexithymia as a dispositional deficit in self-disclosure and psychological health. *Journal of Personality and Social Psychology*, **77**, 630–641.

Pennebaker, J.W. (1989). Confession, inhibition, and disease. In L. Berkowitz (ed.), *Advances in experimental social psychology*, Vol. 22 (pp. 211–244). Orlando, FL: Academic Press.

Pennebaker, J.W. (1997). Writing about emotional experiences as a therapeutic process. *Psychological Science*, **8**, 162–166.

Pennebaker, J.W. & Beall, S.K. (1986). Confronting a traumatic event: toward an understanding of inhibition and disease. *Journal of Personality and Social Psychology*, **58**, 528–537.

Pennebaker, J.W., Colder, M., & Sharp, L.K. (1990). Accelerating the coping process. *Journal of Personality and Social Psychology*, **58**, 528–537.

Pennebaker, J.W., Hughes, C.F., & O'Heeron, R.C. (1987). The psychophysiology of confession: linking inhibitory and psychosomatic processes. *Journal of Personality and Social Psychology*, **52**, 781–793.

Pennebaker, J.W., Kiecolt-Glaser, J., & Glaser, R. (1988). Disclosure of traumas and immune function: health implications for psychotherapy. *Journal of Consulting and Clinical Psychology*, **56**, 239–245.

Pennebaker, J.W. & O'Heeron, R.C. (1984). Confiding in others and illness rate among spouses of suicide and accidental death victims. *Journal of Abnormal Psychology*, **93**, 473–476.

Pennebaker, J.W. & Susman, J.R. (1988). Disclosure of traumas and psychosomatic processes. *Social Science and Medicine*, **26**, 327–332.

Petrie, K.J., Booth, R.J., & Pennebaker, J.W. (1998). The immunological effects of thought suppression. *Journal of Personality and Social Psychology*, **75**, 1264–1272.

Petrie, K.J., Booth, R.J., Pennebaker, J.W., Davison, K.P., & Thomas, M.G. (1995). Disclosure of trauma and immune response to a hepatitis vaccination program. *Journal of Consulting and Clinical Psychology*, **63**, 787–792.

Segal, D.L. & Murray, E.J. (1994). Emotional expression in cognitive therapy and vocal expression of feeling. *Journal of Social and Clinical Psychology*, **13**, 189–206.

Smyth, J.M. (1998). Written emotional expression: effect sizes, outcome types, and moderating variables. *Journal of Consulting and Clinical Psychology*, **66**, 174–178.

Smyth, J.M., Stone, A.A., Hurewitz, A., & Kaell, A. (1999). Effects of writing about stressful experiences on symptom reduction in patients with asthma or rheumatoid arthritis. *Journal of the American Medical Association*, **281**, 1304–1309.

Spera, S., Buhrfeind, E., & Pennebaker, J.W. (1994). Expressive writing and job loss. *Academy of Management Journal*, **37**, 722–733.

Spiegel, D., Bloom, J.R., Kraemer, H.C., & Gottheil, E. (1989). Effect of psychosocial treatment on survival of patients with metastatic breast cancer. *Lancet*, **2**(8668), 888–891.

Swanbon, T. (1999). *The physical and psychological health effects of self-disclosure in homosexual males*. Unpublished doctoral dissertation, California School of Professional Psychology, San Diego, CA.

Van der Kolk, B.A. & Ducey, C.R. (1989). The psychological processing of traumatic experience: Rorschach patterns in PTSD. *Journal of Traumatic Stress*, **2**, 259–274.

Watson, J.P. & Marks, I.M. (1972). Relevant and irrelevant fear in flooding: a crossover study of phobic patients. *Behavior Therapy*, **2**, 276–293.

Wong, P.T.P. & Watt, L.M. (1991). What types of reminiscence are associated with successful aging? *Psychology and Aging*, **6**, 272–279.

Wortman, C.B. & Silver, R.C. (1989). The myths of coping with loss. *Journal of Personality and Social Psychology*, **57**, 349–357.

Chapter 4

Emotion suppression and cardiovascular disease

Is hiding feelings bad for your heart?

Iris B. Mauss and James J. Gross

Theorists have long claimed that the free play of emotion is incompatible with civilization (Elias, 1978; Freud, 1961). There has been a lingering suspicion, however, that the emotion control required by civilization may come at a steep price. In the popular literature, this price has often been represented in terms of the adverse consequences emotion inhibition may have for physical health (e.g. Martin, 1998). In the scientific literature, too, there have been reports linking emotion inhibition to a variety of diseases (e.g. Friedman & Booth-Kewley, 1987; Pennebaker & Traue, 1993). For example, emotion inhibition has been implicated in asthma (Florin *et al.*, 1985; Teiramaa, 1978), cancer (Denollet, 1998; Greer & Watson, 1985; Gross, 1989; Temoshok, 1987), chronic pain disorders (Beutler *et al.*, 1986; Harrison, 1975; Udelman & Udelman, 1981) and cardiovascular diseases (Brosschot & Thayer, 1998; Haynes *et al.*, 1980; Jorgensen *et al.*, 1996; Julius *et al.*, 1986).

Despite a long history of popular and scientific interest in links between emotion inhibition and disease, the complexity of the processes involved in both emotion inhibition and disease has meant that clear conclusions have been hard to come by. Our strategy in this chapter is to focus our discussion in two ways. On the "input" side, we focus on one particularly common type of emotion inhibition, namely emotion suppression, or the inhibition of ongoing emotion-expressive behavior (Gross, 1998). On the "output" side, we focus on cardiovascular diseases. Cardiovascular diseases represent the single most important source of disability and mortality worldwide (Guyton & Hall, 1997; Murray & Lopez, 1997), and they typify the slow-developing, multifactorial disease processes that seem to be most influenced by psychosocial factors such as emotion suppression (Depue & Monroe, 1986; Sapolsky, 1998).

We begin with a selective review of the literature on emotion and cardiovascular disease. This literature suggests that intense emotional responses – whether expressed or suppressed – may play a role in the development and course of cardiovascular disease. To assess whether emotion suppression makes a unique contribution to cardiovascular functioning, we review a series of laboratory studies designed to specify the acute physiological consequences of emotion suppression. These studies show that emotion suppression leads to transient increases in sympathetic activation of the cardiovascular system. Finally, to help bridge the gap between the long-term correlational studies discussed in the first section and the short-term experimental studies discussed in the second section, we offer several possible psychophysiological and psychosocial pathways by which emotion suppression might have a longer-term impact on cardiovascular health.

Emotion and cardiovascular disease

Efforts to link emotional factors to cardiovascular diseases date back to the earliest days of psychosomatic medicine (e.g. Alexander, 1939; Dunbar, 1935). These efforts were given new visibility and credibility when a pair of cardiologists, Friedman and Rosenman, observed that their coronary heart disease patients seemed to be unusually competitive, hard-driving, impatient, and hostile (Friedman & Rosenman, 1974). Friedman and Rosenman referred to this constellation of factors as the Type A behavior pattern. Their hypothesis that the Type A behavior pattern contributed to the development of cardiovascular disease was borne out by a large number of empirical findings, including several large prospective studies (see, for reviews, Booth-Kewley & Friedman, 1987; Cooper *et al.*, 1981; Matthews, 1988; Siegel, 1984).

Emotion experience and expression

Since it was first articulated, the Type A concept has been refined considerably. We now know that anger and hostility seem to be the core features of the Type A behavior pattern. For example, Booth-Kewley and Friedman (1987) found in their quantitative review that anger, hostility, and aggressiveness were significant predictors for coronary heart disease, with combined effect sizes larger than that of any of the other Type A components. Cross-sectional and prospective studies have confirmed that a high level of anger and hostility is a risk factor for the incidence and progression of CHD as well as hypertension (see, for review, Kubzansky & Kawachi, 2000; Matthews, 1988; Miller *et al.*, 1996; Smith, 1992). Adverse cardiovascular health outcomes have been found to be particularly pro-nounced for individuals who openly express their angry feelings (e.g. Harburg *et al.*, 1991; Hecker *et al.*, 1988; Siegman *et al.*, 1987).

More recently, it has become clear that in addition to anger and hostility, other negative emotions seem to be related to cardiovascular disease. Several studies have established that depression (Anda *et al.*, 1993; Barefoot, 1997; Musselman *et al.*, 1998), anxiety (Fleet & Beitman, 1998; Haines *et al.*, 1987; Kawachi *et al.*, 1994) and general emotional distress (Crisp *et al.*, 1984; Gullette *et al.*, 1997; Rosengren *et al.*, 1991) are important factors in the development and progression of coronary heart disease (for reviews, see Barefoot, 1997; Booth-Kewley & Friedman, 1987; Fielding, 1991; King, 1997; Kubzansky & Kawachi, 2000). Despite some negative findings (e.g. Hearn *et al.*, 1989; Helmer *et al.*, 1991; Leon *et al.*, 1988), a consensus has developed that the coronary-prone person experiences and expresses high levels of a variety of negative emotions. As Booth-Kewley and Friedman (1987) concluded, a person prone to coronary heart disease may be not simply a hostile person, but rather a person "with one or more negative emotions: perhaps someone who is depressed, aggressively competitive, easily frustrated, anxious, angry, or some combination" (p. 358).

Emotion suppression

One puzzle has emerged, however. While the studies we have reviewed show that the experience and *expression* of high levels of negative emotion lead to increased risk for cardiovascular disease, other studies have highlighted the role of emotion *suppression* (Brosschot & Thayer, 1998). Thus, Dembroski *et al.* (1985) found that hostility predicted severity of atherosclerosis only in patients who were also likely to suppress feelings of anger ("Anger-in"). Indeed, in several studies now, measures of the inhibition of negative emotions have been found to predict all-cause mortality as well as the incidence of coronary heart disease, hypertension, and related risk-factors (Gallacher *et al.*, 1999; Grossarth-Maticek *et al.*, 1985; Haynes *et al.*, 1980; Julius *et al.*, 1986; Julkunen, 1996; Manuck *et al.*, 1986; Schalling & Svensson, 1984). In their meta-analysis of the literature on emotion and blood pressure, Suls *et al.* (1995) found that anger suppression plays an important role in essential hypertension.

An important qualification recently has been added to this emerging suppression hypothesis, namely that the tendency to inhibit emotions *per se* might not be harmful, only the tendency to inhibit strong emotional impulses (e.g. Burns, 1995). For example, Cottington *et al.* (1986) found that workers with hypertension reported suppression *and* high levels of anger and stress. Denollet and coworkers have hypothesized that the tendency to suppress emotion-expressive behavior in social interactions might interact with the individual's level of emotional distress in determining the progression of coronary heart disease. To test this hypothesis, Denollet *et al.* divided subjects who had survived a myocardial infarction into four groups, depending on their negative affectivity (anxiety, anger, and chronic tension) and social inhibition (the tendency to inhibit the expression of emotions and distress in social interactions). The subgroup scoring high on both dimensions was labeled "Type D" (for *distressed*). It was found that Type D patients had a significantly higher death rate (27 percent) than non-Type D patients (7 percent) (Denollet *et al.*, 1996). It was pointed out that the death rate in patients scoring high on negative affectivity but low on inhibition did not differ significantly from the death rate in patients with low negative affectivity – therefore it was the *negative affectivity by social inhibition interaction* that had an adverse effect on prognosis.

In addition to having an effect on prognosis, this emotional style also seems to be involved in the *development* of risk factors for coronary heart disease. In a meta-analysis, Jorgensen and colleagues (1996) found that taken together, negative affectivity and affect inhibition were the strongest psychological predictors for the development of essential hypertension. Together, these studies suggest that it may be the behavioral suppression of relatively high levels of negative emotions that contributes to the development and progression of cardiovascular disease.

So which is it . . . expression or suppression?

How are we to reconcile the literature which suggests that it is the *expression* of negative emotions that is pathogenic with the literature which suggests that it is the *suppression* of negative emotions that is pathogenic? If suppression is the opposite of expression, how can both be associated with cardiovascular diseases?

One possibility is that suppression and expression are not "opposites", but rather behaviors that *both* may result from the experience of intense negative emotions (Julius *et al.*, 1986; Siegman *et al.*, 1987). Indeed, researchers repeatedly have shown that Anger-in and Anger-out are independent from one another, rather than negatively correlated as lay intuition might suggest (Spielberger *et al.*, 1995; Weidner *et al.*, 1989). Individuals prone to the experience of negative emotions may try to cope with these emotions in different ways, at times inhibiting them and at times expressing them.

The natural confounding of intense negative emotions with emotion suppression in everyday life makes it difficult to assess clearly the unique contribution of emotion suppression to cardiovascular outcomes on the basis of correlational studies such as the ones reviewed in the previous section. To examine the contribution of emotion suppression over and above the contributions of emotion experience and expression, we embarked on a series of laboratory studies designed to assess the acute consequences of emotion suppression. By standardizing our emotion induction procedures, and by randomly assigning participants to either suppression or no suppression conditions, we sought to clarify whether emotion suppression *per se* had any observable impact on cardiovascular responding that might be consistent with longer-term health consequences.

The acute consequences of emotion suppression

Most of what we know about the acute effects of emotion suppression has come from the *facial feedback literature*. This literature has its origins in Darwin's (1872/ 1979) assertion that "the free expression by outward signs of an emotion intensifies it. On the other hand, the repression, as far as this is possible, of all outward signs softens our emotions" (p. 365). As the phrase "facial feedback" suggests, the organizing principle in this literature is that emotion-expressive behavior has feedback effects, such that increasing emotion-expressive behavior should increase the emotion, whereas decreasing emotion-expressive behavior should decrease the emotion (Buck, 1980). Many of the studies in this area have compared suppression with exaggeration (and not with "natural" expression), finding that exaggeration leads to larger responses than suppression. This comparison makes it difficult to discern whether exaggeration and suppression both increase physiological responding (with exaggeration providing the larger boost), or whether – as is typically suggested – suppression actually leads to decreased physiological responding. Unfortunately, studies that have included the critical comparison between suppression and natural responding have focused on positive emotions (such as amusement), and typically have limited themselves to examining the effects of suppression on subjective emotional experience.

Initial studies

To clarify the acute behavioral, experiential, and physiological consequences of suppressing negative emotion, in an initial pair of studies, we used a short film that showed an arm amputation to elicit disgust (Gross & Levenson, 1993). We administered specific instructions to participants who had been randomly assigned to one of two experimental conditions. Watch condition subjects received instructions to simply watch the film clip carefully. Suppression condition subjects received additional instructions to "try to behave in such a way that a person watching you would not know you were feeling anything".

Under normal circumstances, as shown in the top panel of Figure 4.1, subjects move around a bit more when they are watching a disgusting film than they do in the resting baseline. When they suppress, however, they stifle the natural increase in somatic activity associated with disgust, yielding a flatter line for the suppression subjects than for the watch subjects. In the bottom panel of Figure 4.1, we see that suppression subjects' decreased body movement is associated with a slowing of heart rate. Despite these decreases in body movement and heart rate, Figure 4.2 shows that suppression *increased* sympathetic activation. Increases in sympathetic activation are shown both by a theoretically derived composite of sympathetic activation of the cardiovascular system (created by standard scoring finger pulse amplitude, finger temperature, and pulse transit times to the finger and ear) and by skin conductance level (not depicted here).

Testing boundary conditions of emotion suppression

One puzzle is why results from the initial studies were at odds with the facial feedback literature. Why did suppressing disgust increase sympathetic activation? Might the physiological and experiential effects of emotion suppression vary by emotion?

To test the boundary conditions of the effects of emotion suppression, we examined a second negative emotion – sadness. Given widespread agreement that positive emotions serve quite different functions from negative emotions, we also examined a positive emotion, namely amusement. To rule out the possibility that our initial findings were an artifact of the particular suppression instructions we employed, we also gave subjects the same suppression instructions during an affectively neutral film, when there would presumably be no emotion-expressive behavior to suppress (Gross & Levenson, 1997).

We found that watching a sad film leads to decreases in overall body movement. Watching an amusing film, by contrast, leads to increased body movement, as

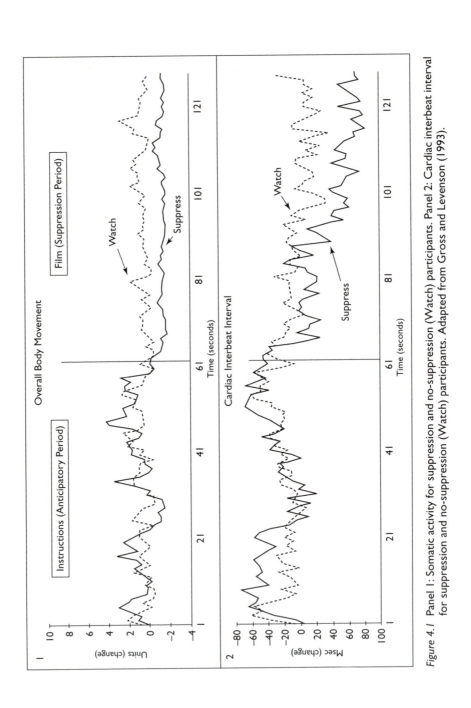

Figure 4.1 Panel 1: Somatic activity for suppression and no-suppression (Watch) participants. Panel 2: Cardiac interbeat interval for suppression and no-suppression (Watch) participants. Adapted from Gross and Levenson (1993).

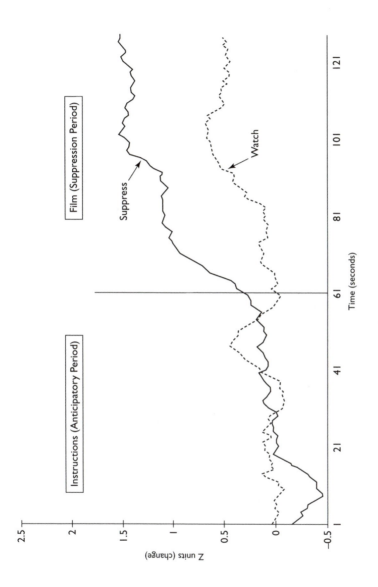

Figure 4.2 Sympathetic activation of the cardiovascular system for suppression and no-suppression (Watch) participants (adapted from Gross & Levenson, 1993).

subjects laugh and move around in their chair (Frijda, 1986). In each case, suppression decreases whatever response tendency is associated with the target emotion. Thus, suppression leads to lesser decreases in body movement during a sad film, and lesser increases in body movement during an amusing film. Heart rate generally follows somatic activity.

Despite decreased body movement and heart rate, as was the case for disgust, suppressing sadness and amusement leads to increased sympathetic activation of the cardiovascular system, including increased systolic and diastolic blood pressure, and decreased finger pulse amplitude, finger temperature, and pulse transit times. Suppressing sadness but not amusement also leads to greater electrodermal responding. Increased sympathetic activation of the cardiovascular system thus appears to be the common core to emotion suppression across emotion contexts, and suppressing either negative or positive emotions exacts a palpable physio-logical cost.

If these results really are the consequence of suppressing ongoing emotion-expressive behavior, suppressing non-emotional behavior during a neutral film should have no such consequences. To test this critical boundary condition, we examined subjects' responses during the neutral film. This film produced low levels of self-reported emotion and non-emotional expressive behavior such as lip-biting and yawning. As expected, suppression decreased non-emotional behavior, and no differences were found between suppress and watch subjects for any of the physiological variables. This is important, because it suggests that the physiological impact of emotion suppression grows out of the counterpoising of attempts to inhibit expression against strong impulses to express. In the absence of a stimulus that produces impulses to express, behavioral inhibition has relatively little impact on physiological responding.

Do all forms of emotion regulation have similar consequences?

Emotion regulation includes very different strategies such as thinking positive thoughts, using drugs, talking with friends, and suppressing emotional expression (e.g. Parkinson et al., 1996; Thayer et al., 1994). Do all these forms of emotion regulation have similar consequences? On the one hand, if the consequences of suppression are due to the effort it takes to override emotion-expressive behavior, other effortful forms of emotion regulation might have similar effects. On the other hand, different forms of emotion regulation could influence the emotion-generative process at different points, and thus have different consequences (Gross, 2001). To test this prediction, we compared emotion suppression with another form of emotion regulation, namely reappraisal, which involves re-evaluating a potentially emotionally evocative situation in order to decrease emotion.

In this study, subjects watched the same amputation film that had been shown in the initial studies. This time, subjects were randomly assigned to view this dis-gusting film under one of three instructional sets (Gross, 1998). In the first, subjects were asked to *think* about what they were seeing in such a way that they did not feel anything at all (reappraisal). In the second, subjects were asked to *hide* their emotional reactions (suppression). In the third, subjects simply watched the films (watch).

Results indicated that emotion suppression and reappraisal could indeed be distinguished. As observed previously, emotion suppression decreased disgust-expressive behavior, and increased sympathetic activation of the cardiovascular and electrodermal systems. Like suppression, reappraisal decreased expressive behavior. Unlike suppression, however, reappraisal had no observable conse-quences in terms of sympathetic activation of the cardiovascular or electrodermal systems. Whereas suppress subjects showed greater increases in sympathetic activation than watch or reappraise subjects, these latter two groups did not differ from one another. Also unlike suppression, reappraisal decreased disgust experi-ence, whereas suppression had no effect on disgust experience. These findings show that the effects of suppression are not simply the result of *any* attempt at influencing one's emotions. How one goes about achieving an emotion regulatory goal may be as important a determinant of the affective consequences of one's efforts as the goal one is trying to achieve – not showing emotion during a social interaction may be a regulatory strategy exacting higher physiological costs than other regulatory strategies. Although much remains to be learned about the details of the physiological consequences of emotion suppression, the available evidence suggests that one core feature of emotion suppression – at least in the passive film and slide-viewing studies conducted to date – is sympathetic activation of the cardiovascular system.

Bridging the gap between acute and longer-term consequences

In the preceding sections, we have shown that (a) in the short term, emotion suppression leads to acute increases in sympathetic activation, and (b) over the longer term, individuals who suppress high levels of negative emotion seem to be at greater risk for cardiovascular disease. Together, these findings are suggestive of a causal link. However, it is far from clear how the acute effects of emotion suppression might translate into longer-term consequences that could promote cardiovascular diseases. In answering this question it is important to keep in mind the heterogeneity of cardiovascular diseases, e.g. primary and secondary hyper-tension, cerebrovascular disease, arrhythmias, or myocardial infarction, as well as the heterogeneity of conditions leading to cardiovascular diseases. Psychosocial factors are almost certainly involved to varying degrees in different cardiovascular diseases and might in some cases either be involved to a very limited extent or not be involved at all.

We consider two kinds of pathways. First, we consider *psychophysiological pathways*, by which emotion suppression could lead to transient increases in sympathetic activation which – if repeated many times – might precipitate a cascade of processes that could directly influence cardiovascular health. Second, we consider *psychosocial pathways*, by which emotion suppression might significantly alter the material and emotional support that social partners provide, thereby indirectly influencing cardiovascular health. The pathways we describe are speculative, and are meant to illustrate rather than exhaust the mechanisms by which emotion suppression might contribute to cardiovascular disease. Although it seems likely that the two kinds of pathways interact (compare Jorgensen *et al.*, 1996; Myers & McClure, 1993), we describe psychophysiological and psychosocial mechanisms separately for the sake of clarity.

Psychophysiological pathways

Any one instance of heightened sympathetic responding, such as that seen in laboratory studies of emotion suppression, would seem unlikely to have deleterious consequences. However, an individual who shows an exaggerated sympathetic response of the cardiovascular system in a laboratory situation might be expected to show exaggerated sympathetic responses in many similar situations in daily life. According to the reactivity hypothesis (see Fredrikson, 1991; Krantz & Manuck, 1984), the cumulative effects of many such instances might be expected to take a toll. It is important to note that sympathetic activation is not always harmful (Dienstbier, 1989). However, if there is no time to recover (e.g. Linden *et al.*, 1997; McEwen, 1998) or if the enhanced cardiac responses are in excess of metabolic demands (e.g. Fisher, 1991; Obrist, 1983; Saab & Schneiderman, 1993), as might be the case in the context of emotion suppression, such increased sympathetic activation might lead to chronic functional and structural changes of the cardiovascular system that compromise its performance.

The available evidence seems to be generally consistent with this reactivity hypothesis. Cardiovascular hyperreactivity to different stressors appears to be involved in the development of essential hypertension (e.g. Everson *et al.*, 1996; Matthews *et al.*, 1993; Wood *et al.*, 1984; see, for review, Fredrikson, 1991) and atherosclerosis (e.g. Keys *et al.*, 1971; Manuck *et al.*, 1983), which are the two major risk factors for myocardial ischemia, infarction, and sudden cardiac death (e.g. Gillum, 1996; Guyton & Hall, 1997; Krantz & Manuck, 1984; Witteman *et al.*, 1998).

In the following sections, we describe how emotion suppression might lead to hypertension and atherosclerosis via exaggerated cardiovascular responding. Our focus is the sympathoadrenomedullary axis, although there is evidence that the adrenocortical axis (e.g. Fredrikson & Tuomisto, 1991; Henry & Stephens, 1977; Herd, 1986; Troxler *et al.*, 1977) and parasympathetic withdrawal (e.g. Brosschot & Thayer, 1998; Horsten *et al.*, 1999; Porges, 1995) also may play important roles in the development and progression of cardiovascular diseases.

The top part of Figure 4.3 shows several pathways by which the frequent incidents of sympathetic hyperreactivity associated with emotion suppression could lead to chronic hypertension. One such pathway was proposed by Folkow (1982),

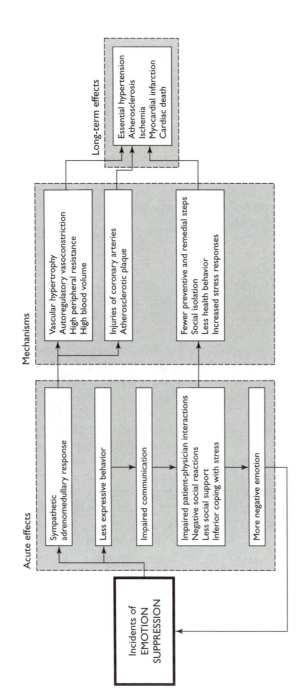

Figure 4.3 Psychophysiological and psychosocial pathways linking emotion suppression and cardiovascular diseases.

who suggested that the repeated pressor episodes exhibited by highly reactive individuals might promote smooth muscle hypertrophy. This process and a concurrent propensity for excessive vasoconstriction can lead to narrowed lumina (Folkow, 1982; Julius, 1993). Furthermore, cardiac output that is excessive relative to metabolic demand can trigger autoregulatory mechanisms, including peripheral vasoconstriction, to prevent tissue overperfusion (Obrist *et al.*, 1983; Sherwood *et al.*, 1986). Both narrowed lumina and excessive vasoconstriction can contribute to chronically heightened peripheral resistance. Moreover, high sympathetic drive might promote sodium and fluid retention through its effects on renal nerve activity. In the long run, this could lead to renal dysfunction with chronically higher blood volume (e.g. Guyton & Hall, 1997; Light *et al.*, 1983). Thus, chronically heightened sympathetic activation, with its attendant smooth muscle hypertrophy, increased peripheral resistance, and increased blood volume, might ultimately contribute to the development of chronic hypertension.

Figure 4.3 also shows pathways by which emotion suppression (and its associated increases in sympathetic activation of the cardiovascular system) could contribute to atherosclerosis. Some of these pathways involve the hemodynamic changes associated with heightened sympathetic activation. Repeated episodes of higher arterial pressure can lead, through hemodynamic forces such as sheer stress and turbulence, to micro-injuries of the coronary arteries at vulnerable points in the arterial tree (e.g. Clarkson *et al.*, 1986). Once the coronary endothelium is damaged, deposition of lipids, platelets, and fibrin (a clotting material in the blood) within the lesioned area can ensue (Guyton & Hall, 1997; Ross, 1993; Schneiderman, 1987). Atherosclerosis can then progress with chronic inflammatory cell proliferation, blood clot formation, and calcification and protrude into the lumen of the artery (Herd, 1986). The altered composition of the intima (the inner layer of the blood vessel) seems to provoke smooth muscles to move into the arterial intima and to proliferate, thereby further decreasing the size of the lumina (Herd, 1986; Ross, 1993; Schwartz *et al.*, 1981). Other possible pathways linking emotion suppression and cardiovascular disease involve the neuroendocrine components of heightened sympathetic medullary activation, in particular plasma catecholamines. Higher levels of circulating catecholamines can directly injure the intimal endothelium of the coronary arteries (Krantz & Manuck, 1984; Schneiderman, 1987), triggering atherosclerotic plaque growth. Catecholamines also induce a release of free fatty acids and lipoproteins into the blood stream, which can be atherogenic if they reach concentrations in excess of metabolic requirements (Carruthers, 1969; Henry & Stephens, 1977; Schneiderman, 1987). These factors contribute to the development of atherosclerotic plaque, which can ultimately completely occlude arteries. This development can become life-threatening, as atherosclerotic obstructive lesions and ensuing thrombosis can trigger myocardial ischemia, infarction, and cardiac death.

Psychosocial pathways

As shown in the bottom of Figure 4.3, emotion suppression also may be linked to cardiovascular disease outcomes via several psychosocial pathways. One particularly important psychosocial pathway is the patient–physician relationship. Roter and Ewart (1992) analyzed patient–physician interviews and found that patients with essential hypertension were less likely to express negative emotions than normotensive subjects. Such suppression of distress in clinical interviews might lead to a delayed detection of disease, less effective patient–physician communication, an underestimation of symptoms, and fewer preventive and remedial steps being taken by the physician to address social and emotional problems (Barsky, 1981; Roter & Ewart, 1992). This in turn could lead to decreased patient satisfaction, and an ensuing tendency of noncompliance with therapy (e.g. Haynes et al., 1987; Lieberman, 1996).

In other relationships, too, emotion suppression could have costs that are relevant to cardiovascular health. Expression of emotions communicates to others a person's wishes and needs. If this communication is interrupted, because emotional expression is inhibited, others may be less accommodating. Individuals with a tendency to inhibit their negative emotions might thus, through reciprocal interactions, inadvertently create an environment provoking the experience of negative emotions (see Smith, 1992). Particularly individuals who exhibit a pattern of inhibition alternating with inappropriately strong expression of emotion could elicit negative social reactions (Davidson et al., 1999). Frequent experience of negative emotions might in turn, as shown in Figure 4.3, prompt the individual to suppress these emotions, thus triggering a positive feedback loop.

In addition, emotional inexpressiveness and introversion have been related to less seeking of social support (Amirkhan et al., 1995; Von Dras & Siegler, 1997). Two models have been proposed that link lessened social support to disease (Schwarzer & Leppin, 1991). On the one hand, social support serves a buffer function against other stressors such as when a person seeks emotional support from her friends after her spouse dies. If an individual has low social support, this buffer function is not afforded anymore and stressors create larger psychological and physiological stress responses (e.g. Jennison, 1992). On the other hand, low social support might have a direct, negative effect on the individual – social isolation might directly lead to heightened negative affect and poorer health-related behavior (e.g. Treiber et al., 1991; Zimmerman & Conner, 1989). Additionally, the non-expression of emotions can have negative effects by preventing the beneficial effects of verbalization, which include restructuring of the emotion-eliciting event (Pennebaker, 1997). Without cognitive restructuring, there may be prolonged rumination, more frequent experience of negative emotions, and inadequate coping with subsequent events (see, for example, Greenglass, 1996; Pennebaker, 1997; Smyth, 1998), further increasing the frequency of harmful physiological responses.

Both consequences of low social support – the missing buffer function and the direct negative effects – could have a detrimental impact on various health outcomes, including cardiovascular diseases (e.g. Adler & Matthews, 1994; Berkman, 1995; King, 1997; Smith & Pope, 1990; Uchino *et al.*, 1996). Such detrimental psychosocial effects might be especially costly *after* a cardiac event, when patients are in a vulnerable state (e.g. Berkman *et al.*, 1992; Orth-Gomér *et al.*, 1988; Ruberman *et al.*, 1984). Suppression thus might contribute both to the development of cardiovascular diseases and to their progression by impairing patient–physician interactions in particular and social relationships more generally.

Summary

The popular press has long urged that emotion suppression may be bad for our health. In this chapter, we have selectively reviewed the scientific literature on emotion and cardiovascular disease, and found that both emotion expression *and* emotion suppression seem to play a role in cardiovascular disease. To examine whether emotion suppression has any unique contribution to cardiovascular responding, we reviewed a series of laboratory studies on the acute consequences of emotion suppression. These studies showed that suppressing negative emotions such as disgust or sadness, or positive emotions such as amusement, leads to acute increases in sympathetic activation of the cardiovascular system. Although any one of these moments of increased activation is unlikely to have any long-term health impact, we have suggested psychophysiological and psychosocial pathways by which the acute effects of emotion suppression might translate into longer term threats to cardiovascular health. One important challenge for future research on emotion suppression and health will be to test these suggestions in the context of rich social interactions, with a broad range of vulnerable and non-vulnerable research participants. Such study will permit a better understanding of the complex health effects of differing patterns of emotion experience, expression, and suppression.

Acknowledgments

This research was supported by Grant MH58147 from the National Institute of Mental Health. The second author began the research program described in the second section of this chapter as a graduate student at the University of California, Berkeley, and gratefully acknowledges the influence of his graduate mentor Robert W. Levenson. Since moving to Stanford University, the second author has continued this line of work on emotion suppression with his own graduate students.

References

Adler, N. & Matthews, K. (1994). Health psychology: why do some people get sick and some stay well? *Annual Review of Psychology*, **45**, 229–259.
Alexander, F. (1939). Emotional factors in essential hypertension. *Psychosomatic Medicine*, **1**, 173–179.

Amirkhan, J.H., Risinger, R.T., & Swickert, R.J. (1995). Extraversion: a "hidden" personality factor in coping? *Journal of Personality*, **63**, 189–212.

Anda, R., Williamson, D., Jones, D., Macera, C., Eaker, E., Glassman, A., & Marks, J. (1993). Depressed affect, hopelessness, and the risk of ischemic disease in a cohort of US adults. *Epidemiology*, **4**, 285–294.

Barefoot, J.C. (1997). Depression and coronary heart disease. *Cardiologia*, **42**, 1245–1250.

Barsky, A.J. (1981). Hidden reasons some patients visit doctors. *Annals of Internal Medicine*, **94**, 492–498.

Berkman, L.F. (1995). The role of social relations in health promotion. *Psychosomatic Medicine*, **57**, 245–254.

Berkman, L.F., Leo-Summers, L., & Horwitz, R.I. (1992). Emotional support and survival following myocardial infarction: a prospective, population-based study of the elderly. *Annals of Internal Medicine*, **117**, 1003–1009.

Beutler, L.E., Engle, D., Oro-Beutler, M.E., Daldrup, R., & Meredith, K. (1986). Inability to express intense affect: a common link between depression and pain? *Journal of Consulting and Clinical Psychology*, **54**, 752–759.

Booth-Kewley, S. & Friedman, H.S. (1987). Psychological predictors of heart disease: a quantitative review. *Psychological Bulletin*, **101**, 343–362.

Brosschot, J.F. & Thayer, J.F. (1998). Anger inhibition, cardiovascular recovery, and vagal function: a model of the link between hostility and cardiovascular disease. *Annals of Behavioral Medicine*, **20**, 326–332.

Buck, R. (1980). Nonverbal behavior and the theory of emotion: the facial feedback hypothesis. *Journal of Personality and Social Psychology*, **38**, 811–824.

Burns, J.W. (1995). Interactive effects of traits, states, and gender on cardiovascular reactivity during different situations. *Journal of Behavioral Medicine*, **18**, 179–303.

Carruthers, M.E. (1969). Aggression and atheroma. *The Lancet*, **2**(7631), 1170–1171.

Clarkson, T.B., Manuck, S.B., & Kaplan, J.R. (1986). Potential role of cardiovascular reactivity in atherogenesis. In K.A. Matthews, S.M. Weiss, T. Detre, T.M. Dembroski, B. Falkner, S.B. Manuck, & R.B. Williams (eds), *Handbook of stress, reactivity, and cardiovascular disease* (pp. 35–47). New York: Wiley.

Cooper, T., Detre, T., & Weiss, S.M. (1981). Coronary prone behavior and coronary heart disease: a critical review. *Circulation*, **63**, 1199–1215.

Cottington, E.M., Matthews, K.A., Talbott, E., & Kuller, L.H. (1986). Occupational stress, suppressed anger, and hypertension. *Psychosomatic Medicine*, **48**, 249–260.

Crisp, A.H., Queenan, M., & D'Souza, M.F. (1984). Myocardial infarction and the emotional climate. *The Lancet*, **1**(8377), 616–619.

Darwin, C. (1872/1979). *The expression of emotions in man and animals*. London: Julian Friedmann. (Original work published in 1872.)

Davidson, K., MacGregor, M.W., Stuhr, J., & Gidron, Y. (1999). Increasing constructive anger verbal behavior decreases resting blood pressure: a secondary analysis of a randomized controlled hostility intervention. *International Journal of Behavioral Medicine*, **6**, 268–278.

Dembroski, T.M., MacDougall, J.M., Williams, R.B., Haney, T.L., & Blumenthal, J.A. (1985). Components of Type A, hostility, and Anger-In: relationship to angiographic findings. *Psychosomatic Medicine*, **47**, 219–233.

Denollet, J. (1998). Personality and risk of cancer in men with coronary heart disease. *Psychological Medicine*, **28**, 991–995.

Denollet, J., Sys, S.U., Stroobant, N., Rombouts, H., Gillebert, T.C., & Brutsaert, D.L.

(1996). Personality as independent predictor of long-term mortality in patients with coronary heart disease. *The Lancet*, **347**, 417–421.

Depue, R. & Monroe, S.M. (1986). Conceptualization and measurement of human disorder in life stress research: the problem of chronic disturbance. *Psychological Bulletin*, **99**, 36–51.

Dienstbier, R.A. (1989). Arousal and physiological toughness: implications for mental and physical health. *Psychological Review*, **96**, 84–100.

Dunbar, H.F. (1935). *Emotions and bodily changes: a survey of literature on psychosomatic interrelationships*. New York: Columbia University Press.

Elias, N. (1978). *The civilizing process: the history of manners*. New York: Urizen Books.

Everson, S.A., Kaplan, G.A., Goldberg, D.E., & Salonen, J.T. (1996). Anticipatory blood pressure response to exercise predicts future high blood pressure in middle-aged men. *Hypertension*, **27**, 1059–1064.

Fielding, R. (1991). Depression and acute myocardial infarction: a review and reinterpretation. *Social Science and Medicine*, **32**, 1017–1027.

Fisher, L.A. (1991). Stress and cardiovascular physiology in animals. In M.R. Brown, G.F. Koob, & C. Rivier (eds), *Stress. Neurobiology and neuroendocrinology* (pp. 463–474). New York: Marcel Dekker.

Fleet, R.P. & Beitman, B.D. (1998). Cardiovascular death from panic disorder and panic-like anxiety: a critical review of the literature. *Journal of Psychosomatic Research*, **44**, 71–80.

Florin, I., Freudenberg, G., & Hollaender, J. (1985). Facial expressions of emotion and physiologic reactions in children with bronchial asthma. *Psychosomatic Medicine*, **47**, 382–393.

Folkow, B. (1982). Physiological aspects of primary hypertension. *Physiological Review*, **62**, 347–503.

Fredrikson, M. (1991). Psychophysiological theories on sympathetic nervous system reactivity in the development of essential hypertension. *Scandinavian Journal of Psychology*, **32**, 254–274.

Fredrikson, M. & Tuomisto, M. (1991). Neuroendocrine and cardiovascular stress reactivity in middle-aged normotensive adults with parental history of cardiovascular disease. *Psychophysiology*, **28**, 656–664.

Freud, S. (1961/1930). *Civilization and its discontents* (J.T. Strachey, trans.). New York: W.W. Norton & Co. (Original work published in 1930.)

Friedman, H.S. & Booth-Kewley, S. (1987). The "disease-prone personality": a meta-analytic view of the construct. *American Psychologist*, **42**, 539–555.

Friedman, M. & Rosenman, R. (1974). *Type A behavior and your heart*. New York: Knopf.

Frijda, N.H. (1986). *The emotions*. Cambridge: Cambridge University Press.

Gallacher, J.E., Yarnell, J.W.G., Sweetnam, P.M., Elwood, P.C., & Stansfeld, S.A. (1999). Anger and incident heart disease in the Caerphilly study. *Psychosomatic Medicine*, **61**, 446–453.

Gillum, R.F. (1996). Coronary heart disease, stroke, and hypertension in a U.S. national cohort: the NHANES I Epidemiologic Follow-up Study. National Health and Nutrition Examination Survey. *Annals of Epidemiology*, **6**, 259–262.

Greenglass, E.R. (1996). Anger suppression, cynical distrust, and hostility: implications for coronary heart disease. In C.D. Spielberger & I.G. Sarason (eds), *Stress and emotion* (pp. 205–224). Washington, DC: Taylor & Francis.

Greer, S. & Watson, M. (1985). Towards a psychobiological model of cancer: psychological considerations. *Social Science and Medicine*, **20**, 773–777.

Gross, J.J. (1989). Emotional expression in cancer onset and progression. *Social Science and Medicine*, **28**, 1239–1248.

Gross, J.J. (1998). Antecedent- and response-focused emotion regulation: divergent consequences for experience, expression, and physiology. *Journal of Personality and Social Psychology*, **74**, 224–237.

Gross, J.J. (2001). Emotion regulation in adulthood: timing is everything. *Current Directions in Psychological Science*, **1**, 214–219.

Gross, J.J. & Levenson, R.W. (1993). Emotional suppression: physiology, self-report, and expressive behavior. *Journal of Personality and Social Psychology*, **64**, 970–986.

Gross, J.J. & Levenson, R.W. (1997). Hiding feelings: the acute effects of inhibiting positive and negative emotions. *Journal of Abnormal Psychology*, **106**, 95–103.

Grossarth-Maticek, R., Bastiaans, J., & Kanazir, D.T. (1985). Psychosocial factors as strong predictors of mortality from cancer, ischemic heart disease and stroke: the Yugoslav prospective study. *Journal of Psychosomatic Research*, **29**, 167–176.

Gullette, E.C.D., Blumenthal, J.A., Babyak, M., Jiang, W., Waugh, R.A., Frid, D.J., O'Connor, C.M., Morris, J.J., & Krantz, D.S. (1997). Effects of mental stress on myocardial ischemia during daily life. *Journal of the American Medical Association*, **277**, 1521–1526.

Guyton, A.C. & Hall, J.E. (1997). *Human physiology and mechanisms of disease* (6th edn). Philadelphia, PA: W.B. Saunders.

Haines, A.P., Imeson, J.D., & Meade, T.W. (1987). Phobic anxiety and ischemic heart disease. *British Medical Journal*, **295**, 297–299.

Harburg, E., Gleiberman, L., Russell, M., & Cooper, M.L. (1991). Anger-coping styles and blood pressure in Black and White males: Buffalo, New York. *Psychosomatic Medicine*, **53**, 153–164.

Harrison, R.H. (1975). Psychological testing in headache: a review. *Headache*, **15**, 177–185.

Haynes, R.B., Wang, E., & Da Mota Gomes, M. (1987). A critical review of interventions to improve compliance with prescribed medications. *Patient Education and Counseling*, **10**, 155–166.

Haynes, S.G., Feinleib, M., & Kannel, W.B. (1980). The relationship of psychosocial factors to coronary heart disease in the Framingham Study. *American Journal of Epidemiology*, **111**, 37–58.

Hearn, M.D., Murray, D.M., & Luepker, R.V. (1989). Hostility, coronary heart disease, and total mortality: a 33-year follow-up study of university students. *Journal of Behavioral Medicine*, **12**, 105–121.

Hecker, M.L., Chesney, M.A., Black, G.W., & Frautsch, N. (1988). Coronary-prone behaviors in the Western Collaborative Group Study. *Psychosomatic Medicine*, **50**, 153–164.

Helmer, D.C., Ragland, D.R., & Syme, S.L. (1991). Hostility and coronary artery disease. *American Journal of Epidemiology*, **133**, 112–122.

Henry, J.P. & Stephens, P.M. (1977). Functional and structural changes in response to psychosocial stimulation. In J.P. Henry & P.M. Stephens (eds), *Health and the social environment. A sociobiological approach to medicine* (pp. 141–166). New York: Springer.

Herd, J.A. (1986). Neuroendocrine mechanisms in coronary heart disease. In K.A. Matthews, S.M. Weiss, T. Detre, T.M. Dembroski, B. Falkner, S.B. Manuck, & R.B.

Williams (eds), *Handbook of stress, reactivity, and cardiovascular disease* (pp. 49–70). New York: Wiley.

Horsten, M., Ericson, M., Perski, A., Wamala, S.P., Schenck-Gustafsson, K., & Orth-Gomér, K. (1999). Psychosocial factors and heart rate variability in healthy women. *Psychosomatic Medicine*, **61**, 49–57.

Jennison, K.M. (1992). The impact of stressful life events and social support on drinking among older adults: a general population survey. *International Journal of Aging and Human Development*, **35**, 99–123.

Jorgensen, R.S., Johnson, B.T., Kolodziej, M.E., & Schreer, G.E. (1996). Elevated blood pressure and personality: a meta-analytic review. *Psychological Bulletin*, **120**, 293–320.

Julius, M., Harburg, E., Cottington, E.M., & Johnson, E.H. (1986). Anger-coping types, blood pressure, and all-cause mortality: a follow-up in Tecumseh, Michigan (1971–1983). *American Journal of Epidemiology*, **124**, 220–233.

Julius, S. (1993). Sympathetic hyperactivity and coronary risk in hypertension. *Circulation*, **21**, 886–893.

Julkunen, J. (1996). Suppressing your anger: good manners, bad health? In C.D. Spielberger & I.G. Sarason (eds), *Stress and emotion: Anxiety, anger, and curiosity* (pp. 227–240). Washington, DC: Taylor & Francis.

Kawachi, I., Graham, A.C., Aschiero, A., Rimm, E.B., Giovannucci, E., Stampfer, M.J., & Willett, W.C. (1994). Prospective study of phobic anxiety and risk of coronary heart disease in men. *Circulation*, **89**, 1992–1997.

Keys, A., Taylor, H.L., Blackburn, H., Brozek, J., Anderson, J.T., & Simonson, E. (1971). Mortality and coronary heart disease in young men studied for 23 years. *Archives of Internal Medicine*, **128**, 201–214.

King, B.K. (1997). Psychologic and social aspects of cardiovascular disease. *Annals of Behavioral Medicine*, **19**, 264–270.

Krantz, D.S. & Manuck, S.B. (1984). Acute psychophysiologic reactivity and risk of cardiovascular disease: a review and methodologic critique. *Psychological Bulletin*, **96**, 435–464.

Kubzansky, L.D. & Kawachi, I. (2000). Going to the heart of the matter: do negative emotions cause coronary heart disease? *Journal of Psychosomatic Research*, **48**, 323–337.

Leon, G., Finn, S.E., Murray, D., & Bailey, J.M. (1988). Inability to predict cardiovascular disease from hostility scores or MMPI items related to Type A behavior. *Journal of Consulting and Clinical Psychology*, **56**, 597–600.

Lieberman, J.A. (1996). Compliance issues in primary care. *Journal of Clinical Psychiatry*, **57** (Suppl. 7), 76–82.

Light, K.C., Koepke, J.P., Obrist, P.A., & Willis, P.W. (1983). Psychological stress induces sodium and fluid retention in men at high risk for hypertension. *Science*, **220**, 429–431.

Linden, W., Earle, T.L., Gerin, W., & Christenfeld, N. (1997). Physiological stress reactivity and recovery: conceptual siblings separated at birth? *Journal of Psychosomatic Research*, **42**, 117–135.

McEwen, B.S. (1998). Protective and damaging effects of stress mediators. *New England Journal of Medicine*, **338**, 171–179.

Manuck, S.B., Kaplan, J.R., & Clarkson, T.B. (1983). Behaviorally induced heart rate reactivity and atherosclerosis in cynomolgus monkeys. *Psychosomatic Medicine*, **45**, 95–108.

Manuck, S.B., Kaplan, J.R., & Matthews, K.A. (1986). Behavioral antecedents of coronary heart disease and atherosclerosis. *Arteriosclerosis*, **6**, 2–14.

Martin, P. (1998). *The healing mind*. New York: Thomas Dunne Books.

Matthews, K.A. (1988). Coronary heart disease and Type A behaviors: update on and alternative to the Booth-Kewley and Friedman (1987) quantitative review. *Psychological Bulletin*, **104**, 373–380.

Matthews, K.A., Woodall, K.L., & Allen, M.T. (1993). Cardiovascular reactivity to stress predicts future blood pressure status. *Hypertension*, **22**, 479–485.

Miller, T.Q., Smith, T.W., Turner, C.W., Guijarro, M.L., & Hallet, A.J. (1996). A meta-analytic review of research on hostility and physical health. *Psychological Bulletin*, **119**, 322–348.

Murray, C.J.L. & Lopez, A.D. (1997). Alternative projections of mortality and disability by cause 1990–2020: Global Burden of Disease Study. *The Lancet*, **349**, 1498–1504.

Musselman, D.L., Evans, D.L., & Numeroff, C.B. (1998). The relationship of depression to cardiovascular disease: epidemiology, biology, and treatment. *Archives of General Psychiatry*, **55**, 580–592.

Myers, H.F. & McClure, F.H. (1993). Psychosocial factors in hypertension in blacks: the case for an interactional perspective. In J.C.S. Fray & J.G. Douglas (eds), *Pathophysiology of hypertension in blacks* (pp. 90–106). New York: Oxford University Press.

Obrist, P.A., Langer, A.W., Light, K.C., & Koepke, J.P. (1983). A cardiac–behavioral approach in the study of hypertension. In T.M. Dembroski, T.H. Schmidt, & G. Blümchen (eds), *Biobehavioral bases of coronary artery disease* (pp. 290–303). Basel: Karger.

Orth-Gomér, K., Unden, A.L., & Edwards, M.E. (1988). Social isolation and mortality in ischemic heart disease. *Acta Medica Scandinavia*, **224**, 205–215.

Parkinson, B., Totterdell, P., Briner, R.B., & Reynolds, S. (1996). *Changing moods: the psychology of mood and mood regulation*. London: Longman.

Pennebaker, J.W. (1997). Health effects of the expression (and non-expression) of emotions through writing. In A.J.J.M. Vingerhoets, F.J. Van Brussel, & A.W.J. Boelhouwer (eds), *The (non)expression of emotions in health and disease* (pp. 267–278). Tilburg, The Netherlands: Tilburg University Press.

Pennebaker, J.W. & Traue, H.C. (1993). Inhibition and psychosomatic processes. In H.C. Traue & J.W. Pennebaker (eds), *Emotion, inhibition, & health* (pp. 146–163). Göttingen, Germany: Hogrefe & Huber Publishers.

Porges, S.W. (1995). Cardiac vagal tone: a physiological index of stress. *Neuroscience and Biobehavioral Reviews*, **19**, 225–233.

Rosengren, A., Tibblin, G., & Wilhelmsen, L. (1991). Self-perceived psychological stress and incidence of coronary artery disease in middle-aged men. *The American Journal of Cardiology*, **68**, 1171–1175.

Ross, R. (1993). The pathogenesis of atherosclerosis: a perspective for the 1990s. *Nature*, **362**, 801–809.

Roter, D.L. & Ewart, C.K. (1992). Emotional inhibition in essential hypertension: obstacle to communication during medical visits? *Health Psychology*, **11**, 163–169.

Ruberman, W., Weinblatt, E., Goldberg, J., & Chaudhary, B.S. (1984). Psychosocial influences on mortality after myocardial infarction. *New England Journal of Medicine*, **311**, 552–559.

Saab, P.G. & Schneiderman, N. (1993). Biobehavioral stressors, laboratory investigation, and the risk of hypertension. In J. Blascovich & E.S. Katkin (eds), *Cardiovascular reactivity to psychological stress and disease* (pp. 49–82). Washington, DC: American Psychiatric Association.

Sapolsky, R. (1998). *Why zebras don't get ulcers* (2nd edn). New York: Freeman.

Schalling, D. & Svensson, J. (1984). Blood pressure and personality. *Personality and Individual Differences*, **5**, 41–51.

Schneiderman, N. (1987). Psychophysiologic factors in atherogenesis and coronary artery disease. *Circulation*, **76** (Suppl. 1), I41–I47.

Schwartz, S.M., Gajdusek, C.M., & Selden, S.C. (1981). Vascular wall growth control: the role of the endothelium. *Arteriosclerosis*, **1**, 107–126.

Schwarzer, R. & Leppin, A. (1991). Social support and health: a theoretical and empirical overview. *Journal of Social and Personal Relationships*, **8**, 99–127.

Sherwood, A., Allen, M.T., Obrist, P.A., & Langer, A.W. (1986). Evaluation of ß-adrenergic influences on cardiovascular and metabolic adjustment to physical and psychological stress. *Psychophysiology*, **23**, 89–104.

Siegel, J.M. (1984). Type A behavior: epidemiologic foundations, and public health implication. *Annual Review of Public Health*, **5**, 343–367.

Siegman, A.W., Dembroski, T.M., & Ringel, N. (1987). Components of hostility and the severity of coronary artery disease. *Psychosomatic Medicine*, **49**, 127–135.

Smith, C.A. & Pope, L.K. (1990). Cynical hostility as a health risk: current status and future direction. *Journal of Social Behavior and Personality*, **5**, 77–88.

Smith, T.W. (1992). Hostility and health: current status of a psychosomatic hypothesis. *Health Psychology*, **11**, 139–150.

Smyth, J.M. (1998). Written emotional expression: effect sizes, outcome types, and moderating variables. *Journal of Consulting and Clinical Psychology*, **66**, 174–184.

Spielberger, C.D., Reheiser, E.C., & Sydeman, S.J. (1995). Measuring the experience, expression, and control of anger. In H. Kassinove (ed.), *Anger disorders: Definitions, diagnosis, and treatment* (pp. 49–67). Washington, DC: Taylor & Francis.

Suls, J., Wan, C.K., & Costa, P.T. (1995). Relationship of trait anger to resting blood pressure: a meta-analysis. *Health Psychology*, **14**, 444–456.

Teiramaa, E. (1978). Psychosocial and psychic factors in the course of asthma. *Journal of Psychosomatic Research*, **22**, 121–125.

Temoshok, L. (1987). Personality, coping style, emotion, and cancer: toward an integrative model. *Cancer Surveys*, **6**, 837–839.

Thayer, R.E., Newman, J.R., & McClain, T.M. (1994). Self-regulation of mood: strategies for changing a bad mood, raising energy, and reducing tension. *Journal of Personality and Social Psychology*, **67**, 910–925.

Treiber, F.A., Baranowski, T., Braden, D.S., Strong, W.B., Levy, M., & Knox, W. (1991). Social support for exercise: relationship to physical activity in young adults. *Preventive Medicine*, **20**, 737–750.

Troxler, R.G., Sprague, E.A., Albanese, R.A., Fuchs, R., & Thompson, A.J. (1977). The association of elevated plasma cortisol and early atherosclerosis as demonstrated by coronary angiography. *Atherosclerosis*, **26**, 151–162.

Uchino, B.N., Cacioppo, J.T., & Kiecolt-Glaser, J.K. (1996). The relationship between social support and physiological processes: a review with emphasis on underlying mechanisms and implications for health. *Psychological Bulletin*, **119**, 488–531.

Udelman, H.D. & Udelman, D.L. (1981). Emotions and rheumatologic disorders. *American Journal of Psychotherapy*, **35**, 576–587.

Von Dras, D.D. & Siegler, I.C. (1997). Stability in extraversion and aspects of social support in midlife. *Journal of Personality and Social Psychology*, **72**, 233–241.

Weidner, G., Istvan, J., & McKnight, J.D. (1989). Clusters of behavioral coronary risk factors in employed women and men. *Journal of Applied Social Psychology*, **19**, 468–480.

Witteman, J.C., D'Agostino, R.B., Stijnen, T., Kannel, W.B., Cobb, J.C., de Ridder, M.A., Hofman, A., & Robins, J.M. (1998). G-estimation of causal effects: isolated systolic hypertension and cardiovascular death in the Framingham Heart Study. *American Journal of Epidemiology*, **148**, 390–401.

Wood, D.L., Sheps, S.G., Elveback, L.R., & Schirger, A. (1984). Cold pressor test as a predictor of hypertension. *Hypertension*, **6**, 301–306.

Zimmerman, R.S. & Conner, C. (1989). Health promotion in context: the effects of significant others on health behavior change. *Health Education Quarterly*, **16**, 57–74.

Chapter 5

The Reality Escape Model

The intricate relation between alexithymia, dissociation, and anesthesia in victims of child sexual abuse

Peter Paul Moormann, Bob Bermond and Francine Albach

Introduction

In the present chapter, we will outline a new model on the sequelae of child sexual abuse, in which dissociation, alexithymia and anesthesia are considered as three different manifestations of the same non-feeling state that is so characteristic of traumatized individuals. The new aspects of the model in particular concern the way several lines of research are combined around the idea that individuals who have been traumatized as a young child may, later in life, apply several psychological mechanisms directed at escaping the terror and the horror of reality.

A significant number of victims of abuse who have been confronted repeatedly with highly threatening and painful events appear to try to escape from reality by inventing a "better" world (Albach *et al.*, 1996). This escape from reality by creating and living in a fantasy world (i.e. in a dissociative state) implies that the normal controlling functions of consciousness are disrupted (Janet, 1911; Kihlstrom, 1992). On the behavioral level, disturbances in conation (loss of initiative), emotion (affective blocking) and cognition (memory impairments) may be observed (Krystal, 1988a). In addition, several hysterical symptoms (Briquet, 1859; Janet, 1911) may be present such as disturbances in sensory perceptions (for instance "les anesthésies" or insensitivity to stimulation from the senses), and disturbances in motor behavior (conversion reactions).

Following Freud and Breuer (1893/1924) and Janet (1911), also in our model, intense anxiety, one of the most painful emotions in human existence, is regarded as the impulse leading to the disruption of the normal controlling functions of consciousness. As early as 1911, Janet gave a detailed description of this disruptive power of intense emotions:

> With respect to this (subject), I have demonstrated the dissolving power of emotions on voluntary decisions, feeling states, and conscious sensations, and I consider this dissociation of memories to be part of the larger group of dissociation of coherent structures by emotions.
>
> (p. 532, translation)

But how can the paradox between, on the one hand, intense affect and, on the other hand, affective blocking be explained? Krystal (1988a) gives the following answer: "The paradox in the traumatic state is that the numbing and closing off are experienced as relief from previously painful affects such as anxiety" (p. 151). Seen from this perspective, this non-feeling state is functional and can be considered as a self-protecting mechanism. The *Reality Escape Model* presented here originated from the idea that the following three different mechanisms may underlie such a non-feeling state.

1   *Splitting of consciousness* (e.g. dissociation) to escape reality: "It is not me who is experiencing this painful emotion. It is another person, and therefore it does not affect me." The consequences are time loss and memory gaps.
2   *Switching off feeling emotions* (e.g. alexithymia) against psychological pain: "Those horrible events don't affect me. I switch off my feeling. I feel nothing." It implies a disconnection of the cognitions belonging to an emotional experience. However, the non-feeling state also affects other areas in life and may therefore lead to anhedonia.
3   *Switching off feeling physical stimulation* (e.g. anesthesia) against physical pain and discomfort: "They may beat me up, but I don't feel the pain." This reaction implies the loss or impairments of sensations, which may result in insensitivity to physical pain. One of the consequences in sexual abuse is frigidity. Another is a heightened risk for getting ill and serious physical problems, because the system that used to warn us against danger is switched off.

All the symptoms described above are generally reported by victims of child sexual abuse. However, individuals suffering from dissociation are mainly persons with a history of repeated abuse for a prolonged period of time, at a very young age. For instance, one of the subjects in our studies reported the following:

My ex-husband said: "You are like a lump of ice." I still am [sexual anesthesia or frigidity]. If my husband would never touch me again, I wouldn't care at all. When I am making love, I am like a sort of doll. I only think about cleaning the windows [escapist fantasy]. It is as if something closes off inside [psychic numbing]. I catch myself thinking "Peter has to take this and that to school tomorrow [escapist fantasy]".

After this brief outline of our model, we will first discuss some important theoretical issues that influenced our thinking. As alexithymia is seen as one of the most important manifestations of the psychological non-feeling state, adequate attention will be paid to this construct. Next, the link between emotion excitability and fantasy or creative imagination will be explained. We then continue with a discussion of research findings on alexithymia in sexually abused women. Although these women appeared to suffer from the cognitive deficiencies found in alexithymia, they reported normal levels of emotion excitability and fantasy. We conclude this contribution by expanding on theoretical issues relevant for our model and research findings that illustrate the interrelationship between alexithymia, dissociation, and anesthesia.

The sequelae of psychotraumata from a historical perspective

During the last decades, there has been a growing interest in the effects of exposure to traumatic events. These studies include victims of the First and Second World Wars (Simmel, 1918; Sargant & Slater, 1941), survivors of the Holocaust (Kardiner & Spiegel, 1947; Krystal, 1968), Vietnam veterans (Keane *et al.*, 1985; MacGee, 1984), and, more recently, soldiers who fought in the Gulf War. The systematic investigation of complaints reported by survivors of war resulted in the description of post-traumatic stress disorder (PTSD). Other investigators have directed their attention at child sexual abuse (Herman, 1981; Draijer, 1990; Ensink, 1992; Albach, 1993). Initially, there were doubts on whether sexual abuse could really be considered as a traumatic event, but nowadays there is considerable consensus that child abuse also should be considered as a trauma (see Albach, 1993; Albach & Everaerd, 1992; Finkelhor & Browne, 1985; Zeitlin *et al.*, 1993). Although the similarity in complaints between victims of war and victims of child abuse is quite remarkable, the following obvious differences cannot be overlooked.

1   *Age of onset.* In contrast with child abuse, the majority of victims of war are generally traumatized in adulthood (exceptions are the children in concentration camps). Being traumatized as a child generally has a greater impact on future personality (as stated in Briquet (1859)), because the organism has not yet fully matured, and therefore is more vulnerable to negative influences (see also Keilson, 1979).
2   The *nature of the trauma*, which is by definition sexual in child sexual abuse. Considering the fact that there is a greater taboo on having sex with children than on making war with enemies, child sexual abuse is "surrounded" by more secrecy, disbelief, and speculation on the exact nature of the traumatic event: "Did it really happen or is it based on fantasy?" In most cases a clear-cut answer cannot be given, as there are no witnesses other than the perpetrator himself/herself, who generally is reluctant to confess.
3   The *theoretical frameworks* behind research on victims of war and victims of child sexual abuse are not identical. PTSD is based on the symptomatology of war victims and originates from psychodynamic thinking (Freud, 1939; Horowitz, 1976/1996). Dissociation is based on accounts of child sexual abuse and originates from Janetian thinking. This has led to the use of different constructs for the description of the same psychological phenomena (for instance dissociative versus psychogenic amnesia). It is interesting to note that over the past decade the impact of Janetian thinking (1889, 1911, 1928) has

become greater. An example of its influence is the fact that in the newest formulation of PTSD psychogenic amnesia (based on the Freudian construct of repression) from the DSM-III-R (American Psychiatric Association, 1987) has been replaced by dissociative amnesia (based on the Janetian construct of dissociation) in the DSM-IV (American Psychiatric Association, 1994). In the Reality Escape Model on the sequelae of child sexual abuse, an effort has been made to embed concepts such as alexithymia, dissociation and anesthesia, originating from different theories, in a new coherent framework.

On subtypes of alexithymia and the implications for psychotherapy

It could be argued that an emotional experience is not complete unless the person is able (i) to experience emotional feelings, (ii) to differentiate between emotional feelings, (iii) to verbalize emotional feelings, (iv) to reflect upon and to some extent analyze these feelings, and (v) to fantasize (e.g. to have a rich fantasy life and creative imagination). Deficits in all these functions are characteristic of alexithymia (Vingerhoets et al., 1995).

Bermond (1995, 1997) reported empirical evidence strongly suggesting the existence of two different types of alexithymia, each with a specific psycho-biological make-up. Type I alexithymia (full-blown alexithymia, in which the emotion excitability is reduced as well) is hypothesized to result from a decreased functioning of the orbito-prefrontal cortex, reduced neural dopaminergic inner-vation of this area, and reduced functioning of the right hemisphere (Bermond's hypothesis of left hemispheric hyperactivity). Type I alexithymia should be distinguished from Type II alexithymia found in victims of sexual abuse, where the emotional experience is present, but the accompanying cognitions are absent (for empirical evidence see Moormann et al., 1997). Type II alexithymia is claimed to be caused by a reduced functioning of the corpus callosum (Bermond's func-tional commissurotomy hypothesis). Among researchers in the field of alexithymia, it has been noted that the cognitive and affective disturbances found in alexithymic patients form a serious and bothersome obstacle to psychotherapy (Groen et al., 1951; Krystal, 1979, 1988b; Ruesch, 1948; Sifneos, 1975; Taylor et al., 1997). However, in our opinion, the type of alexithymia should be taken into account when treatment outcomes are evaluated. Assuming that a successful psychotherapy for alexithymic patients should be directed at restoring disturbed affect regulation, it would be extremely difficult to re-educate Type I alexithymics. Their emotion excitability is seriously impaired and therefore there is not enough potential avail-able from which they can be taught to learn to feel. If there is no emotional arousal, there is no need for cognitive processing of emotions.

The prognosis for Type II alexithymics seems more favorable. With respect to Type II alexithymics, the hypothesis has been put forth that the two hemispheres don't communicate very well with each other. This condition is functional for traumatized individuals, because this specific dysfunction prevents painful emotions from reaching the stage of full awareness, in that way providing an opportunity to escape reality. The point of departure for a successful treatment is that Type II alexithymics are emotionally excitable and therefore possess the required potential to learn to feel. This does not mean that treatment is easy. It is time-consuming and a lot of patience is needed, because psychotherapy in case of Type II alexithymics should be directed at providing the emotional experience with its corresponding cognitions. Furthermore, verbal psychotherapy is useless in the treatment of these patients, as they are unable to describe what they feel. Therefore, other-than-verbal cues (as for instance in art therapy) must be applied in order to stimulate them to express their other-than-verbal consciousness (see Tucker & Sachs, 1993).

The orienting reaction as the key to creative imagination

From the above it could be argued that a lack of emotional arousability is at the core of alexithymia. The subdimensions describing, identifying, and analyzing emotions all are clearly dependent upon the capacity to become emotionally excitable. But is this also the case for reduced fantasizing or the lack of creative imagination? Being deprived of fantasy does not seem to be related to emotions, and therefore it is difficult to grasp why the lack of creative imagination is so characteristic for alexithymia. However, the link between emotion and creative imagination can be found in art theories. Bell (1919/1975), for instance, saw the emotional experience as the source for the creative impulse. In psychodynamic terms, Bell's notion implies that people who become emotionally excited try to discharge this physiological state by engaging in imaginative activities such as daydreaming, wishful thinking and fantasizing. In fact, this is exactly what Freud (1916/50) meant with primary process thinking (a regression in the service of the ego, which enables a return to more primitive, childish ways of thinking with plenty of room for fantasy). According to Krystal (1988b), the kind of operative thinking (*pensée opératoire*) found in alexithymia in combination with the severe blocking of wish-fulfillment fantasy and the limited ability to think abstractly and to use symbols and metaphors has a serious impact on creativity. Krystal held failures in parental bonding, particularly in the mother–child relation, responsible for the development of these symptoms. However, we are more inclined to look for explanations where arousal (and therefore emotion) is involved in creativity.

One of the characteristics of creativity is that it concerns something new, something of value (Murray, 1959). We speculate that creativity in humans evolved from the curiosity drive in animals, which leads to exploratory behavior (for the link between creativity and exploratory behavior we also refer to the laboratory studies on aesthetics done by Berlyne, 1971). In ethology, exploratory behavior is considered to have survival value. A detailed knowledge from the geography of their home area will often mean the difference between life and death to a small mammal or bird as a predator swoops down (Manning, 1972). Exploratory behavior is directed at the detection of novel stimuli, which results in the orienting reaction. Pribram (1967) investigated novelty in humans by using a homeostatic model. He succeeded in teasing apart at least two components of the orienting reaction. One component is an indicator of searching and sampling, while the other is manifest when a novelty is registered. The point to be made is that the two indicators of the orienting reaction, e.g. searching/sampling and novelty, are the parameters *par excellence* to define the creative problem. Often, the creative problem is treated as that of finding a solution to an already defined problem. According to Getzels and Csikszentmihalyi (1976), scientists and artists alike have to be problem-finders in the first place. For them, problem-finding precedes problem-solving.

When the theoretical considerations above are applied to the mechanisms behind alexithymia, the following could be argued. Type I alexithymics suffer from a reduced emotional arousability and will therefore be less inclined to show a strong orienting reaction, which in turn will hamper their creative abilities (i.e. no urge for problem-finding, no curiosity) and self-regulation. This line of reasoning is in agreement with descriptions of alexithymic individuals who are rather dull and mundane. Their weak orienting reactions, due to insufficient arousal, are not likely to lead to extensive exploratory behavior in either overt (expressiveness) or covert behavior (creative thinking and imagination). It is difficult for these individuals to become fascinated or absorbed by a certain topic or subject; they simply lack passion. Furthermore, the weak orienting reaction also implies a lack of initiative, which might explain the deficit in self-regulatory capacities of alexithymics, which is seen as one of the greatest obstacles in psychotherapy (see Krystal, 1988a; Taylor *et al.*, 1997). Already in the nineteenth century, Janet reported this reduced willpower. In his *État Mental des Hystériques*, Janet (1911) described hysterical patients with *les aboulies*, who acted as if experiencing passions was menacing to them and who had a severe diminution of willpower. Janet (p. 105) quotes William Page, who characterized this lack of self-regulation as follows: "I can not" looks like "I will not", but it is "I can not will".

Additional circumstantial evidence favoring the hypothesized relation between emotion arousability and imaginative activities includes the following. (1) Recent research carried out by Vorst & Bermond (2001) on the validity and reliability of the Bermond Vorst Alexithymia Questionnaire (BVAQ) demonstrated that the principal component analysis of subscale interrelations of two language groups (French and Dutch) yields a clear-cut two-factor structure. One comprises an affective component (emotion arousability and fantasizing) and the other a cognitive component (identifying, verbalizing, and analyzing emotions). (2) According to Bermond (1995, 1997), the psychobiological make-up of Type I alexithymics (reduced emotion excitability) differs from that of Type II alexithymics (normal emotion excitability). As mentioned above, Type I is caused by hyperactivity of the left hemisphere and is characterized by a decreased functioning of the orbito-prefrontal cortex, reduced neural dopaminergic innervation of this area, and reduced functioning of the right hemisphere, or possibly reduced functioning of the commisura anterior. As these regions are also known to affect imagination, it is far from surprising that reduced emotion excitability is associated with impoverished imagination in Type I alexithymia. In contrast, Type II alexithymics seem to suffer not from hemispheric deficiencies, but from a communication problem between the two hemispheres. Therefore Type II alexithymics experience difficulties with the cognitive components of emotions, e.g. with verbalizing, identifying and analyzing emotions. However, they (subjects of sexual abuse, for instance) can become emotionally excited, in particular by stimuli which trigger the traumatic experience. They can even draw what excites them, but in most cases they cannot construct a narrative of what they have drawn (personal observation of Albach). In art therapy such patients can be taught to describe in words what they have expressed in their other-than-verbal consciousness (Tucker & Sachs, 1993).

Alexithymia and fantasy

Recent developments (Taylor *et al.*, 1997) seem to suggest that alexithymia not only constitutes an inherent personality aberration in its own right, but also constitutes a secondary accompaniment of trauma, and also emerges secondarily as a consequence of attachment and bonding failures (see Grotstein, 1997). Empirical support for the latter two views can be found in a Dutch study on victims of child abuse (Moormann *et al.*, 1997). These findings seem to support the notion that both psychotraumata (child sexual abuse) and attachment or bonding failures (emotional neglect by both parents) are associated with Type II alexithymia. In Type II alexithymia, where the emotion arousability is intact, a normal level of fantasizing is expected. The concept of fantasy is particularly interesting in the debate on memory recovery of childhood sexual abuse. The "non-believers" (Crombag & Merckelbach, 1996; Loftus, 1997) argue that in memory recovery we are not dealing with real abuse events, but with fabricated stories about sexual abuse which have become implanted memories. It is supposed that those fabricated stories are either suggested to the patient by the psychotherapist (suggestibility hypothesis) or due to fantasy-proneness of the patient (Merckelbach *et al.*, 1998). However, in the studies we have conducted on memory recovery, we failed to find empirical evidence supporting the suggestibility hypothesis (Albach *et al.*, 1996) or the fantasy-proneness hypothesis (Bermond *et al.*, submitted). In the latter study, the Bermond Vorst Questionnaire was administered to 73 women with child sexual abuse ($M = 37.6$ years of age with a range from 20 to 61 years of age). Women with memory recovery did not differ significantly on fantasizing from women who had never forgotten the abuse (M-fantasizing $= 26.20$ (SD $= 8.1$) and 25.97 (SD $= 8.9$), respectively). Moreover, fantasizing scores of both abuse groups did not differ from scores of non-abused age-matched controls (consisting of 206 women taken randomly from the Dutch general population). However, as expected, the women with child sexual abuse suffered from Type II alexithymia: severe reductions in the capacity to verbalize and identify emotions in combination with normal levels of operative thinking, emotion excitability, and fantasy. The point to be made is that alexithymics can have normal levels of fantasy as long as they are emotionally arousable.

Alexithymia, dissociation, and anesthesia: three manifestations of the same "non-feeling" state

Another explanation for the finding that abused women still have their ability to fantasize can be found in the relation between dissociation and alexithymia, particularly in regard to the relation between the dissociative feature "absorption–imaginative involvement" and the alexithymic feature "fantasizing". In dissociation, there is a "disruption of the normal integration of cognition, affect, behavior, sensation and identity". Feelings of depersonalization in the form of detachment from one's physical or psychological being are frequently reported in connection with stressful events (see Boon & Draijer, 1993; Ensink, 1992; Van der Hart, 1991). Traumatized individuals may further suffer from visual and auditory hallucinations, in which they relive parts of the traumatic event. These dissociative phenomena are described for concentration camp survivors (Jaffe, 1968), victims of life-threatening events (Noyes & Kletti, 1977), victims of rape (Rose, 1986), and victims of childhood physical and sexual abuse (Chu & Dill, 1990; Ensink, 1992). There are ample indications that sexual abuse during childhood can result in PTSD and alexithymia (e.g. Albach & Everaerd, 1992; Zeitlin et al., 1993). Moreover, there is evidence that childhood sexual abuse followed by rape or sexual assault during adulthood can result in alexithymia as well (Cloitre et al., 1997). Therefore it is interesting to have a closer look at the relation between alexithymia and dissociation. Berenbaum and James (1994) reported that alexithymia was significantly correlated with dissociative experiences in a group of undergraduates, while Irwin and Melbin-Helberg (1997) found that some aspects of alexithymia could predict dissociation in traumatized children. In a study on self-mutilative behavior, Zlotnick et al. (1996) reported that self-mutilators displayed a greater degree of dissociative symptoms (Dissociative Experience Scale – DES) and alexithymia (Toronto Alexithymia Scale – TAS) and a greater number of self-injurious behaviors, as well as higher rates of childhood sexual abuse than non-mutilators. However, dissociative symptoms and alexithymia were both independently associated with self-mutilative behavior. The results of these studies are inconclusive, which may be explained by the use of different subject samples, methodologies and instruments. Furthermore, information on the relation between the subscales of dissociation and alexithymia is not always presented. It is therefore premature to conclude about the exact nature of the relation between fantasizing and dissociation.

In our study on sexual abuse (58 women), we tried to solve this problem by including the subdimensions of dissociation (DES – Bernstein & Putnam, 1986) and alexithymia (Bermond-Vorst Alexithymia Questionnaire, 1993). In addition, the Confusing Experiencing Scale (Albach, 1993; Ensink, 1992) was administered to measure features of hysteria as described in the nineteenth-century French literature. The CES contains the following four subscales: (i) anesthesia (alpha = .88), (ii) sense of body-fragmentation (alpha = .91), (iii) sexual provocative behavior (alpha = .76), and (iv) sleep disorders (alpha = .77).

Dissociation and its three subdimensions – (1) absorption–imaginative involvement, (2) activities of dissociated states, and (3) depersonalization–derealization – indeed showed substantial correlations with nearly all alexithymic features (for the subscales of the DES we refer to Ross *et al.*, 1995). A striking outcome was the negative correlation between dissociation and the reduced ability to fantasize. After childhood sexual abuse, there appears to be a link between dissociation and what could be called "fantasy-proneness". The absorption–imaginative involvement subscale of the DES had the highest negative correlation ($r = -.44, p < .01$) with the reduced ability to fantasize. This seems quite logical when the content of the items of this DES subdimension is taken into consideration (examples are: "So involved in fantasy that it seems real", and "Not sure whether the remembered event happened or was a dream"). The subscale Activities of Dissociated States (e.g. "Finding oneself in a place, but unaware how one got there", and "Being approached by people one does not know, who call one by a different name") also had a significant negative association ($r = -.33, p < .05$) with the reduced ability to fantasize. Only the subscale depersonalization–derealization (with items such as "Not recognizing one's reflection in a mirror", and "Other people and objects do not seem real") was not significantly correlated ($r = -.10$) with the reduced ability to fantasize. These findings thus suggest that dissociation shares some features with the alexithymia subdimension fantasizing, but is not identical to alexithymia. Recent research by Wise *et al.* (2000) reaffirms the notion that dissociation differs basically from alexithymia.

The following quote from one of the participants in our study nicely illustrates how the relation between fantasy and dissociation may contribute to doubts about the sexual abuse. Janet (1911) refers to this phenomenon as *la folie du doute*:

> I often doubt it, because my mother used to say that I was always making up things. As a child I had fled into a fantasy-world. I loved it. However, my mother sometimes found out things were not true, and then she punished me severely. Therefore I always have the feeling that what I tell isn't true, and with these memories I also have that feeling. It belongs to the fantasy-tales of my childhood, because it is something that can't have happened to me, I think. At the same time I know very well that it did happen. But my mother has been so persistent in denying my fantasies and, at the same time, giving me a feeling of guilt about it. Therefore I still think: It is true, but perhaps it isn't true.

In the section on emotion arousability and creative imagination above, we claim that individuals who become emotionally excited try to discharge this physiological state by engaging in imaginative activities such as daydreaming, wishful thinking, and fantasizing. However, not only do our data fail to support this notion, but the opposite pattern of findings emerged. A reduced rather than an increased emotional excitability was reported as fuelling fantasy emissions, as the BVAQ subscale "reduced emotion excitability" had a substantial positive correlation ($r = .43$, $p < .01$) with "absorption–imaginative involvement" of the DES. Furthermore, the inability to become emotionally aroused appeared to be related to the two other dimensions of the DES as well, e.g. to "activities of dissociated states" ($r = .45$, $p < .01$), and to "depersonalization–derealization" ($r = .46, p < .01$). The latter two findings are not in agreement with what is described by leading theorists on the relation between emotion and dissociation. In short, all three results on emotional arousability contradict what could be expected from art theories (Bell, 1919/1975) and "grand" theories of dissociation. Janet (1911), for instance, states:

> Thus, the previous study showed evidence for a substantial role of emotion in bringing about this dissociation of the mental synthesis; emotion, as I said at another point (Janet, 1889, p. 457), has a dissolving influence of the spirit, it diminishes its synthesis and makes it immediately miserable.
>
> (p. 532, translation)

A related view on the bond between dissociation and emotion is given in the early work of Freud and Breuer (1893/1924). They saw hypnoid states as the *sine qua non* of hysteria:

> There is one thing common to all these hypnoid states and to hypnosis, in spite of all their differences – namely that the ideas, which emerge in them, are marked by *great intensity of feeling*, but are cut off from associative connection with the rest of the content of consciousness.
>
> (p. 35)

How can this seemingly contradictory result be explained? In fact quite simply, when one assumes an influence of the sedating effect of anesthesia in the self-report of physiological arousal. Subjects who suffer from anesthesia have loss or impairments of sensations (on the subscale "anesthesia" of the CES, including items such as "Some people don't have a sensation of cold, even if it is below $-10°C$"). There is physiological reactivity, but this physiological arousal is not perceived as such. In the same vein, one may consider the alexithymic feature of emotion arousability. Suffering from anesthesia implies that the physiological reaction is not perceived. Therefore, individuals with anesthesia are not likely to report (on a questionnaire) that they have become emotionally aroused. This is exactly what we found. Women with a reportedly reduced emotion arousability also indicated to suffer from anesthesia ($r = .43, p < .01$). Hence, it might be expected that, even when persons do not report that they become excited, their physiological indices nevertheless might reveal the contrary. However, note that this is mere speculation, since no physiological measures were included in our study.

Despite this weakness, it is interesting to note that our theorizing is in agreement with Krystal's (1988a) description of the non-feeling reaction. When entering a traumatic state "there is a psychological paralysis that starts with a virtually complete blocking of the ability to feel emotions and pain, as well as other physical sensations, and progresses to inhibition of other mental functions" (p. 151). Here it is explicitly stated that emotions as well as physical sensations are blocked. According to Krystal, these patients are themselves able to observe and describe the blocking of their affective responses – a phenomenon referred to as "psychic numbing", "psychological closing off" (Lifton, 1967), and "affective anesthesia" (Minkowski, 1946).

Additional data confirm that the psychological paralysis progresses to inhibition of other functions as well. In addition to the already discussed relation between emotion arousability and anesthesia, we found that anesthesia was associated with the reduced ability to identify ($r = .45, p < .01$), verbalize ($r = .49, p < .01$), and analyze ($r = .34, p < .05$) emotions. Moreover, anesthesia was rather strongly associated ($r = .75, p < .001$) with dissociation (total score on the DES). The strong link between anesthesia (a conversion) and dissociation is in agreement with Kihlstrom's (1992) assertion that both conversion and dissociative disorders are disruptions in the normal controlling functions of consciousness. To put it differently, dissociation and anesthesia should be regarded as belonging to one disorder (when reading Janet we are inclined to call this disorder hysteria). In Kihlstrom's view, it is a mistake that conversion (somatoform disorder) and dissociation (dissociative disorder) are separately classified in the DSM-IV (see also Davison & Neale, 1998):

> In the dissociative disorders, there is a dissociation between explicit and implicit memory. It is the explicit memory, which refers to a person's conscious recall of some experience, that is disrupted in dissociative disorders. Implicit memory refers to behavioral changes elicited by an event that cannot be consciously recalled.
>
> (p. 172)

Kihlstrom (1992) cites numerous examples of patients with dissociative disorders whose implicit memory remains intact. The same basic disruption of consciousness is found in conversion disorder, in this case affecting perception:

> As in the dissociative disorders, stimuli that are not consciously seen, heard, or felt nevertheless affect behavior (cases of hysterical blindness are taken as an example to make this point). So, we might consider conversion disorder as a disruption in explicit perception with unimpaired implicit perception.
>
> (Kihlstrom, cited in Davison & Neale, 1998, p. 172)

If Kihlstrom is correct, then it seems highly likely that the explicit perception of being emotionally aroused is impaired in cases of anesthesia (a reduced instead of increased emotion arousability is therefore reported on the BVAQ), while the implicit perception might still be unimpaired.

Conclusion

Figure 5.1 shows a graphical representation of the Reality Escape Model. An interesting feature of the model, which has not been discussed yet, concerns the hypothesis that Type I alexithymics (upper part of the model) are less vulnerable to suffering from PTSD related symptoms than Type II alexithymics (lower part of the model). The rationale of this statement is that reduced affect, which is so characteristic of Type I alexithymics, and which is supposed to lead to cognitive deficits in affect regulation, at the same time functions as a protection mechanism against the susceptibility to anxiety disorders.

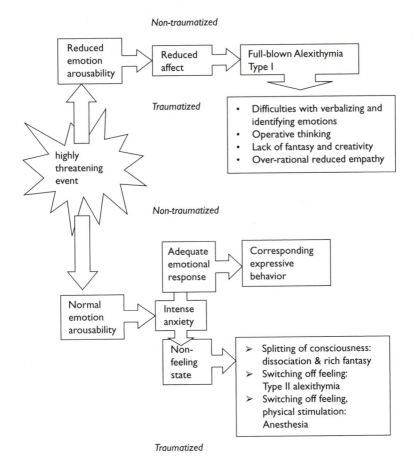

Figure 5.1 Graphical representation of the Reality Escape Model.

Instead it is hypothesized that Type I alexithymics are more prone to develop classical psychosomatic diseases (i.e. peptic ulcer, bronchial asthma, essential hypertension, thyrotoxicosis, ulcerative colitis, rheumatoid arthritis, and neurodermatitis). This statement is based on clinical observations (see for instance Ruesch, 1948, 1957) that many patients (traumatized and non-traumatized) with classical psychosomatic diseases manifest a rather primitive level of psychological organization, and show a lack of imagination in their responses to projective psychological tests. Furthermore, these patients manifest an absence of verbal, gestural, and other symbolic expressions of affects, as well as a tendency to discharge emotional tension through action (Taylor *et al.*, 1997, p. 218). Hence patients with classical psychosomatic diseases fulfill most criteria of Type I alexithymia. Ruesch "contrasted these characteristics (i.e. Type I alexithymia) with the cognitive affective style of psychoneurotic patients, who generally show a high level of expressiveness and relatively easy access to a rich inner life of drive-related fantasies" (Taylor *et al.*, 1997, p. 219). Hence, psychoneurotic patients have normal emotion arousability. Therefore, when traumatized, they are more likely to develop Type II alexithymia.

Our data suggest that symptoms associated with PTSD and psychosomatic diseases seem to fit a diathesis–stress model (see Nolen-Hoeksema, 2001), in which the diathesis or vulnerability factor is caused by early childhood experiences (sexual abuse), biologically determined personality traits (emotion arousability), and possibly hereditary determined (psychosomatic) diseases. Childhood sexual abuse is considered a vulnerability factor here, because the central nervous system has not yet fully matured, which makes it much more vulnerable to future stressors. Threatening events in later life (including abuse), with which organism has to cope, are considered stressors. This model is able to explain why some people are predisposed to react more adversely to environmental stressors.

The most important question is, of course, whether the Reality Escape Model has some surplus value compared with existing models on the sequelae of child sexual abuse. In our opinion, the strength of the Reality Escape Model concerns its eclectic nature and its implications for psychotherapy. Concepts originating from different theories have been embedded in a new coherent framework, around the idea that victims of child sexual abuse try to escape reality by using different psychological mechanisms, all aimed at attaining a non-feeling state. The view that alexithymia, dissociation and anesthesia are different manifestations of this non-feeling state is based on Krystal's (1988a, 1988b) "paradox in the traumatic state", i.e. the paradox between, on the one hand, the intense affect and, at the other hand, the affective blocking. Alternation of affects was initially described by Freud (1939) and later by Horowitz (1976/1996) in his theory of stress response syndromes. Current assessment of PTSD is still based on this alternation between emotional numbing and detachment, on the one hand (avoidance component), and re-experiencing the trauma (intrusions) and hypervigilance (increased arousal), on the other hand. However, the view that the alternation between affective blocking and affective flooding can only happen in Type II alexithymics, i.e. only in individuals who can become emotionally aroused, is new, and suggests a better treatment prognosis for Type II than for Type I alexithymics. The theoretical grounds brought forward to explain why all alexithymic subdimensions, including the subdimension "fantasy or creative imagination", are dependent on emotion arousability is of crucial importance in our theorizing. Of particular relevance is the link between emotion excitability and fantasy, because it bridges the gap between the psycho-dynamic construct of alexithymia and the Janetian constructs of dissociation and conversion. We hope that our alternative conceptualization and integration of concepts will stimulate researchers and clinicians to develop hypotheses and to design studies that will increase our insights into these intriguing clinical phenomena.

References

Albach, F. (1993). *Freud's Verleidingstheorie: Incest, trauma en hysterie [Freud's seduction theory: Incest, trauma and hysteria]*. Amsterdam/Middelburg: Stichting Petra.

Albach, F. & Everaerd, W. (1992). Posttraumatic stress symptoms in victims of childhood incest. *Psychotherapy and Psychosomatics*, **57**, 143–151.

Albach, F., Moormann, P.P., & Bermond, B. (1996). Memory recovery of childhood sexual abuse. *Dissociation*, **9**, 258–269.

American Psychiatric Association (1987). *Diagnostic and statistic manual of mental disorders* (3rd edn, revised). Washington, DC: APA.

American Psychiatric Association (1994). *Diagnostic and statistical manual of mental disorders* (4th edn). Washington, DC: APA.

Bell, C. (1919/1975). The artistic problem (first published in 1919 by Athenaeum). In W.G. Bywater (ed.), *Clive Bell's eye*. Detroit, MI: Wayne State University Press.

Berenbaum, H. & James, T. (1994). Correlates and retrospectively reported antecedents of alexithymia. *Psychosomatic Medicine*, **56**, 353–359.

Berlyne, D.E. (1971). *Aesthetics and psychobiology*. New York: Appleton.

Bermond, B. & Vorst, H. (1993). *The Bermond Vorst Alexithymia Questionnaire*. Unpublished internal report, Department of Psychology, University of Amsterdam.

Bermond, B. (1995). Alexithymia, een neuropsychologische benadering [Alexithymia, a neuropsychological approach]. *Tijdschrift voor Psychiatrie*, **37**, 717–727.

Bermond, B. (1997). Brain and alexithymia. In A.J.J.M. Vingerhoets, F.J. van Bussel, & A.J.W. Boelhouwer (eds), *The (non)expression of emotions in health and disease* (pp. 115–129). Tilburg, The Netherlands: Tilburg University Press.

Bermond, B., Moormann, P.P., & Albach, F. (submitted). *Childhood sexual abuse: Alexithymic complaints and recovered memories*.

Bernstein, E.M. & Putnam, F.W. (1986). Development, reliability, and validity of a dissociation scale. *Journal of Nervous and Mental Disease*, **174**, 727–735.

Boon, S. & Draijer, N. (1993). *Multiple personality disorder in the Netherlands. A study on reliability and validity of the diagnosis*. Amsterdam: Swets & Zeitlinger.

Briquet, P. (1859). *Traité clinique et thérapeutique de l'hystérie [Clinical and psychotherapeutical description of hysteria]*. Paris: Baillière et Fils.

Chu, J.A. & Dill, L.D. (1990). Dissociative symptoms in relation to childhood physical and sexual abuse. *American Journal of Psychiatry*, **147**, 887–892.

Christianson, S.A. & Nilsson, L.G. (1984). Functional amnesia as induced by a psychological trauma. *Memory & Cognition*, **12**, 142–155.

Cloitre, M., Scarvalone, P., & Difede, J. (1997). Posttraumatic stress disorder, self- and interpersonal dysfunction among sexually retraumatized women. *Journal of Traumatic Stress*, **10**, 425–437.

Crombag, H.F.M. & Merckelbach, H.L.G.J. (1996). *Hervonden herinneringen en andere misverstanden [Recovered memories and other misapprehensions]*. Amsterdam: Contact.

Davison, G.C. & Neale, J.M. (1998). *Abnormal psychology* (7th edn). New York: Wiley.

Draijer, N. (1990). *Seksuele traumatisering in de jeugd: Lange termijn gevolgen van seksueel misbruik van meisjes door verwanten [Sexual traumatization in childhood: Long term effects of sexual abuse of girls by relatives]*. Amsterdam: SUA.

Ensink, B.J. (1992). *Confusing realities. A study on child sexual abuse and psychiatric symptoms*. Amsterdam: VU University Press.

Finkelhor, D. & Browne, A. (1985). The traumatic impact of child sexual abuse: a conceptualization. *American Journal of Orthopsychiatry*, **55**, 530–541.

Freud, S. (1916/1950). *Vorlesungen zur Einführung in die Psychoanalyse [Readings for an introduction to psychoanalysis]*. London: Imago.

Freud, S. (1939). Moses and monotheism. In J. Strachey (ed. and trans.), *The standard edition of the complete psychological works of Sigmund Freud*, Vol. 23 (pp. 3–137). New York: Norton.

Freud, S. & Breuer, J. (1893). On the physical mechanism of hysterical phenomena. In Freud, S., *Collected papers*, Vol. 1. London: International Psychoanalytic Press (1924).

Freud, S. & Breuer, J. (1895/1956) *Studies on hysteria*. London: The Hogarth Press.

Getzels, J.W. & Csikszentmihalyi, M. (1976). *The creative vision: a longitudinal study on problem-finding in art*. New York: Wiley.

Groen, J.J., Horst, L. van der, & Bastiaans, J. (1951). *Grondslagen der klinische psychosomatiek [Fundamentals of clinical psychosomatics]*. Haarlem, Netherlands: De Erven F. Bohn.

Grotstein, J.S. (1997). Foreword. Alexithymia: the exception that proves the rule – of the unusual significance of affects. In G. Taylor, M. Bagby, & J. Parker, *Disorders of affect regulation: Alexithymia in medical and psychiatric illness* (pp. 11–22). Cambridge: Cambridge University Press.

Herman, J.L. (1981). *Father–daughter incest*. Cambridge, UK: Harvard University Press.

Horowitz, M.J. (1976/1996). *Stress response syndromes* (2nd. edn) Northvale, NJ: Jason Aronson.

Irwin, H.J. & Melbin-Helberg, E.B. (1997). Alexithymia and dissociative tendencies. *Journal of Clinical Psychology*, **53**,159–166.

Jaffe, R. (1968). Dissociative phenomena in former concentration camp inmates. *International Journal of Psycho-Analysis*, **49**, 310–312.

Janet, P. (1889). *L'automatisme psychologique [Psychological automatism]*. Paris: Félix Alcan.

Janet, P. (1911). *L'état mental des hystériques [The mental state of hysterics]*, 2nd. edn. Paris: Félix Alcan.

Janet, P. (1928). *De l'angoisse à l'extase, études sur les croyances et les sentiments. [From fear to ecstasy, studies on faith and feeling]*. Paris: Félix Alcan.

Kardiner, A. & Spiegel, H. (1947). *War stress and neurotic illness*. New York: Paul Hoeber.

Keane, T.M., Owen, S.W., & Charaoya, G.A. (1985). Social support of Vietnam veterans with PTSD: a comparative analysis. *Journal of Consulting and Clinical Psychology*, **53**, 95–102.

Kihlstrom, J.F. (1992). Dissociative and conversion disorders. In D.J. Stein & J.E. Young (eds), *Cognitive science and clinical disorder* (pp. 247–270). San Diego, CA: Academic Press.

Keilson, H.A. (1979). *Sequentielle Traumatisierung bei Kindern [Sequential traumatization in children]*. Stuttgart: Forum der Psychiatrie.

Krystal, H. (1968). *Massive psychic trauma*. New York: International Universities Press.

Krystal, H. (1979). Alexithymia and psychotherapy. *American Journal of Psychotherapy*, **33**, 17–31.

Krystal, H. (1988a). *Integration and self-healing: Affect, trauma and alexithymia*. Hillsdale, NJ: Analytic Press.

Krystal, H. (1988b). On some roots of creativity. Hemispheric specialization. *Psychiatric Clinics of North America*, **11**, 475–491.

Lifton, R.J. (1967). *Death in life: Survivors of Hiroshima*. New York: Random House.

Loftus, E.F. (1997). Creating false memories: researchers are showing how suggestion and imagination can create "memories" of events that did not actually occur. *Scientific American*, Sept., 50–55.

MacGee, R. (1984). Flashback and memory phenomena. A comment on "flashbacks phenomena" – clinical and diagnostic dilemmas. *Journal of Nervous and Mental Disease*, **172**, 5.

Manning, A. (1972). *An introduction to animal behaviour* (2nd edn). London: Beccles & Colchester.

Merckelbach, H., Muris, P., Schmidt, H., Rassin, E., & Horselenberg, R. (1998). De Creatieve Ervaringen Vragenlijst als maat voor "fantasy proneness" [The Creative Experiences Scale as a measure of "fantasy proneness"]. *De Psycholoog*, **33**, 204–208.

Minkowski, E. (1946). L'anesthésie affective [Affective anesthesia]. *Annales Medico-psychologiques*, **104**, 8–13.

Moormann, P.P., Bermond, B., Albach, F., & van Dorp, I. (1997). The etiology of alexithymia from the perspective of childhood sexual abuse. In A.J.J.M. Vingerhoets, F.J. van Bussel, & A.J.W. Boelhouwer (eds), *The (non)expression of emotions in health and disease* (pp. 139–153). Tilburg, The Netherlands: Tilburg University Press.

Murray, H.A. (1959). Viscissitudes of creativity. In H.H. Anderson (ed.), *Creativity and its cultivation*. New York: Harper.

Nolen-Hoeksema, S. (2001). *Abnormal psychology* (2nd edn). New York: McGraw-Hill.

Noyes, R. & Kletti, R. (1977). Depersonalization in response to life-threatening danger. *Psychiatry*, **18**, 375–384.

Pribram, K.H. (1967). The new neurology and the biology of emotion: a structural approach. *American Psychologist*, **22**, 830–838.

Rose, D.S. (1986). "Worse than death." Psychodynamics of rape victims and the need for psychotherapy. *American Journal of Psychiatry*, **143**, 817–824.

Ross, C.A., Ellason, J.W., & Anderson, G. (1995). A factor analysis of the Dissociative Experience Scale (DES) in dissociative identity disorder. *Dissociation*, **8**, 229–235.

Ruesch, J.E. (1948). The infantile personality. *Psychosomatic Medicine*, **10**, 134–144.

Ruesch, J.E. (1957). *Disturbed communication: the clinical assessment of normal and pathological communicative behavior*. New York: Norton.

Sargant, W. & Slater, E. (1941). Amnesic syndromes in war. *Proceedings of the Royal Society of Medicine, Section of Psychiatry*, **34**, 757–763.

Sifneos, P.E. (1975). Problems of psychotherapy of patients with alexithymic characteristics and physical disease. *Psychotherapy and Psychosomatics*, **26**, 65–70.

Simmel, E. (1918) *Kriegsneurosen und "psychisches Trauma" [War neuroses and "psycho traumata"]*. Leipzig: Otto Nemnich.

Taylor, G.J., Bagby, R.M., & Parker, D.A. (1997). *Disorders of affect regulation: Alexithymia in medical and psychiatric illness*. Cambridge: Cambridge University Press.

Tucker, M. & Sachs, R.G. (1993). Reforming associations: conjunctive treatment of anaclytic depression and alexithymia in the dissociative population. Paper presented at the 10th International Conference on Multiple Personality/Dissociative States, Chicago, IL.

Van der Hart, O. (ed.) (1991). *Trauma, dissociatie en hypnose [Trauma, dissociation and hypnosis]*. Amsterdam: Swets & Zeitlinger.

Vingerhoets, A.J.J.M., Van Heck, G.L., Grim, R., & Bermond, B. (1995). Alexithymia: a further exploration of its nomological network. *Psychotherapy and Psychosomatics*, **64**, 32–42.

Vorst, H.C.M. & Bermond, B. (2001). Validity and reliability of the Bermond-Vorst Alexithymia Questionnaire. *Personality and Individual Differences*, **30**, 413–434.

Wise, T.N., Mann, L.S., & Sheridan, M.J. (2000). Relationship between alexithymia, dissociation, and personality in psychiatric outpatients. *Psychotherapy and Psychosomatics*, **69**, 123–127.

Zeitlin, S.B., McNally, R.J., & Cassiday, K.L. (1993). Alexithymia in victims of sexual assault: an effect of repeated traumatization? *American Journal of Psychiatry*, **150**, 661–663.

Zlotnick, C., Shea, M.T., Pearlstein, T., Simpson, E., Costello, E., & Begin, A. (1996). The relationship between dissociative symptoms, alexithymia, impulsivity, sexual abuse, and self-mutilation. *Comprehensive Psychiatry*, **37**, 12–16.

Chapter 6

Worry, perseverative thinking and health

Jos F. Brosschot and Julian F. Thayer

Introduction

Until recently the concept of worry was mainly studied within the context of test anxiety and anxiety disorders. Worry plays a role in nearly all anxiety disorders and is a core characteristic of generalized anxiety disorder (GAD). Even in the area of anxiety, it was not until the 1980s that the potential etiological importance of the concept became recognized and systematically investigated (see Davey & Tallis, 1994). In this contribution, we will attempt to show that worry may play a much broader role in psychological and somatic health. We will discuss evidence of a wide range of possible long-term health consequences of worry, reaching from anxiety disorders and medically unexplained somatic complaints towards pathophysiological conditions such as cardiovascular disease (CVD). Furthermore, the diverse processes and mechanisms underlying these consequences will be outlined, including some currently known physiological and neurovisceral concomitants of worry. The chapter starts with some theoretical considerations of the definition and nature of worry and related concepts such as rumination. Next we will discuss their etiological role in anxiety, unexplained somatic complaints, and somatic disease, respectively.

Worry, rumination and perseverative thinking

Definitions

Borkovec *et al.* (1983, p. 10) introduced as a working definition of worry: "Worry is a chain of thoughts and images, negatively affect-laden and relatively uncontrollable; it represents an attempt to engage in mental problem-solving on an issue whose future outcome is uncertain but contains the possibility of one or more negative outcomes; consequently, worry is related closely to fear process." Later Davey and Tallis (1994, p. 7) added, "worry is dominated by thought, at the cost of imagery".

The central cognitive–emotional process in this definition, however, is not restricted to worrying over threatening situations *per se*. For example, although worry in this definition is stated to be related to "fear process", fear can be replaced by any other negative emotional state, like depression or anger. In such cases one tends to speak of "ruminative thinking" and "angry brooding" rather than of worry. Although for anxiety theory a worry formulation is the most logical choice, for many other health consequences of worry, or rather the cognitive–emotional process that lies at the heart of the phenomenon, a more encompassing term appears to be called for. For that reason we propose the term "perseverative thinking". The advantage of this term is that it is applicable to many negative emotional situations and, as we will see, is conceptually closer to the central factors that are responsible for the pathogenic processes to be described below. We will use the terms "worry", "rumination" and "perseverative thinking" interchangeably throughout the chapter, often depending on how it is used in the studies to be discussed.

Functions of worry

Worry is thought to serve different functions. The most straightforward or concrete function that is attributed to worry is an attempt at constructive mental problem-solving, albeit a thwarted attempt (Davey, 1994). In support of this function, Davey found a positive correlation between worry and problem-focused coping, but only after partialling out the effect of trait anxiety. Thus, worry was associated with a habitual tendency for active problem-solving combined with low confidence in succeeding in it. Tallis and Eysenck (1991) proposed a tripartite function of worry. They proposed that first, worry serves an alarm function, acting to interrupt ongoing behavior and directing awareness toward an issue demanding immediate solution. Second, worry would have a prompt function, continuously representing unresolved threatening situations to awareness. Third, worry is thought to have a preparation function, anticipating threat and making the organism ready for a situation in which high or even vigorous motor activation is needed. Obviously, such a situation hardly ever occurs in the case of worry, or in most other cases of perseverative thinking. Thus perseverative thinking theoretically leaves the individual in a prolonged state of psychophysiological "action preparation".

Perseverative thinking and psychopathology

Although perseverative thinking is now thought to be implicated in a range of psychopathologies, it has been most explicitly discussed in the context of anxiety disorders. It is only since the early 1980s (Borkovec *et al.*, 1983) that worry has gained importance as a research subject in its own right. Before that time, worry was viewed as an epiphenomenon of anxiety or not more than a cognitive adaptation to the disorder, without etiological importance. The contemporary view, however, is that worry is an important or even core characteristic of many anxiety disorders, especially generalized anxiety disorder (GAD). The feeling of not being able to control worrying, or "meta-worry", is nowadays thought of as the basic manifestation of GAD. This extension of worry with meta-worry can be considered the borderline between normal and pathological worry (Borkovec *et al.*, 1983). For a thorough discussion of the role of worry in GAD the reader is referred to the work of Borkovec and of others (see Davey & Tallis, 1994), while for the role of rumination in depression and psychological trauma the reader is referred to Nolen-Hoeksema and coworkers (e.g. Nolen-Hoeksema *et al.*, 1997). In this chapter, our focus is mainly on the health effects of normal, non-clinical worry, although many of the findings and hypotheses discussed below will also be valid for pathological worry. However, one important general contribution of perseverative thinking to psychopathology should be mentioned here. Long-lasting and intensive worrying or rumination will continuously reactivate the cognitive schemata that lie at the heart of many psychopathologies. Such an abnormal activation "trains" as it were the cognitive apparatus to persistently process bodily or external information congruent with the individual's current psychopathology. In this way perseverative thinking sustains pathology or even induces further pathology. For an extensive account of evidence of this type of cognitive process in psychopathology, and the cognitive biases it produces, the reader is referred to Williams *et al.* (1988). As we will argue later in this chapter, the cognitive "training" effect of perseverative thinking may also have implications for the understanding of medically unexplained somatic syndromes. It suffices here to emphasize that perseverative thinking need not be pathological to have pathogenic effects, for mental as well as for somatic health.

In the development of phobia, perseverative thinking is suggested to play an additional and specific, and possibly unexpected, role. For an exposure therapy to have a successful outcome the phobic individual's so-called fear network has to be fully activated, including the cognitive, affective and physiological levels (Foa & Kozak, 1986). Perseverative thinking, being a predominantly cognitive, verbal and abstract process (Borkovec & Inz, 1990), appears to prevent this full activation, because it interferes with the evocation of imagery and therefore the processing of concrete aspects of the feared stimulus. In this way, perseverative thinking is thought to help to maintain the disorder. Moreover, dispositional worriers or perseverative thinkers may run a higher risk for the development of anxiety disorders because their worrying may prevent them from learning from the multiple occasions that daily life offers for natural exposure to feared situations and objects.

Medically unexplained somatic complaints: "somatisation"

Perseverative thinking may be a crucial etiological factor in yet another area of psychopathology, namely that of medically unexplained somatic complaints. A large part of these complaints goes under the headings of hypochondriasis, somatization or somatization disorder, or several contemporary syndromes such as chronic fatigue syndrome, fibromyalgia, multiple chemical sensitivity, chronic (back-)pain, whiplash and many others. Some authors emphasize that the majority of somatic complaints that are presented to general physicians are subjective and not necessarily related to objectifiable physiopathology (Eriksen *et al.*, 1998), and it might be added that they often continue to be so after the general physician's consultation. In hypochondriasis and in less severe health-related anxieties the role of perseverative thinking is generally similar to that outlined above for phobia and generalized anxiety disorder. Thus, extensive worrying may sustain health-specific fears by creating and strengthening inadequate cognitive pathways, and, as in phobia, it might also prevent fear-specific emotional processing. In addition, in these anxiety-related syndromes as well as in other medically unexplained somatic syndromes, prolonged perseveration about one's putative – or yet to be medically confirmed – illness might sustain complaints in a more direct cognitive way. It might cause long-lasting activation and continuing reactivation of specific (pain- and) illness-related cognitive networks. Just as such a high activation leads to the perception of more threat in anxiety disorders (Williams *et al.*, 1988), activated illness networks might be hypothesized to guide information processing towards overabundant illness perception. As a result, more illness-related internal (bodily) and external cues will be detected, more ambiguous internal and external information will be interpreted in terms of illness, more misattribution of harmless signals to illness will occur, and finally, more and stronger memory traces for illness-related information will be produced. In combination with highly salient and accessible illness information, this might lead to enhanced symptom reporting (see also Pennebaker, 1982). Thus, given the fact that – understandably – most patients suffering from medically unexplained somatic complaints spend a lot of time worrying over their condition, this worrying may continuously activate the cognitive networks. Above a certain level of activation, these networks trigger a feed-forward process in which the experience or perception of illness leads to more and more perception of illness.

The literature provides a limited set of evidence for the role of over-activated cognitive illness networks, also called "cognitive bias" in unexplained or subjective somatic complaints. Cognitive bias can be measured by attentional interference tasks, such as the modified Stroop tasks, or by memory or interpretational bias tasks (Williams *et al.*, 1988). With respect to medically unexplained complaints, higher interference by health-threat words in a modified Stroop task was found in somatoform disorder patients (Lupke & Ehlert, 1998) and the same for pain-related words in chronic pain patients (Pearce & Morley, 1989). Better memory for pain-related words was found in pain patients (cited in Pincus *et al.*, 1998) and an interpretational pain bias regarding ambiguous information was found in pain patients (unpublished PhD and MSc studies cited in Pincus *et al.*, 1998). The notion of a higher (implicit) pain memory and selective attention for pain and enhanced pain perception in pain patients was supported by the finding that pain-related Stroop words, administered peri-threshold, enhanced the N100 to N200 evoked potentials (Flor *et al.*, 1997). In addition, a study by Schmidt *et al.* (1994) suggested that physical symptoms could be induced by attention manipulation alone, without any actual sensory stimulation. Finally, Cioffi and Holloway (1993) supplied some indirect evidence of enhanced pain perception by activation of pain-related cognitive schemata. They found that in undergraduates, suppression of pain after a painful stimulus had the effect that after some delay subsequent pain stimuli were more strongly perceived (more painful) than when the pain was either monitored or distracted from. This apparently paradoxical result can be explained by the well-known phenomenon that suppressing mental content in fact only makes it more accessible, by strengthening its traces in the cognitive network and extending this network by the very information that is used to suppress it. Wegner documented this phenomenon and very appropriately called it an "ironic" process (see e.g. Wegner *et al.*, 1993).

In summary, extensive perseverative thinking about illness or pain, or both, is hypothesized to induce a feed-forward process in which increasingly more illness cues are perceived. The evidence in support of a highly activated cognitive network is still scarce, but seems to be consistent across different cognitive functions such as memory and attention. However, it is not yet clear whether and to what extent a cognitive bias for illness actually contributes to the development or maintenance of medically unexplained complaints. It is also not clear to what extent fear still plays a crucial role in such an etiological process. The findings of Lupke and Ehlert (1998) mentioned above, of a cognitive bias for health-threat words in somatoform disorder patients, raised the question of whether fear of illness is a necessary condition for a cognitive bias to have consequences for illness perception. When this would not be the case, mere over-exposure to illness information or internal rehearsal of it might in itself be enough to produce complaints. Clearly, the answers to these questions might be relevant for clinicians working with patients suffering from medically unexplained syndromes.

Perseverative thinking, somatic illness and physiology

Perseverative thinking in stress–coping–disease theory

Perseverative thinking and the concepts it encompasses, such as worry and rumination or, for example, anticipatory stress, appear to be largely neglected in the area of stress, coping and disease. The bulk of research in this area involves either discrete stressors, such as life events or daily hassles, or discrete coping strategies, or both. When chronic stress, like marital or social-economic stress, is studied, the emphasis is mostly on the stimulus characteristics, or the individual's perception of them, and seldom or never on enduring cognitive processes. In our view, there are several potential reasons for this absence of perseverative thinking or comparable "micro-stress" in this major area of health psychology. One obvious reason is that worry or rumination is not spectacular like major life events or traumatic events. For the same reason, daily hassles have only been recognized as important stressors since the 1980s (e.g. DeLongis *et al.*, 1982), decades after the interest in stressors started with the study of major life events and life changes. Since then, evidence has been accumulating that daily hassles have substantial health consequences (e.g. Graham *et al.*, 1986) that even seem to surpass those of life events (e.g. DeLongis *et al.*, 1982). Worry is even less recognizable as a source of stress than daily hassles. In contrast to daily stressors and life events, worry is usually not associated with very clear emotional tension.

Another, less obvious reason for the absence of perseverative thinking and related concepts in the stress literature is that theoretical models that link stressors to health outcomes lack precision as to the psychobiological mechanisms underlying this link. In particular, a complete model has to account for the chronic pathogenic state that ultimately causes disease. Perseverative thinking may lead to such a state, by acting as an internal or cognitive micro-stressor as well as by acting as a mechanism mediating the effects of other stressors. This seemingly hybrid nature of perseverative thinking, i.e. being both a stressor and a mediating mechanism, is related to its cognitive nature, which it is hoped will become more clear in the sections to follow. Thus, perseverative thinking might facilitate the converting of the immediate psychological and physiological concomitants of life events and daily stressors into prolonged physiological activation, which in turn is necessary for the development of a chronic pathogenic state (Brosschot & Thayer, 1998). Although many theorists may have implicitly agreed that sustained physiological activation is a crucial if not necessary condition for stressors to lead to somatic pathology, only very few have explicitly stated so (e.g. Ursin & Murison, 1983). Instead, numerous investigators have always measured stressors as discrete events and coping behavior as discrete and singular goal-directed strategies, without any purposeful endeavor to study why some events or coping strategies have prolonged effects on physiology.

A final important reason for the neglect of worry and perseverative thinking in stress research is that the dominant measures (life events and daily hassles) always focused on the past (or sometimes on the present). During four decades of stress research, hardly any explicit attempt at measuring anticipatory stress was undertaken. We suspect that this too must be a consequence of the lack of a theoretical precision regarding the psychophysiological mechanism underlying the stress–disease link. There has been a particular failure to recognize the importance of prolonged activation – with the exception mentioned (Ursin & Murison, 1983). An early recognition of the importance of this factor might have stimulated more theorizing about the psychological mechanism underlying sustained activation. The current theory of perseverative thinking may in fact be only one possible theoretical account.

The role of perseverative thinking in stress–coping–disease

As alluded to above, the place of worry or perseverative thinking in stress theory may be right between stressors and health outcomes, mediating the effects of stressors. It is important to note that this is different from coping strategies, which are postulated to modulate the effects of stressors on health outcomes. Coping strategies are regarded as ways either to decrease or to eliminate the effects of stressors by eliminating or reducing the intensity of the stressor, for instance, by changing its meaning. Although some coping strategies, such as expressing or suppressing emotions, are believed to have physiological consequences of their own (the so-called "physiological costs of inhibiting"), they are still not primarily viewed as the mediators of the effects of emotional stressors. Perseverative thinking, on the other hand, can be thought of as a direct mechanism by which the stressor has its effects on physiology. It does this by prolonging the stressor itself, in a representational form that continues to activate the organism. Without perseverative thinking or a comparable mechanism prolonging the activation, an acute, in time limited stressor cannot have an impact on health in a direct manner. In terms of the leading theories on emotion and cognition (Frijda, 1988; Lazarus, 1991; Dalgleish & Power, 1999) perseverative thinking may be regarded as a prolonged state of action readiness that develops when something highly relevant for the individual is at stake. This is primarily a highly vigilant state, without extreme increases in physiological activation. Remember that perseverative thinking is a predominantly verbal, abstract cognitive emotional state that can in fact prevent extreme arousal in a condition like phobia. The crucial pathogenic property then in perseverative thinking is not its intensity or "amplitude", but rather its duration and the inadequate autonomic and emotional regulation associated with it. Later in this chapter we will discuss the (neuro)physiology of perseverative thinking or worry in more detail.

Although its role in the stress–disease process may be different than coping, perseverative thinking is theoretically connected to it. In our view, this relationship can be explained as follows. As mentioned above, perseverative thinking or worry can be regarded as fruitless attempts at mental problem-solving (Davey, 1994). In terms of Lazarus and Folkman's well-known coping theory (Folkman, 1984), worry can be described as a fixation in the phase of "secondary coping". In perseverative thinking, the question "what can I do about this threatening situation?" is constantly and repeatedly asked, but not answered (cf. the "prompt function" mentioned above). Interestingly, if one carefully examines coping instruments, an implicit assumption seems to be that coping is a matter of simply choosing among cognitive and behavioral options and then realizing them. The instruments never ask how long it takes respondents to make their decision, how long they oscillate between options or between actually performed behaviors, or whether they simultaneously use more than one strategy. They also do not ask if and how long respondents feel uncertain about what to do, as often happens in ambiguous situations or in individuals with a high tendency to persevere cognitively. Although seldom or never measured, it might be in fact these intermediate cognitive–emotional states, in which a stressor is repeatedly and fruitlessly reappraised in a primary or secondary fashion (or both at the same time), that are associated with prolonged states of activation, which, when they are frequent or chronic, can have consequences for health. Theoretically then, perseverative thinking is both a stressor (or more precisely, a reappraised stressor) and a mediating mechanism, by the very nature of this reappraisal process.

Perseverative thinking and perceived control

A core characteristic of these perseverative states is the conviction that control over a stressor is threatened. Only when a threat to control is perceived does the stressor's full potential for activating the organism manifest itself, since no way to diminish or change this threat is perceived. Perceived uncontrollability of stress (and associated states such as hopelessness) has been documented as an important if not the most important stressor as well as person characteristic responsible for potentially pathogenic physiological states and health problems (Brosschot *et al.*, 1998; Everson *et al.*, 1996; Frankenhäuser, 1980; Steptoe & Appels, 1989; Ursin & Hytten, 1992). From this perspective, perseverative thinking might be viewed as the cognitive manifestation and nourisher of the deeper underlying experience of perceived uncontrollability. The concept of perseverative thinking may thus be helpful for a better understanding of the health effects of a well-known psychological stress factor, namely perceived uncontrollability, by accounting for the prolongation of its physiological effects. To summarize, we propose that perseverative thinking sustains the physiological response to a stressor by prolonging the uncertain state in the coping process, the state in which low control over the stressor is perceived. Incorporating perseverative thinking in our theorizing means taking into account the importance of the time dimension in stress research. Given this crucial role in the stress–disease link, we would expect associations between perseverative thinking, on the one hand, and disease outcomes and physiological consequences, on the other. In the next sections, we will address these issues.

Worry and risk of somatic disease

Given the short research history of worry and rumination, it is not reasonable to expect a large number of studies linking perseverative thinking with somatic disease. However, there is some recent evidence of the worry–disease link and a PyscInfo search with keywords referring to worry, rumination and anticipatory stress yielded some more relevant findings, scattered over the last decades, mostly from studies that were not explicitly directed at these topics. In fact, the only study that explicitly links worry to disease outcome is one by Kubzansky *et al.* (1997), which showed that a tendency to worry predicted cardiovascular disease (CVD), in this case a second myocardial infarction (MI). More indirectly, worry is a core characteristic of several conditions that are known to be risk factors for CVD, such as anxiety disorders, trait anxiety, and depression (Thayer *et al.*, 1996; Wulsin *et al.*, 1999). Vagal tone is chronically low in these conditions (Thayer *et al.*, 1998; Friedman & Thayer, 1998), just like in states of worry (Lyonfields *et al.*, 1995; Thayer *et al.*, 1996). Since low vagal control is a risk factor for CVD, it has been suggested that worry is a potential mediator of the CVD risk of anxiety disorders and depression (Brosschot & Thayer, 1998; Thayer *et al.*, 1996).

Brosschot and colleagues found some preliminary evidence for a positive association between dispositional worry and general health. In a yet unpublished exploratory study in over 250 psychology students, it was found that a disposition to worry was strongly associated ($r = .64$) with subjective health complaints. The association was much lower, but still significant, when the effect of trait anxiety was controlled for (partial $r = .18$), which suggested that the association was at least partly due to "pure" worry tendency and not entirely due to a tendency to express negative affect. In a related study in older, part-time students we attempted to obtain more evidence in support of a causal role of worry. We instructed seven students to postpone their worrying to a special 30-minute "worry period" later each day, during one week. Compared to the three days prior to the intervention week, the postponement group had significantly fewer health complaints during the last three days of the intervention, as compared to ten control students who only registered their worry periods. These results seem to suggest that a longer time spent worrying might lead to more subjective health complaints. One explanation of the relationship between worry and self-reported health complaints could be over-activated cognitive illness networks due to worrying about health, as discussed in the section on unexplained or subjective somatic complaints. However, this can only be a partial explanation, because the effects of worry postponement were stronger for common cold or flu-like complaints and coughing than for "conventional psychosomatic" complaints such as headache or dizziness. These results instead suggest a psychoneuroimmunological pathway leading from perseverative thinking to infectious disease and probably other immune-related diseases.

Worry, rumination, and physiological functioning

Worry and rumination have been found to be associated with enhanced levels of cortisol. Ruminating before exams was associated with higher salivary cortisol levels (Hellhammer *et al.*, 1985), and worry during sexual stimulation was found to be positively related to plasma cortisol levels (Rowland *et al.*, 1987). Furthermore, a disposition to rehearse or ruminate showed a positive association with urinary cortisol during and after examinations, a relationship that was stronger than between neuroticism and urinary cortisol (Roger & Najarian, 1998). Except for the last study none of the worry studies mentioned so far has tried to distinguish self-reports of worry from more general negative response tendencies such as neuroticism or negative affectivity. On the other hand, it could be speculated that perseverative thinking might be the pathogenic ingredient in these general response tendencies. Both experimental worry and dispositional worry have been found to be associated with low vagal tone (LVT; Borkovec *et al.*, 1998; Lyonfields *et al.*, 1995; Thayer *et al.*, 1996; Kubzansky *et al.*, 1997). As mentioned above, LVT has also been found in depression and anxious states or anxiety disorders that have worry or rumination as a core characteristic. Hence, as we speculated above, worry may mediate part of the CVD risk of these conditions via prolonged cardiovascular activation, especially by chronic decreased vagal control of the heart.

In addition, a more notorious psychological CVD risk factor, hostility (e.g. Miller *et al.*, 1996), might also be partly explained by worry or rumination. Recently, it has been demonstrated that continued rumination about an angering situation prolongs cardiovascular responses to these situations (Glynn *et al.*, 2002). It is reasonable to expect that both hostility and dispositional worry may prolong this activated state by enhancing worry after anger provocation. Thus, these results support the view that perseverative thinking may explain part of the high CVD risk associated with high hostility. As we have proposed before (Brosschot & Thayer, 1998), hostile individuals might be especially prone to anger reactions when no socially appropriate response is possible. We argued that in social reality these situations are far more common than situations in which anger can be freely expressed. This would imply that hostile individuals will have to inhibit their anger far more often than they are able to express it, causing slow cardiovascular recovery or prolonged activation. It is because of this chronic or frequent inhibition of anger, we further hypothesized, that hostile individuals develop the pathogenic physiological state that can result in CVD.

By far the most cardiovascular laboratory experiments on anger have been focused on anger expression and cardiovascular reactivity, rather than on anger inhibition and prolonged activation. Also, hostility and anger questionnaires typically, but often implicitly, refer to situations in which expression options are free. Notwithstanding this longstanding research bias, a reasonable – apparently often ignored – amount of evidence has been built up in the past four decades showing that having no opportunity to express one's anger in frustrating situations is associated with prolonged cardiovascular activation. The line of studies showing this starts with six studies by Hokanson and coworkers in the 1960s (see Megargee & Hokanson, 1970, for a review) and later generally replicated by others. In fact, 13 out of 15 studies found that a lack of opportunity to counteract after being harassed slows cardiovascular recovery after being harassed (see Brosschot & Thayer, 1998). The speed of recovery appeared to be dependent in a complex way on several factors, including characteristics of the subjects and harasser (e.g. Megargee & Hokanson, 1970). An analysis of some of these studies (Brosschot & Thayer, 1998) suggests that the perceived ability to counter-react in a preferred manner, and not actual performance of this behavior, speeds cardiovascular recovery. This seems to underscore the importance of perceived control over the situation, which was mentioned above. In terms of emotion theory, as long as no control is perceived, the organism's psychophysiological state of action readiness is maintained. It could be argued that due to the lack of response opportunity, angered individuals would tend to ruminate, or "brood" or "fume" over the frustrating situation, and that this angry perseverative thinking is in fact the direct cause of their prolonged high CV activation. This effect of perseverative thinking is exactly what the recent study of Glynn *et al.* (2002) demonstrated: rumination after being angered prolongs CV activation.

Undoubtedly, hostile individuals will be especially prone to this type of situation, because they will perceive or even induce many more angering situations and will at the same time be more easily and more intensely angered. Other studies, in which hostility was measured, but in which behavioral response opportunity was not manipulated (and therefore unclear), show that hostility is related to slow recovery after anger provocation tests. The hostility component of the structured interview (SI)-derived Type-A behavior pattern was related to physiological reactivity to and recovery from the SI and a subsequent standard Stroop task (Ganster *et al.*, 1991). Antagonistic, but not neurotic, hostility on the Cook Medley scale was related to greater systolic blood pressure reactivity to and poorer recovery after harassment (Suarez & Williams, 1990). Furthermore, anger that was held in and not anger that was expressed was related to slow recovery in several emotional and cognitive tasks (Vitaliano *et al.*, 1995). The finding that only inhibited anger and antagonistic hostility were related to slow recovery seems to support the emotion-theoretical viewpoint that a dispositional action tendency is the "toxic" characteristic of hostility, via its prolongation of physiological responding after provocation. This view is further supported by the general finding that especially antagonistic hostility or potential for hostility is predictive of CVD and hypertension (Jorgensen *et al.*, 1996).

Anticipatory stress and physiological functioning

A considerable part of daily worrying consists of anticipatory negative thinking. The idea of considering future stressors is conspicuously absent in the bulk of stress research, while it is not difficult to see that it can have important physiological effects. Thus, in addition to the ways that emotion can be extended after stress situations, anticipating stressors and anticipatory worrying are yet other ways to enlarge the duration of physiological responses. In other words, not only the response to a stressor and the recovery afterwards are important from a prolonged activation view on emotional CVD risk factors, but also the start of anticipating the stressor. Even more than is the case with recovery, anticipating stress is difficult to simulate in the laboratory, because either the stressor doesn't have sufficient impact or the subjects have to be kept unaware of the exact manipulation of negative emotions. Not surprisingly, most studies that have included anticipatory stress are ambulatory. One of these, by Hellhammer *et al.* (1985) was already mentioned, and showed that salivary cortisol level was associated with ruminating before examinations. More recently Smyth and colleagues (1998), in an ambulatory study of daily stressors, showed that both the experience of a stressor and anticipating a stressor were associated with enhancement of salivary cortisol. Spangler (1997) showed pre-exam anticipatory cardiovascular, cortisol and immunological responses before an examination. There was also a higher response during the examination, but during the anticipation and recovery phases the differences with a within-subject control situation were larger.

Perseverative thinking: neurovisceral concomitants

Perseverative thinking is repetitive, abstract, involuntary, and represents a failure of inhibitory neural processes. As such, perseverative thinking is a disinhibition of a potentially adaptive mechanism in higher organisms associated with the frontal lobes (Thayer & Lane, 2002). The frontal lobes have reciprocal neural connections with thalamic structures that are associated with more evolutionarily primitive neural circuits that are in part responsible for basic approach and avoidance behavior. When these structures are disinhibited a number of processes associated with threat are unleashed including hypervigilance, fear, and autonomic activity associated with fight or flight such as increased heart rate and blood pressure. When this physiological activation is prolonged, the chronic pathogenic state necessary for the development of disease may ensue.

Thayer and Lane (2002) have recently outlined the neurophysiological concomitants of perseverative thinking. They have proposed a network of neural structures that generate, receive, and integrate internal and external information in the service of goal-directed behavior and organism adaptability. These structures form part of an integrated self-regulation system that allows for the efficient interaction of the organism with its environment – both internal and external.

For example, with respect to cardiovascular disease there are at least two related pathways in which perseverative thinking may be causally related to cardiovascular disease. One pathway is via decreased vagally mediated heart rate variability (HRV). Another pathway is via decreased medial prefrontal cortex activity. Thayer and Lane (2002) have proposed that these two pathways in fact represent the breakdown of a common reciprocal inhibitory cortico-thalamic neural circuit. They described a set of neural structures that serve to link the prefrontal cortex with HRV. This network of reciprocally interconnected neural structures allows the prefrontal cortex to exert an inhibitory influence on thalamic structures associated with defensive behavior and thus allows the organism to regulate its behavior flexibly in response to changing environmental demands. For example, when faced with threat, the tonic inhibitory control of thalamic structures by the prefrontal cortex can be rapidly decreased (disinhibited) leading to sympathoexcitatory fight or flight responses necessary for survival. However, when this tonically inhibitory network is disrupted, a rigid, defensive behavioral pattern is allowed to emerge with its associated perseverative behavior manifesting in attentional, affective, and autonomic inflexibility.

Structurally, this network includes the anterior cingulate, insular, and ventro-medial prefrontal cortices, the central nucleus of the amygdala, the paraventricular and related nuclei of the hypothalamus, the periaquaductal gray matter, the parabrachial nucleus, the nucleus of the solitary tract, the nucleus ambiguus, the ventrolateral medulla, the ventromedial medulla, and the medullary tegmental field. These structures are reciprocally interconnected such that information flows in both directions – top-down and bottom-up. The primary output of this network is mediated through the preganglionic sympathetic and parasympathetic neurons.

Importantly, these neurons innervate the heart via the stellate ganglia and the vagus nerve. The interplay of these inputs to the sino-atrial node of the heart is the source of the complex variability that characterizes the heart rate time series (Saul, 1990), which implies that the output of this network is directly linked to HRV. In addition, sensory information from the peripheral end organs such as the heart are fed back to this set of neural structures, one important example of which is cardiac pain (Foreman, 1999). As such, HRV may be regarded as an index of central–peripheral neural feedback and central nervous system (CNS)–autonomic nervous system (ANS) integration. Perseverative activity in attention, affect, cardiac, and motor behavior have all been linked to disruption of these feedback circuits (Masterman & Cummings, 1997; Spyer, 1989).

Conclusions

In this chapter we have tried to provide the groundwork for a theoretical approach to the relationship between worry or rumination and related concepts, on the one hand, and health, on the other hand. We have introduced the term "perseverative thinking" to describe the core cognitive–emotional process involved in worry, rumination, fuming, and the like, thus allowing this concept to be applied to a wider range of emotional states and dispositions than has previously been done. We have attempted to show that perseverative thinking may play a much broader role in psychological and somatic health than has hitherto been appreciated. Evidence of a wide range of possible long-term health consequences of perseverative thinking including anxiety disorders, medically unexplained somatic complaints, and cardio-vascular disease has been presented. Furthermore, the diverse processes and mechanisms underlying these consequences were outlined, including physiological and neurovisceral processes involved in worry.

The cognitive–emotional process that we have termed perseverative thinking may be the source of prolonged physiological activation that expands the temporal duration of a stressor beyond the traditional reactivity period to include anticipation and recovery. Thus, perseverative thinking may be the missing link in the relation-ship between psychosocial factors and the chronic pathogenic state thought to be causally related to the development of disease.

References

Borkovec, T.D. & Inz, J. (1990). The nature of worry in generalized anxiety disorder: a predominance of thought activity. *Behavioral Research and Therapy*, **28**, 153–158.

Borkovec, T.D., Ray, W.J., & Stöber, J. (1998). Worry: a cognitive phenomenon intimately linked to affective, physiological, and interpersonal behavioral processes. *Cognitive Therapy Research*, **22**, 561–576.

Borkovec, T.D., Robinson, E., Pruzinsky, T., & DePree, J.A. (1983). Preliminary explora-tion of worry: some characteristics and processes. *Behaviour Research and Therapy*, **21**, 9–16.

Brosschot, J.F., Godaert, G.L.R., Benschop, R.J., Olff, M., Ballieux, R.E., & Heijnen, C.J. (1998). Experimental stress and immunological reactivity: a closer look at perceived uncontrollability. *Psychosomatic Medicine*, **60**, 359–361.

Brosschot, J.F. & Thayer, J.F. (1998). Anger inhibition, cardiovascular recovery, and vagal function: a model of the link between hostility and cardiovascular disease. *Annals of Behavioral Medicine*, **20**, 1–8.

Cioffi, D. & Holloway, J. (1993). Delayed costs of suppressed pain. *Journal of Personality and Social Psychology*, **64**, 274–282.

Dalgleish, T. & Power, M.J. (eds) (1999). *Handbook of cognition and emotion*. Chichester: Wiley.

Davey, G.C.L. (1994). Pathological worrying as exacerbated problem-solving. In G.C.L. Davey & F. Tallis, *Worrying. Perspectives on theory, assessment and treatment* (pp. 35–60). New York: Wiley.

Davey, G.C.L. & Tallis, F. (1994). *Worrying. Perspectives on theory, assessment and treatment*. New York: Wiley.

DeLongis, A., Coyne, J.C., Dakof, G., Folkman, S., & Lazarus, R.S. (1982). Relationship of daily hassles, uplifts, and major life events to health status. *Health Psychology*, **1**, 119–136.

Eriksen, H.R., Svendsrod, R., Ursin, G., & Ursin, H. (1998). Prevalence of subjective health complaints in the Nordic European countries in 1993. *European Journal of Public Health*, **8**, 294–298.

Everson, S.A., Goldberg, D.E., Kaplan, G.A., Cohen, R.D., Pukkala, E., Tuomilehto, J., & Salonen, J.T. (1996). Hopelessness and risk of mortality and incidence of myocardial infarction and cancer. *Psychosomatic Medicine*, **58**, 113–121.

Flor, H., Knost, B., & Birbaumer, N. (1997). Processing of pain- and body-related verbal material in chronic pain patients: central and peripheral correlates. *Pain*, **73**, 413–421.

Foa, E.B. & Kozak, M.J. (1986). Emotional processing of fear: exposure to corrective information. *Psychological Bulletin*, **99**, 20–35.

Folkman, S. (1984). Personal control and stress and coping processes: a theoretical analysis. *Journal of Personality and Social Psychology*, **46**, 839–852.

Foreman, R.D. (1999). Mechanisms of cardiac pain. *Annual Review of Physiology*, **61**, 143–167.

Frankenhäuser, M. (1980). Psychobiologic aspects of life stress. In S. Levine & H. Ursin (eds), *Coping and health. Nato Conference Series*, Series III, Vol. 12 (pp. 79–95). New York: Plenum Press.

Friedman, B.H. & Thayer, J.F. (1998). Anxiety and autonomic flexibility: a cardiovascular approach. *Biological Psychology*, **49**, 303–323.

Frijda, N.H. (1988). The laws of emotion. *American Psychologist*, **43**, 349–358.

Ganster, D.C., Schaubroeck, J., Sime, W.E., & Mayes, B.T. (1991). The nomological validity of the Type A personality among employed adults. *Journal of Applied Psychology*, **76**, 143–168.

Glynn, L., Christenfeld, N., & Gerin, W. (2002). The role of rumination in recovery from reactivity: the cardiovascular consequences of emotional states. *Psychosomatic Medicine*, **64**, 714–726.

Graham, N.H.M., Douglas, R.M., & Ryan, P. (1986). Stress and acute respiratory infection. *American Journal of Epidemiology*, **124**, 389–401.

Hellhammer, D.H., Heib, D., Hubert, W., & Rolf, L. (1985). Relationships between salivary cortisol release and behavioral coping under examination stress. *IRCS Medical Science: Psychology and Psychiatry*, **13**, 1179–1180.

Jorgensen, R.S., Johnson, B.T., Kolodziej, M.E., & Schreer, G.E. (1996). Elevated blood pressure and personality: a meta-analytic review. *Psychological Bulletin*, **120**, 293–320.

Kubzansky, L.D., Kawachi, I., Spiro, A., Weiss, S.T., Vokonas, P.S., & Sparrow, D. (1997). Is worrying bad for your heart? A prospective study of worry and coronary heart disease in the Normative Aging Study. *Circulation*, **95**, 818–824.

Lazarus, R.S. (1991). Progress on a cognitive–motivational–relational theory of emotion. *American Psychologist*, **46**, 819–834.

Lupke, U. & Ehlert, U. (1998). Attentional bias towards cues prejudicial to health in patients with somatoform disorders. *Zeitschrift für klinische Psychologie Forschung und Praxis*, **27**, 163–171.

Lyonfields, J.D., Borkovec, T.D., & Thayer, J.F. (1995). Vagal tone in generalized anxiety disorder and the effects of aversive imagery and worrisome thinking. *Behavioral Therapy*, **26**, 457–466.

Masterman, D.L. & Cummings, J.L. (1997). Frontal-subcortical circuits: the anatomical basis of executive, social and motivated behaviors. *Journal of Psychopharmacology*, **11**, 107–114.

Megargee, E.I. & Hokanson, J.E. (eds) (1970). *The dynamics of aggression: Individual, group and international analyses*. New York: Harper & Row.

Miller, T.Q., Smith, T.W., Turner, C.W., Guijaro, M.L., & Hallet, A.J. (1996). A meta-analytic review of research on hostility and physical health. *Psychological Bulletin*, **119**, 322–348.

Nolen-Hoeksema, S., McBride, A., & Larson, J. (1997). Rumination and psychological distress among bereaved partners. *Journal of Personality and Social Psychology*, **72**, 855–862.

Pearce, J. & Morley, S.J. (1989). An experimental investigation of the construct validity of the McGill Pain Questionnaire. *Pain*, **39**, 115–121.

Pennebaker, J.W. (1982). *The psychology of physical symptoms*. New York: Springer.

Pincus, T., Fraser, L., & Pearce, S. (1998). Do chronic pain patients "Stroop" on pain stimuli? *British Journal of Clinical Psychology*, **37**, 49–58.

Roger, D. & Najarian, B. (1998). The relationship between emotional rumination and cortisol secretion under stress. *Personality and Individual Differences*, **24**, 531–538.

Rowland, D.L., Heiman, J.R., Gladue, B.A., Hatch, J.P., Doering, C.H., & Weiler, S.J. (1987). Endocrine, psychological and genital response to sexual arousal in men. *Psychoneuroendocrinology*, **12**, 149–158.

Saul, J.P. (1990). Beat-to-beat variations of heart rate reflect modulation of cardiac autonomic outflow. *News in Physiological Science*, **5**, 32–37.

Schmidt, A.J.M., Wolfs-Takens, D.J., Oosterlaan, J., & van den Hout, M. (1994). Psychological mechanisms in hypochondriasis: attention-induced physical symptoms without sensory stimulation. *Psychotherapy and Psychosomatics*, **61**, 117–120.

Smyth, J., Ockenfels, M.C., Porter, L., Kirschbaum, C., Hellhammer, D.H., & Stone, A.A. (1998). Stressors and mood measured on a momentary basis are associated with salivary cortisol secretion. *Psychoneuroendocrinology*, **23**, 353–370.

Spangler, G. (1997). Psychological and physiological responses during an exam and their relation to personality characteristics. *Psychoneuroendocrinology*, **22**, 423–441.

Spyer, K.M. (1989). Neural mechanisms involved in cardiovascular control during affective behavior. *Trends in Neuroscience*, **12**, 506–513.

Steptoe, A. & Appels, A. (1989). *Stress, personal control and health*. Chichester: Wiley.

Suarez, E.C. & Williams, R.B. (1990). The relationships between dimensions of hostility and cardiovascular reactivity as a function of task characteristics. *Psychosomatic Medicine*, **52**, 558–570.

Tallis, F. & Eysenck, M.W. (1991). Worry: mechanisms and modulating influences. *Behavioural and Cognitive Psychotherapy*, **22**, 37–56.

Thayer, J.F., Friedman, B.H., & Borkovec T.D. (1996). Autonomic characteristics of generalized anxiety disorder and worry. *Biological Psychiatry*, **39**, 255–266.

Thayer, J.F. & Lane, R.D. (2002). Perseverative thinking and health: neurovisceral concomitants. *Psychology and Health*, **17**, 685–695.

Thayer, J.F., Smith, M., Rossy, L.A., Sollers, J.J., & Friedman, B.H. (1998). Heart period variability and depressive symptoms: gender differences. *Biological Psychiatry*, **44**, 304–306.

Ursin, H. & Hytten, K. (1992). Outcome expectancies and psychosomatic consequences. In B.N. Carpenter (ed.), *Personal coping: Theory, research, and application* (pp. 171–184). Westport, CT: Praeger/Greenwood.

Ursin, H. & Murison, R.C. (eds) (1983). *Biological and psychological basis of psychosomatic disease. Advances in the biosciences*, Vol. 42. Oxford: Pergamon Press.

Vitaliano, P.P., Russo, J., Paulsen, V.M., & Bailey, S.L. (1995). Cardiovascular recovery from laboratory stress – biopsychosocial concomitants in older adults. *Journal of Psychosomatic Research*, **39**, 361–377.

Wegner, D.M., Erber, R., & Zanakos, S. (1993). Ironic processes in the mental control of mood and mood-related thought. *Journal of Personality and Social Psychology*, **65**, 1093–1104.

Williams, M., Watts, F., MacLeod, C., & Mathews, A. (1988). *Cognitive psychology and emotional disorders*. New York: Wiley.

Wulsin, L.R., Vaillant, G.E., & Wells, V.E. (1999). A systematic review of the mortality of depression. *Psychosomatic Medicine*, **61**, 6–17.

Part II

Individual differences and assessment

Chapter 7

Different concepts or different words?

Concepts related to non-expression of negative emotions

Bert Garssen and Margot Remie

Introduction

People differ in their tendency to be open about, or to hide, negative emotions. This is an important topic in behavioral medicine, since emotional inhibition is considered a potential health risk factor for disorders as diverse as chronic pain (Beutler *et al.*, 1986), hypertension (Mann & James, 1998), and cancer (Jensen, 1987; Weihs *et al.*, 2000).

The findings in this research area are often presented as if all studies had addressed the same concept. However, the application of the same term does not necessarily imply using the same concept. For instance, the term "denial" has different meanings in the psychodynamic literature compared to behavioral medicine texts. In the former field, it refers to unconsciously denying a threat in general (Vaillant, 1971), while in the latter it is often restricted to, consciously or unconsciously, denying the seriousness of one's disease (Greer *et al.*, 1979, 1990). Neither is it clear to what extent the many different terms used in this area, such as non-expression of negative emotions, repression, suppression, emotional disclosure, concealment, denial, emotional control, emotional inhibition, rationality, anti-emotionality, defensiveness, Type C and Type D response style, alexithymia and emotional numbness, refer to different or similar concepts. Related to this conceptual confusion is the extent to which the various measurement instruments used in this field assess similar or different concepts.

"Non-expression of negative emotions" (NE) is the most general term for the tendency not to express negative feelings. NE refers to a tendency that the person may or may not be aware of (called suppression and repression, respectively, in psychodynamic theories). In behavioral medicine, the term "repression" is often used as a synonym for NE. This is different from its meaning in the psychodynamic literature, where repression specifically refers to an unconscious defence mechanism designed to keep specific memories or experiences, usually involving negative affect, unconscious. In behavioral medicine, consciousness is generally not included in the definition of repression as a distinctive characteristic. For instance, Weinberger stated that "the extent to which this defensive style is characterized by the use of repression relative to other defences such as suppression, denial and negation is not currently known" (Weinberger *et al.*, 1979, p. 370).

Since the uncertainty and confusion about the precise meaning of terms hamper the theoretical development of the area, the present chapter discusses the meanings of the various terms on a conceptual level. The focus is not on the description of the relationship between NE concepts and health and disease, nor does it address assessment issues, except if they are useful for the conceptual discussion. First, a description of NE is provided. Next, an attempt is made to delineate different conceptual dimensions within the area of NE, followed by a characterization of the Type C concepts, which partly overlap with NE but include more elements. Finally, concepts are described that have been related to NE in the literature, but which in our view in fact are clearly distinct from NE.

Non-expression of negative emotions (NE)

The term NE refers to the response style or tendency to inhibit – consciously or unconsciously – the expression of negative emotions, such as anxiety, anger, and depression, in order to avoid that a positive image of oneself and/or the world is threatened. In line with many behavioral medicine texts, we will use the term "repression" here as a synonym. NE includes both self-deception and other-deception (impression management) and also "personal defensiveness" (including emotional control, emotional inhibition, anti-emotionality and rationality), and "social defensiveness". These different aspects will be discussed below.

Some forms of non-expression are not included in this concept, such as those due to shyness, social phobia, and introversion. Shy or social phobic people fear social situations, which inhibits their emotional expression. Repressive people do not typically fear or avoid social situations and their reason for not showing negative emotions is not social fear. Another difference is that shyness, social phobia and introversion refer to non-expression of both negative and positive feelings, while NE refers to non-expression of negative feelings only.

The following interview fragment of a woman with breast cancer is presented as an example of what we mean by NE (I = interviewer; P = patient).

I: You said to have been really shocked when your doctor left you after having told what was wrong. Did you cry then, or were you trembling?

P: Yes, I cried, yes. Oh well, but then I went home quietly anyhow. And then we discussed it shortly in the evening, when my children arrived.

I: Were they also sad?

P: Then, uh . . . But, I am happy that it is over now, and we hope that all stays well. Don't we?

I: Were you frightened about anything concerning your illness?

P: No, uh? . . . No, I have not frightened myself about that ever.

I: Have you ever been angry?

P: No, almost never . . . Oh well, I mean, if you have a good life together, and with your children . . . and we have many friends. So, yes. Well, you hear, I am someone who works it out by myself. I do not give myself away easily. I have been several times in hospitals, but I do not whine about it.

I: Have you ever been sad?

P: . . . well, no. I cannot say so . . . Things go well lately. I did tell you, last time was when my brother-in-law died.

I: You have not been sad about yourself when you discovered having cancer?

P: Well, yes, the first few days. Then I often cried. But only when I was alone.

This fragment describes a woman who shows few emotions about the threatening condition of having breast cancer with its many dramatic effects for herself and her family. It is her general coping style to repress emotions, as she mentions being never angry and rarely sad. She is inclined to emphasize the good side of situations. It is not that she never experiences any emotions, as she remembers having cried briefly after having been informed about her diagnosis. She also remembers the grief about the death of her brother-in-law. This is probably a situation that is distressful but not threatening to her, in contrast to being diagnosed with cancer. It is also remarkable that she reports having experienced sadness about her own situation in the first few days, but only when being alone. She appears to repress her emotions especially in front of her family. One reason for this behavior could be that expressing emotions about a threatening situation, especially toward other people that one is dependent on, increases its threatening character.

On the basis of similar interview findings we would conclude that (1) NE does not preclude the possibility that one is (partly) aware of one's negative emotional feelings; (2) the concept of NE as a response style does not exclude the possibility that the tendency is also situation-dependent; (3) NE is in (a subgroup of) repressors especially prominent in social situations; and (4) a function of NE is to avert the threat of a stressful, often uncontrollable situation.

There are several reasons why people would express their emotions, and several reasons why they would not, and there is no reason to label NE as either positive or negative (cf. Kennedy-Moore & Watson, 1999). Repressive people will generally not bother other people with their problems and may facilitate social situations by their positive attitude. On the other hand, this coping style may impoverish intimate social interactions and may in the long run be negative for their own functioning, because of a lack of insight into their own psychological functioning, a reduced variety of their coping repertoire, and missing signals that would lead to timely seeking of medical help.

Conscious versus unconscious processes

As repressive styles are sometimes distinguished on the basis of a differentiation between conscious and unconscious process, it is important to devote special attention to this topic. The question of whether it is important to make such a distinction has been disputed mainly in psychodynamic theories. Some authors consider it as a self-evident and fundamental difference, and emphasize the distinction by using two different terms: suppression (conscious) and repression (unconscious). Other authors, however, have questioned the usefulness of the distinction. Erdelyi (1993) has argued that this distinction is not supported by empirical findings. For instance, it has never been demonstrated that the psychological or physical health consequences of a more conscious versus a more unconscious defense mechanism are different. Moreover, while many authors have referred to Freud when discussing the difference between repression and suppression this is historically unwarranted, according to Erdelyi, since Freud used these terms interchangeably. Most modern authors describe repression in terms of active cognitive processes, such as selective inattention and motivated forgetting, rather than as an unconscious defense mechanism (Baumeister & Cairns, 1992; Mendolia et al., 1996; Newton & Contrada, 1992).

People generally are not aware of most of their intentions and mental processes, if only for the fact that their capacity for conscious mental operations is limited. Only occasionally may repression account for the fact that a thought content becomes and remains unconscious, especially in the case of a serious traumatic event. Even then, the initial process that causes a person to forget emotionally upsetting material can be conscious and intentional. Consider the example of war victims. When war memories return in veterans years after having "forgotten" the terrifying experiences, they often remember having consciously decided at the end of war "to forget all about it". So, the distinction may be of some relevance with respect to repression of serious traumatic events, but the notion of (un)consciousness seems of limited value with respect to response styles in psychologically healthy people.

For the present discussion it will suffice to conclude that no sharp line can be drawn between conscious and unconscious processes. "Being not clearly aware" or "being not conscious (of one's habitual style)" may be used as descriptive qualifiers, but the distinction between conscious and unconscious processes – in our view – is such a gradual and diffuse one that it is unavailing to use it as a basis for a distinction in repressive response styles.

Self-deception and impression management

So far, NE has been discussed as though it were a unitary concept, while it can be better conceived as a domain. In this domain, one relevant distinction that has been made is between self-deception and other-deception or impression management (Paulhus, 1984; Sackheim & Gur, 1978).

Expression of negative emotions may be deliberately avoided as part of the tendency to make a favorable impression on other people. This tendency is called impression management or, originally, other-deception. It is distinguished from self-deception, in which case the person actually believes his or her positive self-reports (Paulhus, 1984; Sackheim & Gur, 1978). The two concepts can be empirically distinguished. In a study by Paulhus (1984), a secondary factor analysis of several "social desirability" scales yielded two dimensions: lie scales and similar other-deception measures loaded highly on one factor, which was labeled impression management. In addition, a self-deception questionnaire and a repression-sensitization questionnaire loaded both highly on a second factor, labeled self-deception.

Self-deception and other-deception can be considered as reflecting different aspects of NE. Relationships between these concepts and their predictive validity have been studied empirically. An older study showed that impression management is only modestly (and negatively) related to reports of negative emotions and somatic symptoms, while a self-deceptive response style reduces symptom reporting above and beyond the effects of deliberate impression management. Depending on the scale used, impression management explained 3–4 percent of the variance in somatic symptom reports, and 8–10 percent of the variance in psychological symptom reports. Self-deception added 4–6 percent and 8–16 percent explained variance for somatic and psychological symptom reports, respectively (Linden et al., 1986).

A more recent study found that repressors scored high on both other-deception and self-deception questionnaires (Derakshan & Eysenck, 1999). Repressors were defined according to Weinberger et al.'s (1979) classification as scoring low on anxiety and high on "defensiveness", as measured by the Marlowe–Crowne Social Desirability Scale (MC-SDS; Crowne & Marlowe, 1964). However, this study also showed that repressors are more self-deceivers than other-deceivers. This was demonstrated with the so called "bogus pipeline" method, in which the participants are connected via electrodes to a piece of apparatus resembling a lie detector that can allegedly detect whether they are telling the truth. Compared to a control condition, people are more willing to report truthfully about their emotional states in the bogus line condition, even if this report is seen as socially undesirable or embarrassing for the person. If the inhibitory style of repressors was mainly socially determined (determined by impression management), one would expect less expression of negative mood in the control condition, in which favorable reports cannot be checked, than in the bogus pipeline condition. However, repressors generally did not show any difference in anxiety scores between the two conditions. This finding suggests that repressors genuinely perceive themselves as being low in anxiety. On the other hand, self-report data indicated that they also showed some tendency to present themselves deliberately in a socially desirable way. In addition, some repressors did show an increase in anxiety in the experimental condition, suggesting that repressors are not a homogeneous group regarding their tendency to self-deception.

Tomaka et al. (1992) found different physiological patterns for self-deception and for "defensiveness" (measured by the MC-SDS; Crowne & Marlowe, 1964). Self-deception was associated with *decreased* physiological reactivity to a stressful task, while "defensiveness" was associated with *increased* physiological reactivity.

This difference in physiological responding may be the consequence of a basic difference between self-deception and other-deception.

In conclusion, both self-deception and impression management are aspects of NE. Subgroups of repressors may use these two aspects in varying degrees. In addition, some evidence exists that these two aspects may differ regarding their physiological concomitants. Some degree of self-deception, however, is always implied in NE, as NE is defined as emotional inhibition or control "to avoid that a positive image of oneself is threatened".

Social and personal defensiveness

Related to the above, when scrutinizing the descriptions of the different terms used in this field, one gets the impression that some explanations emphasize the social aspect much more than others. For instance, Weinberger and Schwartz (1990), who used the term "self-restraint", stated that it concerns "domains related to socialization and self-control and refers to repression of egoistic desires in the interest of long-term goals and relations with others". In addition, it is stated that self-restraint encompasses "tendencies to inhibit aggressive behavior, to exercise impulse control, to act responsibly, and to be considerate of others" (Weinberger & Schwartz, 1990, p. 382). We propose the term "social defensiveness" to label such tendencies, and define it as the socially related tendency not to express (to inhibit or to control) negative emotions. This tendency may be part of the broader inclination to behave in a socially acceptable way. This should not, however, be conceived as simply the need to follow external norms, but as reflecting a self-concept that depends on the approval of other people.

We suggest using the label "personal defensiveness" for a second category of non-expression of emotions, which is not primarily socially related. We define this category as the general tendency to control one's expression of negative emotions, and not allow oneself to be influenced by these negative feelings. Thus, in contrast to social defensiveness, social goals and motives are largely absent in personal defensiveness. This concept also includes emotional control, as used by Watson and Greer (1983), because their description did not specifically suggest social determination. Another example is rationality, as defined by Spielberger (1988): "The extent to which an individual uses reason and logic as a general approach to cope with the environment." This tendency may likewise occur when the person is alone or in company, i.e. it is not specifically a socially related tendency. Anti-emotionality is defined by Spielberger (1988) as the extent to which an individual uses reason and logic to avoid interpersonally related emotions. This definition gives no certainty where to place this concept. The "use of reason and logic" suggests a close association with rationality, while "interpersonally related emotions" suggests a shift in the direction of social defensiveness, though the definition does not seem to imply "a self-concept that depends on the approval of other people". It is concluded here that anti-emotionality is tentatively placed in the domain of personal defensiveness.

Empirical data are needed to prove the validity of this theoretical division into two types of NE. This would be substantiated if there appeared to be no close relationship between personal defensiveness scales ("emotional control", "emotional inhibition", "rationality" and "anti-emotionality"), and scales assessing social defensiveness ("defensiveness" and "self-restraint"). In addition, we would expect personal defensiveness to be mainly associated with self-deception, whereas social defensiveness should be related to both self-deception and other-deception. In an experimental situation where an honest report of feelings can be publicly checked, a socially defensive person is expected to report a higher level of distress than in more private situations, whereas a person scoring high on personal defensiveness should exhibit consistently low distress scores across situations.

Type C response style

Temoshok and Heller (1981) introduced the concept of Type C behavior, which was hypothesized to be related to the progression of cancer, in a study of psychosocial and epidemiological factors associated with malignant melanoma. Around the same time, British researchers independently had posed the question of whether there might be "a Type C for cancer" (Morris & Greer, 1980). Temoshok (1987, pp. 558–560) describes this coping style as:

> abrogating one's own needs in favor of those of others, suppressing negative emotions, and being cooperative, unassertive, appeasing, and accepting . . . The Type C individual is considered nice, friendly and helpful to others, and rarely gets into arguments or fights . . . The Type C individual may be seen as chronically hopeless and helpless, even though this is not consciously recognized in the sense that the person basically believes that it is useless to express one's needs. The Type C individual does not even try to express needs and feelings; these are hidden under a mask of normalcy and self sufficiency.

One may divide these various characteristics into three domains. The main domain is non-expression of negative emotions, also described as being emotionally contained or controlled. In addition, this is expressed in "maintaining a facade of contentment". A second domain concerns various behaviors directed at other people: being more concerned about the needs of other people than about one's own needs; being self-sacrificing, cooperative, sociable and appeasing; being compliant with external authorities and unassertiveness. The third domain concerns feeling helpless and hopeless in stressful conditions.

The description of the first domain corresponds well to our description of personal defensiveness. The second domain has some similarity to our social defensiveness concept, although being compliant with authorities and unassertiveness have not been included under this heading. The third domain is conceptually different from NE. Not all people who control their feelings and/or do not show them in social situations are inclined to respond in a helpless way to stressful situations. It can be concluded that the Type C coping style is a multidimensional construct, including NE (personal defensiveness and/or social defensiveness) as a core element, to which the dimensions of helplessness and the elements of being compliant with authorities and unassertiveness are added.

Empirical studies have to reveal whether the *combination* of various components into one multidimensional Type C coping style construct has additional value, compared to NE alone (Gross, 1989). This could be realized by demonstrating that the predictive power with respect to external outcome variables, for instance the level of experienced distress or somatic symptoms, or disease progression, is higher for the combination than for the separate components. The predictive power with respect to the development and progression of cancer has been studied for several of these elements separately: repression, depression and other negative emotional states, and helplessness (for an overview, see Garssen & Goodkin, 1999). However, the relative contribution of each of these elements has never been examined simultaneously in one study. Future investigations should address this issue.

One of the repressive types, as distinguished by Weinberger and Schwartz (1990), shows in our view a remarkable resemblance to the Type C coping pattern. Based on a dipartition of distress scores and a tripartition of restraint scores they formed six groups, among others an anxious defensive group (scoring high on both defensiveness and distress) and a repressive group (high on defensiveness, but low on anxiety). Compared to the other groups, the anxious defensive group scored low with respect to assertiveness, ability to express oneself in close relationships, sensitivity to one's own needs and feelings, self-esteem and self-control. They also scored high on avoidant personality (shyness) and dependency (emotional reliance on others and approval dependence). These characteristics resemble the ones described above for individuals employing Type C coping. The repressive group, on the other hand, was characterized by high scores for intimacy, self-esteem, self-control (tendency to use self-management techniques), defensiveness and alexithymia, while low on avoidant personality.

On the basis of the suggested similarity, one would predict that the Type C response pattern is associated with relatively high levels of (reported) distress. This is in line with the inclusion of helplessness and hopelessness in the description of the Type C coping pattern, and places a part of this construct at some conceptual distance from NE.

Concepts different from NE

In this section, we will briefly discuss concepts that seem clearly different from NE: the *acts* of emotional disclosure and suppression, "repressed memories", concealment, type D personality, denial, defense mechanisms, alexithymia, and emotional numbness.

Acts of disclosure and voluntary suppression of emotionally charged material

People can be asked to disclose personal thoughts about an emotional situation or to try not to think about them in an experimental context. Emotional disclosure and thought suppression with respect to a particular situation can also occur spontaneously in normal life. Such acts can be performed incidentally, by people high or low in NE. Therefore, the act should be distinguished from the *habitual response style*.

There is a research tradition studying experimentally the effects of inhibiting emotional behavior (Gross & Levenson, 1993; Mauss & Gross, this volume, Chapter 4) and another research tradition focusing on the effects of thought suppression (Abramowitz *et al.*, 2001). Participants in such studies are asked to refrain from emotional behavior, such as facial expressions, or not to think of a certain image, respectively.

The term "emotional suppression" is used by Gross in the sense of an act. He describes it as the conscious inhibition of behavioral signs of emotion, while emotionally aroused (Gross & Levenson, 1993). The effect of suppression on physiological systems was studied in subjects watching disgust-eliciting films. Instructing participants to suppress any signs of emotions led to decreased body movements and heart rate decelerations (probably due to the restricted movement), and to activation in other physiological systems. Expression of activating emotions, such as anger, is in most studies also associated with increased physiological arousal (see for an overview Gross & Levenson, 1993; Mauss & Gross, this volume, Chapter 4). Thus, experimentally manipulated suppression and expression of emotions may have similar physiological concomitants. It is important to note that the Gross and Levenson study (1993) concerns one form of acute suppression, namely behavioral inhibition; the suppression instruction did not affect the subjective report of the experience of disgust.

The consequences of the acts of emotional disclosure or emotional suppression are not necessarily similar to the psychological and somatic concomitants of being a habitual expressor or repressor, respectively. Long-term effects of emotional disclosure generally include a decrease in reported psychological and somatic symptoms (Smyth, 1998). On the other hand, habitual repressors also report less distress compared to non-repressors (Bleiker *et al.*, 1993; Linden *et al.*, 1986; Mann & James, 1998; Swan *et al.*, 1992; Tomaka *et al.*, 1992; Ward *et al.*, 1988; Weinberger, 1991; Weinberger & Schwartz, 1990). So, the act of *expression* and the response style of *non-expression* are both associated with low reported distress.

On the physiological level, however, there is a similarity between the elevated physiological arousal related to the act of suppression (Gross & Levenson, 1993) and habitual repression (Furnham & Trayner, 1999).

Repressed memories

Repression of memories of traumatic events ("repressed memories"), as described in psychiatric texts, concerns a complex of cognitions and emotions that is mainly limited to a certain theme or event, such as sexual abuse in childhood. This is different from NE, which concerns the tendency not to express negative emotions in general. Repression of memories is initiated by traumatic events, while NE is a habitual style applied in a variety of situations. Repressing the memories of traumatic events could lead to a habitual style of NE, or magnify an existing tendency to NE, but that does not undo the conceptual difference.

The influence of a traumatic event – in the form of being diagnosed with cancer – on habitual NE has been demonstrated by Kreitler *et al.* (1993). They found an increase in number of repressors after notification of a breast cancer diagnosis, which was not found in women who appeared to have no cancer after diagnostic tests.

Self-concealment

Larson and Chastain (1990) have introduced the concept self-concealment as the trait version of the inhibition act, studied by Pennebaker (1989). The authors define self-concealment as "a predisposition to actively conceal from others personal information that one perceives as distressing or negative". In addition, it is said that "Self-concealed personal information is consciously accessible to the individual" (Larson & Chastain, 1990, p. 440).

It is not quite clear whether this concept should be placed within or outside the domain of NE. If included, it is by its voluntary concealment toward other people close to other-deception and social defensiveness. There are some gradual differences with NE:

1   Self-concealment concerns specific, distressing secrets, while NE focuses on negative feelings in general, though it should be admitted that the line between these two elements is rather thin.
2   Self-concealment is explicitly a tendency toward voluntary and conscious inhibition, while NE was conceptualized as incorporating both unconscious and conscious coping strategies. It has also been concluded that NE always includes some degree of self-deception; thus not exclusively the voluntary and conscious form of other-deception.
3   Self-concealment implies the awareness of distressing thought contents, while NE implies that such thought contents are inhibited to become fully aware of.

Empirical findings have supported the supposed conceptual difference. While NE is often negatively related to distress reporting, a positive association has been found between self-concealment and depression, anxiety and physical symptoms (Larson & Chastain, 1990). In addition, a negative relationship has been reported with repression measures (King *et al.*, 1992; Ritz & Dahme, 1996).

Type D personality

The term "Type D personality" was introduced by Denollet (1997) to describe those people who are distressed, but who also inhibit the expression of emotions. Working in the field of cardiovascular disorders, Denollet developed this concept as a combination of two factors that appeared to be predictive for the development of coronary heart disease and hypertension, namely, high distress level (anger, depression, anxiety and vital exhaustion) and social inhibition (of emotional expression). The second factor reflects social inhibition and introversion. In his own research, the two factors in isolation appeared to have no effect on disease progression; it was the interaction that had an adverse effect on prognosis (Denollet, 1997).

It is important to be aware of the fact that Type D individuals consciously suppress their behavior in order to avoid disapproval by others. A critical difference between Type D and Type C is that the negative emotions of anger, anxiety, and depression are experienced consciously but not expressed by the Type D individual, while these emotions are usually unrecognized by the Type C person and repressors. A possible difference is their relationship to repression. While it is not certain whether the Type C response style is closer to the repressive coping style or to the anxious defensive coping style, as we have suggested, the Type D personality style is explicitly of the anxious defensive type.

Denial

Denial is conceived here as denying or minimizing the seriousness of a medical condition, not as denial of negative affect (which would come close to defensiveness; Ketterer et al., 1998). Defined this way, there is a clear difference between denial and NE. The latter concept does not specifically refer to the emotional consequences of a disease, but to negative emotions in general. One might repress emotions, while not denying the seriousness of the disease. In the same line, Greer et al. (1979, p. 786) described denial in breast cancer as: "Apparent active rejection of any evidence about their diagnosis which might have been offered, including the evidence of breast removal, such as 'it wasn't serious, they just took off my breast as a precaution'". Minimizing the impact of the disease either can be an act (an event-driven coping response) or can reflect a habitual style of minimizing the seriousness of unpleasant events.

It is interesting that the consequences of the two phenomena seem opposite in cancer. In studies using a prospective, longitudinal design to investigate the role of psychological factors on the course of cancer, two studies found that NE predicted an unfavorable course (Jensen, 1987; Weihs et al., 2000). On the other hand, in two other studies denial was found to have a favorable influence on the course of cancer (Dean & Surtees, 1989; Greer et al., 1979; 1990).

Defense mechanisms

Defense mechanisms form an important concept in psychodynamic theories. The concept refers to the various ways a person can mentally react to a real or imagined threat, so as to protect him or her from excessive anxiety (Vaillant, 1971). Defense mechanisms include, among other concepts, denial, repression and suppression. As mentioned previously, these terms are used in psychodynamic theories with different meanings than in behavioral medicine. Most of these differences are mentioned above; they are summarized in Table 7.1.

It is difficult, if not impossible, to establish to what extent "defense mechanisms" and "NE" are similar, show some overlap, or are clearly different, due to their origin from completely different backgrounds and frameworks. It is as if the two concepts are described in different languages that are based on different grammars and ways of thinking, which preclude proper translations. Though a complete comparison is impossible, some differences can be indicated.

1 Defense mechanisms are defined as mental strategies that serve the purpose of warding off emotional states by distorting aspects of reality. The mental operation described under the heading NE has most often to do with avoiding threatening information, rather than distorting information.
2 Defense mechanisms refer to processes preventing unconscious impulses from becoming conscious. NE does not imply a sharp distinction between conscious and unconscious thought contents.

Table 7.1 Concepts of non-expression used in both psychodynamic theories and behavioral medicine

	In psychodynamic theories	In behavioral medicine
Denial	An unconscious process leading to negation of a threat	(Often used as:) Denying one's disease or its seriousness; no reference to being conscious or unconscious
Repression	An unconscious process preventing threatening material from becoming conscious	(Often used as:) The tendency not to express negative emotions (NE). This tendency may be based on various (conscious or unconscious) processes
Suppression	Consciously pushing threatening information out of awareness	Sometimes used synonymously to NE, to indicate a response style, but emphasizing that one is or can be aware of one's way of responding. At other times used to indicate the conscious inhibition of the behavioral signs of emotion as an act

3   Defense mechanisms include a variety of intrapsychic processes, whereas NE
     is rarely divided into "subconcepts".
4   In the description of defense mechanisms, a distinction is made between
     "immature" and "mature" defenses. Repressive coping styles are not placed
     into a hierarchy.

Alexithymia

The concept of alexithymia is derived from clinical observations of a cluster of
specific cognitive characteristics among patients suffering from psychosomatic
diseases, substance use disorders, and post-traumatic stress disorders (Bagby
et al., 1997; Nemiah *et al.*, 1976; Taylor, this volume, Chapter 8). It evolved into
a theoretical construct, with the following salient features: (1) difficulty identifying
feelings, (2) difficulty describing feelings, and (3) externally-oriented thinking
(Bagby *et al.*, 1997).

Because of the difficulty in identifying feelings, one might assume that emotions
are not expressed either. However, alexithymic persons should not be considered
as being emotionally flat. Nemiah *et al.* (1976) reported a proneness to sudden
outbursts of crying and anger in these persons, although they were unable to connect
these behaviors with their thoughts and fantasies. Sifneos (1967) reported that these
patients commonly mentioned anxiety or complained of depression. However, they
displayed a limited vocabulary for describing their emotions. The emotions
of alexithymic individuals appear to be rather diffuse, poorly differentiated and not
well represented. Taylor *et al.* (1997) concluded that alexithymia should be regarded
not as a defense against distressing affects or fantasies, but rather as reflecting
an individual difference in the ability to process and regulate emotions cognitively.
They therefore suggested that this construct is different from "other emotion-related
constructs such as inhibition and the repressive–defensive coping style".

The difference between alexithymia and NE is empirically supported. First,
several studies have shown that the Toronto Alexithymia Scale (TAS) – the
most frequently used and well-validated questionnaire for assessing alexithymic
traits – is unrelated or negatively related to various measures of NE, including
social defensiveness, measured by the Weinberger Adjustment Inventory (WAI;
Weinberger, 1991) and the Marlowe-Crowne Social Desirability Scale (Crowne
& Marlowe, 1964; Taylor *et al.*, 1997; Weinberger & Schwartz, 1990), repression,
defined by high defensiveness scores and low anxiety scores (Myers, 1995;
Newton & Contrada, 1994; Taylor *et al.*, 1997), and self-deception and other-
deception (Linden *et al.*, 1996). Second, the discrepancy between subjective and
physiological responses that is characteristic for repressors (heart rate responses
greater than self-reported negative affect) was found in persons scoring *low* on
alexithymia. High alexithymics exhibited a response pattern characteristic of high-
anxious persons (self-reported negative affect greater than heart rate responses;
Newton & Contrada, 1994). High alexithymic persons seem physiologically hypo-
aroused, as indexed by reduced heart rate responses to challenging laboratory

conditions (Linden *et al.*, 1996; Newton & Contrada, 1994). Third, the TAS is unrelated (Linden *et al.*, 1996) or *positively* related to self-reported distress (Taylor *et al.*, 1997), whereas measures of NE are generally *negatively* related to distress (Bleiker *et al.*, 1993; Linden *et al.*, 1986; Mann & James, 1998; Swan *et al.*, 1992; Tomaka *et al.*, 1992; Ward *et al.*, 1988; Weinberger, 1991; Weinberger & Schwartz, 1990).

Thus, based on psychometric and psychophysiological comparisons, alexithymia shows some correspondence with the sensitizing style of high-anxious persons, rather than the avoidant style of repressors. While repressive individuals often report that they are not upset despite objective evidence to the contrary, alexithymic individuals acknowledge that they are upset, but have difficulty in specifying the nature of their distress.

Emotional numbness

The term "emotional numbness" (e.g. Glover, 1992; Litz, 1992) is applied to describe the phenomenon whereby people, having been exposed to a traumatic situation, experience difficulties with experiencing and expressing emotions. It is considered a characteristic of post-traumatic stress disorder and one of its diagnostic criteria is limited affect. Some authors emphasize the connection between emotional numbness and secondary alexithymia, which also has been conceptualized as a disturbance in affective functioning after traumatic experiences (see also Chapter 5).

Summary and discussion

The aim of this chapter was to elucidate, on a conceptual level, the relationships between various constructs related to NE. Self-deception and other-deception are aspects of NE distinguished in the literature. NE may imply a certain degree of impression management or other-deception, but the core of the response style is self-deception: repressors (generally) believe their self-reports. We have also suggested differentiating NE into personal and social defensiveness. The main distinction between personal and social defensiveness is the degree to which the response style is socially related. In personal defensiveness, the tendency to repress negative feelings reflects an intrapsychic need independent of the social context, whereas in social defensiveness the repressive style may reflect the tendency to behave in a socially accepted way and the need for a self-image that largely depends on other people's approval.

The core of *Type C response pattern* is NE, but this multidimensional construct also includes the socially related elements of being more concerned about the needs of other people than one's own needs and being self-sacrificing, cooperative, appeasing, compliant with external authorities, and unassertive. In addition, it includes feeling helpless and hopeless in stressful conditions.

Several concepts have been described as being basically different from NE. The difference may have been sharpened in this chapter, which, it is hoped, will result in more conceptual clarity. First, the acts of emotional disclosure and voluntary suppression have been distinguished from the habitual styles of "expressors" and "repressors", respectively. This distinction not only reflects obvious conceptual differences, but implies a warning against assuming too easily that the psychophysiological concomitants of these acts are similar to the psychophysiological consequences of the corresponding response styles. *Repression of traumatic events* is a concept developed in psychiatry, which refers to repression of feelings and thoughts about a specific event, or series of corresponding events, such as sexual abuse or war situations, leading to psychopathological symptoms. It differs from NE in being also more an act (or series of acts) and in being restricted to certain events.

The *Type D personality and self-concealment* concern the voluntary and conscious tendencies to inhibit the expression of negative emotions and distressing secrets, respectively. They are both associated with high levels of reported distress, in contrast to repression. *Denial* is often used in behavioral medicine in the sense of minimizing the seriousness of the disease, which is clearly different from NE. A person can repress negative emotions while not denying the seriousness of the disease. *Defense mechanisms* refer to a "mini theory" originating from a psychodynamic framework, including (mostly unconscious) processes directed at warding off threatening material and usually preventing it from becoming conscious. It was concluded that the theoretical backgrounds of defense mechanisms and NE are so different that a conceptual comparison is very complicated. *Alexithymia* is not a style of defence against distressing affects, but reflects a dysfunction in processing and regulating emotions cognitively, which is reflected in a limited vocabulary for describing these emotions.

The various concepts discussed in the present chapter are depicted in Figure 7.1, in which they are divided according to the scientific domain they originate from, i.e. *psychiatry (including psychodynamic theories)* and *psychology (including behavioral medicine)*. A second division is into *acts* and *traits (response styles)*. One may also make a division into concepts referring to purely voluntary and conscious forms of inhibition (emotional disclosure, voluntary suppression, Type D personality and self-concealment) and the other concepts, which imply unconscious or mixed forms of emotional inhibition.

Kennedy-Moore and Watson (1999) describe an extensive model of the processes leading from covert emotional experience to overt emotional expression, through a series of cognitive–evaluative steps. The description also involves the disruptions that can occur at different points in these processes, resulting in different forms of non-expression. We will shortly describe their model to compare their description and terminology with those used in the present chapter.

The first step in their model concerns the perception of a threatening condition, the automatic preconscious processing of emotional information and the accompanying physiological changes. One form of non-expression occurs when the person shows no or minimal primary affective reactions (to both positive and

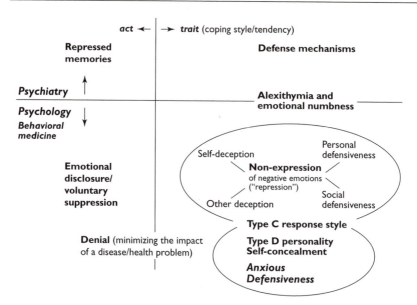

Figure 7.1 Overview of the various concepts, divided into concepts developed in psychiatry or psychology (especially behavioral medicine), respectively; and those describing acts or traits (response styles/tendencies), respectively.

negative events). This form is not included in our framework of NE, since it is automatic and primary (not motivated) and since it refers to both positive and negative emotions. If it describes a trait, in order to differentiate this form from NE, we would prefer another term such as "low affect intensity" or "basal unresponsiveness".

The second step in Kennedy-Moore and Watson's (1999) model refers to the conscious perception of one's affective responses. One might block one's emotional reactions at this step, which is called "motivated lack of awareness". This type of emotional control or inhibition could be part of a general disposition to avoid acknowledging unpleasant emotional experiences. The authors consider the repressive coping style described by Weinberger (1991) as an example of such a disposition. We are more inclined to see the personal defensive style, described above, as more appropriate, because the emotional inhibition at this step is not described as specifically socially motivated.

The third step involves labeling and interpreting the affective response. One may lack the skill to label or interpret one's emotional experiences, which is the core of alexithymia.

The fourth step includes the evaluation of the response in terms of one's beliefs and goals. The evaluation of one's response as unacceptable leads to another form of NE, which in our view is comparable to social defensiveness. This evaluation might stem from a global negative attitude toward emotions, or from more specific beliefs, such as "it is dangerous to express anger".

The perceived lack of opportunity to express emotions is the fifth and last step in the process. The impediment to expression might be situation-specific or more global, for instance when lacking close relationships. We have not included this form of non-expression, since its emphasis is on situational determinants, rather than reflecting an individual's style.

To summarize, Kennedy-Moore and Watson (1991) presented a useful model for describing different forms of (non-)expression. Their theoretical model has the advantage of being comprehensive and showing clearly the diversity of the various forms of non-expression with respect to their underlying processes and consequences. However, it will be extremely difficult to test empirically the link between the various forms of non-expression and the cognitive–evaluative steps of the model. We have been more reserved in presenting theoretical schemes, while preferring the restriction to testable hypotheses regarding the relationships between the various constructs.

It is hoped that the conceptual discussion in this chapter contributes to more clarity in this complex scientific domain. What we further need is a discussion of the various measuring methods developed in this field, analyzing their relationship with the concepts discussed in this chapter. This not only will advance the conceptual thinking regarding NE, but also will aid the construction of specific testable hypotheses regarding potential associations of the various NE constructs with health outcomes.

References

Abramowitz, J.S., Tolin, D.F., & Street, G.P. (2001). Paradoxical effects of thought suppression: a meta-analysis of controlled studies. *Clinical Psychology Review*, **21**, 683–703.

Bagby, R.M., Taylor, G.J., & Parker, J.D.A. (1997). The nomological domain of the alexithymia construct. In A.J.J.M. Vingerhoets, F.J. van Bussel & A.J.W. Boelhouwer (eds), *The (non)expression of emotions in health and disease* (pp. 95–113). Tilburg, The Netherlands: Tilburg University Press.

Baumeister, R.F. & Cairns, K.J. (1992). Repression and self-presentation: when audiences interfere with self-deceptive strategies. *Journal of Personality and Social Psychology*, **62**, 851–862.

Beutler, L.E., Engle, D., Oro'-Beutler, M.E., Daldrup, R., & Meredith, K. (1986). Inability to express intense affect: a common link between depression and pain? *Journal of Consulting and Clinical Psychology*, **54**, 752–759.

Bleiker, E.M.A., Ploeg, H.M. van der, Hendriks, J.H.C.L., Leer, J.-W.H., & Kleijn, W.C. (1993). Rationality, emotional expression and control: psychometric characteristics of a questionnaire for research in psycho-oncology. *Journal of Psychosomatic Research*, **37**, 861–872.

Crowne, D.P. & Marlowe, D. (1964). *The approval motive*. New York: Wiley.

Dean, C. & Surtees, P.G. (1989). Do psychological factors predict survival in breast cancer? *Journal of Psychosomatic Research*, **33**, 561–569.

Denollet, J. (1997). Non-expression of emotions as a personality feature in cardiac patients. In A.J.J.M. Vingerhoets, F.J. van Bussel, & A.J.W. Boelhouwer (eds), *The (non)expression of emotions in health and disease* (pp. 181–192). Tilburg, The Netherlands: Tilburg University Press.

Derakshan, N. & Eysenck, M.W. (1999). Are repressors self-deceivers or other-deceivers? *Cognition & Emotion*, **13**, 1–17.

Erdelyi, M.H. (1993). Repression: the mechanism and the defence. In: D.M. Wegner & J.W. Pennebaker (eds), *Handbook of mental control* (pp. 126–148). Englewood Cliffs, NJ: Prentice Hall.

Furnham, A. & Trayner, J. (1999). Repression and effective coping styles. *European Journal of Personality*, **13**, 465–492.

Garssen, B. & Goodkin, K. (1999). On the role of immunological factors as mediators between psychological factors and cancer progression. *Psychiatry Research*, **85**, 51–61.

Glover, H. (1992). Emotional numbing: a possible endorphin-mediated phenomenon associated with post-traumatic stress disorders and other allied psychopathologic states. *Journal of Traumatic Stress*, **5**, 643–675.

Greer, S., Morris, T., & Pettingale, K.W. (1979). Psychological response to breast cancer: effect on outcome. *Lancet*, 13 Oct., 785–787.

Greer, S., Morris, T., Pettingale, K.W., & Haybittle, J.L. (1990). Psychological response to breast cancer and 15-year outcome. *Lancet*, **335**, 49–50.

Gross, J. (1989). Emotional expression in cancer onset and progression. *Social Science & Medicine*, **28**, 1239–1248.

Gross, J.J. & Levenson, R.W. (1993). Emotional suppression: physiology, self-report, and expressive behavior. *Journal of Personality and Social Psychology*, **64**, 970–986.

Jensen, M.R. (1987). Psychobiological factors predicting the course of breast cancer. *Journal of Personality*, **55**, 317–342.

Kennedy-Moore, E. & Watson, J.C. (1999). *Expressing emotion*. New York: Guilford Press.

Ketterer, M.W., Huffman, J., Lumley, M.A., Wassef, S., Gray, L., Kenyon, L., Kraft, P., Brymer, J., Rhoads, K., Lovallo, W.R., & Goldberg, A.D. (1998). Five-year follow-up for adverse outcomes in males with at least minimally positive angiograms: importance of "denial" in assessing psychosocial risk factors. *Journal of Psychosomatic Research*, **44**, 241–250.

King, L.A., Emmons, R.A., & Woodley, S. (1992). The structure of inhibition. *Journal of Research in Personality*, **26**, 85–102.

Kreitler, S., Chaitchik, S., & Kreitler, H. (1993). Repressiveness: cause or result of cancer? *Psycho-Oncology*, **2**, 43–54.

Larson, D.G. & Chastain, R.L. (1990). Self-concealment: conceptualization, measurement, and health implications. *Journal of Social and Clinical Psychology*, **9**, 439–455.

Linden, W., Lenz, J.W., & Stossel, C. (1996). Alexithymia, defensiveness and cardiovascular reactivity to stress. *Journal of Psychosomatic Research*, **41**, 575–583.

Linden, W., Paulhus, D.L., & Dobson, K.S. (1986). Effects of response styles on the report of psychological and somatic distress. *Journal of Consulting and Clinical Psychology*, **54**, 309–313.

Litz, B.T. (1992). Emotional numbing in combat related post-traumatic stress disorder: a critical review and reformulation. *Clinical Psychology Review*, **12**, 417–432.

Mann, S.J. & James, G.D. (1998). Defensiveness and essential hypertension. *Journal of Psychosomatic Research*, **45**, 139–148.

Mendolia, M., Moore, J., & Tesser, A. (1996). Dispositional and situational determinants of repression. *Journal of Personality and Social Psychology*, **70**, 856–867.

Morris, T. & Greer, S. (1980). A "Type C" for cancer? Low trait anxiety in the pathogenesis of breast cancer [abstract]. *Cancer Detection and Prevention*, **3**, 102.

Myers, L.B. (1995). Alexithymia and repression: the role of defensiveness and trait anxiety. *Personality and Individual Differences*, **19**, 489–492.

Nemiah, J.C., Freyberger, H., & Sifneos, P.E. (1976). Alexithymia: a view of the psychosomatic process. In O.W. Hill (ed.). *Modern trends in psychosomatic medicine* (pp. 430–439). London: Butterworths.

Newton, T.L. & Contrada, R. (1992). Repressive coping and verbal–autonomic response dissociation: the influence of social context. *Journal of Personality and Social Psychology*, **62**, 159–167.

Newton, T.L. & Contrada, R.J. (1994). Alexithymia and repression: contrasting emotion-focused coping styles. *Psychosomatic Medicine*, **56**, 457–462.

Paulhus, D.L. (1984). Two-component models of socially desirable responding. *Journal of Personality and Social Psychology*, **46**, 598–609.

Pennebaker, J.W. (1989). Confession, inhibition and disease. In L. Berkowitz (ed.), *Advances in experimental social psychology* (pp. 211–244). San Diego, CA: Academic Press.

Ritz, T. & Dahme, B. (1996). Repression, self-concealment and rationality/emotional defensiveness: the correspondence between three questionnaire measures of defensive coping. *Personality and Individual Differences*, **20**, 95–102.

Sackheim, H.A. & Gur, R.C. (1978). Self-deception, self-confrontation, and consciousness. In G.E. Schwartz & D. Shapiro (eds), *Consciousness and self-regulation: Advances in research* (pp. 139–197). New York: Plenum Press.

Sifneos, P.E. (1967). Clinical observations on some patients suffering from a variety of psychosomatic diseases. *Acta Medicina Psychosomatica*, **7**, 1–10.

Smyth, J.M. (1998). Written emotional expression: effect sizes, outcome types and moderating variables. *Journal of Consulting and Clinical Psychology*, **66**, 174–184.

Spielberger, C.D. (1988). *The Rationality/Emotional Defensiveness (R/ED) scale: Preliminary test manual*. Tampa, FL: University of South Florida.

Swan, G.E., Carmelli, D., Dame, A., Rosenman, R.H., & Spielberger, C.D. (1992). The Rationality/Emotional Defensiveness Scale – II. Convergent and discriminant correlational analysis in males and females with and without cancer. *Journal of Psychosomatic Research*, **36**, 349–359.

Taylor, G.J., Parker, J.D.A., & Bagby, R.M. (1997). Relationships between alexithymia and related constructs. In A.J.J.M. Vingerhoets, F.J. van Bussel, & A.J.W. Boelhouwer (eds), *The (non)expression of emotions in health and disease* (pp. 103–113). Tilburg, The Netherlands: Tilburg University Press.

Temoshok, L. (1987). Personality, coping style, emotion and cancer: towards an integrative model. *Cancer Surveys*, **6**, 545–567.

Temoshok, L. & Heller, B.W. (1981). Stress and "Type C" versus epidemiological risk factors in melanoma. *Proceedings of the 89th Annual Convention of the American Psychological Association* (Los Angeles, August 1981). Washington, DC: American Psychological Association.

Tomaka, J., Blascovich, J., & Kelsey, R.M. (1992). Effects of self-deception, social desirability, and repressive coping on psychophysiological reactivity to stress. *Personality and Social Psychology Bulletin*, **18**, 616–624.

Vaillant, G.E. (1971). Theoretical hierarchy of adaptive ego mechanisms: a 30-year follow-up study of 30 men selected for psychological health. *Archives of General Psychiatry*, **24**, 107–118.

Ward, S.E., Leventhal, H., & Love, R. (1988). Repression revisited: tactics used in coping with a severe health threat. *Personality and Social Psychology Bulletin*, **14**, 735–746.

Watson, M. & Greer, S. (1983). Development of a questionnaire measure of emotional control. *Journal of Psychosomatic Research*, **27**, 299–305.

Weihs, K.L., Enright, T.M., Simmens, S.J., & Reiss, D. (2000). Negative affectivity, restriction of emotions, and site of metastases predict mortality in recurrent breast cancer. *Journal of Psychosomatic Research*, **49**, 59–68.

Weinberger, D.A. (1991). *Social–emotional adjustment in older children and adults: 1. Psychometric properties of the Weinberger Adjustment Inventory*. Cleveland, OH: unpublished manuscript.

Weinberger, D.A. & Schwartz, G.E. (1990). Distress and restraint as superordinate dimensions of self-reported adjustment: a typological perspective. *Journal of Personality*, **58**, 381–417.

Weinberger, D.A., Schwartz, G.E., & Davidson, R.J. (1979). Low-anxious, high-anxious, and repressive coping styles: psychometric patterns and behavioral and physiological responses to stress. *Journal of Abnormal Psychology*, **88**, 369–380.

Chapter 8

Alexithymia: 25 years of theory and research

Graeme J. Taylor

Introduction

Among the various emotion-related constructs that have been associated with health and disease, alexithymia has the longest history. Formulated by Nemiah *et al.* (1976) in the mid-1970s, the alexithymia construct evolved from clinical observations and theoretical ideas described by Ruesch (1948) and MacLean (1949) more than a half century ago. At that time, and for at least the subsequent two decades, the prevailing psychosomatic theories of disease emphasized the role of intrapsychic conflicts in generating protracted states of emotional arousal that were considered pathogenic to the body. Ruesch and MacLean proposed an alternative theory that unmodulated states of emotional arousal that might adversely affect bodily processes are a consequence of deficits in the capacity to represent emotions within the symbolic system provided by language. In their view, such deficits are evidenced by difficulties in identifying and verbally describing subjective feelings.

Two decades later, Sifneos (1967) and Nemiah and Sifneos (1970) observed that many patients suffering from classic psychosomatic diseases manifest not only a marked difficulty in identifying and describing feelings but also an impoverished fantasy life and a thought content characterized by a preoccupation with the details of objects and events in the external environment. While Sifneos (1973) coined the term "alexithymia" to refer to the former characteristics, the latter characteristics resembled the *pensée opératoire* already described by the French psychosomaticists Marty and de M'Uzan (1963). The entire cluster of characteristics became the salient features of alexithymia in Nemiah *et al.*'s (1976) subsequent definition of the construct. Alexithymia, however, was not considered specific to patients with classic psychosomatic diseases. Similar characteristics were described independently by Bruch (1973) in patients with eating disorders, and by Krystal (1968; Krystal & Raskin, 1970) in many drug addicts and patients with post-traumatic stress disorders (PTSD). Nemiah (1984) later suggested that alexithymia might be associated also with panic disorder.

Although I first heard about alexithymia in the early 1970s, I became better acquainted with the construct in 1976 when I participated in the 11th European

Conference on Psychosomatic Research. Held in the enchanting city of Heidelberg, this conference was devoted almost entirely to theory and research on alexithymia and is considered a landmark event in the history of the field. Prior to this conference, there was only a handful of published papers on alexithymia and very few clinicians and researchers were familiar with the concept. Following the Heidelberg conference, however, interest in alexithymia increased considerably and a large amount of empirical research has now been generated. While about 50 articles were published on alexithymia by the late-1970s, a recent search of the PsycInfo database revealed well over 1000 journal articles on alexithymia.

In this chapter I review the major developments that have occurred in the field of alexithymia theory and research over the past 25 years.

Measurement and validation of the alexithymia construct

Although there was general agreement about the definition of the alexithymia construct at the Heidelberg conference, it was concluded that validational studies, and also reliable and valid methods for measuring the construct, were lacking. It took another 15 years, however, before these deficiencies were overcome. Initially researchers relied on projective techniques or an unvalidated observer-rater questionnaire developed by Sifneos (1973) to assess alexithymic characteristics. Later several self-report measures of alexithymia were introduced, including the MMPI Alexithymia Scale, the Schalling–Sifneos Personality Scale, and the Revised Schalling–Sifneos Personality Scale; these were rather hastily constructed measures that were shown subsequently to lack reliability and/or validity (Taylor *et al.*, 1997).

Recognizing that the development of a reliable and valid measure of a construct is a widely used method of construct validation in personality research, my colleagues and I began a program of research in the mid-1980s aimed at evaluating the validity of the alexithymia construct through the development of a self-report scale for measuring it. The first scale we developed was the 26-item Toronto Alexithymia Scale (TAS), which demonstrated internal consistency and a four-factor structure that corresponded to the salient features of the construct, namely difficulty identifying feelings, difficulty describing feelings, reduced daydreaming, and externally oriented thinking (Taylor *et al.*, 1985). Although the psychometric properties of the TAS were satisfactory and provided considerable support for the validity of the alexithymia construct, in the course of further evaluating the scale we found some limitations that led us to create a larger pool of items from which we developed a revised and improved 20-item version – the Twenty-Item Toronto Alexithymia Scale (TAS-20; Bagby *et al.*, 1994a). Because of limitations of space, I will review the psychometric properties of the TAS-20 only; however, the two versions of the scale are highly correlated.

The Twenty-Item Toronto Alexithymia Scale

The TAS-20 has adequate internal consistency and test–retest reliability and a three-factor structure that is congruent with the theoretical construct of alexithymia – (F1) difficulty identifying feelings; (F2) difficulty describing feelings to others; and (F3) externally oriented thinking (Bagby *et al.*, 1994a). The reduced day-dreaming factor of the TAS is no longer present since all items assessing fantasy and other imaginal activity were eliminated during the process of scale revision because they failed to meet pre-established statistical criteria. Some researchers may mistakenly conclude that without this factor the TAS-20 does not measure alexithymia as it was originally conceptualized; however, the externally oriented thinking factor correlates negatively with a measure of fantasy and imaginal activity and thus appears to assess the reduced fantasy facet of the construct indirectly (Bagby *et al.*, 1994b). This is consistent with Nemiah's (1984) observation that the absence of the capacity to produce fantasies restricts thought content to a preoccupation with external objects, people, and environmental events.

The three-factor structure of the TAS-20 has been replicated by the use of confirmatory factor analysis in English-speaking clinical and nonclinical populations, and also with translated versions of the scale in culturally diverse populations, including Finnish, German, Indian, Italian, Korean, Lithuanian, Portuguese, Spanish, and Swedish. Because the first two factors of the TAS-20 correlate highly, some researchers have questioned the validity of the three-factor structure of the scale. Analyzing data obtained from several different samples, however, we demonstrated that a three-factor model provides a better fit than either a one- or a two-factor model (Taylor *et al.*, 2000).

Convergent validity of the TAS-20 and also of its three factor scales has been demonstrated by significant negative correlations with four closely related constructs, viz., psychological mindedness, need-for-cognition, affective orientation, and emotional intelligence. Moreover, contrary to arguments that alexithymia cannot be assessed adequately by self-report measures, scores on the TAS-20 and its factors show moderate to high levels of agreement with alexithymia ratings by external observers (Taylor *et al.*, 2000).

Inasmuch as the validity of a personality construct cannot be evaluated independently of the tests that purport to measure that construct, the psychometric properties of the TAS-20 provide strong empirical support for the validity of the alexithymia construct itself. The scale is at present the most widely-used alexithymia measure.

New measures

Recently some new measures of alexithymia have been introduced including a California Q-Set Alexithymia Prototype (Haviland, 1998) and the self-report Bermond–Vorst Alexithymia Questionnaire (Bermond & Vorst, 1998). Although the results from preliminary testing of the psychometric properties of these measures are encouraging, as noted elsewhere (Taylor *et al.*, 2000), it is premature to recommend them for clinical or research purposes until there is stronger evidence of their reliability and validity. My colleagues and I (Taylor *et al.*, 2000) developed a modified version of the Beth Israel Hospital Psychosomatic Questionnaire that was introduced initially by Sifneos (1973); while this holds promise as a useful observer-rated measure of alexithymia, it also requires further tests of reliability and validity.

Relationships with other health-related constructs

Several researchers have questioned whether alexithymia is distinct from other personality and emotion-related constructs that have been associated with physical health. For example, Bonnano and Singer (1990) suggested that alexithymia may be part of the better-known repressive coping style, which is identified by high scores on measures of defensiveness and low scores on measures of anxiety despite evidence of high levels of physiological arousal. Subsequent empirical studies have shown that repressors score low on the TAS and TAS-20 and that alexithymia is most similar to the sensitizing style of high-anxious individuals who acknowledge negative emotional experiences but have difficulty regulating them (Myers, 1995; Newton & Contrada, 1994). Alexithymic individuals are distinguished from high-anxious individuals, however, by their difficulties in accurately identifying and communicating subjective feelings, diminished fantasy life, and externally oriented cognitive style.

Also linked with emotional expression and physical health is the construct of inhibition, which is defined by Pennebaker (1989) as a conscious process in which an individual actively restrains, holds back, or in some way exerts effort not to think, feel, or behave. As King *et al.* (1992) point out, this broad definition includes the diverse constructs of constraint, restraint, emotional inexpressiveness, and emotional control. In a study with a nonclinical sample, King *et al.* (1992) found that the TAS correlated positively with a measure of inhibition, negatively with a measure of emotional expressiveness, and was unrelated to a measure of restraint. More recently, Verissimo *et al.* (1998) found that the TAS-20 correlated negatively with a measure of emotional control in a group of patients with inflammatory bowel disease, but alexithymia and emotional control independently influenced the subjective health status of the patients. Indeed, the results suggested that patients who are most aware of their subjective feelings (i.e. least alexithymic), but also exert the greatest control over their emotional reactions, enjoy a higher quality of life than patients who have difficulty knowing what they are feeling and are less able to control their reactions when distressing emotions are experienced.

Some psychologists argue that many of the personality constructs that have been linked with physical illness and health lack uniqueness and can be conceptualized as part of one or more of the broad dimensions within the five-factor model of personality. In a recent study, Luminet *et al.* (1999) examined the relationship between the TAS-20 and the Revised NEO Personality Inventory, which assesses the five major dimensions of personality and also the facets or lower-order traits that constitute each of these dimensions. The results showed that alexithymia is represented not by any single dimension or trait within the five-factor model, but by a cluster of traits across the dimensions and facets. TAS-20 scores were predicted by high scores on the facets of modesty and proneness to depression and by low scores on proneness to positive emotions, assertiveness, openness to feelings, openness to action, altruism, tender-mindedness, and competence. These findings indicate that alexithymia is not redundant with other personality constructs, and support it being conceptualized as an individual difference that may have explanatory power in health research.

Advances in alexithymia theory

The major advances in alexithymia theory over the past 25 years have been to locate the construct within the broad field of emotion theory and to propose ways whereby it might play a role in the development of medical and psychiatric disorders. Several years ago I suggested that the salient features of the construct reflect a deficit in the cognitive processing and regulation of emotions, and that the disorders with which alexithymia is most strongly asssociated be conceptualized as "disorders of emotion regulation" (Taylor, 1994). As my colleagues and I elaborated subsequently in a book (Taylor et al., 1997), this proposal is consistent not only with Ruesch (1948) and MacLean's (1949) idea of a deficit in the symbolic representation of emotion, but also with contemporary models of the cognitive development and organization of emotions.

According to a model outlined by Lane and Schwartz (1987), for example, normal affect development follows an epigenetic sequence in which the emergence of symbolization and the progressive learning of language lead to the formation of cognitive schemata of emotions of increasing complexity that gradually change the subjective experience of emotions from an awareness of bodily sensations and states of tension only to an awareness of blends of feelings and an ability to distinguish nuances of emotions. Although higher degrees of alexithymia correspond to lower levels in this dimensional model, Bucci (1997a) emphasizes that the problem in alexithymia is not simply a lack of words for emotions, but rather a lack of symbols for somatic states. Like Lane and Schwartz (1987), Bucci also argues that during normal affect development the earlier stages of concrete sensory and motor processing of emotions are not abandoned when levels of formal, logical processing are attained.

Drawing on recent knowledge from cognitive science and neuroscience, Bucci (1997b) proposes a "multiple code theory", in which emotions are represented both verbally and non-verbally. The non-verbal emotional schemata develop first and include subsymbolic processes (sensory, visceral, and kinesthetic sensations) as well as symbolic imagery. The verbal emotional schemata develop later and are organized according to the symbolic format of language. Consistent with these theoretical formulations, the deficit underlying alexithymia is manifest not only as a difficulty in describing feelings in words, but also as an impoverished fantasy life, an associated utilitarian thought style, and a dissociation of the (subsymbolic) representations of sensory experiences and patterns of autonomic arousal from (symbolic) images and words.

According to Bucci (1997a), the dissociation between subsymbolic and symbolic within the non-verbal emotion schemata may allow physiological activation to occur during emotional arousal without a corresponding cognitive activation. Moreover, the lack of focus and regulation by symbolic schemata may result in prolonged and repetitive physiological activation. The type of medical or psychiatric disorder that may then arise will depend on the degree of dissociation between somatic and motor patterns of activation and symbolic representations, and also on the interaction with constitutional and other vulnerability factors.

Alexithymia and emotion regulation

Empirical studies over the past decade provide some support for the view that alexithymia reflects deficits in the cognitive processing and regulation of emotion. In exploring the perception and cognitive appraisal of non-verbal emotional stimuli, for example, three experimental studies found that high-alexithymia individuals are less accurate in identifying posed facial expressions of emotion than are low-alexithymia individuals (Jessimer & Markham, 1997; Mann et al., 1994; Parker et al., 1993). In another study, high-alexithymia individuals had significantly lower accuracy rates than did low-alexithymia individuals on a series of tasks that require the matching of verbal or non-verbal emotional stimuli with verbal or non-verbal emotional responses (Lane et al., 1996). Other studies found that alexithymia is associated positively with maladaptive styles of emotion regulation, such as bingeing on food or drinking alcohol, and negatively with adaptive behaviors, such as thinking about and trying to understand distressing feelings or talking to a caring person (Beckendam, 1997; Parker et al., 1998; Schaffer, 1993). There is evidence also that alexithymia is associated with insecure attachment styles, which indicates less effective emotion regulating skills than found in individuals with secure attachment styles (Beckendam, 1997; Schaffer, 1993; Scheidt et al., 1999).

In exploring the proposal that alexithymia involves a dissociation between the cognitive–experiential and physiological components of the emotional response to stressful stimuli, however, experimental studies have yielded inconsistent findings. This may be attributed in part to using different emotion-provoking stimuli (e.g. viewing emotional scenes, performing mental arithmetic, or talking about an upsetting personal experience), and also to monitoring different physiological variables (heart rate, blood pressure, skin conductance, or muscle tension). Whereas in several studies alexithymia was associated with a higher tonic or baseline level of sympathetic activity, most studies found either hypo-arousal or no alexithymia effect during exposure to a stressor (Friedlander et al., 1997; Linden et al., 1996; Roedema & Simons, 1999; Wehmer et al., 1995). In a study that had research participants view an emotional film, however, alexithymia was associated with increased sympathetic arousal, indicated by higher skin conductance (Infrasca, 1997). Such a stimulus is more likely to engage the participants emotionally. In another recent study, Luminet and Rimé (1998) also used an emotional film as the stressor; consistent with the dissociation hypothesis, a higher degree of alexithymia was associated with fewer responses at the cognitive–experiential level, and greater physiological reactivity as indicated by increased heart rate.

Much more research is needed using methodologies that approximate stressful situations in everyday life. One such approach was devised by Troisi et al. (2000), who videotaped the non-verbal behaviors of anxious or depressed patients without their knowledge while they were being interviewed. Although high- and low-alexithymia patients did not differ on self-report ratings of anxiety and depression, the high-alexithymia patients showed significantly more displacement activities such as hand-to-face or hand-to-mouth movements, scratching, fumbling, and biting of lips; these behaviors are presumed to reflect bodily tension or skin sensations associated with emotional arousal (Delius, 1967). Despite the limitation that subjective feelings were assessed immediately prior to rather than during the interview, the results suggest a decoupling of physiological arousal from subjective feeling states.

Relationships with medical and psychiatric disorders

Given that many of the early investigations of alexithymia in clinical populations used measures of questionable validity, I will review only studies that used the TAS or TAS-20. Although alexithymia is considered a dimensional construct, empirically established cutoff scores for these scales enable researchers to compare rates of high alexithymia across studies.

Surprisingly, there have been few methodologically sound investigations of alexithymia and classic psychosomatic diseases, perhaps because of the now known heterogeneity of these disorders. The strongest association is between alexithymia and essential hypertension. In a study conducted in Italy, Todarello et al. (1995) found a rate of 55 percent of alexithymia in a group of hypertensive patients, which contrasted with rates of 33 percent in a comparison group of psychiatric outpatients and 16 percent in a community sample. In a more recent study in Finland, Jula et al. (1999) investigated a group of newly diagnosed and as yet untreated adults with moderate to severe hypertension and found rates of 57 percent in men and 46 percent in women compared with rates of 18 percent in normotensive men and 9 percent in normotensive women.

In another Italian study, Porcelli et al. (1995) found a rate of 35.7 percent of alexithymia in a group of patients with inflammatory bowel disease (IBD), which compared with a rate of 4.5 percent of alexithymia in a control group of healthy adults matched for gender, age, and education. Alexithymia was not related to the duration of illness or the level of disease activity. Although a high degree of alexithymia was present in only slightly more than one third of the IBD group, this finding may signify a subform of IBD that differs psychologically from other subforms.

Despite the clinical impression that patients with medically unexplained somatic symptoms are often alexithymic, there has been little attempt to assess prevalence rates in patients who meet DSM criteria for any of the somatoform disorders. In the one study I am aware of, a rate of 53 percent of alexithymia was found in a group of Canadian patients who met DSM-III-R criteria for somatoform pain disorder (Cox et al., 1994). No rates of alexithymia are reported for patients who meet DSM criteria for diagnoses of hypochondriasis or somatization disorder. However, given that many researchers now conceptualize somatization and hypochondriasis as personality traits rather than diagnostic categories, it is noteworthy that several studies have reported significant positive correlations between the TAS or TAS-20 and dimensional measures of somatization and hypochondriasis (see Taylor, 2000). These associations may be explained by a tendency for alexithymic individuals to focus on, amplify, and misinterpret the somatic sensations that accompany emotional arousal.

Noting that patients with functional gastrointestinal disorders (FGIDs) often complain of numerous unexplained non-gastrointestinal somatic symptoms, and thus show some clinical overlap with patients suffering from somatoform disorders, Porcelli et al. (1999) recently investigated a group of Italian patients with these medical disorders (mainly irritable bowel syndrome and/or functional dyspepsia) and found a rate of 66 percent of alexithymia. The FGID patients were significantly more alexithymic than a comparison group of IBD patients and the difference remained after controlling for higher levels of anxiety and depression in the FGID patients. These results may not be generalizable, however, as the FGID patients were selected from a tertiary-care center and are likely therefore to have had more psychiatric disorders and abnormal illness behavior, and also higher rates of life stress, than FGID patients referred to primary- and secondary-care settings.

Consistent with clinical observations that patients with eating disorders are bewildered by their emotional feelings and often have difficulty describing them, empirical studies have reported rates of alexithymia ranging from 48 percent to 77 percent for patients with anorexia nervosa and 40 percent to 61 percent for patients with bulimia nervosa (see Taylor et al., 1997). Interestingly, alexithymia was associated with the traits of ineffectiveness, (low) interoceptive awareness, and interpersonal distrust in a group of anorexic women, but the construct showed no relationship with attitudes and behavior related to abnormal eating and body weight and shape. The strongest association was with interpersonal distrust, which encompasses not only a reluctance to form close relationships but also a reluctance to express thoughts and feelings to other people (Taylor et al., 1996).

Investigations of other psychiatric populations have yielded empirical support for the early clinical impressions that alexithymia is common also among patients with substance use disorders, PTSD, or panic disorder. Rates of around 50 percent of alexithymia have been reported in groups of men with substance use disorders (see Taylor et al., 1997), which is consistent with the view that many addicts become dependent on alcohol or drugs because of enormous difficulties in regulating distressing, and often poorly-differentiated, affects. Among the anxiety disorders, a rate of 60 percent of alexithymia can be calculated from data collected from a group of male combat veterans with PTSD (Zeitlin *et al.*, 1989); rates of 47 percent and 67 percent of alexithymia have been reported in groups of patients with panic disorder, compared with much lower rates of 12.5 percent in patients with simple phobias and 13 percent in patients with obsessive compulsive disorder (see Taylor *et al.*, 1997). These findings are consistent with the view that panic attacks and some of the intrusive and autonomic arousal symptoms of PTSD are essentially overwhelming floods of undifferentiated emotions that have not been contained by higher order symbolic processes.

State-dependent versus trait alexithymia

Because the TAS and TAS-20 correlate positively with measures of anxiety and depression, some investigators suggest that the association between alexithymia and various medical and psychiatric disorders may reflect a concomitant state reaction secondary to the emotional distress evoked by illness rather than a predisposing or vulnerability factor. Although this distinction can be evaluated adequately only by prospective studies in which alexithymia is assessed before the onset of any disorder, findings from several longitudinal studies support the view that the construct reflects an enduring personality trait. Salminen *et al.* (1994), for example, followed a group of general psychiatric outpatients over a one year period and found a significant decrease in psychological distress, but no significant change in the mean alexithymia score. More recently, Martínez-Sánchez *et al.* (1998) demonstrated that alexithymia scores remained stable over a 17-week period in a group of university students whose levels of emotional and somatic distress initially decreased, and later increased, in association with the timing of university examinations.

It must be noted, however, that these and other longitudinal studies evaluated absolute stability only (i.e. the extent to which personality scores change over time) and not relative stability, which is the extent to which the relative differences among individuals remain the same over time. Furthermore, the changes in levels of emotional distress were relatively small. My colleagues and I therefore conducted a longitudinal investigation of psychiatric outpatients with major depressive disorders; we found a lack of absolute stability of alexithymia as the depressive symptoms lessened in response to antidepressant medications over a 14-week period, but there was strong evidence for the relative stability of alexithymia (Luminet *et al.*, 2001). Thus, while there may be a state-dependent aspect of alexithymia, especially when depression or other negative affects are intense, the demonstration of relative stability supports the conceptualization of alexithymia as a personality trait.

Notwithstanding the findings from these longitudinal studies, it must be emphasized that the associations between alexithymia and the various medical and psychiatric disorders are correlational only and that no causal inferences can be drawn. Some research suggests that the association may be due to the effects of alexithymia on illness behavior (such as symptom awareness and complaints) (Lumley & Norman, 1996), and it is possible that some of the help-seeking for medically unexplained somatic symptoms can be accounted for by neuroticism with which alexithymia is positively associated. Moreover, there is evidence that alexithymia is associated with a reduced ability to cope with stressful situations and with poor relationship skills (Parker et al., 1998; Taylor & Bagby, 2000), which can also influence a person's disposition to illness and disease.

There is preliminary evidence, however, that alexithymia has some value in predicting health changes beyond the predictive ability of other well-known risk factors. In a prospective study of over 2,000 middle-aged Finnish men, alexithymia was predictive of mortality by any cause over five years, independently of behavioral factors (smoking, alcohol consumption, physical activity), physiological factors (hypertension, low-density lipoprotein, high-density lipoprotein, body mass index), socioeconomic status, prior diseases, marital status, perceived health, depression, and social connections. Aside from suicide, homicide and accidents, however, specific causes of death were not reported (Kauhanen et al., 1996).

Neurobiological studies

In some of their early theoretical papers, Nemiah (1977) and his colleagues (Nemiah et al., 1976) suggested that there may be a neurobiological basis for alexithymia. They reiterated a hypothesis advanced many years earlier by MacLean (1949) that the inability to represent emotions symbolically may reflect a lack of adequate connections between the limbic system and the neocortex. At the Heidelberg conference, however, Hoppe and Bogen (1977) described an impoverishment of fantasies and a limited ability to describe feelings in patients who had lost the major connection between the right and left cerebral hemispheres; these patients had previously undergone commissurotomy for treatment of intractable epilepsy and were nonalexithymic before the surgery. Given that the right hemisphere is preferentially involved in the perception and expression of nonverbal emotional behavior, and the left hemisphere preferentially involved in verbal functioning, the observation of alexithymic characteristics in the commissurotomised patients led Hoppe (1977) to suggest that alexithymia in individuals with intact brains may involve an interruption in the flow of information between the two hemispheres; he referred to this as a "functional commissurotomy".

This proposal has now been supported by findings from two experimental studies that used a tactile finger localization task to assess the efficiency of interhemispheric transfer. In both a group of male combat veterans with PTSD (Zeitlin et al., 1989) and a group of undergraduate students (Parker et al., 1999), alexithymia was associated with a deficit in the bidirectional transfer of sensorimotor information between right and left hemispheres. Although these findings need to be replicated for tasks involving the transfer of emotion-laden information, the demonstration that the interhemispheric transfer deficit is bidirectional suggests that the salient features of the alexithymia construct reflect a limited capacity to coordinate and integrate the activities of the two hemispheres. Indeed, while each hemisphere is specialized for different functions, there is an increasing view that most cognitive tasks, including emotional processing and imaginal activity, normally require a varying amount of interhemispheric cooperation (Pally, 1998).

Over the past decade, the development of functional brain imaging techniques has provided investigators with more sophisticated methods for investigating the neural correlates of emotions. Some researchers have begun to use these methods to identify parts of the brain that are associated with subjective emotional experience. In a PET imaging study with a small group of women, Lane et al. (1998) found a positive relationship between high scores on the Levels of Emotional Awareness Scale (LEAS) and increased activity in the right anterior cingulate cortex (ACC) when emotions were induced either by films or by recall of personal experiences. Given that higher scores on the LEAS indicate greater differentiation in the mental representations of emotion and greater awareness of emotional complexity in self and others, the results of the study suggest that the ACC plays an important role in subjective emotional experience.

Although the LEAS was not developed as a measure of alexithymia and correlates only weakly, albeit negatively, with the TAS-20, the results led Lane et al. (1997) to speculate that alexithymia might arise from disruption of transmission of interoceptive emotion information to the ACC. Since the ACC also helps orchestrate the motor, autonomic, and endocrine responses to emotional stimuli, these researchers suggest that altered functioning in this structure might explain the link between alexithymia and disease. They cast doubt on the functional commissurotomy hypothesis of alexithymia, concluding that it does not explain how a failure of interhemispheric transfer could contribute to disease pathophysiology.

Most neuroscientists, however, do not associate the neural processing and regulation of emotion with any one brain structure. As LeDoux (1996), Heilman (1997) and Panksepp (1998) point out, the ACC and other parts of the limbic system do not operate in isolation but are functionally intertwined with higher and lower areas of the brain. Indeed, Panksepp (1999) attributes the generation of emotional feelings not just to the frontal lobe and higher limbic structures, but also to extensive subcortical (including brainstem) command circuits. Moreover, in addition to the role played by the ACC in orchestrating the physiological component of emotional responding, there is evidence that the right hemisphere also mediates autonomic nervous system responses to emotional stimuli (Spence et al., 1996) and that the left hemisphere can modulate an individual's arousal response, perhaps by maintaining some inhibitory control over the right hemisphere (Heilman, 1997). Consequently, rather than discard any of the hypotheses for which there is some empirical support, my colleagues and I proposed a more comprehensive model, which encompasses deficits in interhemispheric integration and coordination as well as a deficit in ACC activity during emotional arousal

(Taylor & Bagby, 2000). There are likely to be other neural correlates as well that may be identified in future brain imaging studies. It must be emphasized, however, that the findings from all of the neurobiological studies are correlational only and do not imply any cause–effect relationships.

Therapeutic considerations

Although it has long been acknowledged that patients with high degrees of alexithymia respond poorly to insight-oriented psychotherapy, there has been little attempt to devise and evaluate alternative treatments for these patients. Sifneos (1996) and Nemiah et al. (1976) favor individual or group psychotherapies that are supportive in nature for alexithymic patients. Krystal (1979; 1982/83), however, recommends a modified form of individual psychotherapy, which uses specific psychoeducational techniques to address deficits in affect awareness and affect tolerance. These include making patients aware of how their subjective experience of emotion differs from that of other people; directing their attention to behavioral expressions of emotion (such as sighs, gestures, and movements); helping them to recognize, differentiate, and label their feelings; teaching them to attend to their dreams; and teaching them to view feelings as information signals that can be reflected upon and used to guide behavior. Some clinicians have applied Krystal's techniques and other approaches in group therapy settings, but reports about their effectiveness are mainly anecdotal.

A recent study evaluated the effectiveness of group psychotherapy in reducing alexithymic characteristics in post-myocardial infarction (post-MI) patients, and also its potential benefits on the subsequent course of coronary heart disease (Beresnevaite, 2000). The techniques that were used during four months of weekly group psychotherapy included relaxation training, role playing, and promoting non-verbal communication, as well as interventions to facilitate verbal emotional expression and attention to dreams and fantasies. A comparison group of post-MI patients received two educational sessions within a period of one month that provided information about coronary heart disease. Although at the start of the study the mean alexithymia scores were similar for the two patient samples, the patients who received group psychotherapy showed a significant reduction in the mean alexithymia score by the end of treatment that was maintained throughout a two-year follow-up period. The comparison sample showed no significant change in mean alexithymia scores between the initial testing and at various intervals during the two-year follow-up. Moreover, those patients whose degree of alexithymia had decreased from high to moderate, or from moderate to low, in response to group psychotherapy experienced fewer cardiac events (reinfarction, sudden cardiac death, or rehospitalization for rhythm disorder or severe angina) than patients whose degree of alexithymia had remained unchanged.

Although this study needs to be replicated by other researchers and with different diagnostic patient groups, the results suggest that specific psychotherapeutic techniques, at least when applied to patients in small groups, can not only modify alexithymia but possibly have positive health benefits as well. Applying Bucci's (1997b) multiple code theory, it is tempting to speculate that the psychotherapeutic techniques that were employed in this study led to an increase in the verbal symbolic elements of emotion representations and to enhanced connections between symbolic and subsymbolic elements.

Conclusions

Alexithymia theory and research have advanced considerably over the past 25 years. There is now strong support not only for the validity of the construct, but also for its association with certain medical and psychiatric disorders that involve problems in emotion regulation. And while the construct continues to interest psychosomatic physicians and health psychologists, it has also begun to capture the attention of emotion theorists and researchers and to benefit from advances in the related fields of cognitive science, neurobiology, and attachment research. Future collaboration between these disciplines is likely to further our understanding of the complex ways whereby alexithymia and emotions might influence physical and mental health.

References

Bagby, R.M., Parker, J.D.A., & Taylor, G.J. (1994a). The Twenty-Item Toronto Alexithymia Scale – I: Item selection and cross-validation of the factor structure. *Journal of Psychosomatic Research*, **38**, 23–32.

Bagby, R.M., Taylor, G.J., & Parker, J.D.A. (1994b). The Twenty-Item Toronto Alexithymia Scale – II: Convergent, discriminant, and concurrent validity. *Journal of Psychosomatic Research*, **38**, 33–40.

Beckendam, C.C. (1997). *Dimensions of emotional intelligence: Attachment, affect regulation, alexithymia and empathy*. Doctoral dissertation, The Fielding Institute, Santa Barbara, CA.

Beresnevaite, M. (2000). Exploring the benefits of group psychotherapy in reducing alexithymia in coronary heart disease patients: a preliminary study. *Psychotherapy and Psychosomatics*, **69**, 117–122.

Bermond, B. & Vorst, H.C. (1998). *Validity and reliability of the Bermond-Vorst Alexithymia Questionnaire*. Unpublished manuscript, University of Amsterdam, The Netherlands.

Bonnano, G.A. & Singer, J.L. (1990). Repressive personality style: theoretical and methodological implications for health and pathology. In J.L. Singer (ed.), *Repression and dissociation: implications for personality theory, psychopathology and health* (pp. 435–470). Chicago, IL: University of Chicago Press.

Bruch, H. (1973). *Eating disorders: obesity, anorexia nervosa, and the person within*. New York: Basic Books.

Bucci, W. (1997a). Symptoms and symbols: a multiple code theory of somatization. *Psychoanalytic Inquiry*, **17**, 151–172.

Bucci, W. (1997b). *Psychoanalysis and cognitive science: a multiple code theory*. New York: Guilford.

Cox, B.J., Kuch, K., Parker, J.D.A., Shulman, I.D., & Evans, R.J. (1994). Alexithymia in somatoform disorder patients with chronic pain. *Journal of Psychosomatic Research*, **38**, 523–527.

Delius, J.D. (1967). Displacement activities and arousal. *Nature*, **214**, 1259–1260.

Friedlander, L., Lumley, M.A., Farchione, T., & Doyal, G. (1997). Testing the alexithymia hypothesis: physiological and subjective responses during relaxation and stress. *Journal of Nervous and Mental Disease*, **185**, 233–239.

Haviland, M.G. (1998). The validity of the California Q-set alexithymia prototype. *Psychosomatics*, **39**, 536–539.

Heilman, K.M. (1997). The neurobiology of emotional experience. *Journal of Neuropsychiatry and Clinical Neuroscience*, **9**, 439–448.

Hoppe, K.D. (1977). Split brains and psychoanalysis. *Psychoanalytic Quarterly*, **46**, 220–244.

Hoppe, K.D. & Bogen, J.E. (1977). Alexithymia in twelve commissurotomized patients. *Psychotherapy and Psychosomatics*, **28**, 148–155.

Infrasca, R. (1997). Alexithymia, neurovegetative arousal and neuroticism. *Psychotherapy and Psychosomatics*, **66**, 276–280.

Jessimer, M. & Markham, R. (1997). Alexithymia: a right hemisphere dysfunction specific to recognition of certain facial expressions. *Brain and Cognition*, **34**, 246–258.

Jula, A., Salminen, J.K., & Saarijärvi, S. (1999). Alexithymia: a facet of essential hypertension. *Hypertension*, **33**, 1057–1061.

Kauhanen, J., Kaplan, G.A., Cohen, R.D., Julkunen, J., & Salonen, J.T. (1996). Alexithymia and risk of death in middle-aged men. *Journal of Psychosomatic Research*, **41**, 541–549.

King, L.A., Emmons, R.A., & Woodley, S. (1992). The structure of inhibition. *Journal of Research in Personality*, **26**, 85–102.

Krystal, H. (1968). *Massive psychic trauma*. New York: International Universities Press.

Krystal, H. (1979). Alexithymia and psychotherapy. *American Journal of Psychotherapy*, **33**, 17–31.

Krystal, H. (1982/83). Alexithymia and the effectiveness of psychoanalytic treatment. *International Journal of Psychoanalytic Psychotherapy*, **9**, 353–388.

Krystal, H. & Raskin, H. (1970). *Drug dependence*. Detroit, MI: Wayne State University Press.

Lane, R.D., Ahern, G.L., Schwartz, G.E., & Kaszniak, A.W. (1997). Is alexithymia the emotional equivalent of blindsight? *Biological Psychiatry*, **42**, 834–844.

Lane, R.D., Reiman, E.M., Axelrod, B., Lang-Sheng, Y., Holmes, A., & Schwartz, G.E. (1998). Neural correlates of levels of emotional awareness: evidence of an interaction between emotion and attention in the anterior cingulate cortex. *Journal of Cognitive Neuroscience*, **10**, 525–535.

Lane, R.D. & Schwartz, G.E. (1987). Levels of emotional awareness: a cognitive developmental theory and its application to psychopathology. *American Journal of Psychiatry*, **144**, 133–143.

Lane, R., Sechrest, L., Reidel, R., Weldon, V., Kaszniak, A., & Schwartz, G. (1996). Impaired verbal and nonverbal emotion recognition in alexithymia. *Psychosomatic Medicine*, **58**, 203–210.

LeDoux, J.E. (1996). *The emotional brain: the mysterious underpinnings of emotional life*. New York: Simon and Schuster.

Linden, W., Lenz, J.W., & Stossel, C. (1996). Alexithymia, defensiveness and cardio-vascular reactivity to stress. *Journal of Psychosomatic Research*, **41**, 575–583.

Luminet, O. & Rimé, B. (1998). *Assessing the empirical validity of alexithymia: its predictive value for various levels of emotional responding when exposed to an eliciting situation and when re-evoking it verbally*. Paper presented at the 10th conference of the International Society for Research on Emotion, Würzburg, Germany.

Luminet, O., Bagby, R.M., Wagner, H., Taylor, G.J., & Parker, J.D.A. (1999). The relationship between alexithymia and the five factor model of personality: a facet level analysis. *Journal of Personality Assessment*, **73**, 345–358.

Luminet, O., Bagby, R.M., & Taylor, G.J. (2001). An evaluation of the absolute and relative stability of alexithymia in patients with major depression. *Psychotherapy and Psychosomatics*, **70**, 254–260.

Lumley, M.A. & Norman, S. (1996). Alexithymia and health care utilization. *Psychosomatic Medicine*, **58**, 197–202.

MacLean, P.D. (1949). Psychosomatic disease and the "visceral brain": recent developments bearing on the Papez theory of emotion. *Psychosomatic Medicine*, **11**, 338–353.

Mann, L.S., Wise, T.N., Trinidad, A., & Kohanski, R. (1994). Alexithymia, affect recognition, and the five-factor model of personality. *Psychological Reports*, **74**, 563–567.

Martínez-Sánchez, F., Ato-García, M., Adam, E.C., Medina, T.B.H., & España, J.S. (1998). Stability in alexithymia levels: a longitudinal analysis on various emotional answers. *Personality and Individual Differences*, **24**, 767–772.

Marty, P. & de M'Uzan, M. (1963). La "pensée opératoire". *Revue Française de Psychoanalyse*, **27** (suppl.), 1345–1356.

Myers, L.B. (1995). Alexithymia and repression: the role of defensiveness and trait anxiety. *Personality and Individual Differences*, **19**, 489–492.

Nemiah, J.C. (1977). Alexithymia: theoretical considerations. *Psychotherapy and Psychosomatics*, **28**, 199–206.

Nemiah, J.C. (1984). The psychodynamic view of anxiety. In R.O. Pasnau (ed.), *Diagnosis and treatment of anxiety disorders* (pp. 117–137). Washington, DC: American Psychiatric Press.

Nemiah, J.C., Freyberger, H., & Sifneos, P.E. (1976). Alexithymia: a view of the psychosomatic process. In O.W. Hill (ed.), *Modern trends in psychosomatic medicine*, Vol. 3 (pp. 430–439). London: Butterworths.

Nemiah, J.C. & Sifneos, P.E. (1970). Affect and fantasy in patients with psychosomatic disorders. In O.W. Hill (ed.), *Modern trends in psychosomatic medicine*, Vol. 2 (pp. 26–34). London: Butterworths.

Newton, T.L. & Contrada, R.J. (1994). Alexithymia and repression: contrasting emotion-focused coping styles. *Psychosomatic Medicine*, **56**, 457–462.

Pally, R. (1998). Bilaterality: hemispheric specialization and integration. *International Journal of Psychoanalysis*, **79**, 565–578.

Panksepp, J. (1998). *Affective neuroscience: the foundations of human and animal emotions*. New York: Oxford University Press.

Panksepp, J. (1999). Emotions as viewed by psychoanalysis and neuroscience: an exercise in consilience. *Neuro-Psychoanalysis*, **1**, 15–38.

Parker, J.D.A., Keightley, M.L., Smith, C.T., & Taylor, G.J. (1999). Interhemispheric transfer deficit in alexithymia: an experimental study. *Psychosomatic Medicine*, **61**, 464–468.

Parker, J.D.A., Taylor, G.J., & Bagby, R.M. (1993). Alexithymia and the recognition of facial expressions of emotion. *Psychotherapy and Psychosomatics*, **59**, 197–202.

Parker, J.D.A., Taylor, G.J., & Bagby, R.M. (1998). Alexithymia: relationship with ego defense and coping styles. *Comprehensive Psychiatry*, **39**, 91–98.

Pennebaker, J.W. (1989). Confession, inhibition, and disease. *Advances in Experimental and Social Psychology*, **22**, 211–244.

Porcelli, P., Taylor, G.J., Bagby, R.M., & De Carne, M. (1999). Alexithymia and functional gastrointestinal disorders: a comparison with inflammatory bowel disease. *Psychotherapy and Psychosomatics*, **68**, 263–269.

Porcelli, P., Zaka, S., Leoci, C., Centonze, S., & Taylor, G.J. (1995). Alexithymia in inflammatory bowel disease. A case–control study. *Psychotherapy and Psychosomatics*, **64**, 49–53.

Roedema T.M. & Simons, R.F. (1999). Emotion-processing deficit in alexithymia. *Psychophysiology*, **36**, 379–387.

Ruesch, J. (1948). The infantile personality. *Psychosomatic Medicine*, **10**, 134–144.

Salminen, J.K., Saarijärvi, S., Ääirelä, E., & Tamminen, T. (1994). Alexithymia – state or trait? One-year follow-up study of general hospital psychiatric consultation outpatients. *Journal of Psychosomatic Research*, **38**, 681–685.

Schaffer, C.E. (1993). *The role of adult attachment in the experience and regulation of affect*. Doctoral dissertation, Yale University, New Haven, CT.

Scheidt, C.E., Waller, E., Schnock, C., Becker-Stoll, F., Zimmerman, P., Lücking C.H., & Wirsching, M. (1999). Alexithymia and attachment representation in idiopathic spasmodic torticollis. *Journal of Nervous and Mental Disease*, **187**, 47–52.

Sifneos, P.E. (1967). Clinical observations on some patients suffering from a variety of psychosomatic diseases. *Acta Medicina Psychosomatica*, **7**, 1–10.

Sifneos, P.E. (1973). The prevalence of "alexithymic" characteristics in psychosomatic patients. *Psychotherapy and Psychosomatics*, **22**, 255–262.

Sifneos, P.E. (1996). Alexithymia: past and present. *American Journal of Psychiatry*, **153**, 137–142.

Spence, S., Shapiro, D., & Zaidel, E. (1996). The role of the right hemisphere in the physiological and cognitive components of emotional processing. *Psychophysiology*, **33**, 112–122.

Taylor, G.J. (1994). The alexithymia construct: conceptualization, validation, and relationship with basic dimensions of personality. *New Trends in Experimental and Clinical Psychiatry*, **10**, 61–74.

Taylor. G.J. (2000). Recent developments in alexithymia theory and research. *Canadian Journal of Psychiatry*, **45**, 134–142.

Taylor, G.J. & Bagby, R.M. (2000). An overview of the alexithymia construct. In R. Bar-On & J.D.A. Parker (eds), *Handbook of emotional intelligence* (pp. 40–67). San Francisco, CA: Jossey-Bass.

Taylor, G.J., Bagby, R.M., & Luminet, O. (2000). Assessment of alexithymia: self-report and observer-rated measures. In R. Bar-On & J.D.A. Parker (eds), *Handbook of emotional intelligence* (pp. 301–319). San Francisco, CA: Jossey-Bass.

Taylor, G.J., Bagby, R.M., & Parker, J.D.A. (1997). *Disorders of affect regulation: Alexithymia in medical and psychiatric illness*. Cambridge: Cambridge University Press.

Taylor, G.J., Parker, J.D.A., Bagby, R.M., & Bourke, M.P. (1996). Relationships between alexithymia and psychological characteristics associated with eating disorders. *Journal of Psychosomatic Research*, **41**, 561–568.

Taylor, G.J., Ryan, D., & Bagby, R.M. (1985). Toward the development of a new self-report alexithymia scale. *Psychotherapy and Psychosomatics*, **44**, 191–199.

Todarello, O., Taylor, G.J., Parker, J.D.A., & Fanelli, M. (1995). Alexithymia in essential hypertensive and psychiatric outpatients: a comparative study. *Journal of Psychosomatic Research*, **39**, 987–994.

Troisi, A., Belsanti, S., Bucci, A.R., Mosco, C., Sinti, F., & Verucci, M. (2000). Affect regulation in alexithymia: an ethological study of displacement behavior during psychiatric interviews. *Journal of Nervous and Mental Disease*, **188**, 13–18.

Verissimo, R., Mota-Cardoso, R., & Taylor, G.J. (1998). Relationships between alexithymia, emotional control, and quality of life in patients with inflammatory bowel disease. *Psychotherapy and Psychosomatics*, **67**, 75–80.

Wehmer, F., Brejnak, C., Lumley, M., & Stettner, L. (1995). Alexithymia and physiological reactivity to emotion-provoking visual scenes. *Journal of Nervous and Mental Disease*, **183**, 351–357.

Zeitlin, S.B., Lane, R.D., O'Leary, D.S., & Schrift, M.J. (1989). Interhemispheric transfer deficit and alexithymia. *American Journal of Psychiatry*, **146**, 1434–1439.

Chapter 9

Emotional intelligence and physical health

Alison Woolery and Peter Salovey

Introduction

Thinkers from King Solomon and Hippocrates to Walter Cannon and Norman Cousins have all suspected that the emotions play an important role in the maintenance of physical health and recovery from disease. Empirical evidence for this idea has accumulated rapidly in the past two decades, and it now appears rather clear that fluctuations in emotional arousal are linked to changes in the immune system (e.g. Herbert & Cohen, 1993; Stone *et al.*, 1996), the interpretation of physical symptoms (e.g. Salovey & Birnbaum, 1989), cardiovascular functioning (e.g. Smith, 1992), the acceptance of health risk information (e.g. Reed & Aspinwall, 1998), health damaging behaviors (e.g. Baumeister, 1991; Brandon, 1994), and other outcomes relevant to health and illness (reviewed by Salovey *et al.*, 2000). Increasingly, investigators have focused on individual differences in the way emotions are experienced as a potential risk factor or protective factor (e.g. Kennedy-Moore & Watson, 1999; Watson, 2000). This chapter will focus on one set of individual differences relevant to emotion – emotional intelligence – and present some preliminary evidence for connections between it and health-relevant outcomes.

What is emotional intelligence?

Emotional intelligence is defined as the ability to understand feelings in the self and others, and to use these feelings as informational guides for thinking and action (Salovey & Mayer, 1990). Our framework of emotional intelligence encompasses a set of emotional competencies, including how people (a) identify and express their own feelings and identify the feelings of others, (b) use emotions to facilitate thinking, (c) understand and analyze emotions, and (d) regulate their own and others' emotions (Mayer & Salovey, 1997). Identification and expression include both verbal and non-verbal behavior. We need to understand what we are feeling, and we need to be able to communicate our feelings using words and non-verbal behaviors. Moreover, we need to understand the feelings of other people – both in their words and in their expressions – and to be able to feel the emotions of other people, i.e. to empathize with them. Second, we must recognize that emotions prioritize thinking, shape memory, create different problem-solving perspectives, and facilitate creativity. Third, to make use of our emotions, we must have a rich emotional vocabulary, and we must be able to understand emotional nuances, blends of feelings, and transitions from one emotion to another. Finally, we need to learn to regulate our emotions so that they are most appropriate to the task or situation at hand, and we need to learn to regulate the emotions of other people, to cheer them up when they are down, to engage them when we want them to listen to us.

Since Salovey and Mayer (1990) first suggested the idea of an emotional intelligence, researchers and the popular media have been quick to propose their own, wide-ranging models of emotional intelligence. Some have gone so far as to turn emotional intelligence into a cluster of personality traits said to determine character and life achievements (e.g. Goleman, 1995, 1998). We prefer our original conceptualization of emotional intelligence, which focuses on mental abilities specific to emotion. This framework helps us to specify what it means when we ask whether emotional intelligence is linked to physical health. What we really want to determine is whether specific emotional competencies enhance health, and whether the absence of these competencies predicts illness or health-damaging behavior. To answer these questions directly, we would need to assess emotional intelligence using skill-based tests that assess these competencies. For example, one test, the Multi-Factor Emotional Intelligence Scale (MEIS), includes tasks that ask people to identify consensual feelings suggested by music and abstract designs, analyze blends and progressions of emotions, and assess how they and other people can best manage their emotions in different scenarios (Mayer *et al.*, 1999).

Because task-based measures such as the MEIS (and its successor, the MSCEIT) are still being refined, many studies of emotional intelligence and health have relied on self-report scales to assess emotional intelligence. Self-report assess-ments have obvious limitations in the study of emotional intelligence; they do not tap directly into people's emotional competencies, but rather assess people's beliefs about how they identify, use, understand, and regulate their own and others' emotions. We would never consider people's beliefs about their intelligence – *"I think I'm a bright person"* – necessarily to be valid measures of IQ; analogous questions about emotional intelligence are similarly troublesome.

Thus, past studies have not explored the link between emotional intelligence *per se* and health, but rather what we have termed perceived emotional intelligence (PEI) – people's beliefs about their emotional intelligence – in conjunction with health variables. Although it does not measure emotional competencies *per se*, PEI is an interesting variable in and of itself. We can think of it as a kind of emotional intelligence self-efficacy. People who report high PEI may be confident that they can successfully apply emotional intelligence skills in diverse situations. This self-efficacy expectation could predict an actual ability to demonstrate emotional competencies, because self-efficacy expectations and ability in general are highly correlated. Seen in this light, the question for us becomes how PEI affects health.

Could people's beliefs about how they identify, understand, and regulate their emotions promote their long-term health and protect them from disease?

Perceived emotional intelligence and health-relevant outcomes

A series of studies conducted in our laboratory suggests that PEI is associated with numerous health-related outcomes. These studies have all assessed PEI using the Trait Meta-Mood Scale (TMMS). The TMMS taps into three aspects of emotional intelligence:

1 *Attention* – the degree to which people report that they typically attend to their moods
2 *Clarity* – the degree to which people report that they can clearly understand and discriminate among their moods
3 *Repair* – the degree to which people report that they can maintain positive and repair negative mood states.

Scores on the TMMS predict recovery from negative mood and ruminative thought following an experimental stressor. Individuals who reported that they experience their feelings clearly were more likely to rebound from induced negative mood and showed a decline in ruminative thought across time when compared to individuals who reported being unclear about their moods (Salovey *et al.*, 1995).

Early studies using the TMMS examined how beliefs about mood affect illness and symptom reporting under stressful conditions (Goldman *et al.*, 1996). Goldman *et al.* assessed 134 student volunteers at three different times during the semester: at the start of the year, during midterm examinations, and during final examinations. At these times, they administered the Trait Meta-Mood Scale (TMMS) as well as measures of stress, physical symptoms, and health center visits. When they divided the sample into three groups of people (those with a high degree of skill in repairing negative moods, those with average skills in this area, and those with low skills), interesting trends in health center visits emerged depending on the level of stress people experienced. When stress was low, the three groups differed very little. As stress increased, those individuals who said that they cannot easily regulate their feelings were more likely to visit the health center, and those individuals who were good at repairing negative moods actually visited the health center less often. Individuals who cannot repair or regulate their feelings may look to others for help in doing so. As a result, they may be more likely to seek the attention of a physician when they are feeling stressed because they do not know how to regulate these feelings themselves. Such individuals may simply be using the health care system as a mood regulation strategy. Of course, it is also possible that these individuals are actually more likely to become physically ill when under stress.

Two recent studies examined the relations among PEI (as measured by the TMMS) and psychophysiological responses to laboratory stressors (Salovey *et al.*, 2002). In one, 60 women were presented with visiospatial puzzles, serial subtraction tasks, and a videotaped speech task under conditions of unrealistic time constraints. Women who reported that they can repair their moods tended to perceive these laboratory stressors as less threatening and used fewer state and trait passive coping strategies. Women who reported that they can perceive their moods clearly tended to release less cortisol at baseline and throughout repeated stress exposures, indicating that Clarity may be associated with lower adrenocortical responses to stress.

In a second study, 48 men and women were randomly assigned to an achievement or interpersonal stress condition (Salovey et al., 2002). People in the achievement condition had to solve difficult arithmetic problems and memorize a complex poem under considerable time constraints. In the interpersonal condition, participants attempted to have conversations with two confederates who intentionally rejected them. People who reported that they can repair their moods were more likely to demonstrate active coping in response to these distressing situations. Self-reported repair was also associated with lower levels of rumination and higher levels of distraction after stressor exposure. People who reported that they frequently attend to their moods showed attenuated cortisol, systolic blood pressure (SBP), and diastolic blood pressure (DBP) reactivity to the laboratory stressors, controlling for baseline levels as well as the other TMMS subscales. These two studies indicate that people who believe that they attend to their moods frequently and/or perceive their moods clearly may show lower adrenocortical responses to stress. People who attend to their moods may also demonstrate a more adaptive cardiovascular response to stress.

A third study in our laboratory extended these physiological findings by examining interactions between PEI and cardiovascular reactivity during an emotional disclosure task. Emotional disclosure is the process of writing or talking about traumatic or other emotional life experiences (e.g. Pennebaker & Beall, 1986). Numerous studies conducted by diverse investigators across multiple populations have demonstrated that engaging in emotional disclosure elicits beneficial health outcomes. Experimentally induced disclosure of thoughts and feelings about emotional life experiences has been associated with fewer college health center visits (King & Miner, 2000; Pennebaker & Beall, 1986; Pennebaker et al., 1990), decreases in self-reported physical symptoms, decreases in distress and depression (e.g. Greenberg & Stone, 1992), adaptive changes in autonomic response (Pennebaker et al., 1987), positive immunological changes (Pennebaker et al., 1988; Petrie et al., 1995), and improvements in the course of asthma and arthritis (Smyth et al., 1999; for a review, see Smyth, 1998; Greenberg & Lepore, this volume, Chapter 3).

Current explanations for positive outcomes following disclosure focus on cognitive processes. According to these explanations, engaging in disclosure facilitates the transduction of traumatic memories into an organized, linguistic structure that reduces the emotional arousal and distress elicited by trauma, such as intrusive thoughts, ruminations, and flashbacks (Pennebaker et al., 1997; Pennebaker & Seagal, 1999; Smyth, 1999; Greenberg & Lepore, this volume, Chapter 3).

Although we do not discount these explanations, we would add that emotional regulatory processes may also be important mechanisms in disclosure.

People disclosing past traumas must regulate their feelings on two levels. First, they must cope with the emotional arousal that disclosure evokes, in part by distinguishing and moderating the moods they are currently feeling as a result of talking about their past experiences. At the same time, they must process and assimilate the emotions surrounding their past experiences into a meaningful cognitive narrative. For example, a male student who writes about failing a class for the first time in his life may remember the intense sadness he felt when the event happened. He may re-experience this sadness as he writes; he may also experience new emotions evoked by his recollection, such as anger at his past failings. He must identify and cope with this anger at the same time that he assimilates his feelings of sadness into a coherent narrative of failing his class. These emotional regulatory processes could necessitate the ability to perceive one's emotions clearly and to understand and discriminate among them (Salovey *et al.*, 1999, 2001). Conversely, this act of processing and imposing structure on traumatic events while coping with current emotional arousal may enhance people's beliefs about their abilities to perceive their emotional states clearly.

Given this potential interaction between emotional intelligence (perceived or actual) and emotional disclosure and in light of our findings in the two stress studies discussed previously, we predicted that people reporting high PEI would demonstrate more adaptive physiological reactivity when writing about emotional life events. Sixty-eight participants were asked to write two ten-minute essays, one about an emotional event in their lives, and the other about a relatively mundane (control) topic (cleaning and doing laundry). Following each writing period, participants sat quietly for a three-minute rest period.

All participants tended to exhibit heightened cardiovascular arousal when they wrote about emotional real-life experiences, relative to the control topic. However, compared to people reporting low Clarity, people who reported that they can perceive their moods clearly tended to show greater SBP increases immediately after writing about their emotional experiences (controlling for baseline). Following the post-writing rest period, people reporting high Clarity had lower SBP than people reporting low Clarity (controlling for baseline and initial reactivity). People who showed the greatest SBP increase immediately after writing, followed by the steepest SBP decrease after the rest period, reported the highest levels of Clarity.

It is particularly interesting that people who reported high Clarity tended to show an increase in SBP immediately after writing about their emotional experiences. These people may simply have been more aroused and engaged in the writing process than were people reporting low Clarity. Alternatively, it may be that everyone was aroused during the emotional writing condition, but that people high in Clarity were particularly open to and/or skilled at perceiving the quality and intensity of the emotions that emerged as they wrote. This heightened awareness of the emotionality of the emotional writing condition may have corresponded to a greater immediate SBP increase.

During the rest period, people reporting high mood Clarity may have processed and assimilated the emotions they experienced while writing. Consequently, their elevated SBP levels tended to recover most efficiently. People reporting low Clarity may have engaged in rumination in an attempt to identify and understand the feelings evoked when they wrote about their emotional experiences (as in the study reported in Salovey et al., 1995); this maladaptive coping style may have resulted in sustained elevation of or even increases in SBP (see Chapter 6, and Carels et al., 1998). People low in Clarity thus had significantly higher SBP levels three minutes after writing about their emotional experiences than people high in Clarity. People who believe they can clearly perceive their moods tend to experience more adaptive cardiovascular responses when they write about emotional life events, compared to people who do not believe that they can perceive their moods.

To summarize, these studies from our laboratory suggest a strong relationship between PEI and physiological outcomes relevant to health. People who believe that they attend to and clearly perceive their moods seem to cope effectively with a wide array of distressing situations, as indicated by their adaptive physiological responses. Over time, these adaptive physiological responses to stress may protect people high in PEI from disease; large increases in physiological responses to acute stressors as well as an inability to habituate to chronic stressors may damage organs and lead to disease (Dienstbier, 1989; Manuck & Krantz, 1984; McEwen & Stellar, 1993). Thus, PEI may be linked to health through psychophysiological stress reactivity: people reporting high PEI may tend to experience adaptive physiological responses in stressful situations, making them less prone to disease in the long run.

Of course, we should be cautious in attributing causality with respect to these physiological findings. The explanations above imply that PEI affects physiological arousal; however, it may be the case that physiological arousal affects people's beliefs about their abilities to attend to, distinguish, and repair their moods. People who experienced adaptive physiological reactions to stress exposure and writing about emotional experiences may have been more willing and/or able to attend to and discern their emotions than people who experienced discomforting, sustained physiological arousal. People experiencing adaptive physiological responses may thus be more likely to report that they attend to their moods and/or can perceive their moods clearly. Future studies could attempt to resolve this causal directionality by "teaching people" Clarity, Attention, and Repair, perhaps through a series of worksheets or verbal instruction. If people who receive this "training" subsequently demonstrate more adaptive physiological responses to stress, relative to a control group, causality from PEI to physiological response could be inferred. Another study design might employ a self-efficacy induction: participants could be primed to believe that they can successfully perceive and repair their moods in emotional situations, and their subsequent physiological reactivity could be compared with that of people not primed with this expectation.

Ultimately, it may be a mistake to assume that the relationship between PEI and health-relevant outcomes is monodirectional, that it either influences or is influenced by the dimensions with which it is correlated. PEI may actually operate within a bidirectional feedback loop. People who believe that they can attend to, clearly perceive, and repair their moods consequently tend to demonstrate adaptive physiological recovery when they confront stressful situations; this adaptive recovery enhances their belief that they can attend to, discriminate, and repair their moods, making it more likely that they will demonstrate these responses to disclosure in the future.

It is important to note that our studies of PEI and health examined short-term, physiological arousal in laboratory settings. We cannot make any absolute claims about the extent to which people's physiological reactivity in these experimental situations predicts their long-term health. Ideally, we would address this issue with a longitudinal study, observing people's physiological reactivity to stress in diverse situations and tracking their health over time. This kind of study would help us determine whether people's PEI predicts the physiological reactivity they typically demonstrate in stressful situations, and whether this reactivity in turn predicts long-term health outcomes.

Traits and styles relevant to emotional intelligence and longer-term health outcomes

In the absence of any longitudinal studies to date examining PEI, physiological reactivity, and health outcomes, we can turn to numerous studies that have looked at long-term health in conjunction with personality traits and coping styles that are conceptually relevant to emotional intelligence. Although few of these studies have examined physiological reactivity to stress as a mediator between any EI-relevant variables and long-term health, they nonetheless provide intriguing support for a possible association between emotional intelligence and health.

In one emotional disclosure study, Pennebaker and colleagues examined whether using specific kinds of words to describe emotional experiences predicts subsequent physical health (Pennebaker et al., 1997). People who used increased numbers of words indicating insight and causal thinking across several days of writing showed improved physical health – as gauged by their symptom reports and how often they visited their doctors – up to six months after writing. Demonstrating insight and causal understanding into emotional life events may require key emotional intelligence skills: in order to analyze an emotional experience in causal terms, a person needs to identify their feelings about the event, understand how those feelings progressed during and after the event, recognize the emotional impact the event had on others and how their emotions, in turn, influenced their experience of the event, and regulate the emotions they experienced while recollecting the event. Armed with these competencies, people high in emotional intelligence may be more likely to use insight and causal words when writing about emotional experiences in their lives, which might optimize their health in the long run.

Other studies have linked cognitive processing and immune outcomes. In one disclosure study, people who showed higher levels of experiential involvement in their disclosure and decreased cognitive avoidance of their stressful topics over the course of three disclosure sessions showed decreased EBV antibody titers (Lutgendorf *et al.*, 1994). Cognitive processing and the discovery of meaning have also been examined among men with HIV who had recently lost a close friend or partner to AIDS (Bower *et al.*, 1998). Men who actively and deliberately thought about the death were more likely to find meaning in the event. They experienced a major shift in values, priorities, or perspectives in response to the loss. Men who found meaning showed less rapid decline in CD4 T-cell levels two and three years later and had lower rates of AIDS-related mortality. Finding meaning in a traumatic event may require the same emotional intelligence skills that we have suggested underlie the use of insight and causal words in emotional disclosure. The men who found meaning in the deaths of their friends and partners may have been particularly apt at identifying, understanding, and regulating their emotions, which allowed them to understand and reinterpret life events in new, meaningful ways. Further research investigating the role of emotional intelligence in cognitive processing and the discovery of meaning is warranted.

Another health area that bears conceptual relevance to emotional intelligence is trait hostility, as it may reflect an inability to regulate negative feelings. Scientific interest in hostility grew out of work on Type A behavior. Now a cliché commonly applied to Wall Street bankers, corporate lawyers, and Ivy League students, the Type A behavior pattern was originally characterized by impatience, time urgency, competitiveness, and easily aroused overt hostility (Friedman *et al.*, 1986). Although many laboratory, clinical, and epidemiologic studies found links between Type A behavior and the prevalence and incidence of coronary heart disease (CHD), more recent work (including re-analysis of past studies) has found that hostility is the only component of Type A behavior that reliably and independently predicts heart disease (Miller *et al.*, 1996).

We suggest that overt hostility is marked by an absence of key emotional intelligence competencies, particularly the abilities to identify and regulate one's emotions. People high in trait hostility express intensely negative reactions to everyday stressors; whether they are waiting in a long line at the bank, arguing with a spouse, or trying to order airline tickets over the Internet, they do not attempt to moderate these reactions. Hostile people might be unable to identify the detrimental impact that their hostility has on themselves and others; in fact, their hostility might be so habitual that they cannot even identify their behaviors as hostile.

Several studies have examined trait hostility and cardiovascular arousal. In numerous laboratory studies comparing hostile and non-hostile populations, hostile people demonstrated greater cardiovascular responses to social provocation, including being interrupted during a task (Suarez & Williams, 1989), facing a disparaging opponent during a rigged game (Glass *et al.*, 1980), role-playing a social conflict (Hardy & Smith, 1988), attempting unsolvable tasks with bad instructions (Weidner *et al.*, 1989), and discussing a marital problem with a spouse (Miller *et al.*, 1999).

A recent study that measured ambulatory blood pressure over three days found that people high in trait hostility consistently showed elevated SBP, DBP, and heart rate regardless of concurrent mood; people low in hostility only exhibited high BP when they experienced negative mood (Raikkonen *et al.*, 1999). This sustained cardiovascular arousal may be one mechanism by which overt hostility and, by extension, Type A behavior increase a person's risk of CHD (Raikkonen *et al.*, 1999).

These findings suggest interesting parallels to our own. Both people low in PEI and people high in hostility have shown heightened physiological arousal after exposure to quite similar laboratory stressors, including social conflict, impossible tasks, and time constraints. Given these shared patterns of response to laboratory stress and our proposed association between hostility and emotional intelligence deficits, some people reporting low PEI may tend to experience heightened cardiovascular arousal on a regular, everyday basis, even in the absence of stressors and negative mood. This sustained reactivity could predispose these people to increased risk of CHD. Note that not all people reporting low PEI necessarily fit this model; whether people who report low PEI but do not demonstrate high trait hostility would show these cardiovascular patterns is unclear. It is also unclear whether PEI would predict cardiovascular arousal independently of hostility in people both low in PEI and high in hostility. Future research should examine potential deficits in emotional intelligence among people high in trait hostility, as well as links between PEI, ambulatory blood pressure, and cardiovascular morbidity and mortality.

Fortunately, the impact of hostility and potential emotional intelligence deficits on CHD might be reversible. In a study by Friedman *et al.* (1986), 592 post myocardial infarction patients received Type A behavioral counseling in addition to group cardiac counseling. At the end of 4.5 years, 35.1 percent of these patients showed reduced Type A behavior, compared to only 9.8 percent of people in a control group. The cardiac recurrence rate for people in the experimental group was only 12.9 percent, compared to 21.2 percent in the control group and 28.2 percent in a standard care group. In a highly publicized study by Ornish and colleagues (1998), patients with moderate to severe CHD participated in an intensive five-year lifestyle modification program that involved a vegetarian diet, exercise, smoking cessation, and – most relevant to this discussion – stress management training and group psychosocial support. Patients in this experimental program evidenced reversals in their coronary atherosclerosis after five years; control group patients showed continued thickening in their arteries and experienced twice as many cardiac events. Ornish has not determined the extent to which each of the program's components (diet, exercise, psychological training, etc.) specifically contributed to cardiac outcomes. However, a recent study connecting Transcendental Meditation training with regression in atherosclerosis indicates that stress management training alone – without diet or exercise interventions – may have a significant impact on cardiac outcomes (Castillo-Richmond *et al.*, 2000).

Each of these interventions emphasized skills relevant to emotional competencies. Friedman and his colleagues counseled people on their Type A behavior; as we have discussed, Type A behavior may involve deficiencies in emotional competencies relevant to the management of hostility, and so counseling that serves to alleviate Type A behavior could also promote emotional intelligence skills, such as identifying and regulating the expression of negative emotions. Patients in Ornish's program very likely learned to moderate their negative emotions in the stress management component of his training sessions, and to express and better understand their feelings through group psychosocial activities. People practicing Transcendental Meditation presumably learned to observe, acknowledge, and release their negative emotions. It thus seems that interventions aimed at cardiovascular patients may foster emotional intelligence skills; because these programs have been shown to enhance long-term health, they might suggest a link between emotional intelligence and health. Unfortunately, these speculations rest on ambiguities about causal directionality and rather unspecified mechanisms. Emotional skills gleaned from psychosocial interventions might enhance health through health behavior, stress physiology, or some other mechanism such as an increased ability to elicit social support from others (Kennedy-Moore & Watson, 1999); or, emotional intelligence and enhanced health may both be independent products of these programs. Future research is needed to clarify these issues.

Psychosocial intervention studies with cancer and AIDS populations also bear relevance to the emotional intelligence–health link. In Spiegel *et al.*'s (1989) now-famous intervention study, metastatic breast cancer patients were randomly assigned to an expressive supportive group therapy condition. The group met weekly for one year and helped patients deal with expressing their thoughts and feelings, coping with illness, enhancing relationships, and directly facing their fears and sadness about cancer. A ten-year follow-up showed that women in this intervention condition survived significantly longer than women in the control group (36.6 months vs. 18.9 months).

Similarly, researchers at the University of Miami randomly assigned 38 post-surgical malignant melanoma patients to a structured psychiatric intervention program that emphasized stress awareness, stress information, enhancement of coping skills and development of coping skills (Fawzy *et al.*, 1990a, 1990b, 1993). Compared to a control group, melanoma patients in the intervention group showed reduced affective distress, more active coping, and enhanced immunity six months later. At a subsequent six-year follow-up, intervention patients had a significantly higher survival rate (91 percent) than people in the control group (21 percent). Increases in active behavioral coping over the six-month intervention period predicted lower rates of recurrence or death.

Other intervention programs of this kind have shown encouraging results for individuals with HIV. For example, Antoni *et al.* (1991) assigned gay men unaware of their HIV serostatus to a cognitive behavioral stress management intervention. Men in the intervention group explored awareness of stress and negative thoughts, cognitive restructuring techniques, and relaxation methods, among other things.

Five weeks into the program, the men were tested for HIV and informed of their serostatus; the intervention continued for another five weeks. Relative to men in the control group, men in the intervention group who discovered that they were HIV positive showed a stress-buffering advantage in their immune titers across the notification period and consistent, positive immune changes over the ten-week intervention period (Antoni et al., 1991; Esterling et al., 1992). Over the next two years, the HIV positive men who coped by engaging denial and were low in adherence during the intervention period (frequently missing group sessions and not practicing relaxation methods, for example) showed faster disease progression, even after controlling for initial disease severity (Ironson et al., 1995).

These studies are only examples of an ongoing area of research; it is worth noting that other psychosocial intervention programs have not always affected the immunity and/or survival rates of cancer and AIDS patients (e.g. Coates et al., 1989; Gellert et al., 1993). Nonetheless, the findings discussed offer support for an association between emotional intelligence and long-term health outcomes. Although the intervention programs were not specifically designed to enhance emotional intelligence, they might have done so indirectly by teaching people to identify and express their emotions in supportive group environments. Moreover, all of the programs emphasized active coping; as we have discussed elsewhere, effective coping involves core emotional intelligence competencies, including understanding the implications of how we are feeling and regulating our emotional experiences (Salovey et al., 1999). These interventions thus seem to have promoted emotional competencies; because they also predicted improved long-term health outcomes, they suggest a link between emotional intelligence and health. Obviously, these suggestions are speculative; future interventions are needed that specifically teach and assess emotional intelligence and its potential relationship to health outcomes. As a start in designing such an emotional intelligence enhancing intervention, one may wish to look at school-based curricula that have been developed with these goals (e.g. Elias et al., 1997; Schilling, 1996).

Conclusion

The skills relevant to emotional intelligence may be linked in significant ways to health and illness. The mechanisms accounting for these connections may be discovered at multiple levels – psychophysiological, cognitive, and behavioral. At present, however, research in this potentially rewarding area has been limited because of the reliance on self-report measures of emotional competencies, including the biases and errors that are a part of the process of reflecting on one's own mental and emotional states and behavioral skills. This issue compromised the conclusions that could be drawn from the burgeoning literature on alexithymia in previous decades, and it threatens to comprise the emotional intelligence area in the present decade as well. It is with pleasure, then, that we recognize the emergence of ability-based assessment tools for capturing individuals' strengths and weaknesses in this domain (e.g. Mayer et al., 1999, 2003). We suspect that by the time this volume is published, these measures will be easily available, and we encourage investigators of links between emotional skills and competencies and health outcomes to take the time to assess patients and healthy participants with them.

King Solomon proclaimed that "a merry heart doeth good like a medicine" (Proverbs 17:22). We suspect, however, that mere merriment will not be enough. Health seems more likely to result from being able to express and appraise emotions clearly, understand them, use them to facilitate cognitive activities, and regulate them adaptively (and not just hedonistically). We look forward to the inevitable breakthroughs and insights supported by systematic inquiry in this field.

Acknowledgments

Preparation of this chapter was facilitated by the following grants: American Cancer Society (RPG-93-028-05-PBP), National Cancer Institute (R01-CA68427), and National Institute of Mental Health (P01-MH/DA56826). We also acknowledge funding from the Ethel F. Donaghue Foundation Women's Health Investigator Program at Yale University.

References

Antoni, M.H., Bagget, L., Ironson, G., LaPerriere, A., August, S., Limas, N., Schneiderman, N., & Fletcher, M.A. (1991). Cognitive–behavioral stress management intervention buffers distress responses and immunologic changes following notification of HIV-1 seropositivity. *Journal of Consulting and Clinical Psychology*, **59**, 906–915.

Baumeister, R.F. (1991). *Escaping the self*. New York: Basic Books.

Bower, J.E., Kemeny, M.E., Taylor, S., & Fahey, J.L (1998). Cognitive processing, discovery of meaning, CD4 decline, and AIDS-related mortality among bereaved HIV-seropositive men. *Journal of Consulting and Clinical Psychology*, **66**, 979–986.

Brandon, T.H. (1994). Negative affect as a motivation to smoke. *Current Directions in Psychological Science*, **3**, 33–37.

Carels, R.A., Sherwood, A., & Blumenthal, J.A. (1998). Psychosocial influences on blood pressure during daily life. *International Journal of Psychophysiology*, **28**, 117–129.

Castillo-Richmond, A., Schneider, R.H., Alexander, C.N., Cook, R., Myers, H., Nidich, S., Rainforth, M., & Salerno, J. (2000). Effects of stress reduction on carotid atherosclerosis in hypertensive African Americans. *Stroke*, **31**, 568–573.

Coates, T.J., McKusick, L., Kuno, R., & Stites, D.P. (1989). Stress reduction training changed number of sexual partners but not immune function in men with HIV. *American Journal of Public Health*, **79**, 885–887.

Dienstbier, R.A. (1989). Arousal and physiological toughness: implications for mental and physical health. *Psychological Review*, **96**, 84–100.

Elias, M.J., Zins, J.E., Weissberg, R.P., Frey, K.S., Greenberg, M.T., Haynes, N.M., Kessler, R., Schwab-Stone, M.E., & Shriver, T.P. (1997). *Promoting social and emotional learning: Guidelines for educators*. Alexandria, VA: ASCD.

Esterling, B.A., Antoni, M.H., Schneiderman, N., Carver, C.S., LaPerriere, A., Ironson, G., Klimas, N.G., & Fletcher, M.A. (1992). Psychosocial modulation of antibody to

Epstein-Barr viral capsid antigen and human herpes viruses type-6 in HIV-1 infected and at-risk gay men. *Psychosomatic Medicine*, **52**, 397–410.

Fawzy, F.I., Cousins, N., Fawzy, N.W., Kemeny, M.E., Elashoff, R., & Morton, D. (1990a). A structured psychiatric intervention for cancer patients: I. Changes over time in methods of coping and affective disturbance. *Archives of General Psychiatry*, **47**, 720–725.

Fawzy, F.I., Fawzy, N.W., Hyun, C.S., Elashoff, R., Guthrie, D., Fahey, J.L., & Morton, D.L. (1993). Malignant melanoma: effects of an early structured psychiatric intervention, coping, and affective state on recurrence and survival 6 years later. *Archives of General Psychiatry*, **50**, 681–689.

Fawzy, F.I., Kemeny, M., Fawzy, N.W., Elashoff, R., Morton, D., Cousins, N., & Fahey, J.L. (1990b). A structured psychiatric intervention for cancer patients: II. Changes over time in immunological measures. *Archives of General Psychiatry*, **47**, 729–735.

Friedman, M., Thoresen, C.E., Gill, J.J., Ulmer, D., Powell, L.H., Price, V.A., Brown, B., Thompson, L., Rabin, D.D., & Breall, W.S. (1986). Alteration of Type A behavior and its effect on cardiac recurrences in post myocardial infarction patients: summary of the results of the Recurrent Coronary Prevention Project. *American Heart Journal*, **112**, 653–665.

Gellert, G.A., Maxwell, R.M., & Siegel, B.S. (1993). Survival of breast cancer patients receiving adjunctive psychosocial support therapy: a 10-year follow-up study. *Journal of Clinical Oncology*, **11**, 66–69.

Glass, D., Krakoff, L., & Contrada, R. (1980). Effect of harassment and competition upon cardiovascular and catecholamine responses in Type A and Type B – individuals. *Psychophysiology*, **17**, 453–463.

Goldman, S.L., Kraemer, D.T., & Salovey, P. (1996). Beliefs about mood moderate the relationship of stress to illness and symptom reporting. *Journal of Psychosomatic Research*, **41**, 115–128.

Goleman, D. (1995). *Emotional intelligence*. New York: Bantam.

Goleman, D. (1998). *Working with emotional intelligence*. New York: Bantam.

Greenberg, M.A. & Stone, A.A. (1992). Emotional disclosure about traumas and its relation to health: effects of previous disclosure and trauma severity. *Journal of Personality and Social Psychology*, **63**, 75–84.

Hardy, J. & Smith, T. (1988). Cynical hostility and vulnerability to disease: social support, life stress, and physiological response to conflict. *Health Psychology*, **7**, 447–459.

Herbert, T.B. & Cohen, S. (1993). Depression and immunity: a meta-analytic review. *Psychological Bulletin*, **113**, 472–486.

Ironson, G., Antoni, M., & Lutgendorf, S. (1995). Can psychological interventions affect immunity and survival? Present findings and suggested targets with a focus on cancer and human immunodeficiency virus. *Mind/Body Medicine*, **1**, 85–110.

Kennedy-Moore, E. & Watson, J.C. (1999). *Expressing emotion: Myths, realities, and therapeutic strategies*. New York: Guilford.

King, L.A. & Miner, K.N. (2000). Writing about perceived benefits of traumatic events: implications for physical health. *Personality and Social Psychology Bulletin*, **26**, 220–230.

Lutgendorf, S., Antoni, M., Kumar, M., & Schneiderman, N. (1994). Changes in cognitive coping strategies predict EBV-antibody titre change following a stressor disclosure induction. *Journal of Psychosomatic Research*, **38**, 63–78.

McEwen, B. & Stellar, E. (1993). Stress and the individual: mechanisms leading to disease. *Archives of Internal Medicine*, **153**, 2093–2191.

Manuck, S.B. & Krantz, D.S. (1984). Psychophysiologic reactivity in coronary heart disease. *Behavioral Medicine Update*, **6**, 11–15.

Mayer, J.D., Caruso, D.R., & Salovey, P. (1999). Emotional intelligence meets traditional standards for an intelligence. *Intelligence*, **27**, 267–298.

Mayer, J.D. & Salovey, P. (1997). What is emotional intelligence? In P. Salovey & D. Sluyter (eds), *Emotional development and emotional intelligence: Implications for educators* (pp. 3–31). New York: Basic Books.

Mayer, J.D., Salovey, P., Caruso, D.R., & Sitacenios, G. (2003). Measuring emotional intelligence with MSCEIT v2.0. *Emotion*, **3**, 97–105.

Miller, G.E., Dopp, J.M., Myers, H.F., Fahey, J.L., & Stevens, S.Y. (1999). Psychosocial predictors of natural killer cell mobilization during marital conflict. *Health Psychology*, **18**, 262–271.

Miller, T., Smith, T., Turner, C., Guijarro, M., & Hallet, A. (1996). A meta-analytic review of research on hostility and physical health. *Psychological Bulletin*, **119**, 322–348.

Ornish, D., Scherwitz, L.W., Billings, J.H., Brown, S.E., Gould, K.L., Merrit, T.A., Sparler, S., Armstrong, W.T., Ports, T.A., Kirkeeide, R.L., Hogeboom, C., & Brand, R.J. (1998). Intensive lifestyle changes for reversal of coronary heart disease. *Journal of the American Medical Association*, **280**, 2001–2007.

Pennebaker, J.W. & Beall, S. (1986). Confronting a traumatic event: toward an understanding of inhibition of behavior. *Journal of Personality and Social Psychology*, **49**, 1427–1433.

Pennebaker, J.W., Colder, M., & Sharp, L.W. (1990). Accelerating the coping process. *Journal of Personality and Social Psychology*, **58**, 528–537.

Pennebaker, J.W., Hughes, C.F., & O'Heeron, R.M. (1987). The psychophysiology of confession: linking inhibitory and psychosomatic processes. *Journal of Personality and Social Psychology*, **52**, 781–793.

Pennebaker, J.W., Kiecolt-Glaser, J.E., & Glaser, R. (1988). Disclosure of traumas and immune function: health implications for psychotherapy. *Journal of Consulting and Clinical Psychology*, **56**, 239–245.

Pennebaker, J.W., Mayne, T., & Francis, M.E. (1997). Linguistic predictors of adaptive bereavement. *Journal of Personality and Social Psychology*, **72**, 863–871.

Pennebaker, J.W. & Seagal, J.D. (1999). Forming a story: the health benefits of narrative. *Journal of Clinical Psychology*, **55**, 1243–1254.

Petrie, K.J., Booth, R.J., Pennebaker, J.W., Davison, K.P., & Thomas, M.G. (1995). Disclosure of trauma and immune response to a hepatitis B vaccination program. *Journal of Consulting and Clinical Psychology*, **63**, 787–792.

Raikkonen, K., Matthews, K.A., Flory, J.D., & Owens, J.F. (1999). Effects of hostility on ambulatory blood pressure and mood during daily living in healthy adults. *Health Psychology*, **18**, 44–53.

Reed, M.H. & Aspinwall, L.G. (1998). Self-affirmation reduces biased processing of health-risk information. *Motivation and Emotion*, **22**, 99–132.

Salovey, P., Bedell, B.T., Detweiler, J.E., & Mayer, J.D. (1999). Coping intelligently: emotional intelligence and the coping process. In C.R. Snyder (ed.), *Coping: the psychology of what works* (pp. 141–164). New York: Oxford University Press.

Salovey, P. & Birnbaum, D. (1989). Influence of mood on health-relevant cognitions. *Journal of Personality and Social Psychology*, **57**, 539–551.

Salovey, P. & Mayer, J.D. (1990). Emotional intelligence. *Imagination, Cognition, and Personality*, **9**, 185–211.

Salovey, P., Mayer, J.D., Goldman, S., Turvey, C., & Palfai, T. (1995). Emotional attention, clarity, and repair: exploring emotional intelligence using the Trait Meta-Mood Scale. In J.D. Pennebaker (ed.), *Emotion, disclosure, and health* (pp. 125–154). Washington, DC: American Psychological Association.

Salovey, P., Rothman, A.J., Detweiler, J.E., & Steward, W.T. (2000). Emotional states and physical health. *American Psychologist*, **55**, 110–121.

Salovey, P., Woolery, A., & Mayer, J.D. (2001). Emotional intelligence: conceptualization and measurement. In G.J.O. Fletcher & M.S. Clark (eds), *Blackwell handbook of social psychology: Interpersonal processes* (pp. 279–307). Malden, MA: Blackwell.

Salovey, P., Woolery, A., Stroud, L., & Epel, E. (2002). Perceived emotional intelligence, stress reactivity, and health: further explorations using the Trait Meta-Mood Scale. *Psychology and Health*, **17**, 611–627.

Schilling, D. (1996). *Fifty activities for teaching emotional intelligence*. Torrance, CA: Innerchoice Publishing.

Smith, T.W. (1992). Hostility and health: current status of a psychosomatic hypothesis. *Health Psychology*, **11**, 139–150.

Smyth, J.M. (1998). Written emotional expression: effect sizes, outcome types, and moderating variables. *Journal of Consulting and Clinical Psychology*, **66**, 174–184.

Smyth, J.M. (1999). Written disclosure: evidence, potential mechanism, and potential treatment. *Advances in Mind–Body Medicine*, **15**, 161–195.

Smyth, J.M., Stone, A.A., Hurewitz, A., & Kaell, A. (1999). Effects of writing about stressful experiences on symptom reduction in patients with asthma or rheumatoid arthritis: a randomized trial. *Journal of the American Medical Association*, **281**, 1304–1309.

Spiegel, D., Bloom, J.R., Kraemer, H.C., & Gottheil, E. (1989). Effect of psychosocial treatment on survival of patients with metastatic breast cancer. *Lancet*, **2**, 888–901.

Stone, A.A., Marco, C.A., Cruise, C.E., Cox, D.S., & Neale, J.M. (1996). Are stress-induced immunological changes mediated by mood? A closer look at how both desirable and undesirable daily events influence sIgA antibody. *International Journal of Behavioral Medicine*, **3**, 1–13.

Suarez, E. & Williams, R. (1989). Situational determinants of cardiovascular and emotional reactivity in high and low hostile men. *Psychosomatic Medicine*, **51**, 404–418.

Watson, D. (2000). *Mood and temperament*. New York: Guilford Press.

Weidner, G., Friend, R., Ficarrotto, T., & Mendell, N. (1989). Hostility and cardiovascular reactivity to stress in women and men. *Psychosomatic Medicine*, **51**, 36–45.

Chapter 10

The repressive coping style and avoidance of negative affect*

Lynn B. Myers and Nazanin Derakshan

Introduction

This chapter presents evidence that individuals who possess a repressive coping style (repressors) avoid negative affect and consequently answer many self-report measures in an overly positive fashion. A potential link between repressive coping and adverse physical health is also discussed.

It has been more than 20 years since interest was renewed in repression as an individual difference variable. Weinberger *et al.* (1979) used measures of trait anxiety and defensiveness to identify a group of individuals who were described as possessing a repressive coping style. Repressors are identified by their low scores on self-report measures of trait anxiety (measured by various trait anxiety scales, e.g. the Bendig version of the Manifest Anxiety Scale; Bendig, 1956) and high scores on defensiveness (usually measured with the Marlowe-Crowne Social Desirability Scale; Crowne & Marlowe, 1964). Apart from the repressor group, three control groups are usually identified using the same typology: a further low trait anxiety group who are low on defensiveness (low-anxious) and two high trait anxiety groups, one of which is low on defensiveness (high-anxious) and one which is high on defensiveness (defensive high-anxious). The seminal Weinberger *et al.* (1979) study and numerous later studies (e.g. Benjamins *et al.*, 1994; Derakshan & Eysenck, 1997; Jamner & Schwartz, 1986; Newton & Contrada, 1992) found that repressors dissociate their somatic reactions from their perceptions of distress, reporting low levels of distress and anxiety but exhibiting high levels of physiological activity; whereas high-anxious participants exhibit the opposite pattern of response and low-anxious participants report similar low levels of distress to repressors but are not high on physiological stress measures. Studies which have included a defensive high-anxious group have found that this group do not show the repressors' style of dissociation (e.g. Asendorpf & Scherer, 1983). As this discrepancy between physiological and self-report measures of distress is one of the defining aspects of possessing a repressive coping style, it is discussed in more detail in the next section.

---

* This chapter is based on Myers, L.B. (2000). Identifying repressors: a methodological issue for health psychology. *Psychology and Health*, **15**, 205–214. (www.tandf.co.uk)

Repressive coping and discrepancies between self-reported anxiety, physiological, and behavioral indices of anxiety

The findings reported in the previous section indicate that repressors appear to be more emotionally reactive than low-anxious individuals and at least as emotionally reactive as the high-anxious individuals. It is believed that repressors employ a wide variety of defensive strategies to minimise the conscious level of experienced anxiety and in fact are capable of not experiencing anxiety at the conscious level of awareness (Derakshan & Eysenck, 1998, 1999). Furthermore, it has been stated that repressors have difficulty coming to terms with this discrepancy. Jamner and Schwartz (1985) reported that it took a number of months for a repressor client to show positive correlations between his subjective experience and his physiological responses of anxiety.

Consequently, "low-anxiety" individuals are no longer a homogeneous group but are divided into repressors and (truly) low-anxious as the low-anxious group do not show the repressor pattern of discrepancy. In anxiety research it has been shown that the high-anxious individuals show a strong tendency to attend selectively to threatening material in the environment (selective attentional bias) and a tendency to interpret potentially ambiguous stimuli in a threatening manner (interpretive bias); on the other hand, the "low-anxiety" group are believed not to show any bias (see Matthew & MacLeod, 1994, for review). In Eysenck's (1997) revised theory of anxiety, it is argued that repressors and not the truly low-anxious show opposite biases to that of the high-anxious, i.e. they are believed to avoid threatening material and interpret ambiguous material in a non-threatening manner. As a consequence of these biases (which are stronger under conditions of high stress), repressors should experience less anxiety and the high-anxious more anxiety. The existence of these biases can help explain in part the discrepancies that are consistently found in the repressor group. In addition, Eysenck (1997) predicted that these biases should apply to internal information (behavior and physiology) as well as external information.

Derakshan and Eysenck (1997, 1999, 2001) conducted a series of experiments to test the above predictions systematically. They examined behavioral anxiety (e.g. bodily movements, facial anxiety, speech anxiety) as well as physiological anxiety. Although physiological and autonomic reactivity can be used to indicate the experience of anxiety, it is not yet understood whether this reactivity is due to excitatory or inhibitory processes or both, and whether it reflects the unconscious or conscious experience of anxiety. The time course for the experience of anxiety is currently being investigated by Derakshan et al. (2002).

Derakshan and Eysenck (1997) examined whether repressors would show opposite interpretive biases for behavioral and physiological measures of anxiety. Repressors, low-anxious, high-anxious, and defensive high-anxious groups were asked to give a public speech in front of a small audience of six, while their heart rate reactivity was recorded and they were videotaped. Various self-reported anxiety measures were taken during the speech. While repressors' heart rate indicated that they were as anxious as the high-anxious and defensive high-anxious individuals, their reported anxiety levels were as low as the low-anxious individuals. When given feedback about their heart rate reactivity, repressors denied that their heart rate ever did increase and claimed that even if it did, the increase was due to the public speech task being exciting and challenging rather than it being threatening and stressful. The high-anxious and defensive high-anxious individuals showed the opposite pattern and the low-anxious did not show any bias.

With respect to behavioral anxiety, two independent judges used the Timed Behavioral Checklist (Paul, 1966) to rate the participants' level of anxiety on various scales such as speech anxiety, facial anxiety, eye contact, and passive and active behavioral anxiety. The judges rated repressors as being as behaviorally anxious as the high-anxious and defensive high-anxious individuals and significantly more anxious than the low-anxious individuals, and this effect was more profound for speech anxiety ratings. However, this was inconsistent with repressors' ratings of their own behavioral anxiety. When asked to rate their behavioral anxiety levels using the videotape, it was found that repressors' ratings for their own behavioral anxiety were much lower than the judges' ratings. However, repressors' ratings of other participants' behavioral anxiety did not differ from those of the judges. This finding indicates that repressors' minimization of threat seems to be confined to "self" and did not extend to ratings of other people's behavioral anxiety.

Repressors' denial of their increased heart rate reactivity during stressful situations, such as the one used above, can indicate that repressors are generally unaware of their internal states. In order to test this hypothesis, Derakshan and Eysenck (2001) manipulated the level of self-focused attention in a public speech task while measuring heart rate and self-focused attention, and videotaping participants. There were two conditions: a self-focus condition, where the participant was instructed to focus on himself or herself, and an "other-focus" condition in which they were instructed to focus on external surroundings. Physiological recordings showed that repressors' heart rate reactivity was highest in the self-focus (stressful) condition and lowest in the other-focus (non-stressful) conditions. However, measurements of self-focused attention and state anxiety indicated that they were lowest on these measures in the self-focus condition, compared to the other groups. It was statistically shown that repressors' low level of self-focused attention accounted for a large part of their low levels of reported anxiety. This finding suggests that in order not to experience high levels of anxiety, repressors may avoid engaging in self-regulatory processes as indicated by their avoidance in focusing on their internal states once directed to do so. The authors also examined discrepancies between standardized scores of physiological reactivity as measured by heart rate, behavioral anxiety (as measured by independent judges using the videotape information), and self-reported anxiety. Repressors had consistently higher levels of behavioral anxiety and physiological reactivity than self-reported anxiety in the stressful condition (self-focus) as opposed to the other conditions.

Discrepancies between heightened levels of behavioral anxiety and low self-reported anxiety can be used as a more direct indication of repressors' experience of anxiety at least from how they appear to an observer/independent judge's view. Overall, it seems that discrepancies between autonomic indicators of stress and reported stress need to be examined more systematically. For example, it is not clear whether physiological reactivity at early stages of information processing reflects vigilance for threat-related material or avoidance of such material. It seems logical to assume, from a motivational perspective, that repressors use their inhibitory or defensive strategies at later stages of processing in order to minimise the impact of early registration of threat. Changes in time course of such processes can be assessed through detailed examination of online physiological recordings accompanied with changes in electrical activities in the brain, e.g. prefrontal brain asymmetry. This needs to be investigated in future studies.

Defining repressive coping

There are a number of important and complex issues in this area of research. Although the Weinberger *et al.* (1979) trait anxiety/defensiveness method has become an increasingly popular method of defining repressive coping, different measures of trait anxiety and defensiveness are used as well as varying ways of identifying repressors and control groups (Myers, 1995).

Trait anxiety

The Manifest Anxiety Scale is a frequently used measure of trait anxiety in repressive coping research, in both its original form (Taylor, 1953; e.g. Weinberger *et al.*, 1979) and the short form (Bendig, 1956; e.g. Davis, 1987). Other trait anxiety measures such as the Spielberger Trait Anxiety scale (Spielberger *et al.*, 1970; e.g. Dawkins & Furnham, 1989) and the Neuroticism Scale of the Eysenck Personality Inventory (EPI, Eysenck & Eysenck, 1964; e.g. Gudjonsson, 1981) have also been used. Measures of trait anxiety have been found to be highly correlated (e.g. Slough *et al.*, 1984; Sullivan & Roberts, 1969).

Defensiveness

The Marlowe-Crowne Social Desirability Scale is invariably used to measure defensiveness. However, the EPI-Lie scale has occasionally been used as a measure of defensiveness. For example, Gudjonsson (1981) used the latter scale, although due to the small number of items on the Lie scale he included the Marlowe-Crowne Social Desirability Scale as an additional defensiveness score. He reported a high positive correlation between the two defensiveness scales ($r = 0.71$).

Other measures

More recently, Weinberger developed the Weinberger Adjustment Inventory (WAI; Weinberger, 1989, reported in Weinberger, 1990) which can be used to measure repressive coping. Derakshan and Eysenck (1997) found that this was a comparable method to the trait anxiety/defensiveness method, with the distress subscale of the WAI correlating highly with trait anxiety (0.79) and the repressive defensiveness and the self-restraint subscales of the WAI correlating with the Marlowe-Crowne Social Desirability Scale (0.68 and 0.47 respectively).

Identifying groups

One of the major difficulties with this area of research is the fact that the trait anxiety/defensiveness method depends on categorizing people into groups based on their location along two dimensions. For example, various studies identify their participants at the beginning of the study by screening a large number of potential participants and choosing extreme scorers on trait anxiety and defensiveness to define repressors, low-anxious, high-anxious and (possibly) defensive–high-anxious groups (e.g. Derakshan & Eysenck, 1997, 1998; Myers & Brewin, 1994, 1995; Myers & Steed, 1999). Other studies have used the entire available pool of participants and hence do not use such stringent measures in defining different groups, usually using median splits on trait anxiety and defensiveness to identify repressors and control groups, thereby not losing any potential participants (e.g. Burns, 2000; Shaw et al., 1986). Therefore, although measuring instruments used to identify repressors are comparable, it is important to note how repressors and control groups have been defined in different studies.

Eliciting information from repressors

Repressors constitute a significant proportion of the population, with prevalence estimates ranging between 10 and 20 percent (Myers & Reynolds, 2000; Phipps & Srivastava, 1997). There is a debate over the best way of eliciting information from repressors, as many studies over the past ten years have shown repressors to be individuals who avoid negative affect and this is reflected in the way that they answer self-report measures. These issues are discussed below.

Repressive coping and avoidance of negative affect

What is the evidence that repressors avoid negative affect? In a comprehensive review, Weinberger (1990) conceptualised the repressive coping style as consisting of "people who fail to recognise their own affective responses . . . who consider maintaining low levels of negative affect central to their self-concept [and] are likely to employ a variety of strategies to avoid conscious knowledge of their genuine reactions" (p. 338). An extensive literature strongly indicates that repressors do indeed avoid negative affect. For example, a number of studies have demonstrated links between the repressive coping style and poor accessibility of negative autobiographical memories (e.g. Davis, 1987; Myers *et al.*, 1992). Other studies using both intentional and incidental recall tasks indicate that these findings are not specific to autobiographical memories and may operate on non-autobiographical negative material as well (Myers & Brewin, 1995; Myers *et al.*, 1998). Repressors have been found to use avoidant style of information processing (e.g. Fox, 1993; Myers & McKenna, 1996) and they appear to employ strategies in maintaining favorable images of their self-concept when this is threatened (Baumeister & Cairns, 1992; Newton & Contrada, 1992), which seems to be due to self-deception rather than impression management (Weinberger & Davidson, 1994). Consequently, repressors' avoidance of negative affect would make it extremely likely that they would answer self-report measures such as questionnaires and checklists in an overly positive fashion.

Repressive coping and self-report instruments

There is a body of research showing that repressors do indeed answer many self-report measures overly positively. Myers and Brewin (1996) were interested in investigating whether repressors would display "illusions of invulnerability" (see Taylor & Brown, 1988) more than nonrepressors. This was investigated with two of the illusions: unrealistic optimism or comparative optimism (the belief that we are more likely to experience pleasant events and less likely to experience negative events than our peers) and overly positive self-evaluations (the finding that individuals evaluate themselves more positively than others). Using self-report measures, repressors showed both of these illusions to a significantly greater extent than nonrepressors for negative self-related material. Myers and Brewin (1996) used mainly extreme-scoring participants on anxiety and defensiveness, omitting nearly 50 percent of the population. In a later study using a whole sample (Myers & Reynolds, 2000), the comparative optimism findings were replicated and extended to solely health-related events (e.g. asthma, bronchitis). Overall, repressors exhibited significantly greater comparative optimism than all nonrepressors for health-related events.

Two studies which used self-report instruments (Gomez & Weinberger, 1986, reported in Weinberger, 1990; Myers, 1996) found that repressors were significantly more likely to rate hypothetical negative events as being caused by a composite of external, unstable and specific factors compared to nonrepressors. This is an "opposite" attributional style to depressive-prone individuals, who typically attribute causality of negative events to internal, stable, and global causes (Abramson *et al.*, 1978).

The relationship between repressive coping and alexithymia was explored in two studies. Alexithymia is a personality style derived from clinical observations of patients with traditional psychosomatic diseases (Nemiah & Sifneos, 1970a; Chapter 8 of this volume). Alexithymic individuals show reduced or absent symbolic thinking as well as difficulties in recognizing and describing their own feelings and difficulties discriminating between bodily sensations and emotional states (see Chapter 8 for detailed descriptions). It has been proposed that alexithymia and repression are similar constructs (Nemiah & Sifneos, 1970b; Weinberger & Schwartz, 1990) or alternatively that alexithymia may be an aspect of repressive coping (Bonanno & Singer, 1990). However, studies using questionnaire measures of alexithymia indicated that repressors score significantly lower on alexithymia than nonrepressors (Myers, 1995; Newton & Contrada, 1994). These results may mean that repressors are truly low on alexithymia, or they may be due to limitations of the questionnaire methodology.

Two recent studies investigated the way in which repressors answer health-related questionnaires (Myers & Vetere, 1997). In the first study, repressors completed the Coping Resources Inventory (CRI; Hammer & Marting, 1988), a 60-item questionnaire used to identify resources currently available to individuals for managing stress. It measures resources in five domains: physical, cognitive, emotional, social, and spiritual/philosophical. Repressors rated themselves as having more total coping resources than nonrepressors. The same pattern of results was exhibited for each of the subscales. In the second study, repressors' responses were extended to other health-related measures. Two questionnaires were used: a measure of psychological symptoms (the 12-item General Health Questionnaire, GHQ-12; Goldberg, 1992) and a measure of physical symptoms (Pennebaker Inventory of Limbic Languidness, PILL; Pennebaker, 1982). Repressors compared to nonrepressors scored significantly lower on the PILL and the GHQ-12, indicating that repressors self-report low levels of both physical and psychological symptomatology.

In a recent study of children with cancer it was noted that repressors self-reported the lowest levels of depression (Phipps & Srivastava, 1997). Similar findings have been reported in earlier studies of patients with cancer (Canning et al., 1992; Jensen, 1987).

It should be noted that the majority of the above studies (Canning et al., 1992; Myers, 1995; 1996; Myers & Brewin, 1996; Myers & Reynolds, 2000; Myers & Vetere, 1997; Phipps & Srivastava, 1997) compared repressors with the high defensive group who are high on anxiety, the defensive high-anxious, and found that repressors significantly differed from this group. This indicated that the findings discussed were due to repressors' unique combination of low trait anxiety and high defensiveness and were not due to repressors' high scores on defensiveness alone.

In summary, the above studies indicate that repressors are overly positive on various self-report measures. These findings may be seen as another manifestation of the repressive coping style which is associated with avoidance of negative affect. Therefore, it appears that self-report measures may be a poor way of collecting data from this group. This is potentially problematic for health psychology as the majority of measuring instruments utilized are self-report instruments.

Other methodologies that have been used
to assess repressive coping

Are there ways to circumvent repressors' avoidance of negative affect? There is some evidence that repressors score differently on questionnaires compared to interview methodology. Firstly, evidence from three studies on repressors' childhood experience indicates that results are very different depending on the method of eliciting information. It was hypothesized that repressors would have had more unpleasant childhood experiences than nonrepressors (Myers & Brewin, 1994). In this study, a semi-structured interview was used which allowed raters to judge reports of childhood experiences according to their own predetermined criteria rather than relying simply on respondents' own judgments about the significance of these experiences. In the interview there are a number of specific questions such as "Do you think your parents approved of you up to the time when you were a teenager?" Independently of whether participants answer yes or no to this question, specific examples of occasions when their parents did/did not approve of them are elicited and form the basis of the interviewer ratings. Consistent with the hypothesis, repressors held a negative view of their fathers, with repressors reporting significantly more paternal antipathy and indifference and being significantly less emotionally or physically close to their fathers compared to nonrepressors (Myers & Brewin, 1994). However, a later study used a questionnaire measure of global childhood experience, the Parental Bonding Instrument (PBI; Parker *et al.*, 1979; Myers *et al.*, 1999). The PBI requires participants to consider generally the whole period of their childhood before they left home. Participants answer a series of questions about their mother and father and consider, for example, whether s/he "made me feel I wasn't wanted", or "frequently smiled at me". Results indicated that repressors reported a much more positive view of their fathers than nonrepressors, depicting their fathers as significantly more caring and less overprotecting (Myers *et al.*, 1999). Similarly, repressors compared to nonrepressors scored significantly lower on paternal overprotection and paternal rejection on another global measure of parenting: the Egna Minnen Beträffande Uppfostran (EMBU; Myers, 1999). The results of the semi-structured interview using specific examples of childhood supported the hypothesis that repressors had experienced unpleasant childhood experiences, compared with the global questionnaire measures in which repressors reported more positive childhood experiences, suggesting that the interview was a more appropriate measure of repressors' childhood experiences. It should be noted that it was not possible to ascertain from these results whether the difference was due to the nature of the questions (specific vs. global) or the nature or the instrument (interview vs. questionnaire), or both. These issues need exploring in further studies.

Secondly, repressors have shown a significantly lower score on a questionnaire measure of Type A behavior (Jenkins Activity Survey; Jenkins *et al.*, 1979) than nonrepressors. However, on an interview measure (the Structured Interview;

Friedman & Powell, 1984), they scored similarly to low-anxious non-repressors, a low-anxious group (Denollet, 1991).

Thirdly, there is some indirect evidence from research on "defensive deniers" (Shedler et al., 1993, p. 1117). Participants were divided into three groups on the basis of clinical assessment and self-report measures of mental health: (1) defensive deniers reported psychological well-being but were judged as distressed; (2) a healthy group reported psychological well-being and were judged as healthy; and (3) a distressed group reported psychological distress and were judged as distressed. Defensive deniers showed significantly higher physiological reactivity than the other two groups; hence, they exhibited a comparable physiological dissociation with low levels of self-reported distress to repressors (e.g. Derakshan & Eysenck, 1997). In addition, the authors proposed that defensive deniers are not healthy but may be prone to physical illness. The possible similarities between repressors and defensive deniers needs to be directly investigated in future studies.

What type of measures should we use?

The studies discussed above which investigated repressors' childhood experiences may give some clues as to how to elicit information from repressors (Myers & Brewin, 1994; Myers et al., 1999). Measures which either require participants to be specific in their answers, rather than making global ratings, or allow an independent rater to judge participants' responses may bypass the problem of repressors' avoidance in reporting negative affect.

One way of achieving this would be by using semi-structured interviews, a methodology gaining popularity in health psychology. For example, a number of researchers (e.g. Coyne & Gottlieb, 1996) have suggested the use of semi-structured interviews in the study of coping as a process, where the use of checklists is problematic. The problems of using checklists to study coping are well discussed in the literature (see Coyne & Gottlieb, 1996; Parker & Endler, 1992). Although it must be recognized that semi-structured interviews are time-consuming, costly and require training of interviewers and raters, some of these problems may be overcome. For example, the Myers and Brewin (1994) study used a brief parenting interview to investigate repressors' childhood experience. This interview overcame many of the potential problems due to its brief administration (approximately 20 minutes) and brief training required (a one-week course). This semi-structured interview identified a number of scales. Inter-rater reliability was calculated for these scales and was found to be good. Kappa was high for each of the ratings (0.90–0.95), with agreement between 92 and 96 percent.

Although there is considerable evidence to support the hypothesis that repressors answer self-report instruments in a positive fashion, repressors may do this less with certain self-report instruments. Repressors' failure to report negative affect may be limited to downplaying the negative rather than overstating the positive. For example, repressors did not differ from nonrepressors in their optimistic bias for positive events and they did not describe themselves more positively when using positive descriptors (Myers & Brewin, 1996). Repressors have been found to be more optimistic than nonrepressors about individual health events which were seen as personally controllable, such as suffering from asthma, but not for uncontrollable events, such as suffering from diabetes (Myers & Reynolds, 2000). In a repertory grid study, repressors compared to nonrepressors were more positive about certain elements in their lives, such as their father, but not others, e.g. "a person I like" (Myers *et al.*, 1999). On a measure of dispositional optimism (the Life Orientation Test; Scheier & Carver, 1985), repressors compared with nonrepressors reported significantly lower pessimism (negative items), but not higher optimism (positive items) (Myers & Steed, 1999).

Other studies suggest that if repressors are allowed to express themselves positively on some items of a self-report measure, they may rate themselves less positively on other items. For example, individuals who exhibit an avoidant adult attachment style have been described as devaluing the importance of relationships, reporting extremely positive relationships with their parents and downplaying the influence of childhood experiences (Dozier & Kobak, 1992), and therefore may be hypothesized as being similar to repressors. In a study investigating avoidant attachment and repressive coping, repressors compared to nonrepressors were significantly more likely to rate themselves as having an avoidant style of romantic attachment (a negative response), as long as they could also rate themselves as having a secure style (a positive response), but this pattern was not seen if they had to exclusively choose one style, where they would rate themselves as securely attached (Myers & Vetere, in press).

Similarly, repressors may rate themselves negatively on some items but not others. For example, a study used the Thought Control Questionnaire (Wells & Davis, 1994) to investigate whether individuals with different coping styles report using different strategies to suppress negative thoughts (Myers, 1998). Repressors compared to nonrepressors reported using significantly more distraction strategies and significantly fewer punishment strategies. Distraction may be seen as less negative than punishment.

Further research should investigate whether other methods are able to bypass repressors' tendency to report less negative affect and, hence, may be a useful way of collecting data from repressors. These methods could include information-processing paradigms which have become popular in pain research. For example, in response to ambiguous cues, pain patients compared to control participants systematically produced more pain-related associations (Pincus *et al.*, 1994). Using an emotional Stroop task, pain patients selectively processed pain-related cues at a strategic level but not an automatic level (Snider *et al.*, 2000). Such information-processing approaches could be extended to other areas of health psychology research. More qualitative methods may also be considered, such as diary studies and focus groups.

Do repressors have significantly worse health outcomes?

There is considerable evidence which indicates that the repressive coping style as defined by Weinberger *et al.* (1979) may be associated with adverse physical health. Some of this evidence is discussed below.

There are a number of studies which suggest a link between repressive coping and cancer. Jensen (1987) conducted a prospective study of women with a history of breast carcinoma who were followed up for two years. Patients exhibiting a repressive coping style were at greater risk of death from cancer: of 11 patients who died during follow-up, eight were repressors and repressors displayed more rapid progression of the disease than nonrepressors (1,755 days' remission for nonrepressors vs. 1,204 days for repressors). Other studies have found an increased incidence of repressors among cancer sufferers in children (Phipps & Srivastava, 1997), adolescents (Canning *et al.*, 1992), and women with breast cancer (Kreitler *et al.*, 1993).

A study by Jamner *et al.* (1988) suggested an association between repressive coping and impaired immune functioning. The authors found that repressors demonstrated decreased monocyte counts and elevated eosinophile counts. Similarly, Brown *et al.* (1989; reported in O'Leary, 1990) found that repressive coping was associated with reduced response to mitogens PHA and ConA.

There is also some evidence linking repressive coping with cardiovascular disease. For example, Shaw *et al.* (1986) examined the relationship between repressive coping, cardiac information and medical complications in predominantly male patients undergoing treatment for narrowed coronary arteries. Six months after treatment, repressors with high knowledge levels about cardiac disease and no history of myocardial infarction had a significantly higher risk of medical complications (e.g. hospitalisation for chest pain, myocardial infarction). Similarly, Niaura *et al.* (1992) found raised blood cholesterol levels in male repressors.

Repressive coping has also been linked to impaired pain perception (Burns 2000; Jamner *et al.*, 1986), high arousal during dental surgery (Fox *et al.*, 1989a) and colonoscopy (Fox *et al.*, 1989b), and changes in the menstrual cycle (Altemus *et al.*, 1988).

Therefore, it appears that possessing a repressive coping style is associated with negative health outcomes. It is postulated that this association is due to repressors not attending to somatic information (e.g. Schwartz, 1990). It seems likely that repressors' failure to pay attention to distress, as demonstrated by their dissociation between self-report and physiological measures of arousal, would produce adverse health outcomes, as somatic signs would be less likely to trigger health behaviors to relieve distress. This may be a critical factor in the development of disease.

Conclusions

A substantial amount of research exists to indicate that people who possess a repressive coping style, who form between 10 and 20 percent of the population, avoid negative affect and answer many self-report measures in an overly positive fashion. Consequently, the exclusive reliance on standard self-report methods is not a satisfactory way of eliciting information from repressors. More than one method of data collection should be used to overcome this problem. These methods may include semi-structured interviews and a carefully constructed self-report measure. These self-report measures should contain some items which allow repressors to express themselves positively so they may rate themselves less positively on other items and, where appropriate, could also require repressors to give descriptions of specific events without allowing them to evaluate those events emotionally. Wherever possible, a third method could be used, such as an information processing approach, or a more qualitative method. Research needs to be conducted on these methods, to determine their advantages and disadvantages in the context of repressive coping.

In addition, the potential link between repressive coping and adverse physical health makes repressors an important group for health psychologists to study in their own right. The implications of understanding the repressive coping style, in terms of its contribution to health outcomes, is crucial. In future studies it may be advisable to identify repressors' specific contribution to the results rather than to ignore this potentially significant source of individual differences.

References

Abramson, L.Y., Seligman, M.E.P., & Teasdale, J.D. (1978). Learned helplessness in humans: critique and reformulation. *Journal of Abnormal Psychology*, **87**, 49–74.

Altemus, M., Wexler, B.E., & Boulis, N. (1988). Changes in perceptual asymmetry with the menstrual cycle. *Neuropsychologia*, **27**, 233–240.

Asendorpf, J.A. & Scherer, K.R. (1983). The discrepant repressor: differentiation between low anxiety, high anxiety, and repression of anxiety by autonomic–facial–verbal patterns of behavior. *Journal of Personality and Social Psychology*, **45**, 1334–1346.

Baumeister, R.F. & Cairns, K.J. (1992). Repression and self-presentation: when audiences interfere with self-deceptive strategies. *Journal of Personality and Social Psychology*, **62**, 851–862.

Bendig, A.W. (1956). The development of a short form of the Manifest Anxiety Scale. *Journal of Consulting Psychology*, **20**, 384.

Benjamins, C., Schuurs, A.H.B., & Hoogtraten, J. (1994). Skin conductance, Marlowe-Crowne defensiveness and dental anxiety. *Perceptual and Motor Skills*, **79**, 611–622.

Bonanno, G.A. & Singer, J.L. (1990). Repressive personality style: theoretical and methodological implications for health and pathology. In J.L. Singer (ed.), *Repression and dissociation* (pp. 435–470). Chicago, IL: University of Chicago Press.

Burns, J.W. (2000). Repression predicts outcome following multidisciplinary treatment of chronic pain. *Health Psychology*, **19**, 75–84.

Canning, E.M., Canning, R.D., & Boyce, T. (1992). Depressive symptoms and adaptive style in children with cancer. *Journal of American Child and Adolescent Psychiatry*, **31**, 1120–1124.

Coyne, J.C. & Gottlieb, B.H. (1996). The mismeasure of coping by checklist. *Journal of Personality*, **64**, 959–991.

Crowne, D.P. & Marlowe, D.A. (1964). *The approval motive: Studies in evaluative dependence*. New York: Wiley.

Davis, P.J. (1987). Repression and the inaccessibility of affective memories. *Journal of Personality and Social Psychology*, **53**, 585–593.

Dawkins, K. & Furnham, A. (1989). The colour naming of emotional words. *British Journal of Psychology*, **80**, 383–389.

Denollet, J. (1991). Negative affectivity and repressive coping: pervasive influence on self-reported mood, health and coronary-prone behavior. *Psychosomatic Medicine*, **53**, 538–556.

Derakshan, N. & Eysenck, M.W (1997). Interpretive biases for one's own behavior and physiology in high trait anxious individuals and repressors. *Journal of Personality and Social Psychology*, **73**, 816–825.

Derakshan, N. & Eysenck, M.W. (1998). Working memory capacity in high trait anxious individuals and repressors. *Cognition and Emotion*, **12**, 697–713.

Derakshan, N. & Eysenck, M.W. (1999). Are repressors self-deceivers or other-deceivers? *Cognition and Emotion*, **13**, 1–17.

Derakshan, N. & Eysenck, M.W. (2001). Manipulation of focus of attention and its effects on anxiety in high-anxious individuals and repressors. *Anxiety, Stress, and Coping*, **14**, 173–191.

Derakshan, N., Feldman, M., Campbell, T., & Lipp, O. (2002). Don't look back to emotion: inhibited to return to emotion. Investigating the time course of attentional bias. Abstract, *Psychophysiology*, **39**, S31.

Dozier, M. & Kobak, R.R. (1992). Psychophysiology in attachment interviews: converging evidence for deactivating strategies. *Child Development*, **63**, 1473–1480.

Eysenck, H.J. & Eysenck, S.B.G. (1964). *The manual of Eysenck Personality Inventory*. London: University of London Press.

Eysenck, M.W. (1997). *Anxiety and cognition: a unified theory*. London: Psychology Press.

Fox, E. (1993). Allocation of visual attention and anxiety. *Cognition and Emotion*, **7**, 207–215.

Fox, E., O'Boyle, C.A., Barry, H., & McCreary, C. (1989a). Repressive coping style and anxiety in stressful dental surgery. *British Journal of Medical Psychology*, **62**, 371–380.

Fox, E., O'Boyle, C.A., Lennon, J., & Keeling, P.W.N. (1989b). Trait anxiety and coping style as predictors of pre-operative anxiety. *British Journal of Clinical Psychology*, **8**, 89–90.

Friedman, M. & Powell, L.H. (1984). The diagnosis and quantitative assessment of Type A behavior: introduction and description of the videotaped Structured Interview. *Integrative Psychiatry*, **2**, 123–129.

Goldberg, D. (1992). *General Health Questionnaire (GHQ-12)*. Windsor: NFER-Nelson.

Gudjonsson, G.H. (1981). Self-reported emotional disturbance and its relation to electrodermal reactivity, defensiveness and trait anxiety. *Personality and Individual Differences*, **2**, 47–52.

Hammer, A.L. & Marting, M.S. (1988). *Manual for the Coping Resources Inventory*. Palo Alto, CA: Consulting Psychologists Press.

Jamner, L.D. & Schwartz, G.E. (1985). Self-regulation and the integration of self-report and physiological indices of affect [abstract]. *Psychophysiology*, **22**, 596.

Jamner, L.D. & Schwartz, G.E. (1986). Self-deception predicts self-report and endurance of pain. *Psychosomatic Medicine*, **48**, 211–220.

Jamner, L.D., Schwartz, G.E., & Leigh, H. (1988). The relationship between repressive and defensive coping styles and monocyte, eosinophile and serum glucose levels: support for the opioid peptide hypothesis of repression. *Psychosomatic Medicine*, **50**, 567–575.

Jamner, L.D., Tursky, B., & Leigh, H. (1986). Discordance between verbal and nonverbal pain indices: the influence of repressive coping strategies [abstract]. *Psychophysiology*, **23**, 419.

Jenkins, C.D., Zyzanski, S., & Rosenman, R.H. (1979). *The Jenkins Activity Survey Manual*. New York: The Psychological Corporation.

Jensen, M.R. (1987). Psychobiological factors predicting the course of breast cancer. *Journal of Personality*, **55**, 317–342.

Kreitler, S., Chaitchik, S., & Kreitler, H. (1993). Repressiveness: cause or result of cancer? *Psycho-oncology*, **2**, 43–54.

Matthew, A. & MacLeod, C. (1994). Cognitive approaches to emotion and emotional disorders. *Annual Review of Psychology*, **15**, 25–50.

Myers, L.B. (1995). The relationship between alexithymia, repression, defensiveness and trait anxiety. *Personality and Individual Differences*, **19**, 489–492.

Myers, L.B. (1996). The attributional style of repressive individuals. *Journal of Social Psychology*, **136**, 127–128.

Myers, L.B. (1998). Repressive coping, trait anxiety and reported avoidance of negative thoughts. *Personality and Individual Differences*, **24**, 299–303.

Myers, L.B. (1999). Are different measures of parenting comparable? *Journal of Genetic Psychology*, **160**, 255–256.

Myers, L.B. & Brewin, C.R. (1994). Recall of early experience and the repressive coping style. *Journal of Abnormal Psychology*, **103**, 288–292.

Myers, L.B. & Brewin, C.R. (1995). Repressive coping and the recall of emotional material. *Cognition and Emotion*, **9**, 637–642.

Myers, L.B. & Brewin, C.R. (1996). Illusions of well-being and the repressive coping style. *British Journal of Social Psychology*, **35**, 443–457.

Myers, L.B., Brewin, C.R., & Power, M.J. (1992). Repression and autobiographical memory. In M.A. Conway, D.C. Rubin, H. Spinnler, & W. Wagenaar (eds), *Theoretical perspectives on autobiographical memory* (pp. 375–390). Dordrecht, The Netherlands: Kluwer Academic Press.

Myers, L.B., Brewin, C.R., & Power, M.J. (1998). Repressive coping and the directed forgetting of emotional material. *Journal of Abnormal Psychology*, **107**, 141–148.

Myers, L.B., Brewin, C.R., & Winter, D. (1999). Repressive coping and self-reports of parenting. *British Journal of Clinical Psychology*, **38**, 73–82.

Myers, L.B. & McKenna, F.P. (1996). The colour naming of socially threatening words. *Personality and Individual Differences*, **6**, 801–803.

Myers, L.B. & Reynolds, R. (2000). How optimistic are repressors? The relationship between repressive coping, controllability, self-esteem and comparative optimism for health-related events. *Psychology and Health*, **15**, 667–688.

Myers, L.B. & Steed, L. (1999). The relationship between dispositional optimism, dispositional pessimism and repressive coping and trait anxiety. *Personality and Individual Differences*, **27**, 1261–1272.

Myers, L.B. & Vetere, A.L. (1997). Repressors' responses to health-related questionnaires. *British Journal of Health Psychology*, **2**, 245–257.

Myers, L.B. & Vetere, A.L. (2002). Repressive coping style and romantic adult attachment in individuals with a repressive coping style. Is there a relationship? *Personality and Individual Differences*, **32**, 799–807.

Nemiah, J.C. & Sifneos, P.E. (1970a). Psychosomatic illness: a problem in communication. *Psychotherapy and Psychosomatics*, **18**, 154–160.

Nemiah, J.C. & Sifneos, P.E. (1970b). Affect and fantasy in patients with psychosomatic disorders. In O. Hill (ed.), *Modern trends in psychosomatic medicine*, Vol. 2 (pp. 26–34). London: Butterworths.

Newton, T.L. & Contrada, R.L. (1992). Repressive coping and verbal-autonomic dissociation: the influence of social context. *Journal of Personality and Social Psychology*, **62**, 159–167.

Newton, T.L. & Contrada, R.L. (1994). Alexithymia and repression: contrasting emotion-focused coping styles. *Psychosomatic Medicine*, **56**, 457–462.

Niaura, R., Herbert, P.N., McMahon, N., & Sommerville, L. (1992). Repressive coping and blood lipids in men and women. *Psychosomatic Medicine*, **54**, 698–706.

O'Leary. A. (1990). Stress, emotion and human immune function. *Psychological Bulletin*, **108**, 363–382.

Parker, G., Tupling, H., & Brown, L.B. (1979). A parental bonding instrument. *British Journal of Medical Psychology*, **52**, 1–10.

Parker, J.D.A. & Endler, N.S. (1992). Coping with coping assessment: a critical review. *European Journal of Personality*, **6**, 321–344.

Paul, G.L. (1966). *Insight versus desensitisation in psychotherapy*. Stanford, CA: Stanford University Press.

Pennebaker, J.W. (1982). *The psychology of physical symptoms*. New York: Springer-Verlag.

Phipps, S. & Srivastava, D.K. (1997). Repressive adaptation in children with cancer. *Health Psychology*, **16**, 521–528.

Pincus, T., Pearce, S., McClelland, A., Farley, S., & Vogal, S. (1994). Interpretation bias in responses to ambiguous cues in pain patients. *Journal of Psychosomatic Research*, **38**, 347–353.

Scheier, M.F. & Carver, C.S. (1985). Optimism, coping and health: assessment and implications of generalized outcome expectancies. *Health Psychology*, **4**, 219–247.

Schwartz, G.E. (1990). Psychobiology of repression and health: a systems approach. In J.L. Singer (ed.), *Repression and dissociation* (pp. 405–434). Chicago, IL: University of Chicago Press.

Shaw, R.E., Cohen, F., Fishman-Rosen, J., Murphy, M.C., Stertzer, S., Clark, D.A., & Myler, R.K. (1986). Psychologic predictors of psychosocial and medical outcomes in patients undergoing coronary angioplasty. *Psychosomatic Medicine*, **48**, 582–597.

Shedler, J., Mayman, M., & Manis, M. (1993). The illusion of mental health. *American Psychologist*, **48**, 1117–1131.

Slough, N., Kleinknecht, R.A., & Thorndike, R.M. (1984). Relationship of the repression-sensitization scales to anxiety. *Journal of Personality Assessment*, **48**, 378–379.

Snider, B.S., Asmundson, G.J.G., & Wiese, K.C. (2000). Automatic and strategic processing of threat cues in patients with chronic pain. *Clinical Journal of Pain*, **16**, 144–154.

Spielberger, C.D., Gorsuch, R.L., & Lushene, R. (1970). *The State Trait Anxiety Scale*. Palo Alto, CA: Consulting Psychologists Press.

Sullivan, P.F. & Roberts, L.K. (1969). Relationship of manifest anxiety to repression-sensitization on the MMPI. *Journal of Consulting and Clinical Psychology*, **33**, 763–764.

Taylor, J.A. (1953). A personality scale of manifest anxiety. *Journal of Abnormal and Social Psychology*, **48**, 285–290.

Taylor, S.E. & Brown, J.D. (1988). Illusion and well-being: a social psychological perspective on mental health. *Psychological Bulletin*, **103**, 193–210.

Weinberger, D.A. (1990). The construct validity of the repressive coping style. In J.L. Singer (ed.), *Repression and dissociation* (pp. 337–386). Chicago, IL: University of Chicago Press.

Weinberger, D.A. & Davidson, M.N. (1994). Styles of inhibiting emotional expression: distinguishing repressive coping from impression management. *Journal of Personality*, **62**, 587–613.

Weinberger, D.A. & Schwartz, G.E. (1990). Distress and restraint as superordinate dimensions of self-reported adjustment: a typological perspective. *Journal of Personality*, **58**, 381–417.

Weinberger, D.A., Schwartz, G.E., & Davidson, R.J. (1979). Low-anxious, high-anxious and repressive coping styles: psychometric patterns and behavioral responses to stress. *Journal of Abnormal Psychology*, **88**, 369–380.

Wells, A. & Davis, M.I. (1994). The Thought Control Questionnaire: a measure of individual differences in the control of unwanted thoughts. *Behavior Research and Therapy*, **32**, 871–878.

Chapter 11

Psychological mindedness

A new index to assess a major emotion-focused coping style

Johan Denollet and Ivan Nyklíček

Introduction

Psychological mindedness can be globally described as a disposition toward thinking about psychological phenomena (Farber, 1985) and to show interest in understanding behavior in psychological terms (Wolitzky & Reuben, 1974). In 1973, Appelbaum stated that psychological mindedness was an elusive construct. Three decades later, little has changed in our understanding of this theoretically elusive but clinically meaningful construct. Investigation of personality variables such as intraception or psychological mindedness has, with few exceptions, been largely absent since the 1960s (Farber, 1985). As a consequence, there is little literature on the relationship of psychological mindedness to mental well-being (Trudeau & Reich, 1995), let alone other domains of well-being such as quality of life and physical health. This chapter is an attempt to understand the construct of psychological mindedness more clearly, and to place it within the framework of clinical research and practice.

Up to now, the limited literature on psychological mindedness has been dominated by the focus on the patient's suitability for psychoanalytical psycho-therapy (Conte *et al.*, 1990; McCallum & Piper, 1990). This therapy involves developing insight into how complaints are the manifestations of underlying psychic conflicts and unconscious defense mechanisms (McCallum & Piper, 1990). Accordingly, there is a broad acceptance of the importance of psychological mind-edness within the area of dynamically oriented psychotherapy (Conte *et al.*, 1995). At its most extreme, this line of reasoning holds that evaluating the patient in terms of psychological mindedness is relevant for this specific kind of treatment but not for other therapies (Rosenbaum & Horowitz, 1983). However, ideas have under-gone a clear development since the start of the 1990s. For example, McCallum *et al.* (1992) stated that individuals scoring low on psychological mindedness are not suited for psychoanalytical psychotherapy but rather may be more attuned to cognitive or behavioral approaches to treatment. In a more recent publication (Piper *et al.*, 1998), however, these authors asserted that psychological mindedness may also be of value to a wide variety of non-dynamic psychotherapies including cognitive, behavioral and/or supportive psychotherapy.

But there is more to psychological mindedness than the mere suitability for and impact on psychotherapeutic interventions. Psychological mindedness may also matter for "normal" individuals in everyday life, impacting on their ability to deal with emotionally stressful situations. There seem to be stable individual differences in people's ability of "reading between the lines of behavior" (Dollinger *et al.*, 1983), and individuals with a high level of psychological mindedness stay better attuned to their emotional world (Farber, 1989). Psychological mindedness involves a sense of intellectual and emotional awareness of both the pleasant and distressful aspects of life (Alvarez *et al.*, 1998). In fact, highly psychologically minded individuals report that they experience a wider range of emotions than less psychologically minded individuals (Farber, 1989). Hence, psychological mindedness is not only a crucial ingredient in psychotherapy; it may also promote psychological health and self-awareness in non-patient populations. Interestingly, this has already been suggested by ancient philosophers (Socrates' "know thyself" is well-known), modern psychologists (e.g. Kabat-Zinn, 1990) and spiritual teachers (e.g. Krishnamurti, 1987) alike. At the same time, being attuned to one's emotional world and being aware of the distressful aspects of one's life may be important keys to ward off the potential deleterious effect of negative affect on health (Denollet, 2000).

Coping with internal mood states

Most research on psychological risk factors for the development and progression of disease has focused on the role of negative emotions such as depression, anxiety, and hostility (Denollet, 2000). In addition to this focus on emotional stress-related disease, there is an urgent need to look at personality traits that may moderate this relationship. In other words, how people cope with negative emotions may be as important in terms of adverse health outcomes as the experience of negative emotion *per se* (Denollet, 2000). The importance of coping has been suggested earlier (e.g. Lazarus & Folkman, 1984), but the theoretical and research emphasis has been on coping with environmental demands rather than with internal negative mood states.

Repressive coping and defensiveness are examples of coping directed at controlling negative affect, the core characteristic of these constructs being the exclusion of negative emotions from awareness (Weinberger *et al.*, 1979). Despite the fact that repressive individuals report *low* levels of negative affect, they still may have an increased risk for adverse health outcomes, as predicted by Alexander (1939) (see also Chapter 10). For example, defensiveness has been associated with elevated blood pressure (e.g. Jorgensen *et al.*, 1996; Nyklíček *et al.*, 1998) and the three-year incidence of hypertension (Rutledge & Linden, 2000). Inclusion of this emotion-focused coping style may uncover an important moderating effect on the negative emotion–disease relationship that otherwise would remain unnoticed.

Apart from repression/defensiveness, there are other emotion regulation-focused personality traits that may moderate the relationship between emotion and disease, such as denial, alexithymia, and social inhibition. Denial is closely related to defensiveness and refers to the under-reporting of emotional distress (Ketterer *et al.*, 1998). Alexithymia is a multifaceted concept that consists of difficulties identifying emotions, difficulties describing emotions, and a cognitive style emphasizing environmental details rather than paying attention to internal feelings and moods, called externally oriented thinking (Bagby *et al.*, 1994). A key feature of alexithymic individuals is a deficit in their ability to recognize emotional stimuli and to process them adequately (Lane *et al.*, 1996). Social inhibition refers to the tendency to inhibit the expression of emotions and behaviors in social interaction (Denollet, 2000). All of these emotion-focused coping styles are directed at avoidance or disability of processing and expressing negative emotions and have been associated with adverse health outcomes, such as cardiovascular disease and all-cause mortality (Denollet, 2000; Kauhanen *et al.*, 1996; Ketterer *et al.*, 1998; Lumley *et al.*, 1997).

In contrast, less attention has been devoted to the postulated positive effects of paying attention to and expressing one's inner thoughts and feelings. Systematic research has been conducted in this area, especially on Pennebaker's writing paradigm showing health-promoting effects of writing in depth about traumatic or other emotionally relevant topics (Pennebaker & Beall, 1986; see for a review Smyth, 1998). In general, evidence suggests that inadequate coping with negative emotions may have adverse health effects, while coping with one's affective states adaptively and intelligently may promote health (Salovey & Mayer, 1990; Smyth, 1998; Chapter 9 of this volume).

Theoretical framework

It is argued here that psychological mindedness is another adaptive emotion-focused coping style that needs to be studied in its own right in relation to health and disease. This statement raises a number of issues.

1   What is psychological mindedness and does it cover a unique portion of variance within emotion-focused coping?
2   Is it measurable and, if so, how?
3   Is there any evidence available linking constructs conceptually related to psychological mindedness with health or disease?

These issues will be discussed in the following paragraphs.

What "psychological mindedness" is about

The term "psychological mindedness" lacks precise definition until now, and is sometimes considered synonymous with insight-related terms such as introspection or self-awareness (Hall, 1992). Psychological mindedness has various referent attributes including ability and motivation for change, focusing on the meaning of one's own behavior and that of others, access to one's feelings, and willingness to be open with others about one's problems (Conte *et al.*, 1990). The study of Dollinger *et al.* (1983) failed to support the notion that psychological mindedness is a unitary construct. Hence, psychological mindedness is often conceptualized as a multifaceted construct that deals with adaptive psychological functioning in general (Conte *et al.*, 1995).

The definitions of psychological mindedness as used in the literature are far from consistent (Conte *et al.*, 1995). Psychological mindedness has variously been described as an ability or a disposition. Appelbaum (1973), for example, defines psychological mindedness as a person's ability to see relationships among thought, feelings and behaviors. McCallum and Piper (1990) define psychological mindedness as the ability to identify intrapsychic components and to connect them to one's own or others' problems. According to Farber (1985), psychological mindedness is the disposition to reflect upon the meaning and the motivation of feelings and behaviors in oneself and others. Both elements are combined in the definition of Hall (1992): psychological mindedness is the *interest* in and *ability* to be reflective about psychological processes across affective and intellectual dimensions. The following paragraphs will discuss these various components of psychological mindedness, resulting in a working definition of the construct and a short self-report measure. Finally, the findings of a pilot study examining the psychometric properties of this self-report measure will be presented.

Ability or motivation?

It has been argued that psychological mindedness is a competence that requires abstract "interiorized" thinking. Originally, this competence was strictly related to the psychodynamic domain: the ability to identify *dynamic* components and to relate them to one's difficulties (McCallum & Piper, 1990). This notion of psychological mindedness refers to those individuals who are skilled at seeing through self-protective defense mechanisms (Dollinger *et al.*, 1983). Nowadays, this ability is more broadly conceptualized to have a beneficial effect *regardless of the nature* of the difficulties being explored (Piper *et al.*, 1998). This notion of the construct implies that those individuals who are high in psychological mindedness are capable of looking behind the surface of overt behavior for underlying psychological meaning (Dollinger *et al.*, 1983). Hence, psychological mindedness reflects a general competence to analyze problems in a psychological way (Piper *et al.*, 1998).

But there is more to psychological mindedness than a mere ability. In fact, psychological mindedness is closely related to the willingness to accept the influence of intrapsychic processes on behavior and on coping with the stress of everyday life. Although psychological mindedness may develop in an unconscious manner, this does not mean that individuals are unaware of their general attitude toward the notion that psychological factors may impact on their lives (Conte *et al.*, 1995). There exist substantial individual differences with respect to this general attitude. Some people deny the idea that intrapsychic processes (which partly are unconscious) may be influencing their current feelings and behavior. In addition, they sometimes cannot even tolerate the idea that there are processes in their brain that may be unconscious (Coltart, 1988). In contrast, other people are highly motivated to monitor and analyze their emotions.

It will be argued here that this motivation is the core of the concept of psychological mindedness. According to Wolitzky and Reuben (1974), psychological mindedness is not an ability but a tendency to show interest in understanding behavior in psychological terms. In a similar vein, Farber (1985) conceptualizes psychological mindedness as a disposition toward thinking about psychological phenomena rather than ability to do so correctly. Still other authors will argue that true psychological mindedness involves both components, i.e. an interest in understanding the relationships between thoughts, feelings, actions, and causes of behaviors as well as an ability to discern these relationships and causes (Appelbaum, 1973; Hall, 1992).

Cognitive or affective style?

Another conceptual issue deals with the cognitive and affective components of psychological mindedness. That is, authors not only have disagreed regarding the role of ability versus motivation; they similarly have disagreed on the intellectual versus affective components of psychological mindedness (Hall, 1992). As pointed out by Farber (1985), the intellectual component of psychological mindedness refers to the cognitive understanding of psychological issues, i.e. the knowledge *about* psychological matters rather than knowledge *of* such matters. Accordingly, some researchers have highlighted this cognitive component by referring to psychological mindedness in terms of social–cognitive competencies (Dollinger *et al.*, 1983). By analogy, research on private self-consciousness (Fenigstein *et al.*, 1975) has focused on the nature of self-reflection as a cognitive style that is related to psychological mindedness. According to Hall (1992), the cognitive component of psychological mindedness can be defined as intellectual reflectivity about psychological processes, relationships, and meanings.

Overemphasis on the intellectual component of psychological mindedness may result in lack of spontaneity and affectivity, however (Farber, 1985). At its extreme, this form of psychological mindedness may lead to rationalization as a form of maladaptive defensiveness. The affective component of psychological mindedness refers to the emotional understanding of psychological issues, i.e. knowledge *of* psychological matters rather than knowledge *about* such matters (Farber, 1985). Hall (1992) defines this component as affective reflectivity about psychological processes. Hence, this component refers to the capacity to experience one's inner psychological life and to be in touch with the thoughts and feelings of oneself and of other people. Or, as put by Appelbaum (1973), psychological mindedness necessarily includes "the ability to allow affects their rightful place".

Most researchers assert that being psychologically minded involves both an intellectual and an affective process (Hall, 1992). According to Appelbaum (1973), for example, psychological mindedness refers to the talent that some people have, and others lack, to *"know"* and *"feel"* covert psychological events. Farber (1985) also views psychological mindedness as consisting of an intellectual and an affective component; a person who fails to evidence either one of these components thus fails to evidence accurate psychological mindedness. This analysis of components that make up psychological mindedness was used by Hall (1992) to devise a theory-driven conceptualization of this multifaceted construct. We used this model as a starting point for our definition and operationalization of psychological mindedness in the present chapter.

The conceptual model of Hall (1992)

The ability/motivation and intellect/affect dimensions were integrated quite inventively by Hall (1992) in her conceptual model of psychological mindedness. With respect to the first dimension, Hall argues that we should think of *interest–motivation* and *ability* as separate but related constructs, each contributing to accurate psychological mindedness. She places these constructs in a *"ceiling" model* of psychological mindedness, stressing the contributive and limitative manner in which interest and ability can be understood in relationship to one another.

This ceiling model is one of necessary but insufficient conditions. Specifically, a lack of interest in being psychologically minded (the motivational component) puts a ceiling on an individual's ability to be psychologically minded. A lack of ability to be psychologically minded (the competence component), in turn, puts a ceiling on the occurrence of accurate behavior. Both the motivation to show interest in psychological phenomena and the ability to be accurate are facets of psychological mindedness, with the latter being limited by the lack of the former.

Concerning the affective and cognitive components of psychological mindedness, Hall (1992) asserts that the affective component is the more basic of the two. The ceiling model holds that the extent to which individuals fail to be accurately *affectively* psychologically minded (i.e. the emotional component) puts a ceiling on an individual's ability to be accurately *intellectually* psychologically minded (i.e. the cognitive component). Hence, accurate psychological mindedness is especially contributed to by the affective dimension of this construct. According to Hall, the danger of a relative lack of psychological mindedness does not mainly stem from a lack of ability to think about psychological processes on an intellectual level, but rather from a lack of accurate affective psychological mindedness.

Instead of considering interest/ability and affect/cognition in isolation, Hall (1992) crosses these dimensions in a comprehensive model of psychological mindedness. In other words, psychological mindedness is displayed by an individual to the extent that he/she displays both the interest in and ability for reflectivity about psychological processes across affective and intellectual dimensions. In this model, interest in being affectively psychologically minded is the most basic component: it contributes to the ability to be affectively and intellectually psychologically minded and, as such, is the cornerstone of accurate psychological mindedness.

A working hypothesis of psychological mindedness

Based on the assumption that psychological mindedness is an emotion-focused coping style that may also matter in the context of physical health, we decided to include this variable in our own research on heart disease. Building on the work of others, we first devised a basic working definition of psychological mindedness that can be integrated easily in psychosomatic research. We used the following elements to conceptualize psychological mindedness:

1 it is a disposition (Farber, 1985)
2 its central element is the motivation to focus on and show interest in psychological processes (Wolitzky & Reuben, 1974)
3 its affective component is more basic than its cognitive component (Hall, 1992)
4 it enhances an individual's immediate adaptation to his/her difficulties (Piper et al., 1998).

This approach resulted in the following definition: *Psychological mindedness refers to the intrinsic motivation to be in touch with one's inner feelings and thoughts by monitoring and analyzing them in an adaptive way.*

We readily acknowledge that this definition is only one of many possible approaches to psychological mindedness. However, we wanted to have a simple, straightforward definition that clearly stressed the minimal requirements to infer accurate psychological mindedness.

Psychological mindedness and related constructs

Psychological mindedness can be distinguished from other emotion-related personality differences. First of all, psychological mindedness is hardly related to repressive coping (Denollet, 1991; Weinberger et al., 1979), which will be demonstrated empirically below. Furthermore, psychological mindedness can clearly be distinguished from two of the components that make up alexithymia (Bagby et al., 1994; Taylor et al., 1997), i.e. difficulties identifying and describing feelings, since they refer to a psychopathological deficit rather than an intrinsic motivation. Psychological mindedness is, however, expected to be negatively related to the third component of alexithymia, i.e. externally oriented thinking style or *la pensée opératoire*, since this component involves preoccupation with details from the environment rather than paying attention to one's internal states. Psychological mindedness can also be distinguished from social inhibition. While inhibition is inversely related to the personality domain of extraversion (Denollet, 2000), psychological mindedness is hypothesized to be more closely related to the personality domain of openness to experience (Bagby et al., 1994).

Some relation is expected between psychological mindedness and emotional intelligence (Davies *et al.*, 1998; Salovey & Mayer, 1990). In particular, the component of "Attention to one's and another person's emotions" overlaps conceptually with psychological mindedness. A modest correlation would be anticipated with "Clarity", which seems to emphasize the ability, not the motivation, to perceive one's emotions clearly. Finally, "Repair" is expected not to correlate substantially with psychological mindedness, since the core issue here involves deliberately altering one's inner psychological contents, which is not typical for psychological mindedness. Anyway, the relation between psychological mindedness and other emotion-focused coping styles should be examined in future research in order to gain insight into the extent to which psychological mindedness covers a unique part of the variance of emotion-focused coping. This is also relevant regarding the potential associations of psychological mindedness with health outcomes.

Psychological mindedness and health

Indirect evidence for a link between psychological mindedness and health has been provided by a few studies on the relationship between related constructs and health outcomes. Externally oriented thinking, but not the other components from the alexithymia concept, has been associated with silent myocardial ischemia among cardiac patients (Torosian *et al.*, 1997) and unmedicated hypertension in a population-based screening sample consisting of 967 women (unpublished data by second author). The controversial results of Grossarth-Maticek *et al.* (1985) indicated that rationality/anti-emotionality, a construct presumably inversely related to psychological mindedness, was a strong predictor of cancer mortality. However, an attempt to replicate this finding was far less successful, yielding a rather modest association (Bleiker *et al.*, 1996). Lack of psychological mindedness is also a component of the Type C coping pattern, which has been associated with a poor prognosis in melanoma patients (Temoshok *et al.*, 1985). Although these illustrative results suggest a possible link, it is clear that more systematic research should be conducted on the relationship between psychological mindedness and physical health. But this requires a clear operationalization of the construct in the first place.

Theory-driven operationalization and assessment

There have been relatively few attempts to operationalize psychological mindedness (McCallum & Piper, 1996). Moreover, the operational definitions of the construct have varied widely, rendering the research results nearly impossible to summarize (Hall, 1992). Overall, there have been three general approaches to assessing psychological mindedness: (1) assessment of variables that are conceptually related to the construct, (2) self-report measures that were specifically developed to assess psychological mindedness, and (3) clinical diagnostic interviews.

inner feelings and thoughts by monitoring and analyzing them in an adaptive way". Central to this operationalization is the notion that the affective component of psychological mindedness is more basic than its cognitive component (Hall, 1992). Furthermore, the items had to cover the tendency to monitor one's own feelings (Swinkels & Giuliano, 1995) and the motivation to analyze these feelings (Wolitzky & Reuben, 1974). In contrast to existing scales, this scale was specifically designed to measure the relative *lack* of psychological mindedness. Such a lack may hamper an individual's adaptation to his/her difficulties (e.g. Piper *et al.*, 1998), which, in turn, may increase the risk of stress-related disease.

An initial pool of 20 items was derived from the literature on psychological mindedness (Conte *et al.*, 1990), and related concepts such as emotional intelligence (Salovey & Mayer, 1990), openness to experience (McCrae, 1994) and externally oriented thinking (Apfel & Sifneos, 1979; Bagby *et al.*, 1994). In addition, several items were specifically written for the purpose of the present research. Subjects were asked to rate the extent to which they agreed with each item on a five-point Likert scale (ranging from 0 = false to 4 = true). Principal components and internal consistency analyses were used to produce a short and reliable ten-item scale reflecting the relative lack of psychological mindedness. Given the focus of this scale, it was termed the *Lack of Psychological Mindedness* (LPM) index. The items of the LPM are shown in Table 11.1. The next section of this chapter will describe some empirical findings from a pilot study in which the LPM was used to examine psychological mindedness in healthy young men and women.

A psychometric study of the LPM

The present study examined the internal consistency and structural validity of the LPM in a sample of 127 undergraduate medicine students from the University of Antwerp: 89 (70 percent) women and 38 (30 percent) men. The mean age of this sample was 22.2 years (SD = 1.7; range 20–30). These subjects also filled out the Repressive Defensiveness (REP) index to assess the unconscious exclusion of negative emotions from awareness as another emotion-focused trait (see Denollet, 1991). The purpose of this first study was (a) to document the factor structure and internal consistency of the LPM and (b) to examine the external validity of the LPM against two hypotheses that were derived from the psychological mindedness literature.

Psychological mindedness scales are often saturated with a tendency to deny unfavorable qualities of the self (Dollinger *et al.*, 1983). Therefore, the LPM was specifically designed to be unconfounded by repressive coping. Hence, it was hypothesized that the LPM was largely *unrelated* to repressive defensiveness as a distinct emotion-focused style (Denollet, 1991). In a number of studies, a gender difference favoring women emerged on the various psychological mindedness scales (Hatcher *et al.*, 1990). Compared with men, women were superior at describing other people in psychological terms (Dollinger *et al.*, 1983) and showed

Table 11.1 Lack of Psychological Mindedness (LPM) index (N = 127)

Facet scale	FA*		FA†		Internal consistency‡
	F1	F2	I	II	
Lack of monitoring					
Pays much attention to feelings	**-.69**	-.36	**-.76**	-.04	.63
Doesn't care much about what he/she is feeling	**.63**	.40	**.74**	.01	.62
Experiences little or no emotion most of the time	**.51**	.36	**.60**	.12	.51
Is out of touch with innermost feelings	**.64**	.16	**.57**	-.07	.46
Being in touch with emotions is essential	**-.79**	.01	**-.57**	-.09	.45
Lack of analyzing					
Prefers to act rather than to discuss feelings	.31	**.71**	**.70**	.10	.63
Prefers talking about daily activities rather than feelings	.46	**.51**	**.65**	.17	.58
Does not tend to analyze his/her own feelings	.35	**.59**	**.67**	.10	.57
Seldom thinks in depth about his/her behavior	.28	**.57**	**.72**	.09	.50
Puts out of his/her mind things that may bother him/her	-.06	**.83**	**.52**	.20	.44
					alpha = **.83**

* Factor analysis of the ten "Psychological Mindedness" items; items assigned to a facet scale are in boldface.
† Factor analysis of the 20 "Psychological Mindedness" and "Repressive Defensiveness" items; items assigned to a factor are in boldface.
‡ Corrected item–total correlations for the "Psychological Mindedness" scale.

a less externally oriented thinking style (Nyklíček & Vingerhoets, 2000). Note that externally oriented thinking indicates lack of psychological mindedness (Bagby et al., 1994). Although these gender differences are not always found (Trudeau & Reich, 1995), it was hypothesized that men would score higher on the LPM than women (indicating less psychological mindedness).

Statistical analyses

The LPM items were analyzed on two levels in the hierarchy of constructs (Comrey, 1988): the first-order level where each item is more or less an alternate form of each other item, and the second-order level that is defined by the overlap among the facets that define the construct. Principal components analysis with varimax rotation was used to examine the accuracy of both the first-order level (i.e. loading of items on both monitoring of feelings and analyzing of feelings) and second-order level (i.e. loadings of the facets on the general construct of psychological mindedness as opposed to repressive defensiveness) of the LPM. For the second-order level analyses, items were summed to comprise total scores for the LPM and REP scales, respectively. Scores on the items "Pays much attention to feelings" and "Being in touch with emotions is essential" were reversed before adding them to the LPM score; scores on the items "Reacts without thinking" and "Loses his/her self-control" were reversed before adding them to the REP score. Scree plot and eigenvalue criteria were used to decide on the optimum number of factors to retain. Cronbach's α and corrected item–total correlations were used to obtain internal-consistency estimates of reliability. Unpaired t-tests, crosstabulation and logistic regression were used to examine gender differences in psychological mindedness and defensiveness.

Results and discussion

The first step in data analysis (factor analysis of the ten LPM items) indicated that five items were related to the lack of monitoring and five items to the lack of analyzing facets (Table 11.1; F1 and F2). Principal components analysis of the combined pool of 20 LPM and REP items clearly indicated that all of the LPM items loaded on the first factor (Table 11.1; I and II). This factor had an eigenvalue = 5.3 and explained 26 percent of the total variance. All of the LPM items had low loadings on the repressive defensiveness factor with seven of ten items loading ≤.10, documenting their divergent validity. Finally, Cronbach's α (= .83) and corrected item–total correlations in the range of .44 to .63 indicated a high level of internal consistency for the LPM (Table 11.1, last column).

Factor analysis of the REP indicated that five items were related to behavioral constraint and five items to repression of hostility (Table 11.2; F1 and F2). Principal components analysis of the combined pool of 20 LPM/REP items indicated that all of the REP items loaded on the second factor (Table 11.2, II; eigenvalue = 3.2; 16 percent total variance). Cronbach's α (= .83) and item–total correlations

Table 11.2 Repressive Defensiveness (REP) index (N = 127)

Facet scale	FA*		FA†		Internal consistency‡
	F1	F2	I	II	
Constraint					
Reacts without thinking	**-.67**	-.32	.00	**-.70**	.59
Keeps within the bounds of reason and logic	**.75**	.18	.11	**.65**	.56
Loses his/her self-control from time to time	**-.75**	-.20	-.11	**-.66**	.56
Never loses his/her patience with other people	**.48**	.37	.02	**.59**	.49
Has his/her behavior under perfect control	**.81**	.02	.25	**.56**	.48
Repressed hostility					
Has never deliberately said something to hurt anyone	.34	**.61**	-.03	**.69**	.56
Never feels the urge to tell someone off	.22	**.71**	.15	**.64**	.54
Never says bad things about other people	.13	**.75**	.08	**.62**	.51
Has never intensely disliked anyone	.20	**.66**	.13	**.59**	.49
Has never taken advantage of other people	.06	**.70**	.03	**.53**	.43
					alpha = **.83**

* Factor analysis of the ten "Repressive Defensiveness" items; items assigned to a facet scale are in boldface.
† Factor analysis of the 20 "Psychological Mindedness" and "Repressive Defensiveness" items; items assigned to a factor are in boldface.
‡ Corrected item–total correlations for the "Repressive Defensiveness" scale.

indicated a high level of internal consistency for the REP as well (Table 11.2, last column).

Next, items were summed to comprise the four LPM and REP facet scales. Lack of monitoring feelings correlated with lack of analyzing feelings ($r = .62$) but these LPM facet scales were largely unrelated to behavioral constraint or repressed hostility ($r < .22$). Second-order analysis of the LPM and REP facet scales indicated that these facets loaded highly only on the general construct they belong to (i.e. loadings $> .85$), not on the other construct (i.e. loadings $< .15$). Hence the first hypothesis was confirmed, i.e. lack of psychological mindedness emerged as an emotion-focused variable that could be clearly distinguished from repressive defensiveness.

With respect to the second hypothesis, men scored significantly higher on the LPM than women: $M = 13.6$ (SD = 6.8) versus $M = 10.3$ (SD = 5.8), t (125) = -2.54, $p = .01$. In contrast, their REP scores were not significantly different (i.e. $M = 20.1$ versus $M = 18.5$, $p = .28$), once again suggesting that psychological mindedness can be distinguished from repressive defensiveness. Using median splits, scores were dichotomized to identify low psychologically minded (i.e. LPM ≥ 10) and defensive (i.e. REP ≥ 19) subjects, respectively. Seventy-one percent of the men versus 48 percent of the women were classified as being relatively low on psychological mindedness (OR = 2.63, 95 percent CI = 1.16–5.93, $p = .02$). No differences were found for repressive defensiveness.

Overall, these preliminary findings suggest that the LPM is a psychometrically sound tool, that psychological mindedness is largely unrelated to repressive defensiveness (hypothesis 1), and that men display a relative lack of psychological mindedness (hypothesis 2).

Concluding remarks

The primary aim of this chapter is to highlight the potential role of psychological mindedness as a distinct emotion-focused coping style. We readily acknowledge the limitations of this study. The empirical research reported here was an initial test of the psychometric properties of the LPM, using only young, healthy students and only one other emotion-focused coping measure. Future studies should examine the validity of the LPM in other populations, including patient samples, and against related measures, such as the Psychological Mindedness Scale (Conte et al., 1990) or the Openness to Experience Scale from the NEO (McCrae, 1994). Research also needs to define the overlap between the LPM and related constructs such as self-consciousness (Fenigstein et al., 1975), emotional intelligence (Salovey & Mayer, 1990), mood awareness (Swinkels & Giuliano, 1995), and externally oriented thinking (Bagby et al., 1994).

Likewise, it is important to examine the divergent validity of the LPM with respect to constructs related to non-expression of emotions, such as alexithymia (Taylor et al., 1997), defensiveness (Weinberger et al., 1979), and ambivalence over emotional expression (King & Emmons, 1990). In addition, future research needs to find out the value of the LPM to assess individual differences in emotional experience (Gohm & Clore, 2000). Does this concept offer a motivational explanation for differences in self-reflection (Franzoi *et al.*, 1990)? And can psychological mindedness really account for a unique part of the variance related to well-being and somatic health?

Nevertheless, two things seem to have emerged from the present study. First, lack of psychological mindedness is not driven by the repression of negative emotions, but reflects a distinctly different emotion-focused trait. Second, there exist substantial gender differences in psychological mindedness (Feldman Barrett *et al.*, 2000). Besides the need for thorough psychometric studies on the LPM, future research should focus on the role of psychological mindedness as a moderator of the relationship between negative affect and physical health. Clinicians often seek to promote psychological mindedness in their patients as a means of increasing self-acceptance (Farber, 1989) and mental health (Alvarez *et al.*, 1998). However, promoting psychological mindedness may also result in enhanced awareness of discrepancies between the real and the ideal self, thereby resulting in decrements in emotional well-being (Farber, 1989). In a similar vein, adaptive psychological mindedness may have favorable effects whereas excessive preoccupation with oneself and rumination may be detrimental to one's mental health (see Trapnell & Campbell, 1999). Hence, at the clinical level, we still need to find out whether we should give our patients the advice:

"Mind your mind".

References

Abramowitz, S.L. & Abramowitz, C.V. (1974). Psychological mindedness and benefit from insight-oriented group therapy. *Archives of General Psychiatry*, **30**, 610–615.

Alexander, F. (1939). Emotional factors in arterial hypertension. *Psychosomatic Medicine*, **1**, 175–179.

Alvarez, J.R., Farber, B.A., & Schonbar, R.A. (1998). The relationship of psychological mindedness to adult perceptions of early parental rejection. *Journal of Clinical Psychology*, **54**, 1079–1084.

Apfel, R.J. & Sifneos, P.E. (1979). Alexithymia: concept and measurement. *Psychotherapy & Psychosomatics*, **32**, 180–190.

Appelbaum, S.A. (1973). Psychological mindedness: word, concept, and essence. *International Journal of Psychoanalysis*, **54**, 35–46.

Appelbaum, S.A. (1976). The dangerous edge of insight. *Psychotherapy*, **13**, 202–206.

Bagby, R.M., Taylor, G.J., & Parker, J.D. (1994). The twenty-item Toronto Alexithymia Scale – II. Convergent, discriminant, and concurrent validity. *Journal of Psychosomatic Research*, **38**, 33–40.

Bleiker, E.M.A., Van der Ploeg, H.M, Hendriks, J.H.C.L., & Adèr, H.J. (1996). Personality factors and breast cancer development: a prospective longitudinal study. *Journal of the National Cancer Institute*, **88**, 1478–1482.

Coltart, N.E. (1988). The assessment of psychological mindedness in the diagnostic interview. *British Journal of Psychiatry*, **153**, 819–820.

Comrey, A.L. (1988). Factor-analytic methods of scale development in personality and clinical psychology. *Journal of Consulting and Clinical Psychology*, **56**, 754–761.

Conte, H.R., Buckley, P., Picard, S., & Karasu, T.B. (1995). Relationships between psychological mindedness and ego functioning: validity studies. *Comprehensive Psychiatry*, **36**, 11–17.

Conte, H.R., Plutchik, R., Jung, B., Picard, S., Karasu, T.B., & Lotterman, A. (1990). Psychological mindedness as a predictor of psychotherapy outcome: a preliminary report. *Comprehensive Psychiatry*, **31**, 426–431.

Cough, H.G. (1957). *California Psychological Inventory*. Palo Alto, CA: Consulting Psychological Press.

Davies, M., Stankov, L., & Roberts, R.D. (1998). Emotional intelligence: in search of an elusive construct. *Journal of Personality and Social Psychology*, **75**, 989–1015.

Denollet, J. (1991). Negative affectivity and repressive coping: pervasive influence on self-reported mood, health, and coronary-prone behavior. *Psychosomatic Medicine*, **53**, 538–556.

Denollet, J. (2000). Type D personality: a potential risk factor refined. *Journal of Psychosomatic Research*, **49**, 255–266.

Dollinger, S.J., Reader, M.J., Marnett, J.P., & Tylenda, B. (1983). Psychological mindedness, psychological construing, and the judgement of deception. *Journal of General Psychology*, **108**, 183–191.

Farber, B.A. (1985). The genesis, development, and implications of psychological mindedness in psychotherapists. *Psychotherapy*, **22**, 170–177.

Farber, B.A. (1989). Psychological mindedness: can there be too much of a good thing? *Psychotherapy*, **26**, 210–217.

Feldman Barrett, L., Lane, R.D., Sechrest, L., & Schwartz, G.E. (2000). Sex differences in emotional awareness. *Personality and Social Psychology Bulletin*, **26**, 1027–1035.

Fenigstein, A., Scheier, M.F., & Buss, A.H. (1975). Public and private self-consciousness: assessment and theory. *Journal of Consulting and Clinical Psychology*, **43**, 522–527.

Franzoi, S.L., Davis, M.H., & Markwiese, B. (1990). A motivational explanation for the existence of private self-consciousness differences. *Journal of Personality*, **58**, 641–659.

Gohm, C.L. & Clore, G.L. (2000). Individual differences in emotional experience: mapping available scales to processes. *Personality and Social Psychology Bulletin*, **26**, 679–697.

Grossarth-Maticek, R., Bastiaans, J., & Kanazir, D.T. (1985). Psychosocial factors as strong predictors of mortality from cancer, ischemic heart disease and stroke: the Yugoslav prospective study. *Journal of Psychosomatic Research*, **29**, 167–176.

Hall, J.A. (1992). Psychological mindedness: a conceptual model. *American Journal of Psychotherapy*, **20**, 131–140.

Hatcher, R., Hatcher, S., Berlin, M., & Okla, K. (1990). Psychological mindedness and abstract reasoning in late childhood and adolescence: an exploration using new instruments. *Journal of Youth and Adolescence*, **19**, 307–326.

Jorgensen, R.S., Johnson, B.T., Kolodziej, M.E., & Schreer, G.E. (1996). Elevated blood pressure and personality: a meta-analytic review. *Psychological Bulletin*, **120**, 293–320.

Kabat-Zinn, J. (1990). *Full catastrophe living*. New York: Delacorte.

Kauhanen, J., Kaplan, G.A., Cohen, R.A., Julkunen, J., & Salonen, J.T. (1996). Alexithymia and risk of death in middle-aged men. *Journal of Psychosomatic Research*, **41**, 541–549.

Ketterer, M.W., Huffman, J., Lumley, M.A., Wassef, S., Gray, L., Kenyon, L., Kraft, P., Brymer, J., Rhoads, K., Lovallo, W.R., & Goldberg, A.D. (1998). Five-year follow-up for adverse outcomes in males with at least mimimally positive angiograms: importance of "denial" in assessing psychosocial risk factors. *Journal of Psychosomatic Research*, **44**, 241–250.

King, L.A. & Emmons, R.A. (1990). Conflict over emotional expression: psychological and physical correlates. *Journal of Personality and Social Psychology*, **58**, 864–877.

Krishnamurti, J. (1987). *The awakening of intelligence*. San Francisco, CA: Harper.

Lane, R.D., Sechrest, L., Reidel, R., Weldon, V., Kaszniak, A., & Schwartz, G.E. (1996). Impaired verbal and nonverbal emotion recognition in alexithymia. *Psychosomatic Medicine*, **58**, 203–210.

Lazarus, R.S. & Folkman, S. (1984). *Stress, appraisal, and coping*. New York: Springer.

Lumley, M.A., Tomakowsky, J., & Torosian, T. (1997). The relationship of alexithymia to subjective and biomedical measures of disease. *Psychosomatics*, **38**, 497–502.

McCallum, M. & Piper, W.E. (1990). The Psychological Mindedness Assessment Procedure. *Psychological Assessment*, **2**, 412–418.

McCallum, M. & Piper, W.E. (1996). Psychological mindedness. *Psychiatry*, **59**, 48–64.

McCallum, M., Piper, W.E., & Joyce, A.S. (1992). Dropping out from short-term group therapy. *Psychotherapy*, **29**, 206–215.

McCrae, R.R. (1994). Openness to experience: expanding the boundaries of Factor V. *European Journal of Personality*, **8**, 251–272.

Nyklíček, I. & Vingerhoets, A.J. (2000). Alexithymia is associated with low tolerance to experimental painful stimulation. *Pain*, **85**, 471–475.

Nyklíček, I., Vingerhoets, A.J., Van Heck, G.L., & Van Limpt, M.C. (1998). Defensive coping in relation to casual blood pressure and self-reported daily hassles and life events. *Journal of Behavioral Medicine*, **21**, 145–161.

Pennebaker, J.W. & Beall, S.K. (1986). Confronting a traumatic event: toward an understanding of inhibition and disease. *Journal of Abnormal Psychology*, **95**, 274–281.

Piper, W.E., Joyce, A.S., Azim, H.F., and Rosie, J.S. (1994). Patient characteristics and success in day treatment. *Journal of Nervous and Mental Disease*, **182**, 381–386.

Piper, W.E., Joyce, A.S., McCallum, M., & Azim, H.F. (1998). Interpretative and supportive forms of psychotherapy and patient personality variables. *Journal of Consulting and Clinical Psychology*, **66**, 558–567.

Rosenbaum, R.L. & Horowitz, M.J. (1983). Motivation for psychotherapy: a factorial and conceptual analysis. *Psychological Theory, Research, and Practice*, **20**, 346–354.

Rutledge, T. & Linden, W. (2000). Defensiveness status predicts 3-year incidence of hypertension. *Journal of Hypertension*, **18**, 153–159.

Ryan, E.R. & Cicchetti, D.V. (1985). Predicting quality of alliance in the initial psychotherapy interview. *Journal of Nervous and Mental Disease*, **173**, 717–725.

Salovey, P. & Mayer, J.D. (1990). Emotional intelligence. *Imagination, Cognition, and Personality*, **9**, 185–211.

Smyth, J.M. (1998) Written emotional expression: effect sizes, outcome types, and moderating variables. *Journal of Consulting and Clinical Psychology*, **66**, 174–184.

Swinkels, A. & Giuliano, T.A. (1995). The measurement and conceptualization of mood awareness: monitoring and labeling one's mood states. *Personality and Social Psychology Bulletin*, **21**, 934–949.

Taylor, G.J., Parker, J.D., & Bagby, R.M. (1997). Relationships between alexithymia and related constructs. In A. Vingerhoets, F. Van Bussel, & J. Boelhouwer (eds): *The *(non)expression of emotions in health and disease* (pp. 103–113). Tilburg, The Netherlands: Tilburg University Press.

Temoshok, L., Heller, B.W., Sagebiel, R.W., Blois, M.S., Sweet, D.M., DiClemente, R.J. & Gold, M.L. (1985). The relationship of psychosocial factors to prognostic indicators in cutaneous malignant melanoma. *Journal of Psychosomatic Research*, **29**, 139–154.

Tolor, A. & Reznikoff, M. (1960). A new approach to insight: a preliminary report. *Journal of Nervous and Mental Disease*, **130**, 286–296.

Torosian, T., Lumley, M.A., Pickard, S.D., & Ketterer, M.W. (1997). Silent versus symptomatic myocardial ischemia: the role of psychological and medical factors. *Health Psychology*, **16**, 123–130.

Trapnell, P.D. & Campbell, J.D. (1999). Private self-consciousness and the Five-Factor Model of personality: distinguishing rumination from reflection. *Journal of Personality and Social Psychology*, **76**, 284–304.

Trudeau, K.J. & Reich, R. (1995). Correlates of psychological mindedness. *Personality and Individual Differences*, **19**, 699–704.

Weinberger, D.A., Schwartz, G.E., & Davidson, R.J. (1979). Low-anxious, high-anxious, and repressive coping styles: psychometric patterns and behavioral and physiological responses to stress. *Journal of Abnormal Psychology*, **88**, 369–380.

Wolitzky, D.L. & Reuben, R. (1974). Psychological mindedness. *Journal of Clinical Psychology*, **30**, 26–30.

Chapter 12

The Stanford Emotional Self-Efficacy Scale – Cancer

Reliability, validity, and generalizability

Janine Giese-Davis, Cheryl Koopman, Lisa D. Butler, Jennifer Joss, Catherine Classen, John Roberts, Richard Rosenbluth, Gary R. Morrow and David Spiegel

Introduction

The ability to utilize strong emotional reactions in traumatic situations, to focus one's thoughts and actions, communicate distress to others, and become fully aware of potential future dangers may be a skill that provides protection (Gottman *et al.*, 1996; Greenberg, 1993; Greenberg *et al.*, 1996). This skill may involve awareness, tolerance, and acceptance of one's own emotional reactions (Greenberg & Safran, 1987; Greenberg *et al.*, 1996) combined with the confidence to use this emotional information to act on one's own behalf (Greenberg, 1993). We have created a self-report scale measuring emotional self-confidence in the face of serious illness. Three theoretical perspectives informed its construction: Bandura's self-efficacy (Bandura, 1977, 1982, 1991); emotional intelligence (Mayer & Salovey, 1993; Salovey & Mayer, 1990; Salovey *et al.*, 1995); and existential psychotherapy (Yalom, 1980).

According to Bandura, "perceived self-efficacy refers to beliefs in one's capabilities to mobilize the motivation, cognitive resources, and courses of action needed to meet given situational demands" (Wood & Bandura, 1989). Self-efficacy is important because it influences people's choice of behaviors, the amount of effort invested in executing them, perseverance in engaging in actions when obstacles arise, aspirations, and self-evaluations. People with higher self-efficacy experience fewer anxiety or trauma symptoms (Ozer & Bandura, 1990; Wood & Bandura, 1989), rebound quicker from dysphoria (Salovey *et al.*, 1995), experience less pain and suffering (Bandura *et al.*, 1987), and achieve more satisfaction with social relationships (Greenberg, 1993). Such self-efficacy for confronting and managing affect in highly emotional situations might also affect endocrine and immune functioning (Pennebaker *et al.*, 1988; Wiedenfeld *et al.*, 1990).

In creating an emotional self-efficacy scale (the Stanford Emotional Self-Efficacy Scale – Cancer SESES–C), we also utilized emerging emotional intelligence theory which postulates that "individuals differ in the skill with which they can identify their feelings and the feelings of others, regulate these feelings, and use the information provided by their feelings to motivate adaptive social behavior" (Salovey et al., 1995, p. 126). In so doing, we sought to measure confidence in one's ability to perform a set of emotional tasks. People frequently experience aversive emotional arousal in response to a threat to life (Spiegel, 1990). To cope successfully with this aversive affect, it would be ideal for those facing a life-threatening illness to acknowledge the reality of the threat by tolerating and expressing the feelings it provokes while retaining a sense of self-efficacy about the management of this affect that allows positive action to go forward. Such confidence may enable more active participation in the treatment process (Ferrero et al., 1994; Watson et al., 1991), perseverance in obtaining the best medical treatment, and assertiveness in gaining support from close others through disclosure of their emotional distress (Classen et al., 1996; Pennebaker, 1995).

Lastly, the specific types of tasks for this scale come from work with patients coping with a life-threatening cancer diagnosis who were participating in existential supportive–expressive psychotherapy. In developing this measure, we combined knowledge gathered from clinical observation, patient reports, previous studies, and existential theory regarding important domains in facing life-threatening illness (Spiegel & Glafkides, 1983; Yalom, 1980) to select these three domains of self-efficacy. These domains also reflect emerging affect-regulation theories in which disclosing (communicating emotions), modulating (focusing in the present moment), and tolerating emotion (confronting death and dying issues) (Greenberg & Safran, 1987; Greenberg et al., 1996; Horowitz, 1986; Mahoney, 1995; Pennebaker, 1995) are found to be important. Although we intend to use this scale with other serious illness populations, the current chapter presents our psychometric work with cancer patients.

Communicating emotions

Communicating emotional distress to others may be particularly important for both quality of life and physiological functioning in medically ill patients. A long history of clinical research has found an association between repression of negative emotions and higher incidence and faster progression of cancer (Derogatis et al., 1979; Goldstein & Antoni, 1989; Greer & Morris, 1975; Jensen, 1987; Kneier & Temoshok, 1984; Morris et al., 1981; Servaes et al., 1999) (for reviews, see Giese-Davis & Spiegel, 2003; Gross, 1989; Spiegel & Kato, 1996). Conversely, disclosure or expression of negative emotions to others is associated with better psychological and physiological functioning in cancer patients and in other traumatized populations (Pennebaker et al., 1988).

Remaining focused in the moment

Relaxation and meditation exercises which focus one's thoughts, and thereby modulate one's aversive affect, have been effective in reducing patients' experience of pain (Lang et al., 1996; Spiegel & Bloom, 1983). The perception of pain can also be affected by treatments bolstering self-efficacy for withstanding or reducing pain (Bandura *et al.*, 1987; Litt, 1988). Research on meditation and hypnosis (Lang *et al.*, 1996; Spiegel & Bloom, 1983) suggests that anxiety, pain, and suffering are lessened by the ability to "take one day at a time" or focus on the present moment without being overwhelmed with debilitating images of a catastrophic future. Self-efficacy in modulating affect enough to focus one's thoughts on goals and priorities in the present may help people coping with physical symptoms to be able to focus on obtaining the best medical treatment, continuing to enjoy those people with whom they are intimate, and continuing to experience a quality of life that is not undermined by the persistence of trauma symptoms or acute pain.

Confronting death and dying issues

Converging evidence indicates that confronting imagined and actual traumas in a way that encourages experiencing and expressing emotions at some depth within a relatively safe and supportive environment can lessen the psychosocial disturbance and damaging physiological effects associated with trauma (Greenberg *et al.*, 1996; Pennebaker *et al.*, 1989; Wiedenfeld *et al.*, 1990). Research with breast cancer patients has found that directly facing concerns about death and dying decreases fear and anxiety and increases positive affect (Spiegel *et al.*, 1981; Spiegel & Glafkides, 1983). Increasing one's self-efficacy by directly confronting what is fearful has also been shown to enhance immune functioning (Wiedenfeld *et al.*, 1990), which may be important to medically compromised patients.

Facing death is inherently traumatic, triggering deep instinctual fight or flight responses in most mammals (Cannon, 1929). In the case of a life-threatening illness, patients must cope with the disease process and treatment, including whatever physical changes these entail, and their impending death. Coping with the threat of death can have emotional sequelae similar to coping with past trauma including intrusive thoughts, avoidant reactions, anxiety and depression (Butler *et al.*, 1999; Cella *et al.*, 1990; Cordova *et al.*, 1995).

Previous cancer self-efficacy scale

The Cancer Behavior Inventory (CBI: Merluzzi & Sanchez, 1997) is a measure of self-efficacy and coping that was developed specifically for use with patients with cancer and has been shown to have satisfactory internal consistency and validity. The CBI assesses the perceived ability to implement cognitive and behavioral strategies (Taylor, 1995), treatment-related coping, and maintaining a positive attitude, whereas the SESES–C focuses on emotion modulation and expression in coping with cancer.

Method

Three studies determined whether the SESES–C met acceptable psychometric standards: Study I examined scale structure, internal consistency, and test–retest reliability; Study II evaluated predictive validity following intervention; and Study III investigated generalizability. For these analyses, we utilized two samples of primary and one sample of metastatic breast cancer patients.

Participants

Sample 1: Randomized primary breast cancer patients

This sample of respondents was used to test the initial factor structure, internal consistency, construct validity, and test–retest reliability of the SESES–C. Participants were 348 women who had been diagnosed with primary breast cancer and who were recruited at participating 12 sites of the Community Clinical Oncology Program (funded by the National Cancer Institute) and two academic medical settings to take part in a randomized multicenter intervention trial to assess the psychosocial benefits of a brief supportive–expressive group psychotherapy (this sample hereafter referred to as the "randomized primary sample" or "RP"). Patients had documented, biopsy-proven, breast cancer of stages I (45 percent), II (48.8 percent), or III (6.1 percent) diagnosed up to one year prior to recruitment with initial surgical treatment completed. Subjects were ineligible if there was any lingering detectable disease or metastasis beyond adjacent lymph nodes, including chest wall involvement, bone, or viscera. Women were also excluded if any other cancers had been diagnosed (except basal cell or squamous cell carcinoma of the skin or *in situ* cervical cancer) within the past ten years, or if they had other medical problems likely to limit life expectancy to less than ten years; if there was a history of major psychiatric illness for which they were hospitalized or medicated, with the exception of depression or anxiety treated for a period of less than one year; or if they had attended a cancer support group for more than two months.

Of these women, 89.5 percent were Caucasian, 2 percent Asian, 2.9 percent African American, 0.9 percent Hispanic, and 4.7 percent Native American. The majority were married (76.9 percent), with 10.4 percent single and 12.7 percent separated, divorced, or widowed. Annual household income approximated a normal distribution with 55.4 percent earning less than $60,000. Of these women, 67.7 percent received chemotherapy, 40.8 percent hormone, and 48.3 percent radiation treatments. Estrogen receptor status was positive for 66.1 percent. All of the RP sample who had completed baseline assessments prior to randomization were used for an initial principal components analysis (PCA) on the 15-item Total Scale and for Cronbach's alpha on the Total Scale and three 5-item subscales. Five subjects were not included in this sample due to incomplete data. Chi square and *t*-test comparisons of demographic and medical variables indicated that the non-completers were significantly older (non-completers: $M = 62$ years of age;

completers: $M = 49$) and were less likely to have had chemotherapy. They did not differ on group assignment (treatment or control), time from diagnosis, marital status, educational level, ethnicity, stage of disease, income, or receiving hormone or radiation treatment. Subjects assigned to the control condition, who had completed baseline and three-month follow-up questionnaires ($N = 139$), were utilized to conduct item-level, Total Scale, and subscale three-month test–retest reliability assessments. Thirty-six subjects in the control condition did not complete the three-month follow-up and therefore were not included in the test–retest analysis. Chi square and *t*-test comparisons indicated that non-completers entered the study significantly earlier in their cancer process (non-completers: $M =$ eight months; completers: $M =$ twelve months since diagnosis) but did not differ on any of the other medical or demographic variables.

Sample 2: Non-randomized primary breast cancer patients

This sample of women ($N = 114$) was used to assess both predictive validity (Study II) and generalizability (Study III) of the SESES–C following an intervention specifically targeted toward increasing self-efficacy in the three domains. Similarly to the sample described above, these women were recruited through the same national multicenter sites, but, in this case, with the request to participate in a pilot non-randomized intervention trial in which they received three months of supportive–expressive group therapy (hereafter, they are referred to as the "non-randomized primary sample" or "NRP"). Participants were 114 primary breast cancer patients who had been diagnosed with biopsy-proven stage I (46.5 percent) or II (53.5 percent) breast cancer and who were within one year of the initial diagnosis. The same exclusion criteria reported above applied to this study. Assessments were at baseline, three months, and six months.

Of these women, 93.9 percent were Caucasian, 0.9 percent Asian, 2.6 percent African American, 1.8 percent Hispanic, and 0.9 percent Native American. The majority were married (67.5 percent), with 10.5 percent single and 20.3 percent separated, divorced, or widowed. Annual household income was approximately normally distributed with 63.7 percent earning less than \$60,000. To assess comparability of these samples, distributions of demographic and medical variables of the NRP sample (who all received an intervention) were compared to those of the treatment condition in the RP sample (Study I). No differences were found. Of the 115 subjects in the baseline NRP sample, one subject had not completed all questionnaires and was not included in calculations. We utilized slopes (from baseline to six months) of the SESES–C to test the relationship of change in self-efficacy to post-intervention dependent measures for predictive validity. Of 115 subjects, 12 subjects were not included in the slopes analysis due to incomplete data. These 12 women had significantly less education (non-completers: 8 percent with less than a high school diploma and 0 percent with advanced degrees; completers: 0 percent with less than a high school diploma and 17 percent with advanced degrees) and were significantly older (non-completers: $M = 58.4$ years of age; completers: $M = 50.0$) than the sample used for the predictive validity analyses.

Sample 3: Randomized metastatic breast cancer patients

This sample of respondents was used to assess generalizability of the SESES–C to use with advanced disease. Participants were 64 women diagnosed with metastatic breast cancer (hereafter referred to as the "randomized metastatic sample" or "RM") participating in an intervention trial designed to study the effect of group psychotherapy on psychosocial adjustment and survival time. Patients had documented, biopsy-proven, breast cancer with metastasis to bone, viscera, or other sites beyond adjacent lymph nodes, muscle, and skin. They had a Karnofsky score (Karnofsky & Burchenal, 1949), a physician rating of physical disability, of at least 70 percent, and were proficient in English. Detailed exclusion criteria are discussed elsewhere (Classen *et al.*, 1996).

Of these women, 87.3 percent were Caucasian, 6.3 percent Asian, 0 percent African American, 1.6 percent Hispanic, and 3.2 percent Native American. The majority were married (49.2 percent), with 12.7 percent single and 36.5 percent separated, divorced, or widowed. Annual household income was approximately normally distributed with 69.3 percent earning less than $60,000. Of these women, 54 percent received chemotherapy, 73 percent hormone treatment. Estrogen receptor status was positive for 73 percent. We used all respondents who had completed baseline assessments prior to randomization ($N = 64$) for confirmatory alpha and Total Score-to-subscale correlation analyses on the 15-item Total Scale and the three five-item subscales. We used the RM control group who completed three-month follow-up at the time of this analysis ($N = 19$) to conduct test–retest assessments. Controls not completing this follow-up ($N = 17$) did not differ from completers on demographic or medical variables.

Measures

Demographic and medical variables

We assessed comparability among samples using demographic (age, marital status, ethnicity, and household income) and medical (months elapsed since diagnosis or between diagnosis and recurrence, disease stage, treatment received, and estrogen receptor status) variables.

Emotional self-efficacy

The SESES–C was specifically developed to measure three domains of coping self-efficacy used by patients who are facing a life-threatening illness: (i) Communicating Emotions in Relationships (CE), (ii) Focusing on the Present Moment (FP), and (iii) Confronting Death and Dying Issues (CD). It measures patients' confidence in their ability on each of 15 items (e.g. CE: "Ask for the emotional support I need from my spouse/partner or closest friend"; FP: "Stay calm while waiting for the results of medical tests"; CD: "Directly consider the thought that I might die"). Each item is rated on a 0–100 point Likert-type scale in increments of ten ranging from "not at all confident" to "completely confident." Subscale scores are the mean of the five subscale items. Total Score is the mean of all 15 items.

Suppression of affect

The Courtauld Emotional Control Scale (CECS; Watson & Greer, 1983) is a 21-item questionnaire measuring the extent to which individuals control emotions. Subscales are consistent with primary negative emotions: Anger, Depressed mood, and Anxiety.

Mood disturbance

The Profile of Mood States (POMS; McNair *et al.*, 1992) was used to assess the predictive validity of the SESES–C. A Total Mood Disturbance Score (TMD) was based on six subscales: Anxiety, Depression, Hostility, Confusion, Vigor, and Fatigue. Alpha for the NRP sample for TMD was .91 at baseline and .94 at six months.

Trauma symptoms

We also used the Impact of Event Scale (IES; Horowitz *et al.*, 1979), to assess predictive validity of the SESES–C. In this study, respondents were asked to estimate the frequency of experiencing a variety of intrusive and avoidant symptoms during the past seven days in response to having cancer. Intrusion and Avoidance symptoms combined give a Total IES Score (IES). Alpha for the NRP sample for IES was .85 at baseline and .88 at six months.

Pain and suffering in the moment

Pain and Suffering were assessed with two single-item questions from the Pain Scale (Spiegel & Bloom, 1983) and were used to assess predictive validity. Respondents rated their experience of Pain at this Moment and Suffering at this Moment on ten-point Likert-type scales anchored at the endpoints by "not noticeable" and "excruciating – worst ever", and "easily bearable" and "agonizing – unbearable" respectively.

Item selection and prior scale development for self-efficacy scale

Items selected for the current 15-item SESES–C were taken from a larger pool of items generated for a 56-item Stanford Cancer Self-Efficacy Scale (SCSES) (Joss *et al.*, 1993). Each item was retained on the basis of meeting three criteria: (a) providing a match in content to one of the three domains, (b) showing a strong correlation to the initial overall scale and subscale scores based on the larger pool of items, and (c) lacking reference to a specific serious illness (i.e. cancer). As we had no theoretical justification for unequal weighting, each domain has five items.

Items for the 56-item SCSES were derived from conversations with clinicians and women with breast cancer. Items were also based on clinical observation of nine metastatic breast cancer patients participating in a year-long pilot trial of supportive–expressive group psychotherapy. Patient discussions focused on themes of expression and management of strong emotion, communication in relationships, coping with emotional and physical pain, and death and dying issues. Group members also learned and practiced a short self-hypnosis exercise to improve their ability to focus and cope in the presence of pain and ruminative thoughts and emotions. Women in the pilot filled out the SCSES and provided feedback on the items. Content validity of the SCSES was additionally assessed by reviewing items with psychotherapists treating cancer patients, as well as consulting with Albert Bandura. An initial analysis demonstrated adequate internal consistency and reliability of these items.

Results

Study I: scale structure

Three-month test–retest Spearman rank order correlation coefficients were obtained for each item for the 139 women in the RP control condition. Because each item reliability was acceptable for entry (range: $r = .47–.66$), all 15 were included in a principal components analysis with Varimax rotation utilizing the pre-randomization data of the primary sample of 348 women.

The analysis revealed three orthogonal factors equivalent to the a priori subscale domains: Factor 1 – Communicating Emotions in Relationships (CE) (eigenvalue = 3.43); Factor 2 – Focusing on the Present Moment (FP) (eigenvalue = 3.06); and Factor 3 – Confronting Death and Dying Issues (CD) (eigenvalue = 2.70) (Table 12.1). One item ("how confident I am to: cry or express other emotions I feel about dying when I am talking with someone close to me"), originally conceptualized within the CD subscale, loaded more highly on the CE factor (.63). Because it also loaded highly on the CD factor (.55) and alphas for this subscale were not lowered by its inclusion, we decided that future subscale use could proceed with the originally conceived five items in each scale.

Further interpretation of this factor analysis, however, revealed that all items loaded highly (all >.41) on a single factor in the unrotated solution which also

Table 12.1 Results of principal components analysis of SESES–C: Randomized primary sample (N = 348) using Varimax rotation

SESES–C item	Factor 1: Communicating emotion	Factor 2: Focusing on present	Factor 3: Confronting death
15 Ask for the emotional support I need from family members	**.86**	.20	.13
4 Ask for the emotional support I need from my spouse/partner or closest friend	**.79**	.30	.04
13 Express sadness or cry with my family members	**.75**	.11	.26
7 Express love, affection, caring to my spouse/partner or closest friend	**.57**	.49	.10
1 Let my friends know when I am angry because of something they did	**.41**	.26	.25
6 Consider any issue at all while remaining calm and feeling centered	.07	**.79**	.26
5 Focus my full attention on one thing at a time	.20	**.75**	.02
12 Truly enjoy activities or people that are meaningful to me	.43	**.68**	.07
3 Be with people or do things without being distracted by painful emotions or anxious thoughts	.25	**.62**	.21
10 Stay calm while waiting for the results of medical tests	.05	**.56**	.49
8 Talk about my possible death with my spouse/partner or closest friend	.41	.10	**.76**
2 Directly consider the thought that I might die	.02	.09	**.67**
11 Face my fears about the thought that I might die without feeling anxious all day or all night	.10	.45	**.66**
9 Talk to my doctor about fears that I have about dying	.36	.20	**.66**
14 Cry or express other emotions I feel about dying when I am talking with someone close to me	.63	.03	**.55**

Table 12.2 Spearman rank-order correlations among cancer SESES–C subscales and total score in RP (*N* = 348), NRP, and RM (*N* = 64) samples

	Communicating emotion			Confronting death			Focusing on the present		
	RP	NRP	RM	RP	NRP	RM	RP	NRP	RM
Communicating emotion	–	–	–						
Confronting death	.61**	.47**	.44**	–					
Focusing on the present	.55**	.53**	.41*	.57**	.55**	.40*	–		
SESES–C total	.84**	.79**	.75**	.89**	.84**	.83**	.78**	.80**	.70**

$* p < .001, ** p < .0001.$

selected three factors above an eigenvalue of 1. This single factor accounted for most of the variance before rotation (42 percent of total variance) with an eigenvalue of 6.24 (the other two factors dropped to 1.54 and 1.42 respectively). Together, three factors accounted for 61 percent of the variance. A moderately high level of correlation with the total score and between subscales was confirmed (Table 12.2). These results indicate that subscale scores should probably be used only in cases where an intervention targets that specific subscale domain.

Alphas were obtained for the total score and each of the three a priori five-item subscales. All 348 primary breast cancer patients in the pre-randomization baseline were included. Each alpha result was within adequate range (Total Score .89, CE .82, CD .80, FP .79) with the total scale score showing the highest consistency.

Three-month test–retest reliabilities were obtained utilizing the 139 women in the primary control condition. Spearman rank order correlation coefficients for Total Score and for each of the three a priori five-item subscale scores showed adequate three-month test–retest reliability (Total Score .69, CE .71, CD .67, FP .57).

Study II: concurrent and predictive validity

Concurrent validity was not measured extensively due to the absence of another relevant self-efficacy scale with which to compare the SESES–C at the time of data collection, and because it is theoretically less important than predictive validity in the development of self-efficacy scales (Bandura, personal communication, January 1997). Concurrent validity was assessed utilizing the RP sample. We hypothesized that the CECS (Watson & Greer, 1983), a scale commonly used to assess chronic suppression of emotion in cancer patients, would be negatively correlated with the SESES–C. The Pearson Product Moment correlation was ($r = -.43, p < .001$), indicating that those who suppress their emotions report less emotional self-efficacy.

To assess predictive validity, we utilized a pilot sample of respondents who each participated in a three-month trial of supportive–expressive group therapy. Multiple-regression analyses were performed. We predicted that those who increased on the SESES–C would decrease on our primary dependent measures at six-month follow-up, including POMS, TMD, IES, Pain in the Moment, and Suffering in the Moment. Three independent variables for each analysis included (i) SESES–C Total Score slopes to measure change (from baseline to six months), (ii) SESES–C Total Score intercepts to approximate baseline level, and (iii) baseline scores of each relevant dependent measure. Simultaneous data entry was used as a conservative test of Bandura's scale development model (Bandura, 1977) in the analysis.

Results of the multiple regressions indicated that both lower six-month TMD and IES were significantly predicted by increasing slopes of change in SESES–C following intervention in combination with higher baseline scores of the dependent variables (see Table 12.3). In addition, the higher Self-Efficacy intercept also predicted lower IES at six months, but not TMD. Neither Pain nor Suffering in the Moment was predicted by Self-Efficacy (see Table 12.3).

Study III: generalizability

Generalizability was tested using the following two samples: (i) NRP breast cancer patients and (ii) metastatic breast cancer patients recruited to participate in a randomized clinical trial of supportive–expressive psychotherapy. We hypo-thesized that all three samples (including the initial RP) would be comparable in internal consistency, in construct validity utilizing the CECS, and in mean levels. We also hypothesized that the control group for the RM sample would be comparable to the RP in test–retest reliability. To test mean levels of self-efficacy, Baseline SESES–C Total Scores were compared using a univariate ANOVA and a group (three different samples) × age (> 50 years or < 50 years) × ethnicity (minority vs. non-minority) × household income (three levels of income) × marital status (married vs. unmarried) design.

Total Score and all subscale alpha results for both generalizability samples were adequate (NRP: Total .88, CE .86, CD .79, FP .78; RM: Total .88, CE .79, CD .86, FP.78) and comparable to alphas for the RP sample. Similar to the RP sample in Study I, the Total Score showed the highest level of internal consistency in both samples. Correlations between the CECS and SESES–C were comparable in magnitude across samples: RP ($r = -.43, p < .001$), NRP ($r = -.34, p < .001$), RM ($r = -.48, p < .001$). Spearman rank correlation coefficients for Total Score and each of the three subscale scores showed high three-month test–retest reliability with the RM control sample (Total .95, CE .88, CD .90, FP .80), similar to the RP sample.

However, the overall Omnibus ANOVA model was significant, indicating differences in Total Score for both group and income factors (Omnibus: $F\,(7, 460)$ = 7.53, $p < .0001$; group: $F\,(2, 460) = 18.99$, $p < .0001$; income: $F\,(2, 460) = 6.42$, $p < .002$). Age, ethnicity, and marital status were not related to Self-Efficacy scores.

Main effect for group: Mean baseline SESES–C Total Scores for the non-randomized and metastatic samples were both significantly higher than for the RP sample, though they did not differ from each other in Least Squares *post hoc* tests (LS): RP sample (RP): $M = 67.03$, S.D. = 17.39; NRP sample (NRP): $M = 77.2$, S.D. = 14.14; metastatic sample (RM): $M = 76.10$, S.D. = 15.09; NRP vs. RP: $t = -5.55$, $p < .0001$; RM vs. RP: $t = -3.98$, $p < .0001$; RM vs. NRP: $t = .52$, $p < .60$.

Table 12.3 Results of multiple regression analysis for predictive validity on mood disturbance, trauma symptoms, and pain using NRP sample ($N = 103$)

	Beta	t
Dependent variable: POMS TMD at six months		
Independent variables:		
SESES–C slope 0–6 months	−.28	−3.50***
SESES–C intercept	−.12	−1.40
POMS Total Score at baseline	.67	8.76***
Overall F-value (3, 99) = 43.74***		
Adjusted overall R^2 = .56		
Dependent variable: IES total score at six months		
Independent variables:		
SESES–C slope 0–6 months	−.26	−2.64**
SESES–C intercept	−.24	−2.34*
IES Total Score at baseline	.47	5.34***
Overall F-value (3, 97) = 15.66***		
Adjusted overall R^2 = .31		
Dependent variable: Pain in the moment at six months		
Independent variables:		
SESES–C slope 0–6 months	−.10	−1.00
SESES–C intercept	−.01	0.11
Pain in the moment at baseline	.53	6.20***
Overall F-value (3, 95) = 13.40***		
Adjusted overall R^2 = .28		
Dependent variable: Suffering in the moment at six months		
Independent variables:		
SESES–C slope 0–6 months	−.22	−1.93
SESES–C intercept	−.20	−1.73
Suffering in the moment at baseline	.09	.91
Overall F-value (3, 98) = 1.69		
Adjusted overall R^2 = .02		

* p <.05, ** p <.01, *** p <.001

Main effect for income: Mean baseline SESES–C Total Score for the lowest income group was significantly lower than the other two income groups though the two higher income groups did not differ from each other in LS *post hoc* tests: low income (LO) < $40,000 annually for total household income; middle (MID) = $40,000–$79,000; high (HI) > $80,000. Descriptive statistics for Self-Efficacy Total Scores: LO: $M = 67.82$, S.D. $= 18.25$; MID: $M = 70.71$, S.D. $= 17.09$; HI: $M = 73.37$, S.D. $= 14.83$; MID vs. LO: $t = 1.96, p < .05$; HI vs. LO: $t = 3.12, p < .002$; HI vs. MID: ns.

Discussion

The aim of the present study was to obtain information about the psychometric qualities of the SESES–C, an instrument designed to measure emotional self-efficacy in the face of serious illness. Overall, the findings indicate that the SESES–C meets acceptable psychometric standards in structure, internal consistency, test–retest reliability, concurrent and predictive validity, and generalizability among patients with breast cancer.

Bandura (1986, p. 372) has stated that "self-efficacy in psychosocial functioning is best elucidated by self-efficacy measures tailored to particular domains of functioning, rather than as global disposition assessed by an omnibus test". The SESES–C does this in two ways. First, it offers a measure of patients' overall perceived self-efficacy to cope with the emotional aspects of the existential challenges they face. In addition, the subscale scores offer a more fine-grained look at the domains in which these emotional challenges manifest themselves: specifically, communicating a full range of emotions to loved ones, maintaining one's focus in the present moment without distraction or diminution of pleasure, and confronting feelings and concerns related to death and dying.

We found that one factor accounted for most of the variance in the unrotated solution in our factor analysis on items, and that subscales were highly inter-correlated. The SESES–C Total Score also demonstrated higher internal consistency than did any of the individual subscales in both primary (randomized and un-randomized) and metastatic breast cancer samples, suggesting that there is a strong association among women's estimates of their emotional self-efficacy across domains even at different levels of illness severity. Thus, it would seem that the Total Score is the most appropriate measure of emotional self-efficacy in the face of serious illness. However, it is worth noting that the items and their subscale placement were derived a priori to correspond to the domains toward which a supportive–expressive group therapy intervention is explicitly directed (Spiegel & Glafkides, 1983), and the conceptual independence of these three factors was confirmed in the rotated factor analysis. Consequently, the subscale scores may be useful to measure hypothesized changes in these domains when they have been specifically targeted for change.

Three-month test–retest assessments for both randomized control groups demonstrated adequate reliability of the measure. However, the RM sample was small ($n = 17–19$) and non-completers in the RP sample were older and also earlier in the cancer process than completers. These sample considerations may limit generalizability. On the other hand, internal consistency and reliability across samples with different levels of illness severity confirm the generalizability of this measure. Predictive validity was confirmed following a three-month supportive–expressive psychotherapy intervention targeting the three domains of the SESES–C. Increases in levels (slopes) of self-efficacy over six months significantly predicted both lower mood disturbance and trauma symptoms over and above their prediction from respective baseline scores. Higher baseline level (intercept) of perceived self-efficacy was predictive of trauma symptoms at six months, although not of mood disturbance. Neither self-efficacy slopes nor intercepts predicted level of pain or suffering at six months.

Empirical studies have found that perceived self-efficacy may be changed by such factors as direct mastery experiences, vicariously learned social comparative information, and social persuasion (see Bandura, 1986 for a review). Each of these factors may be present in the supportive–expressive group therapy experience and may have contributed to the changes in self-efficacy that influenced overall mood disturbance and trauma symptoms. One incidental, and perhaps cautionary, finding was the significantly lower baseline levels of self-efficacy in the randomized primary sample when compared to the two other samples. Further research is needed to elucidate the individual or circumstantial differences that might lead to different levels of self-efficacy across populations with differences in illness type or severity. The comparability of the internal consistency and reliability findings from this randomized sample with the nonrandomized primary and metastatic samples, despite significant differences in baseline self-efficacy, further confirms the generalizability of this measure.

A possible criticism of the SESES–C item characteristics is that they are all worded in the same direction and therefore may be prone to a response bias. Our choice of this format was due to the apparent incomprehensibility that would be elicited by asking subjects to rate their confidence in their abilities *not* to engage in the behaviors described. Given this practical limitation, we believe that our wording represents the best (and perhaps only) way to assess the domains described. A major limitation to our conclusions from the psychotherapy intervention (in the pilot sample) is the absence of a control group (because no control pilot group was conducted). Consequently the observed changes may be unrelated to the intervention. Our findings in this case can only be considered tentative until further tested in randomized trials.

Our hypothesis that increasing self-efficacy would be associated with lower reported pain levels was not supported. Although this appears to be at odds with the well-established laboratory and clinical evidence that strong perceptions of efficacy to manage pain increase pain tolerance (Bandura *et al.*, 1987; O'Leary, 1985), it should be noted that we did not specifically measure perceived self-efficacy to manage pain. Our prediction was based on the finding that enhancing general self-efficacy can reduce pain (Smarr *et al.*, 1997) and that inhibition of emotion may intensify pain (Kerns *et al.*, 1994). Our single-item pain measures may lack psychometric stability, thereby limiting our ability to assess this hypothesis. Future research could utilize a more comprehensive pain measure, as well as a self-efficacy scale particularly aimed at confidence in managing pain.

Finally, it is our belief that the domains tapped by the SESES–C represent relevant concerns for all those suffering from serious illnesses, and therefore this scale is appropriate across diverse medical populations. However, to date our reported norms represent only two populations of breast cancer patients differing in illness severity. Future research is needed to assess the utility of the SESES–C empirically with other seriously medically ill populations. In summary, we believe we have constructed a reliable and valid measure that uniquely gauges breast cancer patients' self-confidence to cope with the emotional demands that challenge them in their lives and treatment. Supportive–expressive therapy specifically targets increasing or maintaining these coping skills even as physical health declines; however, we believe that this scale would be useful in psychotherapy outcome research with people with cancer regardless of therapy orientation. For many people, if not specifically probed, it would be difficult for them to bring up the issues represented in this scale. We therefore believe that it would be useful clinically as a screening tool when beginning to work with someone with cancer who has a poor prognosis, and as an opening for exploration of these important issues.

Acknowledgments

This research was supported by grants from the National Cancer Institute (CA61309) and MacArthur Foundation awarded to David Spiegel; the Cummings Foundation and NCI (CA37420) to Gary R. Morrow; and a postdoctoral fellowship grant to the first author from the Breast Cancer Research Program of California. We acknowledge helpful consultations with Helena Kraemer, PhD and Albert Bandura, PhD on data analyses. We are grateful for the technical support of Sue DiMiceli, Ami Atkinson, Diana Edwards, and those involved in data collection and entry for these studies. Lastly, we wish to thank the participants who took time to fill out our instruments despite their illness.

References

Bandura, A. (1977). Self-efficacy: toward a unifying theory of behavioral change. *Psychology Review*, **84**, 191–215.

Bandura, A. (1982). Self-efficacy mechanism in human agency. *American Psychologist*, **37**, 112–147.

Bandura, A. (1986). The explanatory and predictive scope of self-efficacy theory. *Journal of Social and Clinical Psychology*, **4**, 359–373.

Bandura, A. (1991). Social cognitive theory of self-regulation. *Organizational Behavior and Human Decision Processes*, **50**, 248–287.

Bandura, A., O'Leary, A., Taylor, C.B., Gauthier, J., & Gossard, D. (1987). Perceived self-efficacy and pain control: opioid and nonopioid mechanisms. *Journal of Personality and Social Psychology*, **53**, 563–571.

Butler, L.D., Koopman, C., Classen, C., & Spiegel, D. (1999). Traumatic stress, life events, and emotional support in women with metastatic breast cancer: cancer-related traumatic stress symptoms associated with past and current stressors. *Health Psychology*, **18**, 1–6.

Cannon, W.B. (1929). *Bodily changes in pain, hunger, fear, and rage* (2nd edn). New York: Appleton.

Cella, D.F., Mahon, S.M., & Donovan, M.I. (1990). Cancer recurrence as a traumatic event. *Behavioral Medicine*, **16**, 15–22.

Classen, C., Koopman, C., Angell, K., & Spiegel, D. (1996). Coping styles associated with psychological adjustment to advanced breast cancer. *Health Psychology*, **15**, 434–437.

Cordova, M.J., Andrykowski, M.A., Redd, W.H., Kenady, D.E., McGrath, P.C., & Sloan, D.A. (1995). Frequency and correlates of posttraumatic-stress-disorder-like symptoms after treatment for breast cancer. *Journal of Consulting and Clinical Psychology*, **63**, 981–986.

Derogatis, L.R., Abeloff, M.D., & Melisaratos, N. (1979). Psychological coping mechanisms and survival time in metastatic breast cancer. *Journal of the American Medical Association*, **242**, 1504–1508.

Ferrero, J., Barreto, M., & Toledo, M. (1994). Mental adjustment to cancer and quality of life in breast cancer patients: an exploratory study. *Psycho-Oncology*, **3**, 223–232.

Giese-Davis, J. & Spiegel, D. (2003). Emotional expression and cancer progression. In R.J. Davidson, K.R. Scherer, & H. Hill Goldsmith (eds), *Handbook of affective sciences* (pp. 1053–1082). Oxford: Oxford University Press.

Goldstein, D. & Antoni, M. (1989). The distribution of repressive copying styles among non-metastatic and metastatic breast cancer patients as compared to non-cancer patients. *Psychology and Health*, **3**, 245–258.

Gottman, J.M., Katz, L.F., & Hooven, C. (1996). Parental meta-emotion philosophy and the emotional life of families: theoretical models and preliminary data. *Journal of Family Psychology*, **10**, 243–268.

Greenberg, L. (1993). Emotion and change processes in psychotherapy. In M. Lewis & J.M. Haviland (eds), *Handbook of emotions* (pp. 499–519). New York: Guilford Press.

Greenberg, L.S. & Safran, J.D. (1987). *Emotion in psychotherapy*. New York: Guilford Press.

Greenberg, M.A., Wortman, C.B., & Stone, A.A. (1996). Emotional expression and physical health: revising traumatic memories or fostering self-regulation? *Journal of Personality and Social Psychology*, **71**, 588–602.

Greer, S. & Morris, T. (1975). Psychological attributes of women who develop breast cancer: a controlled study. *Journal of Psychosomatic Research*, **19**, 147–153.

Gross, J. (1989). Emotional expression in cancer onset and progression. *Social Science and Medicine*, **28**, 1239–1248.

Horowitz, M.J. (1986). Stress response syndromes: a review of posttraumatic and adjustment disorders. *Hospital Community Psychiatry*, **37**, 241–249.

Horowitz, M., Wilner, N., & Alvarez, W. (1979). Impact of Event Scale: a measure of subjective stress. *Psychosomatic Medicine*, **41**, 209–218.

Jensen, M.R. (1987). Psychobiological factors predicting the course of breast cancer. *Journal of Personality*, **55**, 317–342.

Joss, J.E., Spira, J.L., & Spiegel, D. (1993). *Stanford Cancer Self Efficacy Scale* (unpublished manuscript). Stanford, CA: Stanford University.

Karnofsky, D.A. & Burchenal, J.H. (1949). *The clinical evaluation of chemotherapeutic agents in cancer.* New York: Columbia University Press.

Kerns, R.D., Rosenberg, R., & Jacob, M.C. (1994). Anger expression and chronic pain. *Journal of Behavioral Medicine,* **17**, 57–67.

Kneier, A.W. & Temoshok, L. (1984). Repressive coping reactions in patients with malignant melanoma as compared to cardiovascular disease patients. *Journal of Psychosomatic Research,* **28**, 145–155.

Lang, E., Joyce, J., Spiegel, D., Hamilton, D., & Lee, K. (1996). Self-hypnotic relaxation during interventional radiological procedures: effects on pain perception and intravenous drug use. *The International Journal of Clinical and Experimental Hypnosis,* **44**, 106–119.

Litt, M.D. (1988). Self-efficacy and perceived control: cognitive mediators of pain tolerance. *Journal of Personality and Social Psychology,* **54**, 154–160.

McNair, D.M., Lorr, M., & Droppelman, L. (1992). *Edits manual for the profile of mood states.* San Diego, CA: Educational and Industrial Testing Service.

Mahoney, M.J. (1995). Emotionality and health: lessons from and for psychotherapy. In J.W. Pennebaker (ed.), *Emotional, disclosure, and health* (pp. 241–254). Washington, DC: American Psychological Association.

Mayer, J.D. & Salovey, P. (1993). The intelligence of emotional intelligence. *Intelligence,* **17**, 433–442.

Merluzzi, T.V. & Sanchez, M.A.M. (1997). Assessment of self-efficacy and coping with cancer: development and validation of the Cancer Behavioral Inventory. *Health Psychology,* **16**, 163–170.

Morris, T., Greer, S., Pettingale, K.W., & Watson, M. (1981). Patterns of expression of anger and their psychological correlates in women with breast cancer. *Journal of Psychosomatic Research,* **25**, 111–117.

O'Leary, A. (1985). Self-efficacy and health. *Behavioral Research Therapy,* **23**, 437–451.

Ozer, E.M. & Bandura, A. (1990). Mechanisms governing empowerment effects: a self-efficacy analysis. *Journal of Personality and Social Psychology,* **58**, 472–486.

Pennebaker, J.W. (ed.) (1995). *Emotion, disclosure, and health.* Washington, DC: American Psychological Association.

Pennebaker, J.W., Barger, S.D., & Tiebout, J. (1989). Disclosure of traumas and health among Holocaust survivors. *Psychosomatic Medicine,* **51**, 577–589.

Pennebaker, J.W., Kiecolt-Glaser, J.K., & Glaser, R. (1988). Disclosure of traumas and immune function: health implications for psychotherapy. *Journal of Consulting and Clinical Psychology,* **56**, 239–245.

Salovey, P. & Mayer, J.D. (1990). Emotional intelligence. *Imagination, Cognition, and Personality,* **9**, 185–211.

Salovey, P., Mayer, J.D., Goldman, S.L., Turvey, C., & Palfai, T.P. (1995). Emotional attention, clarity, and repair: exploring emotional intelligence using the trait meta-mood scale. In J.W. Pennebaker (ed.), *Emotional, disclosure, and health* (pp. 125–154). Washington, DC: American Psychological Association.

Servaes, P., Vingerhoets, A.J.J.M., Vreugdenhil, G., Keuning, J.J., & Broekhuijsen, A.M. (1999). Inhibition of emotional expression in breast cancer patients. *Behavioral Medicine,* **25**, 23–27.

Smarr, K.L., Parker, J.G., Wright, G.E., Stucky-Ropp, R.C., Buckelew, S.P., Hoffman, R.W., O'Sullivan, F.X., & Hewett, J.E. (1997). The importance of enhancing self-efficacy in rheumatoid arthritis. *Arthritis Care and Research*, **10**, 18–26.

Spiegel, D. (1990). Facilitating emotional coping during treatment. *Cancer*, **66**, 1422–1426.

Spiegel, D. & Bloom, J.R. (1983). Group therapy and hypnosis reduce metastatic breast carcinoma pain. *Psychosomatic Medicine*, **45**, 333–339.

Spiegel, D., Bloom, J.R., & Yalom, I. (1981). Group support for patients with metastatic cancer. A randomized outcome study. *Archives of General Psychiatry*, **38**, 527–533.

Spiegel, D. & Glafkides, M.C. (1983). Effects of group confrontation with death and dying. *International Journal of Group Psychotherapy*, **33**, 433–447.

Spiegel, D. & Kato, P. (1996). Psychosocial influences on cancer incidence and progression. *Harvard Review of Psychiatry*, **4**, 10–26.

Taylor, S.E. (1995). *Health Psychology* (3rd edn). New York: McGraw-Hill.

Watson, M. & Greer, S. (1983). Development of a questionnaire measure of emotional control. *Journal of Psychosomatic Research*, **27**, 299–305.

Watson, M., Greer, S., Rowden, L., Gorman, C., Robertson, B., Bliss, J.M., & Tunmore, R. (1991). Relationships between emotional control, adjustment to cancer and depression and anxiety in breast cancer patients. *Psychological Medicine*, **21**, 51–57.

Wiedenfeld, S.A., O'Leary, A., Bandura, A., Brown, S., Levine, S., & Raska, K. (1990). Impact of perceived self-efficacy in coping with stressors on components of the immune system. *Journal of Personality and Social Psychology*, **59**, 1082–1094.

Wood, R. & Bandura, A. (1989). Impact of conceptions of ability on self-regulatory mechanisms and complex decision making. *Journal of Personality and Social Psychology*, **56**, 407–415.

Yalom, I.D. (1980). *Existential psychotherapy*. New York: Basic Books.

Part III

Developmental aspects

Chapter 13

Attachment representation and affect regulation

Current findings of attachment research and their relevance for psychosomatic medicine

Carl Eduard Scheidt and Elisabeth Waller

Introduction

Deficits of affect regulation and affect recognition have been considered as vulnerability factors for the development and course of psychosomatic illness. In the present chapter, the affect regulation is considered from an attachment theory perspective. We claim that the expression and recognition of affects are central features of the infant–mother interaction. Affects regulate distance and closeness and signal the infant's need for support and reassurance. The mother's sensitivity towards the infant's affective signals has turned out as an influential predictor of the infant's attachment security in later development. It may be assumed that the capacity for affect recognition and affect expression and the development of attachment security share a common developmental pathway.

In the following paragraphs, we will first summarize some of the basic concepts of attachment theory. We will then discuss the issue of mental representation of attachment, which is particularly important for the study of attachment in adulthood. Finally, we will outline the contribution of attachment research to the understanding of psychopathological conditions in adulthood with special reference to psychosomatic illnesses.

Basic concepts of attachment theory

Bowlby (1975) defined attachment as an innate system of motivation and behavior with the function to provide those who are not yet self-viable after birth with a sense of closeness and security as protection against external dangers. The term "attachment" refers to a system of behavior serving to establish or protect the close vicinity to an attachment person, generally, the mother. With humans, in the first months of life this behavior is characterized by sucking, clinging, crying, and smiling. By the end of the first year, the different reactions small infants show to separation from the attachment person demonstrate varying behavior patterns. Individual differences in the attachment behavior are brought into the foreground during this period. Empirical descriptions of individual differences in attachment behavior can be found in studies conducted by the Canadian development psychologist M.D.S. Ainsworth (Ainsworth *et al.*, 1971, 1978; Ainsworth & Wittig, 1969). Ainsworth found different characteristics in reactions of 12-month-old children to a short separation from the mother. While some children break out into helplessness and anxiety, others can tolerate the separation much better. Ainsworth related these different reactions to separation to the security of infant bonding with the mother. To examine this hypothesis empirically, she developed a research paradigm, which has become known as the "Strange Situation". In the Strange Situation, the behavior of the child is observed systematically, especially when separated from the mother for a while and after reunion. Based on her observations, Ainsworth *et al.* (1978) were able to categorize the infant bonding behavior into three main groups. She differentiated children with *secure* attachment (B-category), children with *insecure–avoiding* attachment (A-category) and children *with insecure–ambivalent* attachment (C-category). Children in the B-category could use the mother as a "secure base" in the periods of free play and exploration. At the reunion after both separation periods the children demonstrated welcoming behavior through laughing, calling and actively moving towards the mother. These children quickly allowed their mothers to calm them and soon returned to their play and exploration activities. Children in the A-category demonstrated a surprisingly low anxiety reaction. At the reunion, however, they noticeably avoided closeness and interaction: the mother was either totally ignored upon return or the greeting was with avoidance behavior such as turning away, walking past or avoiding eye contact. Children in the C-category reacted to the separation from the mother with a great amount of protest. Even before the separation, the exploring behavior was limited due to the search for closeness and contact. At the reunion the children behaved ambivalently: they tried on the one hand to establish physical contact and on the other hand discouraged this through annoying behavior such as kicking, pushing themselves away etc. These children were difficult to calm after the separation and showed delayed return to the play and exploring activities.

To be sure that the behaviors observed in the Strange Situation were similar to real-life situations of infant–mother interaction and were not an artefact of the laboratory situation, Ainsworth also observed the interaction between mother and child in the home environment. Results were obtained which validated the Strange Situation observations: in the home, the mothers of B-children applied more physical contact and were more sensitive, cooperative and approachable than the mothers of insecure avoiding children. The mothers of A-children often reacted with delay to the cries of their babies and observed these even less often after the reunion (Ainsworth *et al.*, 1978). They also allowed more undercurrent anger and undercurrent annoyance, and showed a higher degree of rigidity and rejection to their children than mothers of securely attached children. Scoring the maternal behavior in the dimension of responsiveness towards the infant (Ainsworth, 1973, 1977; Ainsworth *et al.*, 1971, 1978), maternal sensitivity proved to be a significant influential factor of attachment security (for the construct of maternal sensitivity see Ainsworth *et al.*, 1978; Belsky, 1984; Egerland & Faber, 1984; Grossmann *et al.*, 1985). The connection between maternal sensitivity and quality of attachment during the first year has been confirmed in numerous further studies (Belsky, 1984; Egerland & Faber, 1984; Grossmann *et al.*, 1985).

Further observations in the 1980s led to a discovery of another attachment behavior pattern, which was termed the *disorganized attachment behavior*. Researchers working with maltreated and psychologically conspicuous parents had realized that some children, who had been maltreated, had been scored as "secure" in their attachment behavior although they simultaneously demonstrated behavior patterns typical for insecure–avoiding as well as insecure–ambivalent children (Crittenden, 1985; Radke-Yarrow *et al.*, 1985). Main and Weston (1981) reported that some 13 percent of the children of the "Bay Area sample" could not be categorized according to the usual rules of classification by Ainsworth. A later reanalysis of the videotapes showing children who were difficult to categorize proved that the majority of non-categorized children demonstrated disorganized attachment behavior in the presence of the parents (Main & Solomon, 1986, 1990). This disorganized attachment behavior appears to be associated with non-directed or broken-off movements, vocalizations to the stranger while the mother left the room during the Strange Situation, non-directed hits to the face (often the eyes) of the parents, movement stereotypes, asymmetrical and temporally uncoordinated movement and posture abnormalities, freezing, staring expressions or a generally slowed movement and movement of expression. These behaviors were labeled disorganized because they were not regarded as a distinct, consistent, and coherent attachment strategy (Main, 1995). In non-clinical samples, the percentage of children showing disorganization lies at 15–25 percent. In samples of maltreated children, however, the percentage amounts to 80 percent (Carlson *et al.*, 1989; Lyons-Ruth *et al.*, 1991). Such findings suggest that disorganization is a consequence of trauma affecting attachment behavior.

The mental representation of attachment

In later child and adult life the cognitive processing of social experience as well as the use of symbolical communication becomes increasingly important. This led to attachment research from the mid-1980s becoming increasingly interested in examining the quality of attachment at levels of mental, symbolical representation of the attachment experience. This cannot be assessed by the observation of behavior only. Rather it was assumed that in adulthood individual differences of attachment reveal themselves in the linguistic discourse on attachment experiences, such as during an in-depth interview. Securely attached individuals would be able to give access to experiences with attachment figures in childhood in a more complete and coherent manner than individuals with an insecure attachment representation.

The development of the interview method of examination to record the differences of attachment representation in adult life served to examine the transgenerational continuity of individual differences in the quality of attachment. In a series of studies, it was shown that the attachment representation of the mother, or the main attachment person, did indeed provide a relatively reliable prediction of the attachment security of the infant in the Strange Situation at the age of 12 months (Ainsworth & Eichberg, 1991; Fremmer-Bombik, 1987; Fonagy *et al.*, 1991; Grossmann *et al.*, 1988; Ward & Carlson, 1995).

The ontogenetic continuity of the attachment behavior, i.e. the prediction of security in the quality of attachment in later child and adult years, was the topic of numerous studies. The results showed that the ontogenetic continuity of attachment organization varied between different age groups. In the age range between 12 and 18 months (Main & Weston, 1981; Waters, 1978), between one year and six years (Main & Cassidy, 1988; Wartner *et al.*, 1994) and between one year and ten years a high to very high stability in the attachment behavior (over 80 percent) could be proved. The results of long-term studies examining the continuity of the quality of attachment between 12 months and 16, 17, and 21 years are contradictory. Two studies established a stable quality of attachment even over these very long time periods (Hamilton, 2000; Waters *et al.*, 1995). However, one investigation found no connections (Zimmermann *et al.*, 1995). The discussion about how these contradictory results can be explained still continues.

The Adult Attachment Interview (George *et al.*, 1995), which is used in many of the quoted studies, is a half-structured interview consisting of 15 questions relating to attachment experience during childhood and its influence on further personal development. The interview makes the assumption that attachment security in adults is reflected in the differences in accessibility to the attachment experience from childhood. The accessibility to the attachment experience is judged with respect to its completeness, extensiveness and coherence of description in the interview (Main & Goldwyn, 1996).

The typology of attachment representation in adulthood is based on the infant model of attachment behavior in the Strange Situation. It shows that individuals with an *insecure–dismissing* attachment representation often couldn't substantiate their general judgement on attachment experience via episodic memory. Relationship experience was idealized in general descriptions without being supported by correlating episodic recollection. Furthermore, attachment experience was considered of little relevance for one's own personal development. A *secure–autonomous* attachment representation, however, allowed for an extensive, clear and precise account of the different facets of previous attachment experience. The account was complete and coherent. General and episodic descriptions showed a clear correspondence. The participants behaved cooperatively in the interview. Positive as well as negative aspects of the relationship with their parents were discussed frankly, while the focus of attention during the interview changed flexibly between the questions posed by the interviewer and the participants' personal recollections and thoughts (Main & Goldwyn, 1996). Persons with *insecure–ambivalent* attachment representation, in contrast, are not able to describe experiences with attachment figures in a coherent and objective way due to the involvement in previous attachment experiences. Instead, the description of the attachment persons changes in quick succession between positive and negative judgements. The subjects lose the line of discussion without realizing this themselves. They are unable to abstract specific experiences and recollections and to draw general conclusions. The interview is characterized by mainly episodic memories, which are not brought together with one coherent general picture of the attachment history.

Analogously to the *disorganized (D)* category of infant attachment behavior, an *unresolved (U)* category for adulthood was set up (Main & Goldwyn, 1996; Main & Hesse, 1990). The main characteristic of the disorganized and unresolved attachment representation is the unsuccessful or incomplete working through of loss or trauma (maltreatment or misuse by the attachment person), which has led to a disorganized behavior or thinking process. In discussing the experiences of loss or trauma in the interview, disorganization is demonstrated by a change in the logical and linguistic structure of the discourse, whereby facts in connection with loss or maltreatment are mixed up, denied, brought into question or falsified.

To conclude, observations from attachment research suggest that individual differences in attachment show a considerable stability over time. Differences of attachment style may be considered as central organizing patterns of social behavior and emotional experience. In adulthood, attachment must be considered on the level of representational processes. In the following section we will report on some clinical implications of attachment theory with special reference to psychosomatic illness.

Attachment theory and psychosomatic research

From the perspective of attachment theory, three questions present themselves for psychosomatic research, which will be discussed further on. These questions are:

(1) Is the prevalence of insecure patterns of attachment increased in clinical conditions and in particular in patients with psychosomatic disturbances?
(2) Does attachment security differentially affect physiological arousal in response to stress?
(3) Is insecure attachment associated with disturbances of affect regulation, etiologically relevant for psychosomatic illness?

Differences in attachment representation between clinical and non-clinical groups

The assumption that the quality of previous attachment experience has an influence on the coping with later developmental tasks is a fundamental postulate of attachment theory. Numerous studies confirm the connection between attachment behavior in early childhood and later socioemotional development (see Schieche, 1996, for an overview). These investigations generally suggest a more favorable course of psychological and social adaptation in children with a secure pattern of attachment in early infancy. It therefore seemed reasonable to examine the prevalence of secure or insecure attachment representation in clinical groups. Studies included infants and adolescents with conduct disorders (Crowell & Feldman, 1991; Rosenstein & Horowitz, 1993) as well as adults with various symptoms such as sleeping disorders (Benoit *et al.*, 1992), depression (Patrick *et al.*, 1994; Rosenstein & Horowitz, 1993), borderline disorder (Fonagy, 1993) and others (Crittenden *et al.*, 1991; Fonagy, 1993). Van IJzendoorn and Bakermans-Kranenburg (1996) summarize 14 clinical studies in which a total of 439 participants were examined with the Adult Attachment Interview. Only 13 percent of them proved to have a secure attachment representation, 41 percent had an insecure–dismissing, and 46 percent an insecure–ambivalent attachment representation. The frequency of the two insecure attachment patterns varied in the individual studies depending on the type of disorder. In borderline patients, for example, a high proportion of subjects with an insecure–ambivalent attachment representation was observed (Fonagy, 1993; Patrick *et al.*, 1994), while patients with sleeping disorders (Benoit *et al.*, 1992) more frequently had an insecure–dismissing attachment representation.

There are almost no studies to date on attachment representation in psychosomatic syndromes. One exception is a study by Slawsby (1995), in which patients with chronic atypical facial pain and patients with neuralgia of the trigeminus nerve were compared. A significantly higher prevalence of insecure attachment representation was found in patients with atypical facial pain.

In conclusion, substantial empirical evidence supports the hypothesis that insecure patterns of attachment are significantly more frequent in clinical than in non-clinical populations. In addition, some studies suggest a differential prevalence of the two insecure patterns in different clinical conditions. For instance, the insecure ambivalent pattern seems more prevalent in borderline personality disorder, whereas in psychosomatic and somatoform disorders an insecure dismissing attachment representation prevails.

Patterns of attachment and psychophysiological arousal in response to stress

Research on the psychobiology of attachment has provided evidence that the formation and disruption of social relationships has important physiological consequences. The physiological reactions, which were observed subsequent to separation in young primates, include changes in body temperature, heart rate, endocrine and immune functions, body weight and sleep patterns (Coe, 1993; Coe *et al.*, 1985; Hofer, 1973, 1984, 1994; Reite & Boccia, 1994). Considering the psychobiologic aspects of attachment in humans, Bowlby (1969) suggested that the attachment behavior system is interrelated with physiological systems in a sequential–hierarchical manner: physiological responses occur if the behavioral adaptation to changes in the environment is insufficient. According to this hypothesis, physiological arousal in response to separation indicates that cognitive and behavioral coping strategies are exhausted.

Evidence from developmental psychological research points out that during the early stages of development the regulation of physiological processes strongly depends on the quality of the attachment relationship to a primary care provider. Particularly, maternal sensitivity has been demonstrated to influence the infants' physiological response to stress. Children of less sensitive mothers showed significantly higher levels of salivary cortisol than children of sensitive mothers during periods of free play and exploration in the age of three to six months (Spangler *et al.*, 1994). At the age of 12 months, observations during the Strange Situation (Ainsworth *et al.*, 1978) showed that infants with insecure–avoidant attachment behavior have higher levels of salivary cortisol in response to separation than securely attached infants (Spangler & Grossmann, 1993).

Studies investigating the link between attachment and the psychophysiological response to stress in adults demonstrated that subjects with dismissing attachment show a significantly higher increase in the level of skin conductance while answering questions referring to separation, rejection or threat from the parents than subjects with secure attachment (Dozier & Kobak, 1992). Furthermore, heart rate and blood pressure levels were elevated in insecure–dismissing and insecure–ambivalent subjects during a stressful laboratory task, when their romantic partners were present (Carpenter & Kirkpatrick, 1996).

In sum, these findings suggest that insecure patterns of attachment and in particular an insecure–dismissing attachment pattern might be a determinant of an elevated psychophysiological response to stress and therefore should be considered as a risk factor predisposing to physical illness.

Affect regulation and psychosomatic illness

The suppression of affect expression is also considered as being an important factor in the etiology and course of psychosomatic illness. The assumption of an inverse relationship between emotional expression and physiological arousal in response to stress historically can be traced back to Alexander (1949). This author postulated that physiological processes belonging to non-realized fight-or-flight reactions changed into a dysfunctional permanent activation if they were not realized by action.

The clinical findings that persons suffering from a psychosomatic illness often are not able to realize and express their feelings led Nemiah and Sifneos (1970) to the concept of alexithymia. These authors characterized a personality structure marked by a disturbance in the experience and recognition of emotions. The concept includes the idea that in alexithymic individuals affects have lost their function as links between psychological and physiological processes. As descriptive characteristics of alexithymia, a narrowing and paralysis of the emotional and fantasy life were emphasized (Lesser, 1981). In addition, authors of the French psychosomatic school (Marty & de M'Uzan, 1963) brought forward the cognitive characteristics of "operational thought" (*pensée operatoire*), which manifest themselves in a deficit of fantasy and an inner life which centered on the details of external reality. Taylor (1994) cites empirical evidence which suggests that a decisive aspect of alexithymia consists of deficiencies in the interpersonal regulation of emotions. Patients scoring high on alexithymia showed a "dissociation of the physiological and subjective response to stressful stimuli as well as high tonic levels of sympathetic activity that are not modulated by a changing environment" (Taylor, 1994, p. 63). However, alexithymic characteristics are etiologically relevant for psychosomatic illnesses in only a minority of cases. Alexithymia therefore should be understood more generally as one component among several in a model of *vulnerability* for psychosomatic illness.

Due to a lack of appropriate assessment tools, for long alexithymia did not get attention in psychophysiological research. Hypotheses on an inverse link between affect expression and physiological activation were not systematically elaborated in alexithymia research. However, the clinical validity of the concept together with the more recent availability of a reliable measure (Bagby *et al.*, 1994a, 1994b) has contributed to the most recent series of studies that have been carried out on this issue (see Chapter 8).

Another important emotional non-expression construct is the "repressive coping style" (Byrne, 1961; Weinberger, 1990; Weinberger *et al.*, 1979). Repression relates explicitly to the connection between affect regulation and physiological arousal. Repression is a habitual personality characteristic that regulates the processing of fear-arousing or stress-related information (Weinberger, 1990). Persons with a repressive coping style suppress fear-releasing information that could lead to a contradiction in self-perception. The opposite pole to a repressive coping-style is a "sensitizing" information processing style. This is connected to a strengthened focus on fear-arousing information (Aspendorf & Scherer, 1983; Krohne & Rogner, 1985). The validity of the repression construct has been demonstrated in various psychophysiological studies: repression has been associated with increased cardiovascular reactivity (King *et al.*, 1990), increased plasmalipids (Niaura *et al.*, 1992) and a reduced cellular immune competence (Esterling *et al.*, 1990). A repressive coping style is also connected to specific characteristics of autobiographical memories: persons with higher repression have less access to their childhood memories. On the whole, they report fewer recollections, especially of negative experiences, and they need longer to recollect negative experiences than non-repressors (Myers & Brewin, 1994).

The relationship between affect expression and physiological arousal has been repeatedly studied over the past years (Anderson, 1981; Sänger-Alt *et al.*, 1989; Traue, 1989). Berry and Pennebaker (1993) concluded in a review paper that persons who suppress emotional expression for whatever reason have a high risk for a number of illnesses. However, to date no evidence has been provided for the idea that the suppression of affects is specifically related to psychosomatic illness (Anderson, 1981) or that the selective suppression of negative emotions is more frequent in patients with psychosomatic illnesses than in other persons (Sänger-Alt *et al.*, 1989).

One can conclude that there have been studies linking deficits in affect regulation and expression to physiological functioning and health. However, this has not been obtained exclusively for psychosomatic symptoms and illnesses.

Insecure attachment and affect regulation

From the attachment theory perspective, the realization and expression of affects serves to conserve the relationship to the attachment person. Normally, affective expression – especially the expression of negative affects – is an important signal in order to receive support from parents (Cassidy, 1994). However, if the expression of emotions specially intended to attract the care of the attachment person (e.g. expressions of fear and anger) continuously leads to rejection, a style of affect behavior develops that is based on minimizing affect expression and masking of negative emotions. Based on findings of Ainsworth *et al.* (1978) with respect to the origin of attachment behavior in insecure–avoiding infants, it can be assumed that the avoiding-attachment behavior develops as a consequence of rejection towards the infant's search for closeness and contact. The minimizing of attachment behavior and emotional expression, and the masking of negative affects, allows the infant to preserve perceived closeness to the attachment figure, in spite of the rejection (Main, 1981; Main & Weston, 1981). The narrowing of emotional expression in insecure–avoiding infants can be understood as part of a communicative strategy to indicate that the child stakes no claims (Cassidy, 1994). Escher-Gräub & Grossmann (1983) tested the behavior of two-year-old infants and their mothers during an episode of free play and observed that the mothers of securely attached infants only participated in the play and supported this when the infants showed signs of negative affects (tension and annoyance). In contrast, the mothers of insecure–avoiding infants participated especially when the infants were satisfied and withdrew when negative affects were expressed. It can be concluded that in the interaction with the mother, infants with avoiding attachment find less support than securely attached infants in tolerating negative emotions and learning to cope with them.

Recent studies on the psychosocial conditions in which alexithymia arises showed a connection between a low emotional expressiveness in the family and higher scores of alexithymia in the offspring. In addition, a lower sense of security was observed within the family relationships of alexithymic individuals (Berenbaum & James, 1994). Moreover, an association was found between alexithymic characteristics of infants or adolescents and their mothers (Lumley & Norman, 1996), suggesting a transgenerational link for alexithymia. Finally, in patients with idiopathic spasmodic torticollis, secure attachment representation correlated negatively, and an insecure–dismissing attachment strategy correlated positively, with alexithymia (Scheidt *et al.*, 1999).

It can thus be concluded that convergence can be observed between the results of (i) attachment research into dyadic affect regulation in childhood, suggesting an association between insecure attachment and narrowing of emotional expressiveness, especially with respect to negative affect, and (ii) the retrospective tests into the origins of alexithymia, pointing at potential links with the presence of alexithymia in the parents and with feelings of insecurity within the family. Further studies are necessary to clear the relationship between developmental roots of attachment representation and the clinically described disturbances of affect-regulation later in life.

Conclusion

The application of attachment theory concepts and methods in psychosomatic medicine is still in an early stage. The aim of this chapter is to indicate that psychosomatic research could make better progress when incorporating findings from attachment research. The attachment theory offers a scientific framework for the developmental and etiological aspects of psychosomatic disturbances, which are frequently encountered in clinical practice. Previously developed methods for attachment research should be applied also in clinical psychosomatic research. Only then will it be possible to undertake empirical studies on a pathogenetic model of psychosomatic illnesses based on psychological developmental concepts.

References

Ainsworth, M.D.S. (1973). The development of infant–mother attachment. In B.M. Caldwell & H.N. Ricciuti (eds), *Review of Child Development Research*, Vol. 3 (pp. 1–99). New York: Sage.

Ainsworth, M.D.S. (1977). Skalen zur Erfassung mütterlichen Verhaltens: Feinfühligkeit versus Unempfindlichkeit gegenüber den Signalen des Babys [Scales to assess maternal behavior. Sensitivity versus insensitivity for the baby's signals]. In K.E. Grossmann (ed.), *Entwicklung der Lernfähigkeit [Development of Learning Skills]* (pp. 96–107). Munich: Kindler.

Ainsworth, M.D.S. & Wittig, B.A. (1969). Attachment and the exploratory behavior of one-year-olds in a strange situation. In B.M. Foss (ed.), *Determinants of infant behavior*, Vol. 4 (pp. 113–136). London: Methuen.

Ainsworth, M.D.S., Bell, S.M., & Stayton, D. (1971). Individual differences in strange-situation behavior of one-year-olds. In H.R. Schaffer (ed.), *The origins of human social relations* (pp. 17–57). New York: Academic Press.

Ainsworth, M.D.S., Blehar, M., Waters, E., & Wall, S. (1978). *Patterns of attachment*. Hillsdale, NJ: Lawrence Erlbaum.

Ainsworth, M.D.S. & Eichberg, C.G. (1991). Effects on infant–mother attachment of mothers' unresolved loss of attachment figure, or other traumatic experience. In C.M. Parkes, J. Stevenson-Hinde, & P. Marris (eds), *Attachment across the life cycle* (pp. 160–183). London, New York: Tavistock, Routledge.

Alexander, F. (1949). *Psychosomatische Medizin. Grundlagen und Anwendungsgebiete [Psychosomatic medicine. Basics and fields of application]*, 4th edn (1985). Berlin: de Gruyter.

Anderson, C.D. (1981). Expression of affect and physiological response in psychosomatic patients. *Journal of Psychosomatic Research*, **25**, 143–149.

Aspendorf, J.B. & Scherer, K.R. (1983). The discrepant repressor: differentiation between low anxiety, high anxiety, and repression of anxiety by autonomic–facial–verbal patterns of behavior. *Journal of Personality and Social Psychology*, **45**, 1334–1346.

Bagby, R.M., Parker, J., & Taylor G.J. (1994a). The twenty-item Toronto Alexithymia Scale – I. Item selection and cross-validation of the factor structure. *Journal of Psychosomatic Research*, **38**, 23–32.

Bagby, R.M., Parker, J., & Taylor G.J. (1994b). The twenty-item Toronto Alexithymia Scale – II. Convergent, discriminant, and concurrent validity. *Journal of Psychosomatic Research*, **38**, 33–40.

Belsky, J. (1984). The determinants of parenting. A process model. *Child Development*, **55**, 718–728.

Benoit, D., Zeanah, C.H., Boucher, C., & Minde, K. (1992). Sleep disorders in early childhood: association with insecure maternal attachment. *Journal of the American Academy of Child and Adolescent Psychiatry*, **31**, 86–93.

Berenbaum, H. & James, T. (1994). Correlates and retrospectively reported antecedents of alexithymia. *Psychosomatic Medicine*, **56**, 353–359.

Berry, D.S. & Pennebaker, J.W. (1993). Nonverbal and verbal emotional expression and health. *Psychotherapy and Psychosomatics*, **59**, 11–19.

Bowlby, J. (1969). *Attachment and loss, Vol. 1: Attachment*. New York: Basic Books.

Bowlby, J. (1975). *Bindung. Eine Analyse der Mutter-Kind-Beziehung [Attachment. An analysis of the mother–infant relationship]*. Munich: Kindler.

Byrne, D. (1961). The repression–sensitization scale: rationale, reliability, and validity. *Journal of Personality*, **29**, 334–349.

Carlson, V., Cicchetti, D., Barnett, D., & Braunwald, K. (1989). Disorganized/disoriented attachment relationships in maltreated infants. *Developmental Psychology*, **25**, 525–531.

Carpenter, E.M. & Kirkpatrick, L.A. (1996). Attachment style and presence of a romantic partner as moderators of psychophysiological responses to a stressful laboratory situation. *Personal Relationships*, **3**, 351–367.

Cassidy, J. (1994). Emotion regulation: influences of attachment relationships. In N.A. Fox (ed.), *The development of emotion regulation: biological and behavioral considerations. Monographs of the Society for Research in Child Development*, **59**, 228–249.

Coe, C.L. (1993). Psychosocial factors and immunity in nonhuman primates: a review. *Psychosomatic Medicine*, **55**, 298–308.

Coe, C.L., Wiener, S.G., Rosenberg, L.T., & Levine, S. (1985). Endocrine and immune responses to separation and mental loss in nonhuman primates. In M. Reite & T. Field (eds), *The psychobiology of attachment and separation* (pp. 223–255). Orlando, FL: Academic Press.

Crittenden, P.M. (1985). Maltreated infants: vulnerability and resilience. *Journal of Child Psychology and Psychiatry*, **26**, 85–96.

Crittenden, P.M., Partridge, M.F., & Claussen, A.H. (1991). Family patterns of relationship in normative and dysfunctional families. *Development and Psychopathology*, **3**, 491–512.

Crowell, J.A. & Feldmann S.S. (1991). Mother's working models of attachment relationships and mother and child behavior during separation and reunion. *Developmental Psychology*, **27**, 597–605.

Dozier, M. & Kobak, R.R. (1992). Psychophysiology in attachment interviews: converging evidence for deactivating strategies. *Child Development*, **63**, 1473–1480.

Egerland, B. & Faber, E.A. (1984). Infant–mother attachment. Factors related to its development and changes over time. *Child Development*, **55**, 753–771.

Escher-Gräub, C.D. & Grossmann, K.E. (1983). *Bindungssicherheit im zweiten Lebensjahr. Die Regensburger Querschnittsuntersuchung [Attachment security in the second year of life. The Regensburger cross-sectional study]*. Unpublished report, University of Regensburg.

Esterling, B.A., Antoni, M.H., Kumar, M., & Schneiderman, N. (1990). Emotional repression, stress disclosure responses, and Epstein-Barr viral capsid antigen titers. *Psychosomatic Medicine*, **52**, 397–410.

Fonagy, P. (1993). *The relationship between the emotional development of the child and the history and current mental function of the parents*. Paper presented at the Symposium on Personality: Developmental Psychology and Developmental Psychopathology, Leiden, The Netherlands.

Fonagy, P., Steele, H., & Steele, M. (1991). Maternal representations of attachment during pregnancy predict the organization of infant–mother attachment at one year of age. *Child Development*, **62**, 891–905.

Fremmer-Bombik, E. (1987). *Beobachtungen zur Bindungsqualität im zweiten Lebensjahr und ihre Bedeutung im Lichte mütterlicher Kindheitserinnerungen [Observations of the attachment quality in the second year of life and their meaning in the light of mother's memories]*. Unpublished Master's Thesis, Universität Regensburg.

George, C., Kaplan, N., & Main, M. (1995). *Adult attachment interview*. Unpublished manuscript, Department of Psychology, University of California, Berkeley.

Grossmann, K., Fremmer-Bombik, E., Rudolph, J., & Grossmann, K.E. (1988). Maternal attachment representations as related to patterns of infant–mother attachment and maternal care during the first year. In R.A. Hinde & J. Stevenson-Hinde (eds), *Relationships within families: mutual influences* (pp. 241–260). Oxford: Clarendon Press.

Grossmann, K., Grossmann, K.E., Spangler, G., Suess, G., & Unzner, L. (1985). Maternal sensitivity and newborns' orientation responses as related to quality of attachment in northern Germany. In I. Bretherton & E. Waters (eds), *Growing points of attachment theory and research. Monographs of the Society for Research in Child Development*, **50**, 1–2.

Hamilton, C.E. (2000). Continuity and discontinuity of attachment from infancy through adolescence. *Child Development*, **71**, 690–694.

Hinde, R.A. & Stevenson-Hinde, J. (eds). (1988). *Relationships within families: Mutual influences*. Oxford: Clarendon Press.

Hofer, M.A. (1973). The effects of brief maternal separations on behavior and heart rate of two week old rat pups. *Physiology and Behavior*, **10**, 423–427.

Hofer, M.A. (1984). Relationships as regulators: a physiobiologic perspective on bereavement. *Psychosomatic Medicine*, **46**, 183–197.

Hofer, M.A. (1994). Hidden regulators in attachment, separation and loss. *Society of Research on Child Development*, **59**, 192–207.

King, A.C., Taylor, C.B., Albright, C.A., & Haskell, W.L. (1990). The relationship between repressive and defensive coping styles and blood pressure responses in healthy, middle-aged men and women. *Journal of Psychosomatic Research*, **34**, 461–471.

Krohne, H.W. & Rogner, J. (1985). Mehrvariablen-Diagnostik in der Bewältigungs-forschung [Multi-variable diagnostics in coping research]. In H.W. Krohne (ed.), *Angstbewältigung in Leistungssituationen* (pp. 45–62). Weinheim, Germany: Edition Psychologie.

Lesser, I.M. (1981). Review of the alexithymia concept. *Psychosomatic Medicine*, **43**, 531–543.

Lumley, M.A. & Norman, S. (1996). Alexithymia and health care utilization. *Psychosomatic Medicine*, **58**, 197–202.

Lyons-Ruth, K., Repacholi, B., McLeod, S., & Silva, E. (1991). Disorganized attachment behavior in infancy: short-term stability, maternal and infant correlates, and risk-related subtypes. *Development and Psychopathology*, **3**, 377–396.

Main, M. (1981). Avoidance in the service of attachment: A working paper. In G. Immelmann, G. Barlow, M. Main, & L. Petrinovich (eds), *Behavioral development: the Bielefeld interdisciplinary project* (pp. 651–693). New York: Cambridge University Press.

Main, M. (1995). Recent studies in attachment: overview with selected implications for clinical work. In S. Goldberg, R. Muir, & J. Kerr (eds), *Attachment theory. Social, developmental and clinical perspectives* (pp. 407–474). Hillsdale, NJ and London: The Analytic Press.

Main, M. & Cassidy, J. (1988). Categories of response with the parent at age six: predicted from infant attachment classifications and stable over a one-month period. *Developmental Psychology*, **24**, 415–426.

Main, M. & Goldwyn, R. (1996). *Adult attachment scoring and classification systems* (6th edn). Unpublished manuscript, University of California, Berkeley.

Main, M. & Hesse, E. (1990). Parents' unresolved traumatic experiences are related to infant disorganized attachment status: is frightened and/or frightening parental behavior the linking mechanism? In M.T. Greenberg, D. Cicchetti, & E.M. Cummings (eds), *Attachment in the preschool years: Theory, research and intervention* (pp. 161–182). Chicago, IL: University of Chicago Press.

Main, M. & Solomon, J. (1986). Discovery of a new, disorganized/disoriented attachment pattern. In T.B. Brazelton & M. Yogman (eds), *Affective development in infancy* (pp. 95–124). Norwood, NJ: Ablex.

Main, M. & Solomon, J. (1990). Procedures for identifying infants as disorganized/disoriented attachment pattern during the Ainsworth Strange Situation. In M.T Greenberg, D. Cicchetti, & E.M. Cummings (eds), *Attachment in the preschool years: Theory, research and intervention* (pp. 121–160). Chicago, IL: University of Chicago Press.

Main, M. & Weston, D.R. (1981). The quality of the toddler's relationship to mother and father related to conflict behavior and readiness to establish new relationships. *Child Development*, **52**, 932–940.

Marty, P. & de M'Uzan, M. (1963). Das operative Denken. [Operative thinking]. *Psyche*, **32**, 974–984.

Myers, L.B. & Brewin, Ch.R. (1994). Recall of early experience and the expressive coping style. *Journal of Abnormal Psychology*, **103**, 288–292.

Nemiah, J.C. & Sifneos, P.E. (1970). Psychosomatic illness: a problem in communication. *Psychotherapy and Psychosomatics*, *18*, 154–160.

Niaura, R., Herbert, P.M., McMahon, N., & Sommerville, L. (1992). Repressive coping and blood lipids in men and women. *Psychosomatic Medicine*, **54**, 698–706.

Patrick, M., Hobson, R.P., Castle, P., Howard, R., & Maughan, B. (1994). Personality disorder and the mental representation of early social experience. *Development and Psychopathology*, **6**, 375–388.

Radke-Yarrow, M., Cummings, E.M., Kuczynski, L., & Chapman, M. (1985). Patterns of attachment in two- and three-year-olds in normal families and families with parental depression. *Child Development*, 56, 591–615.

Reite, M. & Boccia, M.L. (1994). Physiological aspects of adult attachment. In M.B. Sperling & W.H. Berman (eds), *Attachment in adults: Clinical and developmental perspectives* (pp. 98–127). London, New York: Guilford Press.

Rosenstein, D.S. & Horowitz, H.A. (1993). *Working models of attachment in psychiatrically hospitalized adolescents: Relation to psychopathology and personality.* Paper presented at the sixth Meeting of the Society for Research in Child Development, New Orleans, LA.

Sänger-Alt, C., Steimer-Krause, E., Wagner, G., & Krause, R. (1989). Mimisches Verhalten psychosomatischer Patienten [The facial expression of psychosomatic patients]. *Zeitschrift für Klinische Psychologie*, 18, 243–256.

Scheidt, C.E., Waller, E., Schnock, Ch., Becker-Stoll, F., Zimmermann, P., Lücking, C.H., & Wirsching, M. (1999). Alexithymia and attachment representation in idiopathic spasmodic torticollis. *Journal of Nervous and Mental Disease*, 187, 47–52.

Schieche, M. (1996). *Exploration und physiologische Reaktionen bei zweijährigen Kindern mit unterschiedlichen Bindungserfahrungen [Exploration and physiological reactions of two year old infants with different attachment experiences].* Unpublished doctoral dissertation, University of Regensburg, Germany.

Slawsby, E.A. (1995). *Psychosocial factors of pain in chronic atypical facial pain.* Unpublished doctoral dissertation. University of Massachusetts, Boston.

Spangler, G. & Grossmann, K.E. (1993). Biobehavioral organization in securely and insecurely attached infants. *Child Development*, 64, 1439–1450.

Spangler, G., Schieche, M., Ilg, U., Maier, U., & Ackermann, C. (1994). Maternal sensitivity as an external organizer for biobehavioral regulation. *Developmental Psychobiology*, 27, 425–437.

Taylor, G.J. (1994). The alexithymia construct: conceptualization, validity and relationship with basic dimensions of personality. *New Trends in Experimental and Clinical Psychiatry*, 10, 61–74.

Traue, H.C. (1989). *Gefühlsausdruck, Hemmung und Muskelspannung unter sozialem Streß: Verhaltensmedizin myogener Kopfschmerzen [Expression of emotion, inhibition and muscle tension under social stress: Behavioral medicine of myogenous headache].* Göttingen, Germany: Hogrefe.

Van IJzendoorn, M. & Bakermans-Kranenburg, J. (1996). Attachment representations in mothers, fathers, adolescents and clinical groups: a meta-analytic search for normative data. *Journal of Consulting and Clinical Psychology*, 64, 8–21.

Ward, M.J. & Carlson, E.A. (1995). Association among adult attachment representations, maternal sensitivity, and infant–mother attachment in a sample of adolescent mothers. *Child Development*, 66, 69–79.

Wartner, U.G., Grossmann, K., Fremmer-Bombik, E., & Suess, G. (1994). Attachment patterns at age six in South Germany: predictability from infancy and implications for preschool behavior. *Child Development*, 49, 483–494.

Waters, E. (1978) The reliability and stability of individual differences in infant–mother attachment. *Child Development*, 49, 483–494.

Waters, E., Merrick, S.K., Albersheim, L., & Treboux, D. (1995). *Attachment security from infancy to early adulthood: a 20-year longitudinal study.* Poster presented at the Biennial Meeting of the Society for Research in Child Development, Indianapolis, IN.

Weinberger, D.A. (1990). The construct validity of the repressive–defensive coping style. In J.L. Singer (ed.), *Repression and dissociation: Defense mechanisms and personality styles* (pp. 337–386). Chicago, IL: University of Chicago Press.

Weinberger, D.A., Schwartz, G.E., & Davidson, R.J. (1979). Low-anxious, high-anxious, and repressive coping styles. Psychometric patterns and behavioral and physiological responses to stress. *Journal of Abnormal Psychology*, **88**, 369–380.

Zimmermann, P., Fremmer-Bombik, E., Spangler, G., & Großmann, K.E. (1995). *Attachment in adolescence: a longitudinal perspective*. Poster presented at the Biennial Meeting of the Society for Research in Child Development, Indianapolis, IN.

Chapter 14

Children's conception of the emotion process

Consequences for emotion regulation

Hedy Stegge, Mark Meerum Terwogt,
Albert Reijntjes and Nathalie van Tijen

Introduction

Contemporary emotion theories consider emotions to be basically adaptive. They signal the relevance of events to personal concerns and prepare the individual to respond so as to ensure the satisfaction and protection of these concerns (Frijda, 1986). The essential function of an emotion is organization: once the system is switched on, it coordinates the activity of disparate response systems (physiology, perception, motor behavior, expression, and also higher mental processes) in order to deal appropriately with the emotion-eliciting event (Levenson, 1999; Scherer, 1984).

Emotions are not only regulatory, they also need to be adequately regulated. Recently, Levenson (1999) has eloquently explicated this conception of emotions as both regulatory and regulated phenomena. In his "two system design of human emotions", Levenson distinguishes a core system that functions quite automatically and provides quick, standard solutions to a limited number of prototypical life problems. By synchronizing the activity of the relevant response modes, the core system enables us to escape a danger, adapt to a loss, or fight an attack. However, the script-like, stereotypical emotional response of the core system often will be modified by the activity of the surrounding control system in order to provide a more adequate fit with the prevailing situation. According to Levenson, emotion regulation refers to "the lifelong process of working out an etiquette of action and interaction between the two emotion systems" (p. 491). As human beings we have the need to feel, while at the same time experiencing a sense of control over our emotional life (Tomkins, 1962). Being able to accomplish adaptive goals in emotionally arousing situations is one of the most important tasks the developing person faces. An emotionally competent individual is capable of reflective regulation of emotion to promote personal growth and the quality of social relationships (Mayer & Salovey, 1997; Saarni, 1999).

Emotions become increasingly self-regulated as a result of neurophysiological maturation, the growth of language and cognition, and the development of emotional understanding (Gross, 1999). In this chapter, we will discuss the development of children's view of the emotion process within the context of emotion regulation.

Meta-emotive understanding stimulates the emergence of self-regulatory processes that can be employed deliberately and with strategic purpose in a variety of situations (Mayer & Salovey, 1997; Meerum Terwogt & Olthof, 1989). Two research areas are of interest for the domain under study here: (i) the stress and coping tradition, which focuses on the way in which people deal with stressful situations, and (ii) the popular research tradition that has become known as the study of the "child's theory of mind". We will provide a short overview of the most important findings from each of these research domains.

The coping tradition

In their "stress and coping" model, Lazarus and Folkman (1984) define coping as the cognitive and behavioral efforts to manage a troubled person–environment relationship. In classifying people's coping behaviors, these authors distinguish two broad categories: problem-focused coping and emotion-focused coping. Problem-focused coping concerns the use of strategies aimed at diminishing the actual problems presented by the situation. Emotion-focused coping, on the other hand, involves behavior that is directly aimed at improving the resulting emotional state. A closely related dichotomy was introduced by Rothbaum *et al.* (1982), who distinguish primary control from secondary control. Primary control involves a change in the actual conditions that gave rise to the emotional experience, whereas secondary control concerns a maximization of one's goodness of fit with the conditions as they are. Most problem-focused strategies can be considered examples of primary control, while the greater part of the emotion-focused strategies can be thought of as instances of secondary control.

In the coping literature, it has consistently been reported that whereas even young children acknowledge the usefulness of problem-focused or primary coping strategies, the value of emotion-focused or secondary coping options is appreciated only with increasing age (Band & Weisz, 1988). This age shift can be explained by children's increasing understanding of emotions as a mental process (Meerum Terwogt & Stegge, 1995). Primary control strategies involve a change in the actual conditions in the outside world and can be applied even without an understanding of the inner emotional experience that motivates the child's coping behavior. In secondary coping, on the other hand, the child tries to influence its subjective reaction to the emotion-eliciting event and may use cognitive manipulations to reach this regulatory goal. In order to acknowledge the usefulness of these cognitive strategies, the child needs a conception of emotion as a mental process. It has to understand that an emotional reaction is not determined by the objective situation as such, but rather by one's appraisal, the interpretation of the event.

In the past two decades, psychologists have extensively studied children's acquisition of knowledge about the mental world. This flourishing research area has become known under the heading of the child's theory of mind (ToM). In the next section, we will discuss the development of a mentalistic conception of emotion as studied within this tradition.

The child's theory of mind tradition

Researchers studing "theory of mind" development have mainly focused on children's conceptions of two fundamental components of the mind, desires and beliefs, and their knowledge of how these mental states are causally linked to behavior and to other mental states such as emotions. It has been shown that between the ages of three and six, children rapidly acquire an understanding of the desire- and belief-dependent nature of emotions. First, they come to understand the link between desires and emotion: getting what you want results in a positive emotion (happiness), whereas not getting what you want causes a negative emotion such as sadness or anger (Stein & Levine, 1989, 1999). Initially, this knowledge is limited in that desires are conceived of as being rather objective: young children assume that everyone will be happy about getting a piece of chocolate to eat and rather unhappy about getting potatoes (Rieffe *et al.*, 2001). It is only when they have come to understand adequately the subjective nature of desires that they realize that person A may be happy when getting a present because it is something that (s)he's wanted to have all along, whereas person B may be unhappy with the same present because (s)he prefers something else. Still somewhat later, as children have also come to understand the relation between beliefs and emotions, they know that it is not the actual situation that determines how you feel about it, but rather your thoughts about it. If you believe that the closed mug in your hand contains your favorite drink, you'll be happy, even if your belief is mistaken because someone has secretly switched the content (Harris *et al.*, 1989). By the age of six, children are quite able both to explain and to predict a person's emotional state on the basis of his or her subjective desires and beliefs. They have acquired a mentalistic conception of the emotion process (Harris, 1989).

Until now, the link between desires and beliefs on the one hand and emotions on the other has never been examined from an emotion regulation perspective. Partly, this may be caused by the fact that theory of mind researchers have mainly focused on the demonstration of the early knowledge of basic principles among young children, rather than the application of this elementary knowledge to more complex problems, such as a situation in which a child needs to change a negative feeling state. It is this applied theory of mind focus (Flavell, 2000) that we have adopted in our research on emotion regulation.

Children understand that emotions are caused by a person's subjective desires and beliefs rather than by the objective situation somewhere around the age of six. However, to date it is unknown whether knowledge about the links between subjective mental states and emotions is also applied in their reasoning about emotion regulation. If emotions are caused by desires, beliefs or thoughts about a situation, one possible way of changing an unwanted emotion is by changing one's desires, beliefs, or the content of one's thoughts.

A review of past research on emotion regulation strongly supports an age-related trend toward an increased preference for cognitive or mental strategies of emotion regulation. In an early interview study (Harris *et al.*, 1981), it was shown that whereas six-year-old children mainly suggest situational or behavioral changes when asked how to regulate a negative feeling state, ten-year-olds also acknowledge the usefulness of mental manipulations. The general developmental shift to an emphasis on cognitive strategies of emotion regulation has been replicated in numerous other studies since then (for recent reviews see Denham, 1998; Saarni, 1999).

In developmental psychology, the focus of studies on age-related changes in emotion regulation has largely been confined to the broad distinction between situational or behavioral strategies versus mental strategies (or "external" versus "internal" strategies, as Brenner and Salovey (1997) have called them). Relatively little attention has been paid to developments within the extensive domain of cognitive manipulations. Nonetheless, it is quite plausible that some cognitive strategies are more easily understood than others. These developments are the focus of the present chapter. We will examine to what extent children of different ages consider various kinds of mental manipulations useful to change a negative feeling state. Based on the results of empirical research, we will present some important changes in children's conception of the emotion process, seen from a regulation perspective.

Children's perspective on the strategic control of emotions: the use of cognition

In a first interview study, age changes in children's theorizing about the usefulness of different strategies of emotion regulation were examined (Stegge & Meerum Terwogt, 1998). Children (four-year-olds, $N = 39$; six-year-olds, $N = 58$; ten-year-olds, $N = 59$) and adults ($N = 44$) were presented with two negative stimulus situations, one intended to elicit anger and one intended to elicit sadness. For sadness, two prototypical situations were used: the death of a pet dog and the move of one's best friend to another town. A situation in which a promise was broken (a trip to the beach was cancelled) and a situation in which a valued possession was damaged by a younger sibling were used to elicit anger. Half of the subjects from each age group answered questions about the situation in which the protagonist was sad because his/her pet dog died and the situation in which the story character was angry about a broken promise. The other half of the subjects were presented with the two parallel stimulus situations.

After the stimulus situation was described, subjects were presented with six alternative reactions. In each case, they were asked whether or not the strategy offered would result in a decrease in the protagonist's negative feeling state and why that would or would not be the case. These six reactions were:

1   behavioral avoidance (e.g. go and play outside with a friend)
2   behavioral confrontation (e.g. put away the belongings of the dog that died)
3   mental avoidance (e.g. try to forget about what had happened)
4   mental confrontation (e.g. go to sit down and think of your beloved pet)

5   a positive reappraisal (remembering the good times you spent with your pet friend)

6   a negative reappraisal (thinking that you can never play with your dog anymore).

In Table 14.1, children's evaluations of the different regulation options presented are summarized.

Table 14.1 Mean percentages of participants in each age group that predicted an increase or decrease in the intensity of the negative emotion as a result of the use of different regulation strategies

	4-year-olds	6-year-olds	10-year-olds	Adults
Decrease by behavioral avoidance	81%	78%	88%	88%
Increase by behavioral confrontation	40%	60%	72%	62%
Reappraisals*	63%	71%	90%	92%
Decrease by mental avoidance (anger)	80%	82%	95%	80%
Increase by mental confrontation (anger)	58%	50%	91%	93%
Decrease by mental avoidance (sadness)	76%	79%	89%	36%
Increase by mental confrontation (sadness)	34%	60%	84%	45%

*Mean percentages of participants who correctly predicted mood improvement (positive reappraisals) or mood deterioration (negative reappraisals).

Behavioral avoidance and confrontation

Children of all ages, as well as adults, were of the opinion that seeking distraction is an effective strategy to regulate both anger and sadness. Inspection of the justifications showed that four-year-olds mainly explained their answers in terms of situational responses ("the person feels better because he or she is going to do an activity"), whereas ten-year-olds and adults almost exclusively referred to the mental process ("the person feels better because he or she forgets about what has happened"). The group of six-year-olds gave both situational and mentalistic justifications. Thus, whereas the majority of subjects from all age groups were able to predict that a person feels better when he or she engages in some pleasant activity, older subjects evidenced greater knowledge of how mental activity can change a person's emotions.

Clear age differences were found in children's thoughts about the effect of behavioral confrontation. As age increased, subjects more often indicated that the negative emotional reaction would be intensified by being confronted with something that would remind one of the negative stimulus situation. Inspection of the justifications showed that this reflects an increasing understanding of the mechanism that is referred to in the literature as cognitive cueing (Whittaker et al., 1985). Whereas four-year-olds, and to a lesser extent six-year-olds, often did not seem to realize that confrontation with an otherwise neutral element related to the original stimulus situation would remind one of the negative event, ten-year-olds and adults proved to be well aware of this effect.

Reappraisals

Next to the behavioral strategies, different types of cognitive strategies were presented. The so-called reappraisals are examples of what is called "pure cognition" in the coping literature (Lazarus & Folkman, 1984). We asked the children to evaluate the effect of both strategies that supposedly would decrease the negative feeling state (positive reappraisals) and strategies that would probably intensify the negative reaction (negative reappraisals). The strategies offered concerned a further interpretation of the way in which the negative outcome was achieved (for example, the protagonist thought that the other person had damaged a car on purpose) or a reappraisal of the negative outcome itself (for example, the protagonist thought that the damaged car wasn't that nice anyway). Consistent with our hypothesis, the understanding of the effect of the reappraisals increased significantly with age (see Table 14.1).

Inspection of children's justifications provides us with an insight into some of the problems that young children face in understanding the effect of the reappraisals. Both four- and six-year-olds seem to be inclined to interpret the cognitive change in perspective presented as a change in reality. When asked, for example, to explain why it would help to think that you can always visit your friend who has been moved, they argue that it helps because it is nice to visit your friend and play with him or her. In contrast, older subjects (ten-year-olds and adults) most of the time explicitly refer to a change in perspective: "you realize that your friend is still your friend, even though (s)he's living far away now". The two youngest age groups seem to have substantial difficulties understanding the possibility of such a deliberate change in perspective. When asked, for example, whether it would help to think that you didn't like the destroyed car that much anyway, they either deny that such a change is possible (but he did like the car), or they say "no" and argue that you'd feel more sad because of a negative experience ("you don't like the car"). The two oldest age groups, in contrast, correctly argue that such a change in perspective (a previously very much appreciated car "is made" less valued) would make you feel less sad, as losing something that you didn't like very much is not as bad as losing something that you really loved. It seems as if young children base their answers on the positive or negative content of the phrase as such, whereas older participants actually compare the differential effect of two different appraisals of the same situation on the resulting emotional reaction.

Cognitive avoidance and confrontation

Finally, we asked subjects whether or not mental avoidance or mental confrontation would decrease the intensity of the negative emotion. As the judgments in this case proved to be dependent on the type of emotion, we present the results for sadness and anger separately.

In the case of anger, the results parallel those obtained with the strategies of behavioral avoidance and behavioral confrontation. Even four-year-olds understand that a negative emotion decreases if one tries to stop thinking about the situation that caused the emotion. When asked to justify their answers, the three oldest age groups (and even some of the four-year-olds) referred to the relation between feeling and thinking: when you stop thinking about a negative situation, you'll feel better. In contrast, the effect of mental confrontation is often not adequately evaluated by the two youngest age groups. Almost half of the younger children do not understand that cognitive confrontation increases the negative feeling state. Inspection of children's justifications revealed that young children's problems are caused by their reliance on the specific negative, neutral or positive content of the thoughts presented. When asked whether it would help to think about the beach in case of the cancelled trip, they argue "yes, because it is nice to think about the beach". Older subjects, in contrast, correctly argue "no, because that only reminds you of how much you wanted to go to there".

For sadness, similar results were found, with one exception. A substantial proportion of the adults felt that mental avoidance is not an effective strategy to regulate feelings of sadness, whereas mental confrontation is considered to be a useful strategy for dealing with this emotion. The analysis of the justifications showed that adults typically refer to the long-term consequences of the different strategies. Whereas avoidance may be effective in the short run, the long-term consequences are considered to be more negative. One has to face the loss in order to be able to come to terms with one's sadness. Quite a number of adults opted for this long-term perspective, arguing that confrontation (both behavioral and mental) is an effective way of dealing with sadness, whereas avoidance will be effective in the short run but problematic as time passes by.

The results of this study convincingly show an increase in children's under-standing of the usefulness of cognitive strategies of emotion regulation, based on their understanding of the link between situation, cognition and emotion. The findings seem to suggest the following developmental sequence.

Negative/positive situations

Children understand that engaging in a pleasant activity or withdrawing from a distressing one results in mood improvement.

Negative/positive thoughts

Children have acquired an insight into the relation between thinking and feeling: a negative feeling state can be improved by thinking of something pleasant or not thinking of something unpleasant. Similarly, a negative emotion will be intensified by thinking of something unpleasant.

Cognitive cueing

Children know that an otherwise neutral or even positive stimulus (real or mental) may intensify a negative feeling state, as it triggers thoughts about the original negative stimulus situation.

Change in perspective

Children understand that one can deliberately change one's subjective perspective on the original situation in the service of mood improvement. As mentioned above, emotional understanding is especially important for the deliberate, strategic control of negative feeling states. We will now discuss some of the implications of children's growing understanding of the mechanisms described above.

First, knowing that the engagement in pleasant activities results in a pleasant feeling state allows children to seek these kinds of activities wilfully and avoid unpleasant ones. When, in the next step, children also come to understand the elementary link between thinking and feeling, situational changes are not necessary anymore. You can also opt for a mental change in order to feel better (for example, thinking of something more pleasant in a boring or otherwise negatively valenced situation, when it is not allowed to actually leave the situation). Subsequently, children may come to realize that certain stimuli (real ones and mental ones alike) may trigger other thoughts. Understanding the principle of cognitive cueing not only helps children to better understand their own emotional reactions, but also allows them to anticipate future reactions more precisely. As a person realizes that certain objects or thoughts will remind him or her of an earlier negative experience, these stimuli can be avoided strategically. Some participants in this study actually referred to these future anticipations by stating, for example, that it would be wise to put away the belongings of your beloved dog in order not to be reminded too often about what had happened. Finally, children also come to understand the so-called reappraisals. Some reappraisals are relatively easy to understand. To some extent, all children appear to know that focusing on a positive aspect of the stimulus situation diminishes the negative feeling state. Young children's understanding seems to be limited, however, in that they are tied to one cognitive representation of reality. They do not seem to realize that one can switch perspective deliberately in order to influence one's emotions. In the case of a valued loss, for example, they either deny a possible change in perspective (but he did like the car), or they base their judgments on the absolute valence (positive or negative) of the thoughts presented. Thus, although they know that the loss of something unimportant will not make you feel sad, it is not very likely that they will actively try to reach such a state of mind. Older participants (adults and, to a somewhat lesser extent, ten-year-olds) actually keep several perspectives in mind and compare their differential effects on the target emotion. This knowledge of the coexistence of different perspectives is also reflected in their appreciation of the short-term versus the long-term effects of different strategies.

Given the developmental changes in children's reasoning about emotion regulation, one would expect some strategies to be used more frequently at younger ages, whereas others will be used more frequently (or maybe even exclusively) at older ages. Although we do not have data yet allowing us to relate children's understanding of emotion regulation to their actual use of different strategies, the developmental sequence presented here was supported by another set of data.

Before they evaluated the usefulness of the regulation options presented above, the participants were asked to generate all the possible strategies they could think of that would be useful to diminish their sadness or anger in the prevailing stimulus situations. Behavioral distraction was frequently mentioned by all age groups, including four-year-olds. Mental avoidance was frequently mentioned by six- and ten-year-olds, and to some extent by four-year-olds, whereas adults did not mention this strategy very often and referred to mental reappraisals instead. Mental reappraisals were frequently mentioned by this oldest age group and, to a certain extent, also by ten-year-olds, whereas this strategy was completely absent in the two youngest age groups. Finally, only adults (and a few ten-year-olds) spontaneously mentioned confrontation as an effective strategy in response to loss.

To summarize, two major age changes became evident in the present study: (i) a growing understanding of the effect of mental manipulations, especially those that rely heavily on the understanding of the representational nature of mental processes, and (ii) an increased tendency to acknowledge the long-term effects of confrontational strategies as opposed to the short-term usefulness of avoidant behavior. Children initially seem to assume a one-to-one correspondence between situation, thought content and emotion: a sad situation evokes sad thoughts and results in a sad feeling state. In the next step, children are able to disconnect these relationships to some extent. By association, even a neutral stimulus may evoke sadness. And the confrontation with a sad situation need not evoke sad thoughts and thus sad feelings. The person may focus on a different aspect of the situation or even adopt a completely different perspective, thereby changing the resulting feeling state.

In this study, the main focus was on the cognitive–experiential component of the emotion process. An additional component of the emotion process that may be influenced by regulatory activities is the emotional expression (Brenner & Salovey, 1997). In the next section, we will discuss some empirical findings concerning age-related changes in children's views on the (non-)expression of emotion.

Children's theorizing about the (non-)expression of emotion

In studies on children's understanding of emotion regulation, their ideas about the expressive component of the emotion process and its usefulness for regulation purposes have been relatively neglected so far. Work that has been done in the area of emotional expression has predominantly concentrated on children's knowledge of display rules (Saarni, 1999). This certainly is an important topic, as rules about the expression of emotion play an important role in the regulation of daily social interaction. However, from a functionalist perspective on emotion, it has been argued that the expressive component serves other regulatory functions as well, both intrapsychic and interpersonal. Some examples of widely acknowledged functions are the reduction of tension, the support of emotion-specific action tendencies, and the communication of the personal feeling state in the service of problem solution (Frijda, 1986; Gross, 1998; Philippot & Rimé, 1998). We therefore investigated age changes in children's theorizing about the usefulness of the (non-)expression of emotion for regulation purposes.

As part of the study on regulation described above, we asked children whether or not the expression of the emotion (for example going to one's room and starting to cry, or running upstairs and slamming the door) would diminish the intensity of the subjective feeling state. Similarly, in a second question, they were asked whether or not the non-expression of the emotion (no longer putting on an angry face, stopping to cry and wiping one's eyes) would help to diminish its intensity.

Table 14.2 gives the mean percentages of participants in each of the age groups who consider the expression or non-expression of the emotion to be effective. Inspection of Table 14.2 shows that adults are convinced that expressing the negative emotion is effective in diminishing its intensity, whereas the inhibition of the expression will not be effective. For children, it's exactly the other way round. By analyzing the participants' justifications, it was found that children of all ages consider the expression of the emotion to be intrinsically linked up with other components of the negative emotional experience. They seem to see little opportunity for regulation of the negative feeling state by means of the expressive component. Age changes were nonetheless evident. It was shown that with increasing age, the expressive component is linked with different and probably more essential aspects of the emotional experience. The emphasis on situational changes makes way for a relative emphasis on cognitive content and the subjective feeling state. Characteristic of children's theorizing is that they assume a one-to-one-correspondence between the emotion-specific expression and the inner experience. Thus, although research within the ToM tradition shows that even children younger than six are able to distinguish inner experience and outer expression (Harris & Gross, 1988), the results of this study suggest that they do not consider the distinction relevant when asked about the effects of expression on the intensity of the subjective feeling state. Rather, they seem to assume a one-to-one correspondence between the two components of the emotion process. Consequently, if the aim is to improve the subjective feeling state, the emotional expression should first be made consistent with the direction of this change. That is, stopping expressing the negative emotion is a first requirement.

Adults, in contrast, seem to consider the expressive component to be relatively independent from other aspects of the emotion process. They frequently argue that not expressing the emotion does not necessarily diminish its intensity, because the expression of emotion does not coincide with its inner experience. In addition, they feel that the expression of emotion has a function of its own. Most adults argue that the emotion should be expressed in one way or another, and refer to the

Table 14.2 Mean percentages of participants that predicted an increase or decrease in the intensity of the negative emotion as a result of (non-)expression of the emotion

	Children	Adults
Increase by expressing the emotion	80%	17%
Decrease by expressing the emotion	20%	83%
Increase by not expressing the emotion	30%	62%
Decrease by not expressing the emotion	70%	38%

negative mental health consequences of suppression. In fact, they are referring to the notion of catharsis, which should be understood not so much – or at least not only – as short-term impulse release, but also as a renewed confrontation needed to see the situation in terms of what it really means to the person. Crying, for example, is an essential part of what is called the work of grief, which may help the person to come to grips with a loss (Frijda, 1986).

The results of this study suggest some interesting age changes in implicit theories about the expressive component of the emotion process, its relation to other components, and its regulatory functions. Obviously, there is an intrinsic link between expression and emotional experience. We have seen that children up to the age of ten are inclined to stress this intrinsic relationship between expression and other components of the emotion process: crying prevents one from engaging in positive activities (link between situation and expression), triggers negative thoughts (link between expression and cognition), and makes you feel miserable (link between expression and subjective feeling state). In fact, their relative preference for non-expression because of these factors indicates that they mainly consider the short-term effects of expression: giving free rein to anger or sadness may instate a self-reinforcing cycle, where the expression of the emotion intensifies the negative experience. However, in the long term, there is much to gain by expressing the emotion: it may allow for a renewed confrontation with the stimulus situation, open up the possibility for cognitive change (as in reliving a traumatic event and learning how to deal with it) and thereby prevent negative mental health consequences (Pennebaker, 1995; Pennebaker & Hoover, 1985; Philippot & Rimé, 1998).

Conclusion

The emotional core system as described by Levenson (1999) comprises of a set of response tendencies in different domains (physiological, expressive, behavioral, cognitive) that are intrinsically linked and whose activity is choreographed carefully so as to deal successfully with prototypical stimulus situations. The control system can change the course of the core system by acting on one or several of the different components. In line with such a two-system view of emotion, Brenner and Salovey (1997) define emotion regulation as "the process of managing responses that originate within cognitive–experiential, behavioral–expressive and physiological–biochemical components [of the emotion process]" (p. 170). In this chapter, we have focused on children's theorizing about regulation strategies that act upon the first two components of the emotion system.[1]

The research presented here has shown that in their reasoning about emotion regulation, young children (four- and six-year-olds) assume a one-to-one correspondence between different components of the emotion process: the confrontation with a sad event triggers sad thoughts, a sad expression, a sad feeling state and problematic functioning (you can't play, you can't concentrate when you are sad). The presence of one of these negatively valenced components is considered to be the starting point of an associative chain of negative elements. In order to improve a negative feeling state, then, young children argue that one should avoid the negative stimulus, expel negative thoughts and/or think of something fun instead, and stop expressing the negative emotion. Older children, in contrast, no longer seem to be committed to these one-to-one relationships between different components of the emotional experience. With age, children increasingly consider confrontation to be the starting point of an emotional process that is regulated by cognition: being confronted with something sad, thinking about something sad, or expressing a negative emotion may indeed trigger negative feelings at first, but also open up new perspectives. As older children have a better understanding of the mind as an interpretative device (Carpendale & Chandler, 1996), they understand that one can actually try to see things from different angles, and compare the effect of different interpretations of one and the same situation on the prevailing mood state.

The development of an adequate inner theory of emotion (Meerum Terwogt & Stegge, 1997) requires two levels of knowledge: (i) an understanding of the prototypical associations between different components of the emotional experience, and (ii) the ability to disconnect these relationships at least partially and to understand that every single element within the emotion process can become the target of regulatory activities. During the course of development, children first acquire knowledge about the prototypical elements of different emotional experiences. They learn, for example, what makes them angry, what an angry face or voice looks like, and which behaviors are characteristic of an angry person. This type of knowledge enables children to recognize anger in themselves and others and to know when regulation is called for (Meerum Terwogt & Olthof, 1989). Concerning the question of how to regulate, we argue that a strong focus on the intrinsic relations between situation, expression, behavior and emotion as evidenced in young children's theorizing about emotion will stimulate regulatory activities aimed at "keeping a distance" from the negative experience. In order to regulate their anger, young children will choose to leave the aversive situation, to direct

---

1 The physiological–biochemical component can be considered less relevant within the framework of emotional understanding (Brenner & Salovey, 1997).

their attention elsewhere, and to refrain from angry expressions or behaviors. In contrast, older children's theorizing will allow for more confrontative regulation options: paying attention to the negative event and/or the negative emotion will help you solve the problem by putting it in (a different) perspective.

For children to be able to function in a complex world, the development of emotion regulation capacities is critical. Indeed, behavioral or emotional problems are often associated with an inability to regulate negative emotions adequately (Cole *et al.*, 1994; Oatley & Jenkins, 1996; Stegge *et al.*, 1998). In line with the increased interest in emotional competence, in both the scientific community and the society at large (Goleman, 1995), affective education nowadays forms an integrative part of prevention and intervention programs (e.g. Greenberg *et al.*, 1995; Lochman & Wells, 1996; Stark & Kendall, 1996). The ultimate goal of most of these training courses is to teach children how to better regulate emotional distress so as to promote subjective well-being and improve the quality of social relationships. Empirical research may provide practitioners with valuable suggestions to further develop and validate the ingredients of their programs. Our studies on children's reasoning about emotion regulation have shown that some strategies are more demanding than others, in terms of both children's knowledge of the emotion process and their willingness to endure at least some amount of negative affect. Knowledge of the developmental trends outlined in this chapter can be used not only to direct children of different ages to use appropriate strategies, but also to determine the optimal sequencing of the strategies to be proposed to a single individual: a depressed child needs to start out with trying relatively "safe" strategies allowing him or her to avoid a confrontation with the negative event and turn to something pleasant instead. Similarly, after an aggressive child has learned to become aware of his or her own anger, (s)he will initially need to be instructed to react by leaving the situation. In either case, it is only at a later moment in time that the therapist can turn to the more demanding regulation options of confrontation and cognitive restructuring (Stegge *et al.*, 2001).

References

Band, E.B. & Weisz, J.R. (1988). How to feel better when it feels bad: children's perspectives on coping with everyday stress. *Developmental Psychology*, **24**, 247–253.

Brenner, E.M. & Salovey, P. (1997). Emotion regulation during childhood: developmental, interpersonal and individual considerations. In P. Salovey & D.J. Sluyter (eds), *Emotional development and emotional intelligence.* New York: Basic Books.

Carpendale, J.I. & Chandler, M.J. (1996). On the distinction between false belief understanding and subscribing to an interpretative theory of mind. *Child Development*, **67**, 1686–1706.

Cole, P., Michel, M.K., & O'Donnell-Teti, L. (1994). The development of emotion regulation and dysregulation: a clinical perspective. In N. Fox (ed.), *Monographs of the Society for Research in Child Development*, **59**, 73–103.

Denham, S.A. (1998). *Emotional development in young children.* New York: Guilford Press.

Flavell, J.H. (2000). Development of children's knowledge about the mental world. *International Journal of Behavioral Development*, **24**, 15–23.

Frijda, N.H. (1986). *The emotions*. Cambridge: Cambridge University Press.

Goleman, D. (1995). *Emotional intelligence*. New York: Bantam Books.

Greenberg, M.T., Kusche, C.A., Cook, E.T., & Quamma, J.P. (1995). Promoting emotional competence in school-aged deaf children: the effects of the PATHS Curriculum. *Development and Psychopathology*, **7**, 117–136.

Gross, J.J. (1998). Antecedent- and response-focused emotion regulation: divergent consequences for experience, expression, and physiology. *Journal of Personality and Social Pyschology*, **74**, 224–237.

Gross, J.J. (1999). Emotion and emotion regulation. In L.A. Pervin & O.P. John (eds), *Handbook of personality: Theory and research* (pp. 525–552). New York: Guilford Press.

Harris, P.L. (1989). *Children and emotion: the development of psychological understanding*. Oxford: Blackwell.

Harris, P.L. & Gross, D. (1988). Children's understanding of real and apparent emotion. In J.W. Astington, P.L. Harris & D.R. Olson (eds), *Developing theories of mind* (pp. 205–314). Cambridge: Cambridge University Press.

Harris, P.L., Johnson, C.N., Hutton, D., Andrews, G., & Cook, T. (1989). Young children's theory of mind and emotion. *Cognition and Emotion*, **3**, 379–400.

Harris, P.L., Olthof, T., & Meerum Terwogt, M. (1981). Children's knowledge of emotion. *Journal of Child Psychology and Psychiatry*, **22**, 247–261.

Lazarus, R.S. & Folkman, S. (1984). *Stress, appraisal and coping*. New York: Springer.

Levenson, R.W. (1999). The intrapersonal functions of emotions. *Cognition and Emotion*, **13**, 481–504.

Lochman, J. & Wells, K. (1996). A social–cognitive intervention with aggressive children: prevention effects and contextual implementation issues. In R. Peters & R. McMahon (eds), *Preventing childhood disorders, substance abuse and delinquency* (pp. 111–143). Thousand Oaks, CA: Sage.

Mayer, J.D. & Salovey, P. (1997). What is emotional intelligence? In P. Salovey & D.J. Sluyter (eds), *Emotional development and emotional intelligence* (pp. 3–34). New York: Basic Books.

Meerum Terwogt, M. & Olthof, T. (1989). Awareness and self-regulation of emotion in young children. In C. Saarni & P.L. Harris (eds), *The child's understanding of emotion* (pp. 209–237). New York: Cambridge University Press.

Meerum Terwogt, M. & Stegge, H. (1995). Children's understanding of the strategic control of negative emotions. In J.A. Russell (ed.), *Everyday conceptions of emotions. NATO ASI Series* (pp. 373–390). Dordrecht, The Netherlands: Kluwer.

Meerum Terwogt, M. & Stegge, H. (1997). De positie van emoties binnen de "Theory of Mind" [The position of emotions within the "Theory of Mind']. *Tijdschrift voor Ontwikkelingspsychologie*, **23**, 183–192.

Oatley, K. & Jenkins, J.M. (1996). *Understanding emotions*. Cambridge: Blackwell.

Pennebaker, J.W. (1995). *Emotion, disclosure and health*. Washington, DC: American Psychological Association.

Pennebaker, J.W. & Hoover, C.W. (1985). Inhibition and cognition: toward an understanding of trauma and disease. In R.J. Davidson, G.E. Swartz, & D. Shapiro (eds), *Consciousness and self regulation*, Vol. 4 (pp. 107–136). New York: Plenum Press.

Philippot, P. & Rimé, B. (1998). Social and cognitive processing in emotion: a heuristic for psychopathology. In F. Flack & J.D. Laird (eds), *Emotions in psychopathology: Theory and research* (pp. 114–129). Oxford: Oxford University Press.

Rieffe, C., Meerum Terwogt, M., Koops, W., Stegge, H., & Oomen, A. (2001). Preschoolers' appreciation of uncommon desires and subsequent emotions. *British Journal of Developmental Psychology*, **19**, 259–274.

Rothbaum, F.M., Weisz, J.R., & Snyder, S.S. (1982). Changing the world and changing the self: a two-process model of perceived control. *Journal of Personality and Social Psychology*, **42**, 5–37.

Saarni, C. (1999). *The development of emotional competence*. New York: Guilford Press.

Scherer, K.R. (1984). On the nature and function of emotions: a component process approach. In K.R. Scherer & P. Ekman (eds), *Approaches to emotion* (pp. 293–317). Hillsdale, NJ: Erlbaum.

Stark, K. & Kendall, P.C. (1996). *Treating depressed children: Therapist manual for "taking action"*. Ardmore, PA: Workbook Publishing.

Stegge, H. & Meerum Terwogt, M. (1998). Pespectives on the strategic control of emotions: a developmental account. In A. Fischer (ed.), *Proceedings of the Xth conference of the International Society for Research on Emotions* (pp. 45–47). Würzburg: ISRE Publications.

Stegge, H., Meerum Terwogt, M., & Bijstra, J. (1998). Emoties als aangrijpingspunt voor de diagnostiek van psychische stoornissen [Emotions as starting point for the assessment of psychopathology]. In W. Koops & W. Slot (eds), *Van lastig tot misdadig* [From difficult to criminal] (pp. 67–80). Houten, The Netherlands: Bohn Stafleu van Loghum.

Stegge, H., Meerum Terwogt, M., & Koops, W. (2001). Affect-educatie: Ontwikkelings-psychologische ondersteuning voor recente ontwikkelingen binnen de cognitieve gedragstherapie. In H. van Leeuwen, W. Slot, & M. Uijterwijk (eds), Antisociaal gedrag bÿ jeugdigen [Antisocial behavior in adolescents] (pp. 125–147). Lisse, The Netherlands: Swets & Zeitlinger.

Stegge, H., Reijntjes, A., & Meerum Terwogt, M. (1997). De ontwikkeling van het inzicht in emotieregulatie. *Tijdschrift voor Ontwikkelingspsychologie*, **23**, 129–140.

Stein, N.L. & Levine, L.J. (1989). The causal organisation of emotional knowledge: a developmental study. *Cognition and Emotion*, **3**, 343–378.

Stein, N.L. & Levine, L.J. (1999). The early emergence of emotional understanding and appraisal: implications for theories of development. In T. Dalgleish & M. Power (eds), *Handbook of cognition and emotion* (pp. 383–408). New York: Wiley.

Tomkins, S.S. (1962). *Affect, imagery and consciousness*. New York: Springer.

Whittaker, S., McShane, J., & Dunn, D. (1985). The development of cueing strategies in young children. *British Journal of Devlopmental Psychology*, **3**, 153–161.

Chapter 15

Emotional information processing in boys with disruptive behavior disorders

Bram Orobio de Castro, Willem Koops
and Mark Meerum Terwogt

Introduction

Aggressive behavior, vandalism, extreme stubbornness, and other disruptive behavior problems (DBP) are among the most frequent grounds for admission to child mental health services. At present, DBP in children are rated among the largest concerns of the general public in Western countries (e.g. for the Netherlands, Sociaal en Cultureel Planbureau (SCP), 1999), not least because their prevalence seems to have increased markedly in recent decades (Rutter, 1997; SCP, 1999). Researchers in psychology, psychiatry, criminology, sociology, and biology have increasingly cooperated to study the nature, causes, consequences, and variability of DBP.

To date, there is strong evidence that there is no single sufficient cause for disruptive behavior in children. Rather, complex interactions between multiple environmental and biological factors seem to cause various kinds of disruptive behavior (e.g. Loeber & Hay, 1997; Rutter, 1998). Once manifested, DBP seem to be exceptionally stable over time (Dishion *et al.*, 1995; Kazdin, 1995). Children with these problems run an increased risk of becoming delinquent, addicted to substances, rejected by peers; of dropping out of school, becoming unemployed, experiencing depressive episodes, and developing antisocial personality disorder (Dishion *et al.*, 1995; Loeber & Hay, 1997). Children with persistent DBP may thus cause considerable psychological, physical, and material damage to themselves, their direct environment, and society at large.

A promising approach to further our understanding of these behavior problems is the study of emotion and social cognition. These constructs are believed to play important parts in the development of disruptive behavior (e.g. Rutter, 1998). Furthering our understanding of emotion and social cognition in this group of children may help to increase the effectiveness of promising cognitive behavioral and emotion-focused interventions (Kazdin, 1995; Lochman & Lenhart, 1993). Such intervention programs are becoming increasingly popular and are evaluated relatively favorably (Greenberg *et al.*, 1995; Kazdin, 1995). These programs may be improved considerably by a better understanding of the relations between emotion, social cognition, and disruptive behavior.

A great deal of research has already been conducted on social cognition in disruptive boys. Yet little attention has been paid to the roles of emotion in behavior problems, as the dominant theory concerning the social emotional development of these boys, the "social information processing" theory ("SIP"; Dodge, 1986), was originally oriented more toward cognitive than toward emotional aspects of behavior problems.

In this chapter, we aim to demonstrate that emotions play important roles in disruptive behavior. To this end, we first review theories concerning social cognition and emotion in disruptive behavior, then we describe a series of experiments that we have recently conducted on the roles of emotion in disruptive boys' social information processing, and finally, we integrate theories and findings in a tentative model of emotional information processing in DBP boys.

Theoretical approaches to emotion and social cognition

During the past decade, the dominant theory on social cognition and behavior problems has been the social information processing theory (SIP; Crick & Dodge, 1994; Dodge, 1986). This theory proposes that, in order for one to react appropriately to social situations, social information has to be processed in an orderly fashion. First, the information has to be *encoded* accurately. Second, the encoded information has to be *represented* correctly. Third, response alternatives have to be *generated*. Fourth, these response alternatives have to be *evaluated* against *interaction goals*, and from these responses an optimal response has to be selected. Finally, the selected response has to be *enacted*. The theory proposes that disruptive boys have, through interactions of organismic and environmental influences, developed deviant SIP styles that make them act problematically in specific situations.

The SIP approach has several advantages over traditional approaches. It accommodates the possibility that children develop qualitatively different social cognitive styles rather than "deficiencies" on a single developmental dimension, and it is clearly embedded in existing knowledge of the development of disruptive behavior.

Numerous studies have been conducted concerning children's SIP following provocation by peers (for reviews, see Crick & Dodge, 1994; Orobio de Castro et al., 2002). These studies demonstrate that boys with DBP differ from their peers in encoding, representation,[1] response generation, response evaluation, and response enactment. As to differences in interaction goals, two studies (Erdley & Asher, 1996; Lochman et al., 1993) established that aggressive children were more inclined to pursue goals of dominance and revenge and were less willing to pursue prosocial goals than nonaggressive children.

---

1 Representation has primarily been studied in the narrow sense of representing other children's intentions (also known as "attribution of intent" and "hostile attribution bias").

Several authors have noted the marked contrast between the subordinate role of emotions in the SIP approach to disruptive behavior and the experience of many clinicians that anger, tension, and disappointment play an important role in the development of disruptive behavior (Crick & Dodge, 1994; Gottman, 1986). In psychology, the importance of emotions is currently being reappraised to such an extent that an "affect revolution" has been said to be taking place (Tangney & Fischer, 1995). Emotions are increasingly seen as fundamental to human behavior, in that they constitute the basic action programs that drive behavior and enable social interaction. Emotions seem to be fundamental to the regulation of social interactions. Indeed, Campos *et al.* (1989, p. 395) propose that "emotions are not mere feelings, but rather are processes of establishing, maintaining, or disrupting the relations between the person and the internal or external environment, when such relations are significant to the individual". In this view, emotional involvement and "hot cognition", rather than "cold", rational decision-making, determine our social behavior.

The present SIP model does not incorporate this eminent role of emotion explicitly. Emotions may be implicitly present in the model as "energy" driving the whole process (Dodge, 1991), but the model does not propose how this energy influences information processing. Accordingly, the model provides no clear, testable hypotheses concerning the roles emotions play in determining one's responses to situations. Furthermore, in popular cognitive behavioral interventions, the recognition and regulation of emotions play an important role. Examples can be found in Promoting Alternative Thinking Strategies (PATHS; Greenberg *et al.*, 1995) and in the Anger Coping Program (Lochman & Lenhart, 1993). However, at present it is difficult to draw links between Dodge's cognitive model and these treatment techniques focusing on emotions.

Theoretically, a variety of interactions between emotions and SIP may play a role in the development of disruptive behavior. Before discussing these roles of emotion, the term "emotion" first needs to be defined. An emotion can be regarded as comprising an experiential/cognitive component, a motor/behavioral component, and a neurophysiological component. The experiential/cognitive component represents the subjective experience of the emotion: the experience of being happy, angry or sad. The motor/behavioral component, also called "action tendency", represents a specific drive to perform a certain action – which is characteristic of emotions. A defining component of rage, for example, is the action tendency to rebel against the immediate environment, and a component of shame is the action tendency to creep away and hide. The neurophysiological component of emotion represents specific levels of the physical arousal characteristic of emotions. These three components are not mutually independent, but are considered different manifestations of the same process (Fischer *et al.*, 1990).

Exactly how emotions arise is the subject of wide debate. A central question concerns the causal relationship between emotion and cognition. One school of thought is that a relevant stimulus directly evokes an emotion, which then evokes a specific cognition. An alternative view is that a stimulus is first represented cognitively and that this representation then evokes a specific emotion. There is evidence in favor of both standpoints. A stimulus can elicit different emotions independently of the way it is represented, and different emotions can call up different representations of stimuli (Fischer *et al.*, 1990).

Models incorporating both these positions (e.g. Frijda, 1993) distinguish two types of representation. A stimulus can be perceived and a rudimentary representation can be realized almost immediately. This primary representation leads to a specific action tendency, which initiates behavior. The action tendency also influences subsequent information processing. Before or during enactment of the action tendency, a second type of representation can take place: the action tendency itself can be observed and represented, resulting in an altered action tendency and other behavior. Various authors suggest that most children learn to use such secondary representation in order to regulate their emotions (e.g. Campos *et al.*, 1989; Dodge, 1989).

Boys with disruptive behavior problems, however, may fail to perceive their own action tendencies, fail to represent them as running counter to their goals, or be unable to regulate them. Suggested causes for these possible deviations are that representation and emotion regulation skills were never learned, perhaps because it was never necessary for these boys to learn such skills, having grown up in environments where emotion regulation did not have any beneficial effects. With regard to attention deficit hyperactivity disorder (ADHD), it is suggested that children with ADHD may not be able to develop secondary representation because they are unable to inhibit or delay their first action tendency, which means that they never reach the stage of secondary representation (Barkley, 1994).

It is notable that the above accounts of emotion in disruptive boys are very similar to Dodge's SIP model. Both models postulate stimulus representation, which leads to certain behavior. Several authors (Crick & Dodge, 1994; Lochman & Lenhart, 1995) have tried to integrate the two models by extending Dodge's original model to incorporate emotional action tendencies or a changed arousal level. According to these adapted models, in children with behavior problems a stimulus representation will lead to enhanced intensity of emotions or level of arousal, increasing the likelihood of aggressive responses by these children.

In the above models, emotions exist on the basis of representations. However, it is likely that salient cues may lead to basic emotions *without* representations first being formed. These so-called precognitive emotions are thought to arise immediately as stimuli are encoded and to activate dominant responses automatically (Ledoux, in Goleman, 1995). This "precognitive" information processing shows clear differences from the revised SIP model. Here, the stimulus is of course not represented, and instead of an optimal response being selected through comparison of several alternatives, a single dominant response is directly activated. It is possible that boys with DBP react aggressively to salient stimuli sooner than their peers because "precognitive" anger is more likely to be activated in them and because the dominant response evoked by anger is aggressive.

Empirical studies of emotional information processing in children with behavior problems

As described above, to a certain extent emotions are incorporated in SIP. DBP are thought to be related to inaccurate encoding and representation of other people's emotional states, greater intensity of own anger, and lack of adequate regulation of own emotions. However, research on these issues is scarce, particularly for children with severe behavior problems:

> Relatively little research has been conducted from an integrative perspective on social information processing and emotion. That is, few investigators have assessed the relation between social information processing and emotion and the impact of this relation on social adjustment. . . . Clearly, it will be important for future research to consider carefully the role that emotion plays in social information processing and adjustment.
>
> (Crick & Dodge, 1994, pp. 81–82)

In this section, we first give a short overview of existent research of emotional information processing in disruptive children. Then we present the main findings of a number of studies we recently conducted concerning emotional information processing, the differences between emotional and reflective information processing, and the influence of emotional state on information processing.

Even though emotion is not specifically included in Dodge's model, emotional aspects of information processing have often been indirectly involved in research designs. It seems that deviations in SIP occur only when boys are *personally* involved in the situation presented (Orobio de Castro *et al.*, 2002), and that these deviations increase when participants feel threatened. The influence of participant involvement in presented situations was investigated in two studies with aggressive, rejected boys (Dodge & Frame, 1982; Dodge & Somberg, 1987). In the first investigation, the study participants were asked to imagine themselves as being either an onlooker or the injured party in vignettes presented to them. Hostile representation of intent was found only when subjects imagined themselves as the injured party. In the second study, during a pause in SIP tasks, the boys were confronted with the so-called real problem, staged by the experimenter, that a child in the corridor was threatening to pick a quarrel with the subject. The aggressive–rejected group did not differ from the popular–nonaggressive group in their representation of hostile intent before the threat, but represented more hostile intent after the threat.

Concerning encoding and representation of others' emotions, boys with behavior problems appear to be inaccurate at identifying other children's emotions from pictures of emotion expressions (Cook *et al.*, 1994; Izard *et al.*, 1997). Whether this inaccuracy involves a tendency to systematically misattribute specific emotions (for example, to consider a sad facial expression as representing anger), and whether the inaccuracy also occurs when representing the social situations used in SIP research, is, however, unclear.

We recently conducted a number of empirical studies aimed to clarify emotional aspects of differences in SIP between disruptive and non-disruptive comparison boys. Each of these studies was conducted with 30–55 seven- to 13-year-old participants in child psychiatric care or special education for DBP and 30–60 non-referred participants in regular schools. Each of these studies required participants to listen individually to stories concerning provocation by a peer and to answer questions about these stories. Our main findings concerning emotions in disruptive boys' information processing were as follows.

Representation of emotions in others

As in numerous previous studies, we found that DBP boys more often attribute hostile intentions to other children than their peers do. Moreover, in response to the vignettes we presented, they attributed different emotions to other children. When distressed, disruptive boys more often indicated that other children enjoy their distress, or are at best indifferent to it. The latter finding remains even when disruptive boys attributed benign intentions to the children involved (Orobio de Castro, 2000).

Own emotions

Intense anger in disruptive boys is seen as an important source of their disruptive behavior. Greater intensity of anger in boys with behavior problems may lead these boys to react more aggressively than other children (Graham et al., 1992; Lochman & Lenhart, 1993). However, results of studies on anger after provocation in non-referred samples are inconsistent. While Graham et al. (1992) and Vlerick (1994) did find that aggressive–rejected children became more angry than their non-aggressive peers, other studies (Quiggle et al., 1992; Waas, 1988) did not obtain such results. In our studies (Orobio de Castro et al., 2003a), boys referred for DBP consistently indicated that they become angrier than their non-referred peers after a provocation. Possibly this effect only occurs in severely disruptive children, like the clinically disruptive boys in our studies.

Emotion regulation

Even intense anger does not necessarily lead to aggression. Most children learn to regulate anger and other negative emotions in circumstances where expression of these emotions would have aversive consequences (Campos et al., 1989; Dodge, 1989). In fact, young children are remarkably apt at emotion regulation, for instance by distracting themselves, or by intentionally devaluing the goal they were pursuing (Stegge, 1995). Anger coping programs (e.g. Lochman & Lenhart, 1993) are based on the assumption that boys with behavior problems are less skilled at regulating anger and therefore act aggressively more often when angered than their peers do. There has, however, been surprisingly little research on emotion regulation by boys with behavior problems. Meerum Terwogt *et al.* (1990) found that a hetero-geneous sample of children – including children with DBP – receiving treatment in an institute for child psychiatric care knew fewer strategies to regulate emotions. In a non-referred sample, Hubbard *et al.* (1998) found that aggression was related to lack of skill and motivation to regulate emotion.

In our study (Orobio de Castro, 2000), emotion regulation strategies were assessed by asking participants: *when you feel so [negative emotion mentioned before], can you think of something that could make you feel better? What can you think of?* Answers to these questions were coded as *solution* when an attempt to solve the problem was mentioned (e.g. "I'll go to the teacher and explain what happened"), as *distraction* when a participant made an attempt to find distraction ("go to my room and play my music"), as *cognitive* when a cognitive strategy was suggested ("I'll think it was only a game"), as *aggressive* when any form of aggression was mentioned ("Yes! Beat him up!"), as *by other* when only acts by another person were mentioned ("when he gives me a new one"), or as *don't know/irrelevant* when no answer or irrelevant answers were given.[2] We considered solutions, distractions or cognitive strategies to be adaptive emotion regulation strategies.

As expected, disruptive boys mentioned fewer adaptive emotion regulation strategies than comparison boys. Boys in the comparison group more often mentioned *solutions* and *distraction*, whereas boys in the disruptive group more often *did not know* a strategy to regulate their emotion and more often said that emotion could only be regulated *by others*. More disruptive boys than comparison boys mentioned *aggression* as a way to regulate negative emotions, for example by stating "If I smudge his painting too, then he'll cry and it's my turn to laugh".

Interaction goals and response selection

From a rational stance, the inclusion of "interaction goals" in the social information-processing model makes sense: one can only select an optimal response if one uses a goal as a standard to evaluate possible responses against. However, from an emotional point of view, it is quite possible that disruptive boys' behavior does not result from a deliberate response in order to obtain a goal. Rather, responses may simply result from a strong emotional action tendency that is executed without any goal or outcome in mind. This is exactly what our studies indicate for disruptive boys. These boys generally responded aggressively, did not select responses they expected to have the best outcome, and frequently indicated that their responses resulted from intense anger that "made them" act aggressively (e.g. "I'll go mad with anger"). In contrast, non-disruptive boys generally responded non-aggressively and selected responses that would best help them attain their predominantly prosocial goals.

---

2 All examples are quotes from participants' actual answers.

In sum, on all emotion measures, disruptive boys were found to differ from comparison boys. All the emotion variables studied were also related to teacher-rated DBP. Larger deviations were associated with more severe behavior problems. Controlling for possible confounding effects of group differences in verbal intelligence and socially desirable answering tendencies did not alter these findings.

Differences between emotional and reflective information processing

Appreciation of the importance of emotions in SIP necessitates a reappraisal of results obtained in previous SIP studies. An important aspect of emotions – which was also mentioned by our disruptive participants – is that they take "control precedence" (Frijda, 1988). That is, emotions invoke a tendency to interpret and act on a situation in a specific "emotional" way. Anger, for example, is believed to invoke both a tendency to encode and represent potentially threatening information and a tendency to act aggressively. Such "emotional" processing is clearly different from the extensive, rational information processing the SIP model prescribes. Yet by asking children a series of questions about hypothetical events, studies of SIP have generally tempted children to calmly process information in the way the SIP model prescribes. The results of such studies are then believed to apply to automatic, emotional processing as well, even though there is no evidence to support this claim. This issue is particularly important, since a number of cognitive behavioral intervention programs aim to train children in reflective processing, under the assumption that this will reduce aggressive behavior.

To test this assumption, we conducted two experiments (Orobio de Castro et al., 2003a) on the relation between automatic, emotional, and reflective SIP. In the first of these studies, children's direct automatic responses to hypothetical vignettes were compared to their responses following extensive prompts to reflect, by following the SIP model before responding. The results revealed that reflection did not lead to an overall increase or decrease in aggressiveness of responses. However, response aggressiveness did increase for some children, while it decreased for others. Increased response aggressiveness was found to be associated with hostile attribution of intent in the reflective condition. This suggests that whether reflection decreases or increases aggressiveness depends on what children think during reflection. This finding seems to go against the popular advice that aggressive children should "take another's perspective" before they act: if they take the other's perspective and represent the other's perspective as hostile, perspective taking will only increase aggressiveness.

In a second study we pursued this issue by studying the differential effects of different kinds of reflection in disruptive and comparison boys. Participants were asked to monitor their own feelings and emotion regulation, to consider the other's intentions and feelings, to wait ten seconds, or to answer a distracting question. The effects of reflection were found to depend on the type of reflection required. In line with the previous findings, considering another's emotions and intentions tended to increase aggressiveness in disruptive boys and decreased it in comparison boys. Consistent with the idea that unregulated anger plays an important role in aggressive responding, only monitoring their own emotions and emotion regulation significantly reduced aggressiveness in the disruptive group.

The influence of emotional state on information processing

The influence of emotions on consequent SIP was examined more directly in a third study (Orobio de Castro *et al.*, 2003b). In this experiment, a manipulated computer game was used to induce negative emotions in boys with severe behavior problems, aggressive boys in regular education, and nonaggressive boys. Both before and after the affect manipulation, participants completed SIP tasks comparable to those used in the previous experiments. The affect manipulation led to an increase in hostile attributions of intent for the disruptive boys, but not for the other groups. Although the increased hostile attribution was not followed by increased response aggressiveness, this experiment clearly showed that disruptive boys are particularly susceptible to the effect of negative emotions on subsequent information processing.

Toward an extension of the SIP model

Over the past decade, the dominant theory on social cognition and disruptive behavior has been the SIP theory. Unfortunately, emotional processes are only implicitly acknowledged in SIP theory, even though they are considered influential aspects of both SIP and disruptive behavior. In fact, the "core business" of emotions may be considered as predisposing a person to react adequately to social information. Theoretical work on emotions shows this relatedness between SIP and emotion: models of emotion processes and SIP are in certain respects quite similar.

In theory, several roles of emotion in SIP are plausible. One important aspect concerns representation of one's own and other people's emotions. Different representations may trigger different subsequent emotions, which will result in generating, selecting, and enacting specific responses. However, in the case of intense emotions, an individual may be impelled to generate a single response and enact it without any generation of, or selection from, alternative responses. Finally, emotions are at the focus of an important class of responses: responses aimed to regulate one's own emotions.

Results of the studies described in this chapter clearly show that disruptive boys deviate from the process prescribed by Dodge (1986). Emotions play important roles in these deviations. Aggressive responses to social situations are associated with intense anger, limited knowledge of adaptive emotion regulation strategies, and distorting effects of negative feelings on internal representations. Even in the "normal" comparison groups in our studies, individual differences in aggressiveness were consistently related to intensity, regulation, and representation of emotions.

Rational decision-making processes seem to play only a limited role in disruptive boys' SIP. These boys do not indicate that they "select" certain responses to pursue a specific goal, and respond in ways they themselves expect to have negative consequences.

The important roles of emotions are only implicitly addressed in the present SIP models of Dodge (1986) and Crick and Dodge (1994). If one considers these models as "idealized" prescriptions for rational decision making, the virtual absence of emotions in the models is understandable. However, the usefulness of such prescriptive models for understanding children's actual information processing seems limited if they do not resemble children's actual information processing. In practice, the SIP models are rarely used as idealized *prescriptive* decision models, but rather as *descriptive* models of how "normal" children process social information and how disruptive children should learn to process information as well (consider, for example the cognitive "steps" children are taught in cognitive programs such as PATHS). If the SIP models are used in this broader descriptive sense, then the absence of emotions in the models is problematic. An economic model of SIP should include the most important facets of information processing, and leave out unimportant aspects that add little to its explanatory value.

What would a SIP model look like if multiple roles of emotion were included? We feel that emotional aspects of information processing can be integrated easily with the SIP model, resulting in an integrative SIP model (see also Orobio de Castro, 2003). Figure 15.1 gives an example of such a model.

In this "emotional information processing" model, responses are partly determined by characteristics of the social situation a child is in. Relevant information is then encoded. Encoding does not only concern aspects of the situation, but also "internal" information concerning one's own emotional state and action tendency, for example muscle tension, heart rate, and body movements. Moreover, the quality of encoding depends on one's emotional state.

As in the SIP model, a representation of the meaning of the situation is formed on the basis of the encoded information. This representation does not only concern other people's intentions, but also an estimate of their emotional state, and – from the encoded information about one's own state – a representation of one's own emotions. In many cases, such an in-depth representation is not made, but only a rough appraisal of the encoded information as beneficial or detrimental to one's interests. One's emotional state influences how information is represented.

A certain representation may subsequently trigger a specific emotional response-tendency. If the representation signals that something relevant to one's interests is happening, the representation triggers an emotion. The type and severity of the emotion triggered depends on the representation. If, for example, a situation is represented as a deliberate and unjust attack on vital interests, intense anger will be triggered, which comprises a tendency to respond aggressively. Representations

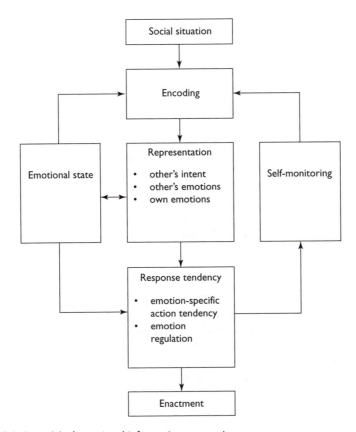

Figure 15.1 A model of emotional information processing.

of one's own emotional state similarly trigger emotions. If, for example, one encoded having strong muscle tension, screaming, and running towards another person, a representation might be formed of being extremely angry and about to fight, which in turn might trigger fear and the response tendency to back off from the situation.

In contrast with the existing SIP model, only a single emotion-specific response tendency is triggered at this time, so there is no comparison and selection of a "best" response from multiple alternatives. The emotional response tendency is directly enacted, unless the response tendency itself is encoded, represented as detrimental to one's interests, and thereby changed. This process of "self-monitoring" (Fischer *et al.*, 1990), prevents most people from uninhibitedly enacting their emotional response tendencies in situations where this would be maladaptive.

One's emotional state may have a profound influence on SIP, as it influences encoding and representation and functions as a "base rate" from which emotional response tendencies arise.

As in the SIP model, emotional information-processing in a specific situation is thought to be determined by characteristics of the situation, a child's information processing capacities, and schemata in a so-called "database". An additional determinant of emotional information processing may be a child's "emotionality", i.e. the general intensity and duration of emotions a child experiences. It appears from the literature (e.g. Fischer *et al.*, 1990) that there are stable, trait-like inter-individual differences in emotionality. These differences would have a profound influence on emotional information processing as described here. Children with more intense emotions would exhibit more extreme response tendencies than other children, even if they represented a situation in the same way. Emotional information processing in children whose emotions tend to recede more slowly would be influenced by these emotions for a longer period. Whether children with DBP differ from other children in "emotionality" is not yet clear, although there are indications that this may be the case (Eisenberg *et al.*, 1996). Future research on individual differences in duration and intensity of emotions may clarify this issue.

The model in Figure 15.1 is obviously very similar to present SIP (Dodge, 1986; Crick & Dodge, 1994) and emotion models (Fischer *et al.*, 1990; Graham *et al.*, 1992). What's different is that this model enables a description of what usually seems to go on in the average child *and* what seems to happen in a distressed boy with severe DBP. For example, the findings concerning the influence of negative emotion on hostile attribution of intent can more easily be explained by the model in Figure 15.1 than by the original SIP model, because the influence of emotional state on representation is included in this alternative model.

These findings seem particularly relevant to our understanding of the escalation of small conflicts. If a minor annoyance suffices to increase the likelihood that disruptive boys will attribute hostile intentions to other children, and if these hostile attributions in turn amplify negative feelings and aggressive behavior, then for these boys, small misunderstandings can easily escalate to violent incidents. The child will presumably blame these incidents on the "other" to whom he attributed hostile intent. This exact scenario is frequently reported by teachers and caregivers that experience that once children become frustrated or tired, conflicts flare up easily.

Discussion and conclusion

An important limitation of the studies discussed here is that they all concern responses to hypothetical events, rather than to actual situations. This is particularly troublesome, because part of the studies concern emotions, and children would presumably be more emotional in real situations that concern them than when listening to stories about such situations. Care was taken to construct emotionally engaging vignettes and participants generally seemed to become very involved with the stories, but the vignettes are nonetheless unlikely to be as engaging as "the real thing". Fortunately, a number of findings suggest that responses to hypothetical vignettes are related to responses in actual situations. We consistently found deviations in SIP to be associated with real-life teacher-rated disruptive behavior, even while the teacher's ratings did not concern the same situations as the vignettes we presented. Moreover, a recent meta-analysis (Orobio de Castro *et al.*, 2002) suggested that findings on hostile attribution are larger when participants are more involved with the vignettes presented. If this finding also applied for the other SIP variables, the problem of hypothetical vignettes would be easily resolved: in that case, all findings would simply be underestimates of effects in real situations. Notwithstanding these arguments, the relation between findings with hypothetical vignettes and findings in actual situations is far from clear, and requires direct empirical study.

A second limitation of the studies reported here is the heterogeneity of the samples. Disruptive behavior is a very broad term and the disruptive participants in our studies differed considerably with regard to type of behavior problems, developmental history, and severity of associated problems. For example, different SIP patterns have been suggested for reactively aggressive and proactively aggressive children. Explorative analyses of relations between specific kinds of behavior problems and emotional information processing were complicated by the fact that most children presented combinations of many different behavior problems, rendering the discriminant validity of different dimensions of behavior problems small in these samples. The heterogeneity of behavior problems makes it especially important to note that most findings on deviant SIP in disruptive boys presented here did not apply to *all* boys in the disruptive groups, but concern differences between mean scores of groups of children. One of the challenges for future research will be to link specific SIP patterns to children with specific kinds of behavior problems and specific life histories.

In our studies, the accent was on anger and its regulation as determinants of disruptive behavior. In situations that evoke other kinds of disruptive behavior than reactive aggression, other emotions may be more relevant. For example, (lack of) guilt may be associated with proactive and covert disruptive behavior (Loeber & Coie, 2001) and feelings of pride and grandiosity may be associated with disruptive behavior in antisocial peer groups.

In this chapter we only discussed differences between existing groups of disruptive and normal comparison boys. We have not yet completed our ongoing longitudinal studies concerning the development of disruptive behavior. Therefore, we cannot draw any conclusions about the role of deviations in emotional information processing in the development of disruptive behavior. Nonetheless, the deviancies we found are consistent with developmental studies on the roles of SIP in the development of disruptive behavior.

During the past years, several risk factors and developmental pathways of disruptive behavior have been identified (e.g. Lipsey & Derzon, 1998; Loeber, 1990). We still, however, know very little about the mechanisms that cause the development of disruptive behavior. Disturbances in emotional information processing may be part of such a mechanism (Rutter, 1998).

Interactions between limited information-processing capacities, aversive social experiences, and training in deviant SIP by peers or parents may result in the emotional information processing patterns disruptive boys displayed in our studies. The relative contributions of these factors may differ between individual children. For one child, impulsive behavior and attention problems may have prohibited learning of social skills and given rise to rejection by peers, causing the child to expect hostile behavior from these children. Yet another child may have learned hostile attributions and aggressive responses as survival strategies in an abusive and coercive family climate. It has also been suggested (Fischer *et al.*, 1990; Greenberg & Snell, 1997; Lewis, 1990) that such experiences not only influence SIP, but also are reflected in changes in physiological systems associated with emotionality and executive functioning. One way or another, once these deviant patterns have been learned, they may maintain and escalate behavior problems, as they lead to frequent conflicts with and rejection by peers. This limits opportunities to learn social skills and to experience benign social interactions with nondisruptive children. Over time, deviant SIP patterns may become self-fulfilling prophecies: children evoke hostile behavior from others, do not learn social skills other than getting their own way through aggressive behavior, and associate with other disruptive children, who confirm their expectations (Dishion *et al.*, 1995).

This view on deviant emotional information processing as a maintenance factor for disruptive behavior is obviously highly speculative, and certainly does not follow logically from the results of the studies reported here. It does, however, seem a promising starting point for further research. If the proposed causal relations between emotional information processing and the development of DBP can be established, (preventive) interventions aimed at self-monitoring-skills, representation of other's emotions and intentions, emotion regulation, and response repertoire seem particularly promising. However, at this stage, little can be said about the effectiveness of such emotion-focused interventions on the basis of the research discussed here. Evaluative experimental research (cf. Lochman & Lenhart, 1993) is needed to judge the value of these interventions.

References

Barkley, R.A. (1994). Impaired delayed responding: a unified theory of attention-deficit hyperactivity disorder. In D.K. Routh (ed.), *Disruptive behavior disorders in childhood* (pp. 11–57). New York: Plenum Press.

Campos, J.J., Campos, R.G., & Barrett, K.C. (1989). Emergent themes in the study of emotional development and emotion regulation. *Developmental Psychology*, 25, 394–402.

Cook, E.T., Greenberg, M.T., & Kusche, C.A. (1994). The relations between emotional understanding, intellectual functioning, and disruptive behavior problems in elementary-school-aged children. *Journal of Abnormal Psychology*, 22, 205–219.

Crick, N.C. & Dodge, K.A. (1994). A review and reformulation of social information processing mechanisms in children's social adjustment. *Psychological Bulletin*, 115, 74–101.

Dishion, T.J., French, D.C., & Patterson, G.R. (1995). The development and ecology of antisocial behavior. In D. Cicchetti & D.J. Cohen (eds) *Developmental psychopathology, Vol. 2: Risk, disorder, and adaptation* (pp. 421–471). New York: Wiley.

Dishion, T.J., Spracklen, K.M., Andrews, D.W., & Patterson, G.R. (1996). Deviancy training in male adolescents' friendships. *Behavior Therapy*, **27**, 373–390.

Dodge, K.A. (1986). A social information processing model of social competence in children. In M. Perlmutter (ed.), *The Minnesota Symposium on Child Psychology*, **18** (pp. 77–125). Hillsdale, NJ: Lawrence Erlbaum.

Dodge, K.A. (1989). Coordinating responses to aversive stimuli: Introduction to a special section on the development of emotion regulation. *Developmental Psychology*, **25**, 339–342.

Dodge, K.A. (1991). Emotion and social information processing. In J. Garber & K.A. Dodge (eds), *The development of emotion regulation and dysregulation* (pp. 159–181). Cambridge: Cambridge University Press.

Dodge, K.A. & Frame, C.L. (1982). Social cognitive biases and deficits in aggressive boys. *Child Development*, **53**, 620–635.

Dodge, K.A. & Somberg, D.R. (1987). Hostile attributional biases among aggressive boys are exacerbated under conditions of threats to the self. *Child Development*, **58**, 213–224.

Eisenberg, N., Fabes, R.A., Guthrie, I.K., Murphy, B.C., Maszk, P., Holmgren, R., & Suh, K. (1996). The relations of regulation and emotionality to problem behavior in elementary school children. *Development and Psychopathology*, **8**, 141–162.

Erdley, C.A. & Asher, S.R. (1996). Children's social goals and self-efficacy perceptions as influences on their responses to ambiguous provocation. *Child Development*, **67**, 1329–1344.

Fischer, K.W., Shaver, P.R., & Carnochan, P. (1990). How emotions develop and how they organise development. *Cognition and Emotion*, **4**, 81–127.

Frijda, N.H. (1988). The laws of emotion. *American Psychologist*, **43**, 349–358.

Frijda, N.H. (1993). The place of appraisal in emotion. *Cognition and Emotion*, **7**, 357–387.

Goleman, D. (1995). *Emotional intelligence*. New York: Bantam.

Gottman, J.M. (1986). Comments in Dodge, K.A., Pettit, G.S., McClaskey, C.L., & Brown, M.M., Social competence in children. *Monographs of the Society for Research in Child Development*, **51**, 81–85.

Graham, S., Hudley, C., & Williams, E. (1992). Attributional and emotional determinants of aggression among African-American and Latino young adolescents. *Developmental Psychology*, **28**, 731–740.

Greenberg, M.T., Kusche, C.A., Cook, E.T., & Quamma, J.P. (1995). Promoting emotional competence in school-aged children: the effects of the PATHS curriculum. *Developmental Psychopathology*, **7**, 117–136.

Greenberg, M.T. & Snell, J.L. (1997). Brain development and emotional development: the role of teaching in organizing the frontal lobe. In P. Salovey & D.J. Sluyter (eds), *Emotional development and emotional intelligence* (pp. 93–119). New York: Basic Books.

Hubbard, J.A., Parker, E.H., Ramsden, S.R., & Smithmyer, C.M. (1998). *Anger regulation processes in children's peer interaction*. Paper presented at the XVth biennial ISSBD meeting, Berne.

Izard, C.E., Schultz, D., & Ackerman, B.P. (1997). *Emotion knowledge, social competence, and behavior problems in disadvantaged children*. Paper presented at the 1997 Biennial Meeting of the Society for Research in Child Development, Washington DC.

Kazdin, A.E. (1995). *Conduct disorders in childhood and adolescence. Developmental Clinical Psychology and Psychiatry series*, Vol. 9. London: Sage.

Lewis, D.O. (1990). Neuropsychiatric and experiential correlates of violent juvenile delinquency. *Neuropsychology Review*, **1**, 125–136.

Lipsey, M.W. & Derzon, J.H. (1998). Predictors of violent or serious delinquency in adolescence and early adulthood: a synthesis of longitudinal research. In R. Loeber & D.P. Farrington (eds), *Serious and violent juvenile offenders: Risk factors and successful interventions* (pp. 86–105). Thousand Oaks, CA: Sage.

Lochman, J.E. & Lenhart, L.A. (1993). Anger coping intervention for aggressive children: conceptual models and outcome effects. *Clinical Psychology Review*, **13**, 785–805.

Lochman, J.E. & Lenhart, L.A. (1995). Cognitive behavioral therapy of aggressive children: effects of schemas. In H.P.J.G. van Bilsen, P.C. Kendall, & J.H. Slavenburg (eds), *Behavioral approaches for children and adolescents: Challenges for the next century* (pp. 145–166). New York: Plenum Press.

Lochman, J.E., Wayland, K.K., & White, K.J. (1993). Social goals – relationship to adolescent adjustment and to social-problem solving. *Journal of Abnormal Child Psychology*, **21**, 135–151.

Loeber, R. (1990). Development and risk factors of juvenile antisocial behavior and delinquency. *Clinical Psychology Review*, **10**, 1–41.

Loeber, R. & Coie, J. (2001). Continuities and discontinuities of development, with particular emphasis on emotional and cognitive components of disruptive behavior. In B. Maughan & J. Hill (eds) *Cambridge monographs in child and adolescent psychiatry: Conduct disorders* (pp. 379–407). Cambridge: Cambridge University Press.

Loeber, R. & Hay, D. (1997). Key issues in the development of aggression and violence from childhood to early adulthood. *Annual Review of Psychology*, **48**, 371–410.

Meerum Terwogt, M., Schene, J., & Koops, W. (1990). Concepts of emotion in institutionalized children. *Journal of Child Psychology and Psychiatry*, **31**, 1131–1143.

Orobio de Castro, B. (2000). *Social information processing and emotion in antisocial boys* (doctoral dissertation). Amsterdam: PI Research.

Orobio de Castro, B. (2003). The development of social information processing and aggressive behavior: current issues. *European Journal of Developmental Psychology*, **1**, in press.

Orobio de Castro, B., Veerman, J.W., Koops, W., Bosch, J.D., & Monshouwer, H.J. (2002). Hostile attribution of intent and aggressive behavior: a Meta analysis. *Child Development*, **73**, 916–934.

Orobio de Castro, B., Bosch, J.D., Veerman, J.W., & Koops, W. (2003a). The influences of emotion regulation, attribution prompts, and delay, on response aggressiveness in antisocial boys. *Cognitive Therapy and Research*, **27**, 153–166.

Orobio de Castro, B., Slot, N.W., Bosch, J.D., Koops, W., & Veerman, J.W. (2003b). Negative affect exacerbates hostile attributions of intent in highly aggressive boys. *Journal of Clinical Child and Adolescent Psychology*, **32**, 57–66.

Quiggle, N.L., Garber, J., Panak, W.F., & Dodge, K.A. (1992). Social information processing in aggressive and depressed children. *Child development*, **63**, 1305–1320.

Rutter, M.L. (1997). Nature–nurture integration: the example of antisocial behavior. *American Psychologist*, **52**, 390–398.

Rutter, M.L. (1998). Practitioner review: routes from research to clinical practice in child psychiatry: retrospect and prospect. *Journal of Child Psychology and Psychiatry*, **39**, 805–816.

Sociaal en Cultureel Planbureau (SCP) (1999). *Sociale en culturele verkenningen 1999 [Social and cultural explorations 1999]*. Cahier 157. The Hague: SCP.

Stegge, G.T.M. (1995). *Mood dependent social judgments in children.* Unpublished doctoral dissertation, Vrije Universiteit, Amsterdam.

Tangney, J.P. & Fischer, K.W. (eds) (1995). *Self-conscious emotions: the psychology of shame, guilt, embarrassment, and pride.* New York: Guilford Press.

Vlerick, P. (1994). The development of socially incompetent behavior in provocative situations. *Psychologica Belgica*, **34**, 33–55.

Waas, G.A. (1988). Social attributional biases of peer-rejected and aggressive children. *Child Development*, **59**, 969–975.

Part IV

Expression in specific ways and groups

Chapter 16

Crying, catharsis, and health

*Suzanne Stougie, Ad Vingerhoets
and Randolph R. Cornelius*

Introduction

Among both scientists and the lay public, crying,[1] the shedding of emotional tears, is often assumed to be healthy, or at least to have a tension-reducing effect. Cornelius (1986), in his study of crying in the popular press, reviewed 72 articles on crying published in popular media between 1848 and 1985. He found that in the majority of articles crying was considered essential to human health and well-being. The advice of many of the articles, regardless of the time they were published, was not to hold back tears, as this might lead to a variety of negative consequences ranging from unhappiness to ill-health or even death.

Vingerhoets and Scheirs (2001) and Becht and Vingerhoets (2002) provide some nice illustrations of how crying and its functions are perceived, extracted from poems and quotes from popular writings. To mention some examples, crying is considered as the most human and universal of all relief phenomena and as a vital part of a healing or growing process that should not be hindered, or as an inborn healing mechanism. One cancer patient declares that his neck tumor was caused by the inhibition of his tears. Some eminent scientists share this perspective: the famous British physician Sir Henry Maudsley has been quoted as stating that "Sorrows which find no vent in tears, may soon make other organs weep".

In this chapter, we first briefly review the most important scientific theories that have been formulated about crying. We then describe the research conducted in this field and the evidence for the effects of crying on catharsis and health. Finally, we discuss the contradictory research results that have emerged from studies of the relationship between crying and physical and emotional well-being and suggest ways to reconcile some of these contradictory results.

Theories of crying

Theories of crying have been formulated by people from many different backgrounds, including clinicians, social and experimental psychologists, and

---

1 Some authors, including one of us (RRC), prefer the term "weeping".

biochemists (Kottler & Montgomery, 2001; Vingerhoets *et al.*, 2000). The ways in which, according to these theories, crying may contribute to physical and emotional well-being are multiple. Below, some important theories on crying are briefly reviewed. Throughout, emphasis is placed on the postulated effects of crying on health and well-being.

Cathartic theories

Some theories propose that crying results in a form of emotional catharsis. Catharsis may be defined as the experience of relief or release of emotional tension as well as decrease in felt distress or physiological arousal. The word catharsis is derived from the Greek *katharsis*, meaning "purification", and a related word meaning to "cleanse and purify" in a ritual context (Cornelius, 1997). Behind the idea of catharsis lies another idea, namely that withholding crying when it is called for may result in ill health. The emotional tension we have failed to release by crying will be discharged through other means, resulting in a variety of physical and psychological symptoms (see Groen, 1957). Headaches, ulcers, hypertension, and insomnia are some examples of disorders that, according to catharsis theories, will result from the failure to cry. The idea that crying facilitates catharsis is thus entangled with the often assumed positive effects of crying on health. Crying is commonly described as health-promoting in a cathartic way: it alleviates built-up emotional stress, whether this stress is in the form of psychological tension or in the form of toxic waste products resulting from exposure to stressful conditions (cf. Frey *et al.*, 1981).

An early influential theory describing crying as a cathartic process was formulated by Sigmund Freud (1915/1957). According to this author, stimulation of the lacrimal gland would relieve the brain from accumulated stress. Other psychoanalysts, such as Heilbrunn (1955), also endorsed the idea that tears are a physiological means of relieving the state of tension generated by tear-provoking stimuli. Or, as Sadoff (1966) put it, crying is a kind of "safety valve" that allows for the "draining off" of the energy accompanying negative affect. In this description of crying in terms of a hydraulic or overflow process, tears are considered as overflowing emotions that have reached a critical level (see also Breuer & Freud, 1895/1955; Koestler, 1964).

Bindra (1972) claimed that crying takes place when one's emotional state reaches a certain threshold value and becomes too overpowering to allow normal adaptive behavior to proceed. Tears reflect emotions that cannot otherwise be worked off in action. They are thus considered as helping to discharge tension in situations in which an individual is not able to cope effectively. Such a relationship with powerlessness has also been proposed by Crile (1915), Frijda (1986), and Vingerhoets *et al.* (1997).

Reductionist theories

Reductionist theories consider crying in terms of its supposed physiological functions. According to Darwin (1872), children cry out loudly when in need of food or help and partly as a relief from suffering. The secretion of tears is a by-product of firmly contracting the muscles around the eye during the crying episode. Eventually, according to Darwin, suffering alone, through association, can cause the secretion of tears. This author further argues that crying may bring relief in much the same way as "the writhing of the whole body, the grinding of the teeth, and the uttering of piercing shrieks, all give relief under an agony of pain" (p. 175).

Montagu (1959) argued that the intense inhaling and exhaling of air during sobbing would rapidly dry out the mucous membranes of the nose and throat. He considered crying to be a protective mechanism against this drying. Tears draining through the nasolacrimal ducts would keep the membranes moist. However, since sobbing is not present in all crying episodes (see Frey *et al.*, 1983) and no tears are secreted during running or any other physical exercise that increases breathing, it is not likely that the primary function of tears is to protect against the effects of rapid breathing. Montagu also suggested that the antibacterial enzyme lysozyme, found in lacrimal fluid, would protect against upper respiratory infections.

Frey (1985) emphasized that psychogenic lacrimation is an excretory process. He hypothesized that, like other excretory processes such as urinating, defecating, and exhaling, emotional tearing may be involved in removing waste products or toxic substances from the body. According to Frey, the reason why people feel better after crying is that their tears are removing toxic substances and stress hormones that build up during emotional stress. Frey *et al.* (1981) found that emotional tears indeed contain high concentrations of some hormones, including ACTH, prolactin, and endorphins, which was seen as evidence supporting Frey's theory. In addition, differences were found in the composition of emotional and irritant tears, in particular with respect to proteins. This result is, however, difficult to interpret and it is not clear whether this difference has any clinical relevance. Moreover, it is not known whether the biochemical composition of sad tears and tears of joy also differs. Critics, including Murube *et al.* (1999), refute this claim, stating that the amount of tears generally is so limited that it is not reasonable to presume that this process would have any physiological relevance.

Cognitive theories

A third category of theories of crying is more cognitive in nature. Efran and Spangler (1979), for example, outlined a two-factor theory explaining crying in adults. According to this theory, two phases occur in adult crying, emotional arousal and recovery. Crying occurs when a period of either positive or negative arousal is followed by a shift to recovery. Only during this second phase, while tension decreases, will tears flow. In this view, tears do not facilitate recovery, but rather they are merely an epiphenomenon, marking the occurrence of important cognitive changes.

As can be concluded from the theories described above, there has been much speculation on the origin and functions of crying. In contrast, there is remarkable little theoretically guided research and systematic testing of the proposed theories and hypotheses. Until now, most research has not tested specific theories or hypotheses, but must be qualified as exploratory, descriptive and unsystematic. Writings on crying have focused primarily on descriptions of casual observations (e.g. Borgquist, 1906) or speculations about its biological origins and psychological utility (e.g. Montagu, 1959; Sadoff, 1966). However, some scientific research has been done on the relationship between crying and well-being. In what follows we will summarize the results that this research has yielded.

Scientific research on crying, catharsis, and health

Experimental designs are generally considered the best for demonstrating causal associations between behavior and short-term outcome measures. The most important feature of the experimental design is randomization, the procedure of randomly assigning participants to treatment groups. The superiority of a randomized design is based on ensuring the comparability of two (or more) groups of participants on all characteristics except the one(s) under experimental manipulation (Kasl & Jones, 2001). In this way, potential confounding factors are reduced to a minimum.

However, such a randomized experimental design cannot be used in research on crying (see also Scheirs & Sijtsma, 2001). A study participant cannot be forced to cry merely because s/he has been assigned to the "crying" group; they can only be retrospectively assigned to a group. Participants who cried in response to an emotional, tear-eliciting stimulus will be assigned afterwards to the "crying group", while participants who did not cry will be assigned to the "non-crying" group. Since no randomization can take place, there is always a chance of confounding factors; for example, it is not unlikely that individuals who do and do not cry in response to an emotional film differ in certain (personality) characteristics. Thus, since researchers will have to settle for a quasi-experimental design as the best alternative, one still has to be aware of the limitations to drawing definitive conclusions. Vingerhoets and Scheirs (1998, 2001) have described how the relationship between crying and health can be investigated using other research designs than the purely experimental one. These authors feel that quasi-experimental research can yield important information concerning the immediate effects of crying on the psychobiological and mental states of the crying individual. Moreover, the role of reactions of the social environment on these outcome variables can be evaluated. In addition, studies can be designed in which crying proneness – as a more or less stable personality feature – is examined in relation to subjective and objective health status. With regard to this type of (cross-sectional) study design, however, investigators should be aware that crying proneness may be affected by health status, rather than the other way around. Examples are the increased crying proneness of depressed people or patients with certain neurological disorders (cerebrovascular diseases, multiple sclerosis, etc.; see for a review Shaibani *et al.*, 2001). In addition, asthmatic patients may cry less often, because crying may evoke attacks. Furthermore, spurious relationships between crying and health may emerge because personality characteristics act as a so-called "third factor" being related to both crying proneness and to health status.

Studies on crying and well-being that have appeared so far can be divided into two categories based on the research designs used. One category consists of retrospective descriptions based on self-report questionnaires (e.g. Borgquist, 1906); the other consists of more systematic and controlled, sometimes even quasi-experimental studies using well-tested questionnaires and comparing as carefully as possible matched groups. Examples of both kinds of studies are described below.

Retrospective descriptive self-report studies

Theories that describe crying as the cathartic relief of depressed mood and related negative emotions are largely based on anecdotal evidence from clinicians and lay persons. When people are asked to describe how they felt after a recent crying episode, many of them indicate that they felt relieved or more relaxed and report experiencing an increase in positive affect or a decrease in negative affect. In his classic study of crying, Borgquist (1906) asked a sample of university students to describe recent crying experiences and how they affected their well-being. The majority of students in his sample reported positive effects of crying. Bindra (1972) administered a short questionnaire on crying to a sample of university students, and although the questionnaire did not contain a direct question on the matter, some participants reportedly mentioned the fact that crying made them feel better. In a study by Frey and coworkers (1983), focusing on human crying frequency, 85 percent of the female and 73 percent of the male participants indicated they generally felt better after crying. Other researchers have reported similar findings (e.g. Becht & Vingerhoets, 1997; Cornelius, 1981; Lombardo *et al.*, 1983; Kraemer & Hastrup, 1986).

Although the results of these retrospective self-report studies thus suggest that having a good cry can make one feel better, such subjective positive effects of crying have almost never been observed in more controlled studies (see Cornelius, 1997, for an overview).

Controlled studies

A number of controlled studies have focused on the effects of crying on mood as well as other variables, including psychophysiological functioning (see Cornelius, 1997, for a review), physical health, and coping. Laboratory studies typically use a sad film to induce crying in their participants. Before, during, and after the film, participants are asked to report on their mood and sometimes physiological assessments (e.g. heart rate, skin conductance, hormones, immune measures) are made. The data from participants who cried during the film are then compared to the data from those who did not cry. The results obtained by these studies generally fail to support the hypothesis that crying alleviates depressed mood or restores homeostasis. On the contrary, the results generally strongly suggest that crying individuals feel worse after a crying episode. Some examples of these studies are given below.

Crying, mood, and psychophysiological response

Gross *et al.* (1994) evaluated two conflicting views about the relationship of crying to catharsis. The first one, the recovery view, suggests that crying serves homeostasis by facilitating recovery from emotional arousal. The other, the arousal view, suggests that crying produces a state of high physiological arousal. After inducing sadness using a film, several physiological measurements were taken and emotional responses were recorded. The results indicated that participants who cried during the film experienced higher levels of sadness and emotional pain. Crying participants also showed increased somatic and autonomic nervous system activity, indicating that crying was associated with arousal and negative affect.

Similarly, Choti *et al.* (1987), in their examination of the social and personality correlates of crying, found that participants who cried in response to a sad film reported significant increases in sadness, frustration, depression and muscle tension, and a decrease in happiness. Similar findings of decreased happiness, increased sadness, and increased bodily tension were reported by Marston *et al.* (1984).

The interpretation of these findings is, however, difficult because it could of course be argued that those who fail to cry do so because they experience less sadness. Ideally, one would like to compare study participants who appraise the experimental stimulus in exactly the same way and experience the same emotions with the same intensity, but with one group crying and the other not.

Labott *et al.* (1990) conducted a laboratory study on the effects of crying on mood and immunity, more specifically secretory immunoglobulin A (S-IgA), an antibody protecting against respiratory and gastrointestinal tract infections found in saliva. Overt crying turned out to be immunosuppressive; a significant decrease of S-IgA levels in saliva of criers was found when compared to non-criers. Another study of the relationship between crying and S-IgA (Martin *et al.*, 1993) reported similar findings. Again, the occurrence of emotional tears in a laboratory setting appeared to be associated with lowered S-IgA. These data thus show that crying more likely compromises (some functions of) the immune system rather than stimulating it.

Up to now, there has been just one study suggesting that crying indeed may facilitate physiological recovery. Rottenberg *et al.* (2003) measured respiratory sinus arrhythmia (RSA), considered to be a parasympathetic parameter related to emotion regulatory activity, in study participants exposed to a sad movie. It appeared that non-depressed crying individuals exhibited increases in RSA, whereas not crying subjects and depressed crying persons failed to show increases in RSA. It was concluded that crying indeed may serve homeostatic functions, at least in non-depressed persons. In conclusion, the evidence supporting a positive effect of crying on mood or psychobiological functioning is to date weak at best. However, the quality of the studies and in particular also the choice of the parameters is not always optimal. This kind of research is a major challenge for the future.

Crying and physical health

Some studies have investigated the relationship between crying and physical health in a more direct manner. Among the few studies whose results suggest a positive effect of crying on health is that of Crepeau (1980/1981). This investigator examined crying behavior in ulcer patients, colitis patients, and healthy controls. Her results showed that both male and female patients cried less frequently in a variety of situations than did healthy controls. Patients also had a more negative attitude towards tears, regarding crying as a sign of weakness or loss of control. However, the compared groups were not matched carefully and some additional methodological problems prevented a clear and unequivocal interpretation of the results. Most problematically, the retrospective nature of this study does not exclude the possibility that the differences in crying behavior are the consequence rather than the cause of the disease. Therefore, we badly need data from prospective studies. It would be of the utmost importance if investigators included questions on crying behavior in large prospective population studies.

Crying, coping, and subjective health and well-being

In their study of the use of crying as a coping mechanism, Labott and Martin (1987) found that those who cry often in response to negative life events were more likely to report high levels of mood disturbance. Labott and Martin deem it possible that crying "may enhance distress, instead of releasing or reducing it" (p. 162). In a second study, these investigators found additional evidence for increased depressed mood after a crying spell induced by a sad film (Martin & Labott, 1991), as did Kraemer and Hastrup (1988).

Vingerhoets et al. (1993), investigating the links between self-reported crying proneness and personality, coping, and subjective health status, also failed to find support for the hypothesis that crying is healthy. In their study, self-rated health was not associated with crying, but some relationships between crying, on the one hand, and coping and personality, on the other hand, were uncovered. More specifically, negative associations were found between crying proneness and alexithymia and the coping strategy "distancing", whereas crying proneness and the coping factors self-blame, daydreams and fantasies, and expression of emotions/seeking social support, were positively associated.

A final study of interest to the current question has been conducted by Hendriks *et al.* (2001). This group examined the relationship between crying and subjective health status, as similarly done by Vingerhoets *et al.* (1993). However, in their regression analysis with crying frequency as predictor and subjective health status as dependent variable, they also introduced the short-term effect of crying (whether people felt that their well-being after a crying episode generally improved, stayed the same, or deteriorated) as an additional predictor. The results indicated that a positive subjective health status is predicted by a relatively low crying frequency. Surprisingly, the subjective short-term effects of crying failed to have any predictive power and did not show any relationship to health status.

To summarize, the hypothesis that crying generally results in some form of catharsis or positive change in health status could not be verified. Crying in response to a sad film in a controlled setting does not appear to lead to any appreciable decrease in emotional tension or distress, or to an improved psychobiological functioning. Indeed, results of various studies seem to point in the opposite direction, relating crying to increases in arousal, tension, and negative affect. Future studies need to take into account that crying presumably is more likely when the level of distress is higher or people feel more intense emotions. In addition, it cannot be ruled out that immediately after a crying episode, the order of events suggested by James (1984) holds, which implies that people report that they are very sad or distressed, because they have cried. The crucial point is that one should compare the psychological state of people who are totally identical in terms of quality and intensity of mood, but who just differ in crying. This will be a serious challenge for investigators.

Reconciling discrepant research findings

Since there is a major difference in the results of retrospective self-report studies, in which participants are asked to describe a recent crying spell, and more controlled studies that mostly use sad films to induce crying, one may wonder how these differences may be explained. In the former case, people generally report positive effects or no changes in mood after crying, whereas the results of laboratory studies uniformly have yielded that mood is lowered after a crying episode. Several possible factors may be held responsible for this major difference in study outcomes. First of all, in the quasi-experimental studies, there may be insufficient time for crying to bring about its beneficial effects. Perhaps the cathartic effects of crying become first manifest after a longer period than assessments in most controlled studies take place (Gross *et al.*, 1994). Measurements are usually taken immediately after the tear-inducing stimulus has ended, after only a few minutes or, at most, within a few hours. In retrospective self-report studies, participants possibly base their reports of how they felt after crying on a longer span of time (Cornelius, 2001). As far as the time span of the effects of crying is concerned, there is another additional important question. Does crying bring greater relief than the passage of time alone? Possibly, the cathartic effects of crying are due simply to the passage of time. Kraemer and Hastrup (1986) found that depressed affect diminishes in one or two hours regardless of whether people cry or inhibit crying. These issues need further investigation.

Some kind of memory bias could also contribute to the difference in results between retrospective self-report studies and controlled studies. In all self-report studies, participants themselves chose which episodes they described. Since popular accounts of crying suggest we should feel better after crying, respondents may simply have chosen episodes in which they indeed recalled feeling better (Cornelius, 1997). It may also be that crying episodes after which one feels good are more easily or better remembered, or more readily reported, than crying episodes that leave one feeling sad.

Another aspect that needs to be seriously considered as a possible explanation for the different results of the two types of studies concerns the difference in intensity of crying in the two kinds of settings. Most controlled studies were conducted in group sessions in a rather artificial, i.e. laboratory, setting. Feelings of shame and/or social reactions may prevent participants from expressing their emotions overtly during these sessions. Additionally, the kinds of stimuli used to elicit tears in the laboratory are, because of ethical considerations, often necessarily less intense than those in real-life situations. For these reasons, the intensity and duration of crying under laboratory conditions might be considerably less than that under more natural conditions, where crying may involve a prolonged expression of tears, vocalization, and/or respiratory changes (Martin & Labott, 1991).

Finally, Cornelius (1997) argued that "participants in laboratory studies do not feel better after crying because they have no reason to feel better" (p. 307). According to him, participants will only report emotional relief after crying in situations in which the events that caused them to cry in the first place have been resolved, or in which their crying has had some positive effect, for example on the social environment. In the laboratory, participants generally have no control over the events that cause them to cry. In real life, in contrast, crying might lead to a way of resolving the emotional situation. For instance, crying may trigger a social response of comfort or offered help (see Cornelius, 1997; Cornelius & Labott, 2001; Fischer & Manstead, 2000; for a more detailed description of the effects of crying on the social environment). Along similar lines of reasoning, Martin and Labott (1991) argued that crying may have positive effects only when it is accompanied by appropriate cognitive changes and negative effects when it is not. The assumption that crying is either good or bad for one's health or well-being may thus be too simplistic.

Crying and health: exploring possible relationships

As Kasl and Jones (2001) make clear (see also Vingerhoets et al., 2002), before one can conclude that there is a causal relationship between a psychosocial factor and one's health status, certain requirements should be met. The first one implies that the causal factor should precede the consequences. More specifically, one needs to exclude the possibility that the inhibition of crying is a consequence of the affected health status or of the medications that the patients use. Retrospective studies, such as the one by Crepeau (1980/1981), therefore have only limited value for the discussion of whether or not there is a causal effect. One further cannot rule out the possibility that – much as has been proposed in the buffering model of social support – crying is only beneficial if one is in distress and not when someone leads a normal and happy life. Finally, the possibility of the "third variable " should be considered. This implies that there might be a relationship between a third factor (e.g. personality or coping) and, on the one hand, crying, and, on the other hand, health. As a consequence, spurious relationships between crying and health may ensue from such connections. In conclusion, even if one finds a relationship between crying and health, one should always be critical and aware that it may not be a causal relationship.

A second important requirement discussed by Kasl and Jones (2001) that deserves our attention concerns the biological plausibility of the relationship. Given the current state of psychobiological knowledge, how realistic is it that such a relationship really exists? What are the psychobiological mechanisms that mediate cause and effect? This important question, until now, has hardly received any attention. Except for the unlikely hypothesis of Frey (1985) about the removal of toxic substances, hardly any serious alternative has been formulated. Inspired by the work of Panksepp (1998), Vingerhoets and Scheirs (2001) speculate that crying may stimulate the release of endorphins. Panksepp specifically describes as an important function of these substances the facilitation of recovery and restoration of homeostasis after one has been in distress. In addition, endorphins are well-known for their pain-relieving powers. At least theoretically, these two features render this substance a serious candidate as mediating the crying–relief association. However, until now, no studies have systematically tested this hypothesis.

The other requirements discussed by Kasl and Jones (2001) address the need of replication in order to show consistency of the evidence, the strength of the association, and the biological gradient. These requirements gain in relevance once a clear association between crying and well-being or health has been reported. Unfortunately, at present, it is premature to draw any conclusions. Obvious questions are still waiting for answers. For example, how is the self-reported mood improvement related to the emotion that triggered the crying episode? Does the presence of others or, more generally, one's social environment or culture influence how one feels after having cried? One could argue that one's mood is negatively affected after having cried in a context that generally is considered as not appropriate, resulting in strong disapproval. Some preliminary evidence reported by Becht and Vingerhoets (2002) suggests that cultural factors indeed play a role. In their study of country characteristics as predictors of mood after crying, masculinity–femininity and shame (over crying), among others, showed up as predictors, indicating that in more masculine countries, where people experience much shame over crying, one generally reports less mood improvement after a crying episode than in more feminine countries, where crying is more accepted.

To conclude, more effort should be spent designing proper studies focusing on this kind of relevant research questions. In addition, in quasi-experimental studies, adequate attention should be paid to contextual/cultural factors affecting appraisal and pre-crying mood of criers and non-criers.

Summary and conclusions

Summarizing the research that has been conducted so far, it cannot be concluded that crying has a straightforward cathartic function. It does not appear to be necessarily beneficial to one's health either. The relevant studies that have been done so far can be divided into two categories: retrospective, descriptive self-report studies and more controlled, quasi-experimental studies. Results of these studies show a marked discrepancy in their results. In most retrospective self-report studies, at least half of the participants indicated that crying had a relieving and relaxing effect, and that crying led to a decrease in negative mood. Controlled studies, however, failed to yield corresponding findings. In such studies, crying rather appeared to increase depressive feelings and arousal. Thus, as yet, scientific research has not been able to come up with any conclusive results regarding the effects of crying on well-being.

The study of the effects of crying on well-being and health remains a challenge for researchers. Until more well-designed research has been conducted, no definitive conclusions can be drawn about the presumed relationship between crying and catharsis and/or health. Without adequately controlled designs, study results cannot be interpreted properly, and the direction of cause and effect relationships cannot be determined with certainty. This is important because one of the first things any theory of crying must do is to delineate the functions of crying. Indeed, in order to be able to develop any model – not to say comprehensive theory – of crying, we first need to learn more about both the intrapersonal and interpersonal functions of crying. The obvious implication of the state of affairs described above for theories of crying is that we are, unfortunately, still not entirely able to do this given our present knowledge.

References

Becht, M.C. & Vingerhoets, A.J.J.M. (1997). *Why we cry and how it affects mood*. Paper presented at the annual meeting of the American Psychosomatic Society, Santa Fe, NM, March; abstract in *Psychosomatic Medicine*, **59**, 92.

Becht, M.C. & Vingerhoets, A.J.J.M. (2002). Crying and mood change: a cross-cultural study. *Cognition and Emotion*, **16**, 87–101.

Bindra, B. (1972). Weeping: a problem of many facets. *Bulletin of the British Psychological Society*, **25**, 281–284.

Borgquist, A. (1906). Crying. *American Journal of Psychology*, **17**, 149–203.

Breuer, J. & Freud, S. (1895/1955). *Studies on hysteria*. London: Hogarth Press.

Choti, S.E., Marston, A.R., & Holston, S.G. (1987). Gender and personality variables in film-induced sadness and crying. *Journal of Social and Clinical Psychology*, **5**, 535–544.

Cornelius, R.R. (1981). Weeping as a social interaction: the interpersonal logic of the moist eye. *Dissertation Abstracts International*, **42**, 3491–3492B.

Cornelius, R.R. (1986). *Prescience in the pre-scientific study of weeping? A history of weeping in the popular press from the mid-1800's to the present.* Paper presented at the 57th annual meeting of the Eastern Psychological Association, New York, April.

Cornelius, R.R. (1997). Toward a new understanding of weeping and catharsis? In A.J.J.M. Vingerhoets, F.J. Van Bussel & A.J.W. Boelhouwer (eds), *The (non)expression of emotions in health and disease* (pp. 303–321). Tilburg, The Netherlands: Tilburg University Press.

Cornelius, R.R. (2001). Crying and catharsis. In A.J.J.M. Vingerhoets & R.R. Cornelius (eds), *Adult crying: a biopsychosocial approach* (pp. 199–212). Hove, UK: Brunner-Routledge.

Cornelius, R.R. & Labott, S.M. (2001). The social psychological aspects of crying. In A.J.J.M. Vingerhoets & R.R. Cornelius (eds), *Adult crying: a biopsychosocial approach* (pp. 159–176). Hove, UK: Brunner-Routledge.

Crepeau, M.I. (1980/1981). A comparison of the behaviour patterns and meanings of weeping among adult men and women across three health conditions. *Dissertation Abstracts International*, **42**, 137–138B.

Crile, G.W. (1915). *The origin and nature of the emotions.* Philadelphia, PA: WB Saunders.

Darwin, C. (1872). *The expression of the emotions in man and animals.* London: Murray.

Efran, J.S. & Spangler, T.J. (1979). Why grown-ups cry. A two-factor theory and evidence from The Miracle Worker. *Motivation and Emotion*, **3**, 63–72.

Fischer, A. & Manstead, A. (2000). *Voetballers, politici en andere mensen in tranen. Over de functionaliteit van het huilen* [Soccer players, politicians, and other people in tears. On the functionality of tears]. *De Psycholoog*, **35**, 54–59.

Freud, S. (1915/1957). Repression and the unconscious. In J. Strachey (ed.), *The standard edition of the complete psychological works of Sigmund Freud.* London: Hogarth Press.

Frey, W.H. (1985). *Crying: the mystery of tears.* Minneapolis, MN: Winston Press.

Frey, W.H., DeSota-Johnson, D., Hoffman, C., & McCall, J.T. (1981). Effects of stimulus on the chemical composition of human tears. *American Journal of Ophthalmology*, **92**, 559–567.

Frey, W.H., Hoffman-Ahern, C., Johnson, R.A., Lykken, D.T., & Tuason, V.B. (1983). Crying behaviour in the human adult. *Integrative Psychiatry*, **1**, 94–100.

Frijda, N.H. (1986). *The emotions.* New York: Cambridge University Press.

Groen, J. (1957). Psychosomatic disturbances as a form of substituted behaviour. *Journal of Psychosomatic Research*, **2**, 85–96.

Gross, J.J., Fredrickson, B.L., & Levenson, R.W. (1994). The psychophysiology of crying. *Psychophysiology*, **31**, 460–468.

Heilbrunn, G. (1955). On weeping. *Psychoanalytic Quarterly*, **27**, 245–255.

Hendriks, M.C.P., Becht, M.C., Vingerhoets, A.J.J.M., Van Heck, G.L. (2001). *Crying and health.* Poster presented at the Amsterdam Emotion Symposium, Amsterdam.

James, W. (1984). What is an emotion? *Mind*, **19**, 188–205.

Kasl, S.V. & Jones, B.A. (2001). Some methodological considerations in the study of psychosocial influences on health. In: A.J.J.M. Vingerhoets (ed.), *Advances in behavioral medicine assessment* (pp. 25–48). Hove, UK: Brunner-Routledge.

Koestler, A. (1964). *The act of creation.* London: Hutchinson.

Kottler, J.A. & Montgomery, M.J. (2001). Theories of crying. In: A.J.J.M. Vingerhoets & R.R. Cornelius (eds), *Adult crying: a biopsychosocial approach* (pp. 1–18). Hove, UK: Brunner-Routledge.

Kraemer, D.L. & Hastrup, J.L. (1986). Crying in natural settings: global estimates, self-monitored frequencies, depression and sex differences in an undergraduate population. *Behavioral Research Therapy*, **24**, 371–373.

Kraemer, D.L. & Hastrup, J.L. (1988). Crying in adults: self-control and autonomic correlates. *Journal of Social and Clinical Psychology*, **6**, 53–68.

Labott, S.M., Ahleman, S., Wolever, M.E., & Martin, R.B. (1990). The physiological and psychological effects of the expression and inhibition of emotion. *Behavioral Medicine*, **16**, 182–189.

Labott, S.M. & Martin, R.B. (1987). The stress-moderating effects of weeping and humor. *Journal of Human Stress*, **13**, 159–164.

Lombardo, W.K., Cretser, G.A., Lombardo, B., & Mathis, S.L. (1983). Fer cryin' out loud – there is a sex difference. *Sex Roles*, **9**, 987–995.

Marston, A., Hart, J., Hileman, C., & Faunce, W. (1984). Toward the laboratory study of sadness and crying. *American Journal of Psychology*, **97**, 127–131.

Martin, R.B., Guthrie, C.A., & Pitts, C.G. (1993). Emotional crying, depressed mood, and secretory immunoglobulin A. *Behavioral Medicine*, **19**, 111–114.

Martin, R.B. & Labott, S.M. (1991). Mood following emotional crying: effects of the situation. *Journal of Research in Personality*, **25**, 218–244.

Montagu, A. (1959). Natural selection and the origin and evolution of weeping in man. *Science*, **130**, 1572–1573.

Murube, J., Murube, L., & Murube, A. (1999). Origin and types of emotional tearing. *European Journal of Ophthalmology*, **9**, 77–84.

Panksepp, J. (1998). *Affective neuroscience. The foundations of human and animal emotions*. New York: Oxford University Press.

Rottenberg, J., Wilhelm, F.H., Gross, J.J., & Gotlib, I.H. (2003). Vagal rebound during resolution of tearful crying among depressed and nondepressed individuals. *Psychophysiology*, **40**, 1–6.

Sadoff, R.L. (1966). On the nature of crying and weeping. *Psychoanalytic Quarterly*, **40**, 490–503.

Scheirs, J.G.M. & Sijtsma, K. (2001). The study of crying: some methodological considerations and a comparison of methods for analyzing questionnaires. In A.J.J.M. Vingerhoets & R.R. Cornelius (eds), *Adult crying: a biopsychosocial approach* (pp. 277–298). Hove, UK: Brunner-Routledge.

Shaibani, A.T., Sabbagh, M.N., & Khan, B.N. (2001). Pathological human crying. In A.J.J.M. Vingerhoets & R.R. Cornelius (eds), *Adult crying: a biopsychosocial approach* (pp. 265–276). Hove, UK: Brunner-Routledge.

Vingerhoets, A.J.J.M., Cornelius, R.R., Van Heck, G.L., & Becht, M.C. (2000). Adult crying: a model and review of the literature. *Review of General Psychology*, **4**, 354–377.

Vingerhoets, A.J.J.M., Nyklíček, I., & Denollet, J. (2002). Emotion inhibition and physical health: fact or fiction? *Revista Portuguesa de Psicossomatica*, **4**, 71–84.

Vingerhoets, A.J.J.M. & Scheirs, J.G.M. (1998). Huilen en gezondheid [Crying and health]. *De Psycholoog*, **7/8**, 302–307.

Vingerhoets, A.J.J.M. & Scheirs, J.G.M. (2001). Crying and health. In A.J.J.M. Vingerhoets & R.R. Cornelius (eds), *Adult crying: a biopsychosocial approach* (pp. 226–247). Hove, UK: Brunner-Routledge.

Vingerhoets, A.J.J.M., Van den Berg, M.P., Kortekaas, R.Th.J., Van Heck, G.L., & Croon, M.A. (1993). Weeping: associations with personality, coping, and subjective health status. *Personality and Individual Differences*, **14**, 185–190.

Vingerhoets, A.J.J.M., Van Geleuken, A.J.M.L., Van Tilburg, M.A.L., & Van Heck, G.L. (1997). The psychological context of crying episodes: toward a model of adult crying. In A.J.J.M. Vingerhoets, F.J. Van Bussel, & A.J.W. Boelhouwer (eds), *The (non)expression of emotions in health and disease* (pp. 323–336). Tilburg, The Netherlands: Tilburg University Press.

Chapter 17

Femininity, masculinity, and the riddle of crying

Agneta H. Fischer, Marrie H.J. Bekker, Ad Vingerhoets,
Marleen C. Becht and Antony S.R. Manstead

Introduction

We see far more women than men shedding tears on television, in movies, in novels, on paintings, and in everyday life. Although there is no doubt that women cry more often than men, little is known about the major determinants of this difference. Do women encounter more severe negative events? Do they have a lower threshold for crying? Are they more often in negative moods that make them cry, or are their hormones the main cause of their frequent crying? And, finally, is there a relationship with the sex differential in health? In the present chapter various, mainly social, determinants will be considered. We will start with the question how large and robust the sex difference in crying is.

Sex differences in crying

Reviewing the empirical literature on sex differences in adult crying (Bekker & Vingerhoets, 1999; 2001; Vingerhoets & Scheirs, 2000) has led to the conclusion that women indeed shed tears more frequently and more intensely than do men. The average female crying frequency ranges between 2.5 and 5 times a month, whereas the average male frequency varies between 0.5 and 1.5 times a month. None of the reviewed studies showed a reversed effect. Similar differences are found when a broader definition of crying is used. Studies investigating crying tendency in specific situations, i.e. the (self-reported) *likelihood* that one will cry, also demonstrate that women are more likely than men to shed tears. In addition, women confirm that their general crying proneness is higher than that of men.

The question is how universal this phenomenon is. In a recent 30-nation study by Becht *et al.* (2001), there was not one country in which men reported a higher crying frequency than women. This sex difference also concerned the tendency to cry. There were, however, notable differences among countries in the extent to which the two sexes differed. Data from the Netherlands and Switzerland, for example, revealed a large sex difference, whereas in Nepal the self-reported crying frequency of men and women was nearly similar.

The correspondence in the results of all these studies strongly suggests that we are dealing with a universal phenomenon, rendering it likely that there is a biological underpinning for this sex difference. Indeed, it has been proposed that sex differences in adult crying can at least be partially explained by biological (i.e. hormonal) differences between the sexes. In particular, the predominantly female hormone prolactin has been subjected to investigation because of its presumed threshold-lowering effects on shedding tears (Eugster *et al.*, 2001; Frey, 1985; Vingerhoets & Scheirs, 2000), but also the role of other female sex hormones cannot be precluded. In addition, the possible inhibiting influence of male hormones might be relevant. Chickens that received daily testosterone injections uttered fewer distress vocalizations than controls in response to being isolated from the mother. On the other hand, male guinea pigs that had had their sexual glands removed, resulting in a decrease in testosterone levels, exhibited smaller declines in distress vocalization after separation than animals with intact testes and ovaries (Panksepp, 1998). Thus, there are indications that hormonal factors play a role in human crying behavior, but the extent and the mechanism are a mystery. The large cultural variance in sex differences in crying suggests that biological factors are not the only determinants of this sex difference in crying.

Crying, masculinity, and femininity

Crying is an emotional response to helplessness and its supposed primary function is to signal that one needs comfort and care. Crying is considered to be part of the dependency system (Darwin, 1872) and to give a clear signal in order to attract attention of others and to facilitate responsiveness. In other words, people often cry because they are confronted with a negative situation in which they perceive themselves as helpless. Crying can thus be seen as the result of the appraisal of an antecedent. Crying responses – like other emotional responses – can also be regulated (Gross & Munoz, 1995). One may suppress crying by, for example, avoiding situations that make one cry, or by swallowing one's tears. This observation creates room for the influence of cultural and social, or probably more generally spoken, cognitive influences.

The basic idea of the present chapter is that sex differences in crying frequency and crying proneness can be explained in particular in terms of appraisal and regulation processes. Appraisal and regulation involve gender-specific concerns, which are *inter alia* the result of the different relations between gender and power. Traditionally, men's roles in Western societies can be characterized as being independent, in control, and solving problems rationally, whereas women's roles are being dependent on others, emotional and relational. In other words, from childhood onwards, men have learned to gain control over situations, to have confidence in themselves, and to solve problems on their own, whereas for women it is more accepted to be dependent on others, and to be out of control (Fischer & Jansz, 1995). In addition, on average, men still occupy positions or roles with higher status and greater power than do women. As a consequence, women have generally been (seen as) the powerless sex, resulting in a greater tolerance of female helplessness compared to male helplessness.

For women, being helpless or powerless is not associated only with the inability to cope with problems or difficulties, but also with positive characteristics of being modest, submissive, nice, or sensitive to others (Bekker, 1993). In other words, powerlessness fits perfectly with some of the core characteristics of Western femininity. For men, in contrast, powerlessness is a sign of inferiority, of weakness, and – even worse – of injured manliness. Therefore, any display of powerlessness must be concealed in order to preserve one's masculinity, or, as Darwin (1872) put it, "[because of] its being thought weak and unmanly by men . . . to exhibit bodily pain by any outward sign" (p. 153). According to Murube (1997), this stereotypical sex difference may have served an evolutionary function. This author speculated that the sex difference in crying is rooted in early history in which men took up their role as defenders of the tribe and group against aggressors. Therefore, they could not allow themselves to shed tears when they were in danger. Crying would interfere too much with their fighting capacity, making women and children feel unprotected and unsafe. As a consequence, men who did not cry were sexually more attractive than those who rather easily shed tears. In addition to this basically untestable supposition, it makes sense to focus on alternative explanations and to examine the possible role of differential exposure to emotional stimuli and whether these are appraised differently by men and women.

Antecedents and appraisal

Do women have more and other reasons to cry than men? Are they confronted more often with emotionally taxing events, or do they only appraise events differently? It could be argued that women generally experience more negative affectivity (e.g. Gijsbers van Wijk, 1995) for a variety of reasons, and thus have more to cry about. However, it is also not difficult to think of sad or traumatic situations that occur more often to men than to women, such as injury or physical trauma at the workplace or during leisure activities (Gijsbers van Wijk, 1995). Unfortunately, it is not known whether those situations indeed also provoke tears in men. One type of event with a high crying-evoking potential for men (Kottler, 1996) is sports: both victory and defeat appear to elicit high levels of emotional expression in men, including shedding tears. It is tempting to speculate about explanations for this phenomenon. Why are men so selective in their choice of situations in which shedding tears and emotionality are openly displayed and, moreover, shared with other men? Kottler speculates that men almost uniquely cry in response to feelings that are part of their core identity, which, in his opinion, is framed in the roles of provider, protector, warrior, athlete, husband, father, and team player in most cultures. Male tears are thus likely to express pride, bravery, loyalty, victory, and defeat.

However, empirical data suggest that this picture needs some shading. Recent unpublished data of Vingerhoets and coworkers showed that watching sportsmen crying indeed evoked tears in men, both in defeat (as when the players of the Dutch national soccer team let their tears flow after being beaten in the semi-final of the

World Cup in France, 1998) and in victory (as many successful Dutch Olympic athletes did when standing on the platform with their gold medal). However, more women than men cried while watching these scenes. More precisely, in a Dutch population survey, it appeared that 20 percent of the women and 8 percent of the men admitted to having cried when watching the Olympic ceremonies. Remarkably, these figures were 12 percent and 5 percent when watching news reports on a fire in a bar, where many young people were severely wounded or killed.

Although there are some notable exceptions, men generally cry because of the same events as do women (e.g. loss of loved ones, breakup of relationships), although women generally report these events with higher frequencies. In one of our studies (Fischer & Manstead, 1998, 2000) men more often mentioned some-one's death, the breakup of a relationship, and the death of a pet. Women, on the other hand, more often described a conflict with their partner, and stressful or frustrating situations (see Table 17.1). These differences suggest that more men than women only cry when a very negative event, such as someone's death, has occurred, whereas women cry in response to a wider variety of situations.

A typical sex difference in the antecedents of crying concerns the fact that women cry more often during interactions with intimates (e.g. Lombardo et al., 1983). Becht et al. (2001), for example, found that women often cry when they feel humiliated or insulted, or during conflicts with their partner. This may be due to the fact that women have less effective interactional strategies to realize their wishes, but also to their lower power position in marital relationships (Komter, 1985).

One problem with studies on crying antecedents is that it remains unclear which aspect of a situation makes one cry. For example, in a conflict situation, the respondent may have cried because of the bad things that have been said during the conflict, or because of the frustration or powerlessness that the other person does not change his or her behavior, or out of fear that the other will become aggressive, or out of relief when the other is making up. In other words, it seems relevant to distinguish between the event itself and those appraisals of the event that specifically elicit crying (Gore & Colten, 1991). Although not many sex

Table 17.1 Percentages of self-reported crying eliciting antecedents

Crying antecedent	Men (%)	Women (%)
Death of person	27.0	10.0
Breakup of relationship	18.7	8.0
Stress	10.4	30.0
Conflicts	2.0	16.0
Suffering of others	10.4	14.4
Death of pet	10.4	0.0
Farewell	10.4	4.0
Frustration, injustice	2.0	8.0
Book, film	2.0	4.0
Happy event	4.1	4.0

differences have been found in the primary appraisal of emotional stimuli and appraisals of whether or not one can cope with these situations, subsequent coping processes have been found to differ substantially between men and women (Nolen-Hoeksema & Girgus, 1994; Ptacek *et al.*, 1994; Vingerhoets & Van Heck, 1990). In particular, the fact that women tend to focus more and ruminate more on the negative aspects of events may enhance their crying proneness.

Women also more often perceive themselves as more helpless or powerless than do men. This hypothesis was tested by asking respondents to rate their appraisals of powerlessness in response to an event they had spontaneously mentioned and to six vignettes, describing typical incidents in which people are assumed to cry (Fischer & Manstead, 1998, 2000). Results showed that men and women did not differ in their appraisal of the episodes in which they had cried for the last time. This is in line with our expectations, because these were the situations in which both men and women had actually cried. Moreover, the fact that they reported to have cried in these situations may also have affected their appraisal of the situation afterwards. As for the vignettes, we found that women appraised their own role in the situation as more powerless than did men, except in the situation in which a loved one was going to die (see Table 17.2). An explanation for this finding is that the latter situation has such strong impact that sex differences disappear. We also measured crying proneness in response to these vignettes and found that women also thought it more likely than men that they would cry in these situations.

The importance of powerlessness has further been demonstrated in the study by Vingerhoets *et al.* (1997), who analyzed the most recent crying episodes of 260 Dutch and Flemish women. In addition to information about the crying inducing situation and its context, these investigators also inquired about the experienced emotions. It appeared that most often the respondents mentioned a blend of emotions and feelings, in which powerlessness was important. One felt sad and powerless, angry and powerless, or anxious and powerless. These authors concluded that their data yielded support for the notion that tears in particular emerge when emotional energy cannot be worked off in action.

Table 17.2 Appraisal ratings (1 = not powerless; 7 = very powerless) and tendency to cry

	Appraisals		Crying tendency	
	Men	Women	Men	Women
Death of loved one	5.32	5.40	5.19	6.29****
End of relationship	4.62	5.11	5.61	6.48*
Conflict with intimate	3.07	3.56	2.23	5.04****
Burglary	4.01	4.99***	1.63	3.80****
Computer crash	4.16	5.04**	2.07	3.98***
Unjust treatment	3.82	4.63*	1.84	3.27***

*p<.05, **p<.01, ***p<.001, ****p<.0001.

In order to investigate whether appraisals could account for the sex differences in crying tendencies, Fischer and Manstead (1998, 2000) performed a stepwise regression analysis with crying tendency (averaged over all the situations) as dependent variable, and sex, and appraisal scores as predictors. The results showed that, apart from sex, which explains most of the variance in crying, a significant amount of variance was accounted for by appraisals of powerlessness.

Regulation of crying

Men's lower frequency of crying may also be explained by the fact that they regulate their crying in other ways than do women. A first way in which crying can be regulated is by antecedent-focused emotion regulation strategies, i.e. "things that we do before an emotion starts that affect whether a given emotion occurs (e.g. avoiding situations, selective attention, denial), modifying the inputs to the emotional system" (Gross & Munoz, 1995, p. 153). One example of antecedent-focused emotion regulation is men's avoidance of situations in which they may appear weak. Weakness or insecurity is often hidden behind sturdy or indifferent male behavior. For instance, there are indications that men have problems admitting (phobic) anxiety. This masculine avoidance of displaying phobic complaints can at least partially explain the low prevalence of phobias in men (Bekker, 1996). Another, opposite, example of antecedent-focused regulation is consciously stimulating one's tearfulness by watching soap operas and other movies with a high "tear-jerking" capacity. There is some evidence that women are more likely to read sad books and to watch sad movies or television programs (Van der Bolt & Tellegen, 1995–1996). Soap operas can be characterized by *emotional* realism: "What is recognized as real is not knowledge of the world, but a subjective experience of the world: a 'structure of feeling'" (Ang, 1985, p. 45). Meier and Frissen (1988) reported that their female respondents watched certain television series only because they consciously sought their emotion-inducing power. One of them said: "(When I am watching) I am no longer in my own surroundings; I am completely swooning then. I am whining wonderfully. When I am in the right mood, I perfectly like such a swoon movie . . . handkerchief at hand . . . wonderful!"

A second regulation strategy that may account for men's lesser crying is suppressing the crying response itself. This implies that men actively avoid showing their tears by suppressing or swallowing their tears, whereas women may have a greater tendency to intensify their crying or feel less need to hide their tears. An example of the operation of this strategy may be found in the description of the ritual of wailing songs, spontaneous ritual poems that Greek village women sing together in order to express their sadness about having lost their beloved by exile or death (Caraveli, 1986). Characteristic of this ritual is that these women need the other women to make the song successful in eliciting emotionality. While mourning and singing together, their sadness is increased by observing the others' sadness and by being reminded of their own experiences (see also Kuipers (1986) and Darwin (1872) for a description of such a practice by New Zealand's women in the nineteenth century). By means of this common practice, the women strengthen their mutual connectedness, which is expected to alleviate the pain of loss. This type of mutual social support is considered to be an effective way of coping with sadness. It is interesting to note that these female practices focus not only on the expression of emotions *per se*, but also on the social capacity of facilitating others to express their emotions.

Display rules and judgments of male and female tears

Regulation attempts are assumed to be instigated by sex-specific *display rules* telling men that crying is not allowed or may damage their image, and women that it is not too bad to cry. As a consequence, men are expected to feel more ashamed of their crying than are women. Several studies have found support for this assumption. Truijers and Vingerhoets (1999), for example, examined shame-inducing events in adolescents and found that crying was the only event that made boys feel more ashamed than girls. Fischer and Manstead (1998, 2000) also found that men generally report more shameful feelings when crying. Women felt less ashamed of their tears than did men, especially when their computer crashed or when they were confronted with a burglary in their own house.

The traditional male sex role, particularly in the Western world, has been depicted as imposing toughness, strength, and coolness, thereby forbidding any sign of weak emotions (e.g. Jansz, 2000). There are a few studies suggesting that the evaluation of crying and the application of display rules on one's own crying behavior are more dependent on one's sex role than on one's biological sex. Ross and Mirowsky (1984) for example found that non-traditional men cry more frequently than traditional men. More indirect support is provided by Conway *et al.* (1990), who found that higher femininity was associated with more rumination and higher masculinity with more distraction. A similar conclusion is drawn by Bronstein and coworkers (1996), who showed that male adolescents whose families had been emotionally expressive and accepting of emotions were more likely to report displaying sex role-incongruent emotions, including crying.

Sex-specific display rules are assumed to inhibit male crying and to facilitate female crying. Fischer and Manstead (1998, 2000) investigated the influence of display rules on respondents' crying frequency ratings. They hypothesized that if a display rule is made salient (e.g. in a public situation), respondents will downplay their ratings of how likely it is that they will cry. Salience of display rules was operationalized by creating two conditions in which subjects answered questions about their own crying. In the *public* condition, participants gave their answers aloud, in the presence of either a male or a female experimenter. In order to strengthen the impression that their answers would not be anonymous, the interview was taped and it was made clear that someone else would listen to these answers. In the second, *private* condition, subjects were asked to answer questions in the form of a written questionnaire and it was emphasised that their answers were anonymous. Because men's roles generally do not allow crying, it was expected that there would be a larger difference between answers in the private and the public condition in the case of male subjects. The results showed that women reported crying more often in both conditions and all participants reported less frequent crying in the public condition. In line with the expectations, men suppressed their crying more in the public condition than in the private condition, whereas for women there was no difference between the conditions. In addition, an effect for sex of experimenter was found: men reported less crying to a male experimenter than to a female experimenter, whereas women reported less crying to a female experimenter than to a male experimenter. Thus, both male and female participants seemed to be engaging in some degree of impression management. The self presented to an opposite-sex other was more inclined to cry than the self presented to a same-sex other.

The operation of sex-specific display rules also suggests that the crying of men is evaluated more negatively than is women's crying. Kottler (1996) suggests that it is especially men who consider the crying of men as inappropriate and as a sign of weakness. The few studies that have dealt with this question do not support this hypothesis, however. Labott et al. (1991), for example, found that both men and women find a crying man, watching a sad movie, more sympathetic than a crying woman. An explanation for this finding is that men's crying is more exceptional than women's crying, suggesting that the reason for a man to cry must be more severe. To put it differently, when a man cries, it is believed that he has good reasons to do so, resulting in more sympathy or pity for him. There may be cultural differences in this respect, however, as is reflected by the saying in some cultures "never to trust a crying man" (Frey, 1985).

In sum, there is a good deal of evidence that women are more acceptant and tolerant with respect to their own crying, and that they even actively approach situations that make them cry. On the other hand, there are also findings indicating that others evaluate crying women less positively in comparison with crying men, presumably because women's reasons for crying are thought to be less valid and crying by women sometimes is even considered as manipulation or blackmail (Buss, 1992; Frijda, 1997). Therefore, more research is needed to determine how crying, as well as the inhibition of crying, is perceived by the social environment and to what degree these evaluations depend on the specific characteristics of the situation.

Do sex differences in well-being and health relate to differences in crying behavior?

It had been well established that there are considerable gender differences in health status, although in recent publications it is emphasized that this statement needs some shading (e.g. McDonough & Walters, 2001). Vague symptoms, many mental health problems (excluding alcohol and substance abuse and suicide), and specific somatic disorders, such as autoimmune diseases, predominate in women. On the other hand, most lethal diseases including cardiovascular diseases and many cancers show a higher prevalence among men. More generally, investigators tend to explain these differences at least partially by differences in stress, coping, social support, and health behaviors (e.g. Baum & Grunberg, 1991). One may wonder whether there is a relationship between these gender differences in health and differences in their crying behavior. In this context it is important to realize that the shedding of tears may be considered as serving different functions, including being a sign of distress, but also as both an emotion-focused and a problem-focused coping mechanism (Vingerhoets *et al.*, 2001).

In addition, it is important to make a distinction between the supposed short-term effects of crying and its possible consequences for one's health status.

The short-term effects of crying on well-being

The available relevant literature does not support the popular view that crying brings relief and even should be considered healthy and yields a more complex view of this issue (Vingerhoets & Scheirs, 2000; see also Chapter 16 of this volume). Surprisingly, as far as is known, to date no studies have examined whether there may be a differential effect for men and women.

In the ISAC project, Becht and Vingerhoets (see Becht *et al.*, 2001) applied a retrospective approach and asked the participants to report, *inter alia*, how they felt both mentally and physically after their last crying episode. This distinction between mental and physical well-being appeared to make sense, given the remarkable differences in results. Analyzing the data of 1,599 men and 2,258 women (mainly students) revealed a striking similarity in the percentages of men and women who reported a worsened versus improved *mental* feeling after their crying episode: 11 percent and 47 percent and 11 percent and 52 percent for men and women, respectively. The question about experienced changes in *physical* well-being yielded the following results: 17 percent reported a deterioration and 28 percent felt better. For men and women separately, these percentages were 13 percent and 28 percent, and 20 percent and 28 percent, respectively. Remarkably, it also appeared that one generally reported more mood improvement when one cried for positive reasons than for negative reasons. In other words, if one was already in a positive mood, more mood improvement was reported than when one was in a negative mood.

In a second study among a Dutch sample consisting of 751 men and 513 women in the age range of 16 to 87 years, the following results were obtained: 45 percent of the men and 64 percent of the women reportedly felt mentally better after a crying episode, whereas 2.5 percent and 4.5 percent reported a general deterioration in mood. Physical improvement was reported by 26 percent of the men and by 27 percent of the women. The difference in the number of men and women reporting feeling physically worse is remarkable: 6 percent versus 16 percent.

In conclusion, these self-report studies thus suggest that approximately 50 percent to 60 percent of the population feels better mentally after crying, whereas between 4 percent and 11 percent indicates a change in mood for the worse. Men and women differ only slightly in this respect; somewhat more women report an improvement. Focusing on the physical changes, there is an opposite tendency: more women than men report feeling worse physically after a crying spell. We failed to ask for more details, but Borgquist (1906) lists some of the frequently reported somatic problems that arise after a crying episode, such as headache, excessive fatigue, stupor, nausea, sore eyes and sickness. It is not clear how these sex differences can be explained. A first interpretation is that women more easily admit that they suffer from physical symptoms. Alternative obvious – but until now not examined – explanations concern the possible difference in intensity and/or duration of crying (specifically for the difference in physical change) and in how the social environments react to the tears.

Health status and crying

But what about general health status? The few studies that focused on crying and (subjective) health status demonstrated either no association or a weak negative one (see Chapter 16), meaning that those who cry more often generally feel less healthy. However, this is still a largely unexplored area. Theoretically, the nature of a relationship between crying and health may take several forms. Given the nature of the sex differences in health, least likely is that crying affects health status. A serious problem with such a view is that women generally appear to be less healthy, implying that (the inhibition of) crying should play an exclusive causal role in only those diseases, such as heart disease, which are more typical for men. An alternative and more plausible explanation is that the sex difference in crying is the consequence of the differences in, particularly, mental health. If women experience more depression, anxiety, and distress, it is also more likely that they cry more often (Dennerstein *et al.*, 1993; Nolen-Hoeksema, 1987). In addition, crying is an important symptom of some typical female health problems, such as premenstrual disorder, post-partum blues, and (post-partum) depression. Also, a spurious association may result from the fact that women cry more often and at the same time also happen to suffer less from lethal diseases, as a result of unknown factors.

To summarize, with respect to subjective effects of crying on well-being, the gender differences are not impressive, although women generally appear to report somewhat more mood improvement, while at the same time experiencing a decrease in physical well-being. However, apart from the fact that women may cry more often, because they also report more distress and are more depressed, the extent to which the sex differences in crying frequency are related to the differences in health status remains unclear. We feel that at present there is not much reason to assume a causal relationship between crying and health status. We attach more value to recent findings which suggest that, more generally, the non-expression of emotions may have a negative effect on health (see Vingerhoets *et al.*, 2002, for a brief overview). With respect to crying, we feel that the major function is to communicate to others that one is in need of comfort or help. This view fits empirical results showing a greater tendency among women to induce social support. The recent speculation about the specific female tend-and-befriend stress reaction (Taylor *et al.*, 2000), also aimed at generating a social network to induce emotional support, is an additional indication that a specific interpersonal function of crying should not be overlooked.

Conclusion

A review of the literature on sex differences in crying shows that the stereotype about the crying woman and the inhibited man holds a kernel of truth. There is firm evidence that women cry more frequently and intensely than men, independent of culture and social context. However, there is also large cross-cultural and contextual variance in the extent to which men and women differ in their crying frequency or crying proneness. This suggests that, in addition to biological factors, social and cultural factors play an important role. We have suggested and shown evidence for the fact that powerlessness may be a key concept in explaining sex differences in crying. Western masculinity is not compatible with powerlessness, whereas femininity is nearly by definition associated with powerlessness. As a consequence, women seem more likely to appraise their own role in response to negative events as powerless, and they seem more tolerant of displays of powerlessness, of which crying is the most extreme illustration. These observations and women's more frequent crying in intimate relationships are in line with the idea that masculinity and femininity are not natural givens, but have to be established continuously. This "doing gender" (Unger & Crawford, 1996; West & Zimmerman, 1987) implies that gender differences in crying are not merely the result of differences in gender roles and gender identity concerns, but also reflect the dichotomy between male and female identity. Crying can be seen as a core element of Western femininity, because it construes women as helpless, emotional, and labile persons. Gender differences in crying therefore once more confirm the differences in gender roles and male–female power relations.

Concerning the role of crying as a co-determinant of the sex differential in health, we do not feel that there are any clear indications for such a relationship. Crying is a relatively rare behavior and it generally is not very intense and of short duration. This makes it unlikely that there is a significant effect on well-being. On the other hand, we do not discount an important role of crying in acute situations. It has a major impact on the social environment and may change the situation for the better. In addition, although there is to date no research addressing this issue, it would make sense if crying stimulates the release of endorphins, which have mood improving and pain alleviating features. It is clear that a better understanding of the functions of shedding tears also may contribute to a better understanding of the sex difference in crying.

References

Ang, I. (1985). *Watching Dallas: Soap opera and the melodramatic imagination*. London: Methuen.

Baum, A. & Grunberg, N.E. (1991). Gender, stress, and health. *Health Psychology*, **10**, 80–85.

Becht, M., Poortinga, Y.H., & Vingerhoets, A.J.J.M. (2001). Crying across countries. In A.J.J.M. Vingerhoets & R.R. Cornelius (eds), *Adult crying: a biopsychosocial approach.* (pp. 135–158). Hove, UK: Brunner-Routledge.

Bekker, M.H.J. (1993). The development of a new Autonomy scale based on recent insights into gender identity. *European Journal of Personality*, **7**, 177–194.

Bekker, M.H.J. (1996). Agoraphobia and gender, a review. *Clinical Psychology Review*, **16**, 129–146.

Bekker, M.H.J. & Vingerhoets, A.J.J.M. (1999). Adam's tears; the relationship between crying, biological sex and gender. *Journal of Psychology, Evolution and Gender*, **1**, 11–31.

Bekker, M.H.J. & Vingerhoets, A.J.J.M. (2001). Male and female tears: swallowing versus shedding? In A.J.J.M. Vingerhoets & R.R. Cornelius (eds), *Adult crying: a biopsychosocial approach.* (pp. 91–114). Hove, UK: Brunner-Routledge.

Borgquist, A. (1906). Crying. *American Journal of Psychology*, **17**, 149–205.

Bronstein, P., Briones, M., Brooks, T., & Cowan, B. (1996). Gender and family factors as predictors of late adolescent emotional expressiveness and adjustment: a longitudinal study. *Sex Roles*, **34**, 739–765.

Buss, D.M. (1992). Manipulation in close relationships: five personality factors in interactional context. *Journal of Personality*, **60**, 477–499.

Caraveli, A. (1986). The bitter wounding: the lament as social protest in rural Greece. In J. Dubisch (ed.), *Gender and power in rural Greece* (pp. 169–194). Princeton, NJ: Princeton University Press.

Conway, M., Giannopoulos, C., & Stiefenhofer, K. (1990). *Sex Roles*, **22** (9/10), 579–587.

Darwin, C. (1872). *The expression of emotions in man and animals*. London: John Murray (1965).

Dennerstein, L., Astbury, J., & Morse, C. (1993). Psychosocial and mental health aspects of women's health. Geneva: World Health Organization.

Eugster, A., Horsten, M., & Vingerhoets, A.J.J.M. (2001). Menstrual cycle, pregnancy, and crying. In A.J.J.M. Vingerhoets & R.R. Cornelius (eds), *Adult crying: a biopsychosocial approach* (pp. 177–198). Hove, UK: Brunner-Routledge.

Fischer, A.H. & Jansz, J. (1995). Reconciling emotions with Western personhood. *Journal for the Theory of Social Behaviour*, **25**, 59–81.

Fischer, A.H. & Manstead, A.S.R. (1998). Gender, powerless, and crying. In A.H. Fischer (ed.), *Proceedings of the Xth Conference of the International Society for Research on Emotions* (pp. 95–98). Würzburg: ISRE.

Fischer, A.H. & Manstead, A.S.R. (2000). Voetballers, politici, en andere mensen in tranen. Over de functionaliteit van huilen. [Soccer players, politicians, and other people in tears. On the functions of crying]. *De Psycholoog*, **35**, 54–59.

Frey, W.H. (1985). *Crying: the mystery of tears*. Minneapolis, MN: Winston Press.

Frijda, N.H. (1997). On the functions of emotional expression. In A.J.J.M. Vingerhoets, F.J. van Bussel, & A.W.J. Boelhouwer (eds), *The (non)expression of emotions in health and disease* (pp. 1–14). Tilburg, The Netherlands: Tilburg University Press.

Gijsbers van Wijk, C.M.T. (1995). *Sex differences in symptom perception: a cognitive–psychological approach to health differences between men and women.* Unpublished doctoral dissertation, Department of Psychology, University of Amsterdam.

Gore, S. & Colten, M.E. (1991). Gender, stress, and distress: social-relational influences. In: J. Eckenrode (ed.), *The social context of coping* (pp. 139–1630). New York/London: Plenum Press.

Gross, J.J. & Munoz, R.F. (1995). Emotion regulation and mental health. *Clinical Psychology: Science and Practice*, **2**, 151–164.

Jansz, J. (2000). Masculine identity and restrictive emotionality. In: A.H. Fischer (ed.), *Gender and emotion* (pp. 166–186). Cambridge: Cambridge University Press.

Komter, A. (1985). *De macht der vanzelfsprekendheid [The power of obviousness].* The Hague: Vuga.

Kottler, J.A. (1996). *The language of tears.* San Francisco, CA: Jossey-Bass.

Kuipers, J. (1986). Talking about troubles: gender differences in Weyewa speech use. *American Ethnologist*, **13**, 448–462.

Labott, S.M., Martin, R.B., Eason, P.S., & Berkey, E.Y. (1991). Social reactions to the expression of emotion. *Cognition and Emotion*, **5**, 397–419.

Lombardo, W.K., Cretser, G.A., Lombardo, B., & Mathis, S.L. (1983). Fer cryin' out loud – there is a sex difference. *Sex Roles*, **9**, 987–996.

McDonough, P. & Walters, V. (2001). Gender and health: reassessing patterns and explanations. *Social Science and Medicine*, **52**, 547–559.

Meier, U. & Frissen, V. (1988) Zwijmelen tussen de schuifdeuren: televisie kijken. In: L. van Zoonen (ed.), *Tussen plezier en politiek: Feminisme en media* [Between pleasure and politics: feminism and the media]. Amsterdam: SUA.

Murube, J. (1997). Emotional tearing: a new classification. *Rizal Journal of Ophthalmology*, **3**, 27–35.

Nolen-Hoeksema, S. (1987). Sex differences in unipolar depression: evidence and theory. *Psychological Bulletin*, **101**, 259–282.

Nolen-Hoeksema, S. & Girgus, J.S. (1994). The emergence of gender differences in depression during adolescence. *Psychological Bulletin*, **115**, 424–443.

Panksepp, J. (1998). *Affective neuroscience.* New York: Oxford University Press.

Ptacek, J.T., Smith, R.E., & Dodge, K.L. (1994). Gender differences in coping with stress: when stressors and appraisals do not differ. *Personality and Social Psychology Bulletin*, **20**, 421–430.

Ross, C. & Mirowsky, J. (1984). Men who cry. *Social Psychology Quarterly*, **47**, 38–146.

Taylor, S.E., Klein, L.C., Lewis, B.P., Grunewald, T.L., Gurung, A.R., & Updegraff, J.A. (2000). Biobehavioral responses to stress in females: Tend-and-Befriend, not Fight-or-Flight. *Psychological Review*, **107**, 411–429.

Truijers, A. & Vingerhoets, A.J.J.M. (1999). *Shame, embarrassment, personality, and well-being.* Poster presented at the 2nd international conference on The (Non)Expression of Emotions in Health and Disease, Tilburg, The Netherlands.

Unger, R.K. & Crawford, M. (1996). *Women and gender: a feminist psychology.* New York: McGraw-Hill.

Van der Bolt, L. & Tellegen, S. (1995–1996). Sex differences in intrinsic reading motivation and emotional reading experience. *Imagination, Cognition and Personality*, **15**, 337–349.

Vingerhoets, A.J.J.M., Nyklíček, I., & Denollet, J. (2002). Emotional inhibition and physical health: fact or fiction? *Revista Portuguesa de Psicossomatica*, **4**, 71–84.

Vingerhoets, A.J.J.M. & Scheirs J.G.M. (2000). Sex differences in crying: empirical findings and possible explanations. In A.H. Fischer (ed.), *Gender and emotion* (pp. 143–165). Cambridge: Cambridge University Press.

Vingerhoets, A.J.J.M., Van Geleuken, A.J.M.L., Van Tilburg, M.A.L., & Van Heck, G.L. (1997). The psychological context of crying episodes: toward a model of adult crying. In A.J.J.M. Vingerhoets, F.J. Van Bussel, & A.J.W. Boelhouwer (eds), *The (non)expression of emotions in health and disease* (pp. 323–336). Tilburg: Tilburg University Press.

Vingerhoets, A.J.J.M. & Van Heck, G.L. (1990). Gender, coping and psychosomatic symptoms. *Psychological Medicine*, **20**, 125–135.

Vingerhoets, A.J.J.M., Van Tilburg, M.A.L., Boelhouwer, A.J.W., & Van Heck, G.L. (2001). In A.J.J.M. Vingerhoets & R.R. Cornelius (eds), *Adult crying: a biopsychosocial approach* (pp. 115–134). Hove, UK: Brunner-Routledge.

West, C. & Zimmerman, D.H. (1987). Doing gender. *Gender & Society*, **1**, 125–151.

Chapter 18

The heart of the actor

Let it all out or keep a healthy distance?

Elly A. Konijn

Introduction

The relation between the expression and experience of emotions, and the influence of emotional processes on one's health, are important issues in psychology. Buck (1999) emphasizes the importance of emotional competence: the ability to communicate emotions and to understand emotional expressions in others, including (fictional) characters presented in media.

Several studies on emotions used professional actors as the ideal subjects, since they are assumed to be experts in reliving emotions at command (e.g. Ekman *et al.*, 1983; Futterman *et al.*, 1992; Levenson *et al.*, 1990). This idea is much in line with the common actor training programs at American Universities: "Method trained actors are actually perfect for this kind of study, because what they do for a living is get themselves into emotional states" (Kemeny in Moyers, 1994). Some authors have challenged this view, but empirical research to test the opposing views has not been performed until now. It may be interesting to take a look at the actors' emotions from backstage, i.e. from the actor's perspective. Is the actress really experiencing the revenge of her character Medea? And are the actors impersonating Romeo and Juliet also in love with each other? In addition, are the recurrent expressions of emotions beneficial to the actors' health? Or should they keep their distance? How can the emotion processes in professional actors impersonating characters on stage be identified? Are professional actors indeed the ideal subjects to study emotion?

These and related questions will be addressed in the present chapter. Cognitive emotion theory (Frijda, 1986 and Lazarus, 1982, among others) may be helpful to unravel the actor's emotion process while portraying a character–emotion. My focus is from the viewpoint of the actor and considers professional acting during public performances, which should be distinguished from acting in rehearsals and from amateur acting. I will further present the so-called *task–emotion theory* and relevant empirical findings.

Studies on emotional expressions and experiences

There is ample evidence that inhibiting emotional expression increases the risk of health problems (see Chapter 3 for an overview). Verbally expressing traumatic experiences enhances the immune function and improves physical health, which is reflected in fewer medical visits (Berry & Pennebaker, 1998). Likewise, Futterman *et al.* (1992) investigated whether deeply felt emotions affect health in professional actors. They asked the actors to get themselves into a short-term positive (happiness), a negative (anxiety, depression), or a neutral affective state. All affective states induced more variability in all immune parameters than the neutral state, and actually enhanced the immune system. The authors concluded that whatever the emotion, "going through" it might be healthy. An apparent and arguable premise of this kind of study is that the actors really immerse themselves in the emotions they are asked to accomplish. In psychological research, this premise is well established, but my claim is that it is basically unwarranted.

The research of Paul Ekman (e.g. 1982) and his coworkers and followers is also based on this assumption. In particular, Ekman *et al.* (1983) and Levenson *et al.* (1990) have conducted quite influential work by studying emotional facial expressions of professional actors (who were well-trained in method acting). Ekman *et al.* asked the actors to relive past emotional experiences and to make the expressions of some basic emotions, muscle by muscle, one after another without naming them, and simultaneously measured several physiological variables. They found that the voluntary facial expressions of different emotions generated emotion-specific autonomic nervous system activity.

These findings have led many other researchers to use professional actors as ideal subjects to study emotions (e.g. Ekman & Rosenberg, 1997; Gosselin *et al.* 1995; Ruch, 1997). Although Nummenmaa (1990) reported that expressions were more easily identified if the actor did *not* try to feel the emotion too deeply, the actors in subsequent studies were still asked not only to pose, but preferably to "feel" the emotion. This is not surprising when we realize that the underlying assumptions in the studies mentioned above are firmly established by the prevailing actor training in the US, called *method acting* (Brumm, 1973; Chambers, 2000). Method acting is developed by Lee Strasberg (1988), after his interpretation of the Russian director Konstantin Stanislavsky. It advocates that the actor should immerse himself in the emotions of the character he portrays in order to convey a convincing expression. In the remainder of this chapter this position will be discussed and challenged by a competing theory, which is developed in an inter-disciplinary study into the emotional onstage lives of professional actors.

A task–emotion theory on actors' emotional experiences

It is a widespread and popular notion that the emotional experiences of the actors themselves (should) parallel the impersonated character-emotions onstage; the *involvement* viewpoint. However, as far back as 1773 in "Paradoxe sur le comédien", Diderot stated the opposite: the actor of genius feels nothing at all in order to get the audience maximally involved in the staged character-emotions. In today's theatre, this view is expressed by the proponents of *detachment acting* (after Meyerhold, 1922, in Pesochinsky, 1992; Brecht, 1967). As a third mainstream I distinguish *self-expression acting*, with Brook (1968) and Grotowski (1968) as its main advocates. According to this approach, the actor should express his/her authentic self. Thus, the character, to some extent, disappears behind the actor, whereas according to the involvement acting style the actor disappears behind the character. These acting methods, however, describe the actors' emotions from the perspective of the observed character: a spectator's perspective. This implies that they take only the so-called basic or prototypical emotions into consideration (see Ekman, 1982; Izard, 1992); characters usually are carriers of "big" emotions such as love, hate, anger, jealousy, sadness, fear (Polti, 1990).

The actor's point of view onstage is performing a particular task – conveying an image of a character(-emotion) as convincingly and believably as possible to the audience. Cognitive emotion theory (e.g. Lazarus, 1982; Frijda, 1986; 1988) states that emotions arise from an individual's interaction with the environment and that they are functional reactions regarding an individual's concerns in coping with environmental demands. If situational demands impinge on an individual's concerns, an emotion will arise, either because his concerns are threatened or because the situation offers a potential satisfaction of personal interests, motives or goals. The result of the interaction between individual concerns and situational demands is called the situational meaning-structure, which forms the basis of an emotional experience and defines a specific emotion (Frijda, 1986). Therefore, the quality of the actor's real emotions onstage will be determined by the situational meaning-structure of the performance situation, rather than by the emotions of the character. In describing the situational meaning-structure from the perspective of the actor onstage, we must take into account his main concerns, on the one hand, and the particular components in the situational context that impinge on the actor's concerns, on the other hand.

The actor's task concerns

From a psychological point of view, at least four main concerns of professional actors can be traced in the acting situation: (i) competence, (ii) image, (iii) sensation seeking, and (iv) aesthetic concerns. To acquire skills and techniques to cope with environmental demands, one's own desires and emotions, the need for self-development and self-esteem are regarded as central drives related to the concept of competence (Frijda, 1986; White, 1959). It is the actor's concern to be considered as a competent actor, to show in his own peculiar way his competence and skills to portray a character or role, in a direct confrontation with the audience. For an actor it is not possible to conceal lack of competence. The relevance of the competency-concern to an actor gets special emphasis because he has to perform complex tasks in front of evaluative audiences, which demands a high level of competence regarding the task performance (after Zajonc & Sales, 1966; see also Bond & Titus, 1983).

In addition, the actor will be concerned about his image. Image building is closely related to concerns over the impression one creates among others, not wanting to harm one's self-image by "losing face", and the general concern for approval and recognition. Impression management and presentation of self are considered central drives for human behavior in social situations (Goffman, 1959; Snyder, 1974). Conveying the "right" image is important with regard to his reputation as an actor and his self-respect.

Presenting oneself in front of an audience is generally considered as a stressful task (Jackson & Latané, 1981; Martin, 1990). Psychophysiological studies have shown that actors experience very high levels of stress during performances (Konijn, 1991, 1992; Weisweiler, 1983, 1985). Therefore, a third category of primary concerns and driving forces of the actor relate to what is called sensation seeking (Zuckerman, 1979; Zuckerman et al., 1980). Sensation seeking concerns the need for excitement and suspense and the willingness to seek activities that involve a certain risk, either in a physical or a social sense. This drive is presupposed in actors who choose to expose themselves in such stressful situations, almost daily, as a profession.

Finally, the need to "create something beautiful", to be creative and original, is a driving force of the performing artist. This concern of the actor relates to aesthetic motives (Wang, 1984). The actor's aesthetic concerns can be met by reaching high levels in the artistic design of the performance, in beautiful enactment, in a smooth display of character-emotions, and so on, but they can be provoked when the director asks one to perform in a distasteful way. For example, the actor can enjoy the beauty in the way in which he portrays the anger of his character. The object of emotion then is enjoying the act of performing anger in an aesthetic way, rather than involvement in the character-emotion.

Specific components in the performance situation

The situational meaning-structure during stage acting is dominated by the actor's awareness of attentive spectators, who generally have high expectations and a critical, evaluative attitude toward what is shown on stage. Therefore, evaluation of the professional acting situation includes high levels of *objectivity* ("there's no escape") and *reality* of the performance situation, which are necessary to arouse an emotion (Frijda, 1986, 1988). Further, the portrayal of convincing character-emotions and captivating and moving the spectator is a difficult and complex (*high demand*) task. The actor must fulfill a high level of requirements within a relatively short period of time. The actor can show his skills only as long as the performance lasts. This differs from most other working situations. The appraisal of the performance situation as *difficult* and the urgency of demands ("the audience is waiting now!") stir high intensities of emotions in the actor. In addition, the degree of *(un)familiarity* of the performance situation is important to further define the quality and intensity of the specific emotion aroused in the actor. Unfamiliar aspects in the situation, like tonight's particular audience and the alertness of fellow actors, may heighten the demand character. To be able to cope with these high demand aspects of the situation, a high level of *control* over the situation, one's acting skills, and even the spectator's attention, is needed. A positive or negative *valence* of emotions is dependent on one's capacities to overcome potential risks of failure and to transform them into a successful performance. For the actor, both to fail and to succeed will have extreme consequences; his task concerns will be severely threatened or optimally satisfied. Thus, the situational meaning-structure of the performance situation induces intense emotions in the actor related to accomplishment in his profession (see also Konijn, 1994, 2000). Figure 18.1 systematically represents the general emotion process of an actor's emotions on stage during a public performance, from the actor's point of view.

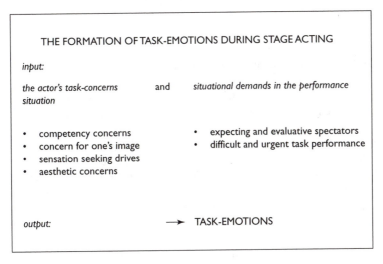

Figure 18.1 The basis of the emotion process while one is acting onstage.

The merging of potential risks, difficulty, and urgency with control, a generally positive valence, a certain degree of unfamiliarity, and a high demand character are components that refer to the meaning-structure of challenge (cf. Frijda *et al.*, 1989). Challenge is considered a central emotion during the performance of acting tasks, provided that rehearsals were successful. This implies that an actor experiences emotions related to challenge: generally positive feelings of concentration, excitement, tension, flow, courage, guts, strength, and so forth. When challenges perceived in a given situation are balanced by one's skills, this leads to the optimal experience of flow (Csikzentmihalyi & Csikzentmihalyi, 1988; Csikzentmihalyi, 1992). Task-emotions such as challenge can be considered real and strong emotions in the acting situation, because they relate to basic concerns associated with relevant components in a performance context. These emotions are dominated by the typical action tendencies related to challenge, such as impulses "to approach and overcome difficulties" and "to go at it" (cf. Frijda, 1986; Frijda *et al.*, 1989).

In conclusion, it will be clear that task-emotions are of a different nature than the emotions the actor has to portray on stage as a character, emerging from different situational meaning-structures. Furthermore, task-emotions may be considered functional to a proper accomplishment of acting tasks.

The theoretical assumptions about emotions in actors have been shown to be based on four different views on acting: involvement, self-expression, detachment, and the task-emotion theory. Based on these views, three hypotheses can be generated.

1 The involvement hypothesis: the emotions of the actor correspond to the portrayed character-emotions (the self-expression view leads to a comparable hypothesis). This hypothesis is most closely related to the hypotheses generated by the psychological studies of emotional expressions and experiences mentioned above.
2 The detachment hypothesis: the actor has no emotions while performing the character.
3 The task-emotion theory: actors don't experience emotions that parallel the portrayed character-emotions, but do experience task-emotions.

In what follows, I will summarize the results of two studies aiming to test these hypotheses.

In both studies, questionnaire data were obtained from random samples of professional actors: 114 in the Netherlands and Flanders (Dutch-speaking part of Belgium) and 227 American stage professionals. The questions concerned emotions during a live performance and pertained to only a small part in a recent role, which provided respondents with a concrete focus to base their answers on. The questionnaire contained guidelines about the conditions the chosen scene needed to meet, such as that the scene had to be played during one of the last performances in a series and not in a premiere. Twenty-six positive and negative emotion words covered both the prototypical emotions (e.g. disgust, sadness, in love, pleasure) and the task-emotions (e.g. challenge, concentration, shame, nervousness). In addition, various levels of enactment were distinguished. This involved asking about (i) which emotions were intended to be portrayed in the role, (ii) which character-emotions were actually realized during performance, and (iii) which emotions the actor experienced just prior to the start of the performance and (iv) during the performance. A comparison of the actor's emotions during and immediately before the performance provided information about the nature of task-emotions.

Further questions concerned the acting style the actor had applied. In order to be able to classify an actor as being primarily an involvement actor or a detachment actor, 20 statements were formulated referring indirectly to either the involvement or detachment style of acting. Information about the general preference for an acting style could be obtained indirectly by asking the actors how they thought other qualified actors achieved their results. The responses about general preference were crosschecked with that actor's responses on acting emotions and the acting style they had applied.

The involvement hypothesis

In order to test the involvement hypothesis, a comparison was made between the actor's own emotions and the represented character-emotions. The comparison concerns the prototypical emotions. Figures 18.2a and b display the results of the Dutch/Flemish actors and the American respondents, respectively.

As can be seen, the mean intensities of the character-emotions on stage were significantly stronger than the actor's own emotional intensities, except for tenderness, pleasure, and cheerfulness. It seemed as though the actors actually experienced these latter emotions when portraying them in characters. However, if mean intensities of emotion do not differ, this does not necessarily imply that the emotions covary, and vice versa. In a similar vein, despite a potential reflection of the character-emotions in the emotions of the actor, the emotions portrayed as a character may be stronger that those experienced by the actor. Consequently, not the means, but the strengths of the associations are more decisive. Therefore, Pearson's correlations were calculated between the actor's emotions and the character-emotions (see Table 18.1).

Because many emotions did not apply to individual actors, only those actors that attributed the emotion under consideration to the character were included in the analysis. For example, only if a character is attributed sadness does it make sense to check whether the actor feels sad as well. It appeared that, applying a criterion of $r = .60$ and $p < .001$ (Konijn, 1994, 1999), none of the actors' emotions can be considered to correspond to the represented character-emotions on stage. Thus, despite the equal average intensities of pleasure in the actor and the character's pleasure presented on stage, they generally do not run in parallel.

Intended and performed character-emotions

It is conceivable that the differences between the portrayed character-emotions and the emotions experienced by actors themselves might be due to "bad acting". To test whether the actors impersonated their characters in a proper way, i.e. the way they had intended to according to their preparations, the intended emotions (as part of the character portrayal) were compared with the actually portrayed emotions (i.e. the character-emotions) during the chosen scenes. The results of this analysis show that the mean intensities of the intended character-emotions are almost identical to the actually performed character-emotions and strong correlations were found between them (see Table 18.1). The lack of correspondence between the

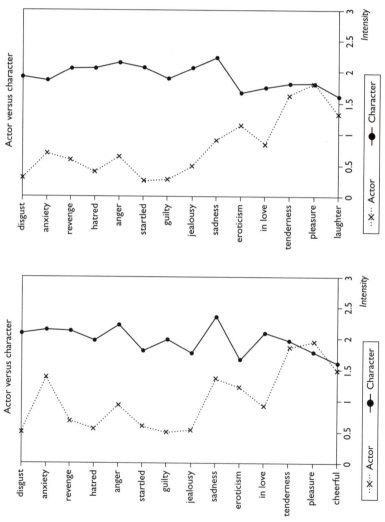

Figure 18.2 Comparison of the actor's emotions with his character-emotions: (a) for Dutch/Flemish actors and (b) for American actors. The solid line represents the mean rated intensities of portrayed character-emotions and the broken line the mean emotional experiences as indicated by the professional actors for themselves. The emotional intensity is represented on a scale ranging from "0" (not at all) to "3" (to a very great extent).

actors' emotions and those of the characters, discussed above, cannot therefore be attributed to an inadequate performance.

The importance of acting style

Since the actors might have different acting styles that might reveal differences in the degree to which the character-emotions and actors' own emotions coincide, additional comparisons were made with two subgroups, based on their responses to the statements referring to the acting styles of detachment and involvement. The quartile percentage groups of actors who predominantly used a style of detachment and those who predominantly used a style of involvement were selected.

As expected, within the detachment group, correspondence was found only incidentally between the portrayed character-emotions and the emotions felt by the actors (see Table 18.1). Surprisingly, however, the same holds for the involvement group. Overall, the results for the two subgroups were not really distinct, despite their opposing acting styles. Remarkably, even among the most adept American "involvement" actors, the actors' emotions hardly relate to the character-emotions.

Task emotions

In the foregoing analyses, the actors' emotions were considered from the viewpoint of the traditional acting theories, which take only the prototypical emotions into consideration. From the viewpoint of the task-emotion theory, one would not expect actors to experience the character-emotions they portray, but rather would expect them to experience task-emotions. The results indeed indicated that the actors experienced positive task emotions intensely, whereas negative task emotions played only a subordinate role. Although the mean intensities almost converged for some emotions, as can be seen in Table 18.1, there were no significant correlations between the emotions of actors and their character-emotions.

Contrary to expectations, the characters were also attributed positive and negative "task-emotions", presumably because characters also attempt to achieve their goals. In order to resolve the (dramatic) conflicts and to overcome hurdles to reach desired results, characters – like actors – must accomplish numerous tasks, which may lead actors to attribute task-emotions to their characters. However, again, it cannot be concluded that there is any similarity between actor and character, because the actors, as predicted, mainly experienced intensely the positive task-emotions (concentration, challenge, strength, certainty) which were not related to those portrayed in the character.

Actors' emotions before and during performance

As a further test of the idea that the emotions actors experience during performances mainly relate to accomplishing acting tasks, the actors' emotions

Table 18.1 Pearson's correlations between emotions of actors and characters

Prototypical emotions[a]

	Actor vs. character during stage acting		Performed and intended character-emotions		Detachment group actor vs. character		Involvement group actor vs. character	
	NL	US	NL	US	NL	US	NL	US
Disgust	.24	.21	.58*	.70**	-.07	.31	.25	.32
Anxiety	.23	.09	.66**	.31	.63**	-.02	.27	.11
Revenge	.28	.25	.68**	.43	.33	.35	.49	.60
Hatred	.15	.16	.76**	.68**	.05	.06	.05	.37
Anger	.19	.23	.73**	.72**	.31	.19	.62	.60*
Startled	.05	.25	.65**	.72**	.76**	.23	-.63	.55
Guilty	.25	.31	.85**	.71**	.38	-.05	-.28	.41
Jealousy	.48	.12	.77**	.67**	.85**	.02	.13	.28
Sadness	.36	.37	.76**	.80**	.35	.14	.20	.04
Eroticism	.55	.49	.68**	.60**	.65	.18	.51	.48
In love	.16	.40	.73**	.79**	-.06	.17	.60	.31
Tenderness	.45	.51	.71**	.73**	.18	.58	.78*	.59*
Pleasure	.24	.18	.58*	.63**	-.41	.17	.93[b]	-.21
Laughter	-.01	.41	.70**	.64**	.17	.58	.87[b]	.20

Task-emotions[a]

	Actor vs. character during stage acting		Actors' emotions before and during stage acting	
	NL	US	NL	US
Neutral	.46	−.35	.22	.49
Ashamed	.04	.38	.26	.50
Listless	−.33	.48	.33	.33
Tired	.18	.29	.25	.50
Nervous	.11	.13	.37	.58*
Tensed	.22	.19	.51	.51
Excited	.28	.34	.54	.56*
With guts	.09	.48	.68**	.55*
Strong	.18	.49	.49	.57*
Concentrated	.30	.14	.31	.26
Challenged	.19	.16	.58*	.56*
Certain	.13	.13	.41	.54

Prototypical emotions[a]

	Actors' emotions before and during stage acting	
	NL	US
Disgust	.36	.14
Anxiety	.46	.52
Revenge	.77**	.59*
Hatred	.54	.38
Anger	.74**	.44
Startled	.48	.32
Guilty	.23	.42
Jealousy	.62**	.41
Sadness	.45	.38
Eroticism	.68**	.67**
In love	.68**	.57
Tenderness	.56*	.64**
Pleasure	.24	.38
Laughter	.48	.44

[a] Ascription of an emotion word to the category of prototypical or task-emotions is done on theoretical grounds. In practice, emotion words cannot be labeled one or the other exclusively (e.g. pleasure can belong to both categories).

[b] When n is very small (<10), r will become hardly significant and is unreliable; n varies per emotion word. NL = Dutch speaking actors (incl. Flanders). US = actors in United States. The NL sample is smaller than the US sample.

* Denotes a significance level of $p < .01$; ** denotes $p < .001$.

just before the performance started were compared to the emotions experienced during the performance. The significant, but moderate, correlations between the positive task-emotions before and during the performance suggest that the emotions during a live stage performance compare to the emotions the actors experience just before the performance starts. In general, there is a substantially stronger relationship between the positive emotions actors experienced before and during the performance than between the portrayed character-emotions and the emotions of the actors themselves (the latter both during performance).

Some emotion words were not categorized as task-emotions in theory, because they belong to the category of the prototypical emotions (such as tenderness, pleasure, and cheerfulness). For these emotions, however, relatively strong relationships between the actors' experiences just before the performance and those during the performance were observed. This finding further supports the task-emotion theory. Apparently, the actors' emotional experiences during the performance were already present just before the performance (and to similar degrees as shown by the mean intensities). Even when the actor did experience so-called prototypical emotions, these generally did not relate to the character-emotions. The emotional experiences of actors during a performance can therefore be interpreted as (mainly) related to the *acting tasks*, even when prototypical emotions are involved.

Concluding comments

The present study examined the validity of the generally accepted assumption that actors experience the represented emotional expressions, usually portrayed as a character, as inner emotions themselves. This research question is scientifically relevant because in emotion studies, professional actors are considered ideal subjects because of their capacity to really experience the emotions they portray. Based on acting theories, three competing hypotheses were formulated:

1   according to the prevailing involvement hypothesis, actors should feel the same emotions as their characters
2   according to the detachment hypothesis, actors don't experience any emotions at all
3   according to the task-emotion theory, actors don't feel the character-emotions, but rather experience task-emotions intensely.

Our results indicate that the actors themselves hardly experience the emotions they represent as characters, whatever emotion they portray, which implies no support for the involvement hypothesis. Rather, the actors experience task-emotions, which is in agreement with the task-emotion theory. Surprisingly, the results showed a remarkable correspondence between Dutch (including Flemish) and American actors. Even the firmest adherents to method acting from the US failed to show a significant correspondence between the emotion they portrayed as character and their own affective states. This indicates that while becoming involved in their character, the actors do not necessarily share comparable emotional experiences with their character.

The actors' emotions while acting can rather be interpreted as resulting from the demands of task accomplishment and the situation of performing on stage. The actors reported that they experienced intense task-emotions of a positive nature, such as excitement, concentration, and challenge, notwithstanding the sad, frightening or tragic fate of their tormented dramatic characters. Seen from this perspective, it is not surprising that Futterman *et al.* (1992; also in Moyers, 1994) found exactly the same patterns of changes in immune functioning during the happy and sad states of their professional actors. Such findings can now be interpreted as the result of experiencing similar task-emotions while trying to meet the task demands of "reliving an emotional experience". Thus, the premise underlying the Futterman *et al.* study can be seriously questioned; professional actors appear to differentiate clearly between their emotional *expressions* and their emotional *experiences*. In the same vein, the underlying premise in Ekman *et al.*'s research can be questioned.

Additional evidence in support of the task-emotion theory can be derived from Boiten (1996). This investigator criticized Ekman *et al.* (1983) and Levenson *et al.* (1990) by pointing at the effects of differential difficulties of producing emotional expressions. Boiten (1996) replicated Ekman *et al.*'s studies with 50 adults and found that the facial expressions most difficult to produce (anger, fear, and sadness) showed larger cardiac accelerations and more pronounced respiratory effects than those that were easy to produce (disgust and surprise); the happiness expression fell somewhere in between. On the other hand, when comparing the heart rates of adults who reported actually feeling the emotion with those who did not, no differences were found. Boiten (1996) therefore concluded that facial activity does not recruit emotion-specific autonomic activity but rather that physiological changes including heart rate are modulated by effort-related changes in respiration.

Further support for the notion of task-emotions has been obtained in previous studies. For example, it has been found that heart rate, reflecting the physiological tension or stress of actors, was significantly higher during public performances than during rehearsals (Weisweiler, 1983; Konijn, 1991). The differences in the physiological stress indicators were, however, not related to specific expressions of character-emotions, but rather to going on and off stage, reaching the highest levels during monologues. Thus, the task at hand determined whether heart rate increased. Fourier spectral analyses of heart rate variability uncovered a considerable increase in mental load right after the performance had begun, compared to about 15 minutes prior to the actual confrontation with the audience (Konijn, 1991).

The present findings may have serious methodological consequences for measurement in emotion studies. Martin (1990) describes how difficult it is to generate spontaneous emotions in participants in laboratory studies. Because of ethical constraints, daily life situations seldom provide an optimal setting for emotion studies. In addition, any "intruder" may serve as an audience and prevent the evoked emotions from being spontaneous (for a discussion on real, pretended, and faked emotion, see Konijn, 2000). As the present studies reveal, actors are not a valid substitute for subjects experiencing spontaneous emotions. Although actors are probably very capable of producing prototypical signs of (outward) emotional expressions, this is perhaps not representative for the way people express emotion in daily life, because their expressions are not necessarily supported by corresponding inner feelings. Their experiences are more likely to be based on the different affective states like task-emotions – which may affect or even distort the outer signs in expression. Differentiating between emotional *expressions* and emotional *experiences* is not just a special gift of professional actors: all people regulate the expression of their true inner feelings according to display rules or feeling rules that exist in their culture. According to Ford (1996, and Chapter 1 of the present volume), lying, self-deception and dissimulation of our emotional expressions even serve to protect our personal vulnerabilities and the sensitivities of others.

Clearly, because of different situational meaning-structures, task-emotions are of a different nature than the emotions the actor has to portray on stage as a character. Typical emotions of characters mainly concern the basic or so-called prototypical emotions (Izard, 1992; Polti, 1990), such as anger, sadness, love, hate, and fear. Moreover, during the play, character-emotions are usually negative ones, only turning into positive ones at the end of the play (when the hero succeeds), whereas task-emotions of actors in performance are usually positive. We can only reflect on how the expression of character-emotions might be understood in the light of the task-emotions of the actor. Following the task-emotion theory, the actual context of the performance situation *in itself* is a source of intense emotions for the actor as a craftsman. The actor may shape his task-emotions so that the display of task-emotions merges with the expression of character-emotions, which are perceived by the spectator. Frijda (1986) considers regulation of emotions in daily life as usually directed at reducing the negative or distorting side-effects of emotional experiences. In contrast, in my view, the actor modifies emotions during stage acting in a positive way. I assume that by shaping his task-emotions so as to fit into the outer or visible form of portrayed character-emotions, the actor's task-emotions lend support to the appearance of "warmth" and "liveliness" of the represented character-emotions. Therefore I would call this phenomenon "shaping of emotions", in order to make a distinction with the regulation of (negative) emotions (Frijda, 1986).

Task-emotions do not have characteristic facial expressions and therefore cannot be interpreted on their own, on the basis of the expression of task-emotions (Konijn, 1994; 2000). The physiological consequences of task-emotions become apparent in details of the expression, like a sharp readiness, an increased awareness, presence, tenseness, alertness, excitement, warmth, goal-orientedness, and so on. They can probably be seen and "felt" by the spectator, but the particular features of task-emotions are not specific to a certain kind of emotion. The general action tendencies accompanying task-emotions, such as impulses to approach, to over-come difficulties and "to go at it", are then in accordance with the presupposed action tendencies involved in approaching the dramatic conflict by main characters in general. They run up against difficulties, attack their antagonists and try to remove obstacles to reach their goals. That is why the (felt impulses of) actors' task-emotions can empower the representation of the (supposed action tendencies of) characters. The radiation of task-emotions of the actor in performance might contribute to his power to convince, to the actor's presence, to the liveliness of the expression, and to the illusion of spontaneity of character-emotions.

It is not yet clear how the shaping of task-emotions occurs precisely, nor how the process of ascribing genuineness to (character-)emotions works, either for actors or observers. Psychological studies on the recognition and credibility of posed and spontaneous emotional expressions show that observers in general are not able to distinguish between feigned and spontaneous emotional expressions and they cannot read the relevant cues in determining whether an emotion is real or feigned (Frijda, 1986; Hess & Kleck, 1990; 1994; Shields, 1984). Observers even sometimes ascribe more credibility to posed emotional expressions than to spontaneous ones (e.g. Wallbott, 1988), and, as Nummenmaa (1990) found, expressions seem to be more easily identified if the actor did *not* try to feel the emotion too deeply. Gosselin *et al.* (1995) reported that the emotional facial expressions of six actors were only half of the time closer to the expression of genuinely experienced emotion than the portrayals of unfelt emotions. More-over, decoders of the actors' emotional portrayals were found to be accurate in recognizing the emotional category but *not* in judging the encoding condition (felt or unfelt; Gosselin *et al.*, 1995). Thus, there appears to be no actual need for an actor to experience character-emotions in order to put across character-emotions to an audience convincingly.

Probably, spectators need additional information from situational cues, the dynamics of the emotional expression, and the context in which the emotion occurs to determine the particular kind of emotion. The behavior and expressions of the actor will thus be analyzed and interpreted in accordance with the dramatic circumstances of the character and the dramatic context of the play, whereas the perceived "authenticity" of the emotional expression may stem from the radiation of underlying real task-emotions and related action tendencies. The latter hypo-thesis in particular needs to be studied in the future.

One may wonder about the possible incompatibility of the two emotion systems in an individual. It might be that, when task-emotions are at hand, prototypical (character) emotions may be prevented from being aroused. Conversely, when one is swamped by prototypical emotions, one may not be able to do a proper task performance, for which task-emotions are needed. This rather speculative hypothesis is also a theme for further research.

Finally, future studies should systematically examine how emotions are communicated, how their genuineness is determined, how their meaning is interpreted and can be altered by the context (Russell, 1991), and how meanings may vary with cultural conventions or display rules (Matsumoto *et al.*, 1999). Experiences of actors playing emotional roles and spectators watching fictional and non-fictional characters may serve as important sources.

Acknowledgments

The Netherlands Organization for Scientific Research (NWO) is kindly acknowledged for grant-funding this research. Gratitude for insightful theoretical discussions on the subject and generous support goes to Nico H. Frijda, Henri Schoenmakers, and Ed S.H. Tan. I owe many thanks to Harrie Vorst, Rein Douze, Astrid Westerbeek, and Johan F. Hoorn for their invaluable help and sensitive comments. Without the support of Actors' Equity and the cooperation of the respondent actors in The Netherlands, Flanders, and the US this endeavor would have been impossible – thanks!

References

Berry, D.S. & Pennebaker, J.W. (1998). Nonverbal and verbal emotional expression and health. In G.A. Fava & H. Freyberger (eds), *Handbook of psychosomatic medicine* (pp. 69–83). Madison, CT: International Universities Press.

Boiten, F. (1996). Autonomic response patterns during voluntary facial action. *Psychophysiology*, **33**, 123–131.

Bond, C.F. Jr & Titus, L.J. (1983). Social facilitation: a meta-analysis of 241 studies. *Psychological Bulletin*, **94**, 265–292.

Brecht, B. (1967). *Gesammelte Werke. [Complete works]. Vol. 15: Schriften zum Theater 1. [Contributions to theatre 1]* (ed. Werner Hecht). Frankfurt am Main: Suhrkamp.

Brook, P. (1968). *The empty space*. Harmondsworth, UK: Pelican, Penguin Books.

Brumm, B.M. (1973). *A survey of professional acting schools in New York City: 1870–1970*, unpublished dissertation, New York University.

Buck, R. (1999). The biological affects: a typology. *Psychological Review*, **106**, 301–336.

Chambers, D. (2000). Acting emotions in an American context (preface). In E.A. Konijn (2000), *Acting emotions* (pp. 8–12). Amsterdam: Amsterdam University Press.

Csikszentmihalyi, M. (1992). *Flow*. Ann Arbor, MI: University of Michigan Press.

Csikszentmihalyi, M. & Csikszentmihalyi I.S. (eds) (1988). *Optimal experience: Psychological studies of flow in consciousness*. Cambridge: Cambridge Univerity Press.

Diderot, D. (1959/1773). Paradoxe sur le comédien. In P. Vernière (ed.), *Diderot: Oeuvres esthétique*. Paris: Éditions Garnier (original work published in 1830).

Ekman, P. (ed.) (1982). *Emotion in the human face*. Cambridge: Cambridge University Press.

Ekman, P., Levenson, R.W., & Friesen, W.V. (1983). Autonomic nervous system activity distinguishes among emotions. *Science*, **221**, 1208–1210.

Ekman, P. & Rosenberg, E.L. (eds) (1997). *What the face reveals: Basic and applied studies of spontaneous expression using the Facial Action Coding System (FACS)*. Series in affective science. New York: Oxford University Press.

Frijda, N.H. (1986). *The emotions: Studies in emotion and social interaction*. Cambridge: Cambridge University Press.

Frijda, N.H. (1988). The laws of emotion. *American Psychologist*, **43**, 349–358.

Frijda, N.H., Kuipers, P., & ter Schure, E. (1989). Relations between emotions, appraisal and emotional action readiness. *Journal of Personality and Social Psychology*, **57**, 212–228.

Ford, Ch.V. (1996). *Lies! lies!! lies!!!: The psychology of deceit*. Washington, DC: American Psychiatric Association.

Futterman, A.D., Kemeny, M.E., Shapiro, D.P., Polonsky, W., & Fahey, J.L. (1992). Immunological variability associated with experimentally-induced positive and negative affective states. *Psychological Medicine*, **22**, 231–238.

Goffman, E. (1959). *The presentation of self in every day life*. Harmondsworth/New York: Penguin.

Gosselin, P., Kirouac, G., & Dore, F.Y. (1995). Components and recognition of facial expression in the communication of emotion by actors. *Journal of Personality and Social Psychology*, **68**, 83–96.

Grotowski, J. (1968). *Towards a poor theatre*. Holstebro, Denmark: Christensen.

Hess, U. & Kleck, R.E. (1990). Differentiating emotion elicited and deliberate emotional facial expressions. *European Journal of Social Psychology*, **20**, 369–385.

Hess, U. & Kleck, R.E. (1994). The cues decoders use in attempting to differentiate emotion-elicited and posed facial expressions. *European Journal of Social Psychology*, **24**, 367–381.

Izard, C.E. (1992). Basic emotions, relations among emotions, and emotion–cognition relations. *Psychological Review*, **99**, 561–565.

Jackson, J.M. & Latané, B. (1981). All alone in front of all those people: stage fright as a function of number and type of co-performers and audience. *Journal of Personality and Social Psychology*, **40**, 73–85.

Konijn, E.A. (1991). What's on between the actor and his audience? Empirical analysis of emotion processes in the theatre. In G. Wilson (ed.), *Psychology and performing arts* (pp. 59–74). Lisse, The Netherlands: Swets & Zeitlinger.

Konijn, E.A. (1992). Waiting for the audience: empirical study of actors' stage fright and performance. In H. Schoenmakers (ed.), *Performance theory, reception and audience studies, Tijdschrift voor Theaterwetenschap*, **8**, 157–182.

Konijn, E.A. (1994). *Acteurs spelen emoties; vorm geven aan emoties op het toneel – een psychologische studie [Actors act emotions; shaping emotions on stage – a psychological study]*. Amsterdam: Boom.

Konijn, E.A. (1995). Actors and emotions: a psychological analysis. *Theater Research International*, **20**, 132–140.

Konijn, E.A. (1999). Spotlight on spectators; emotions in the theater. *Discourse Processes*, **28**, 169–194.

Konijn, E.A. (2000). *Acting emotions*. Amsterdam: Amsterdam University Press.

Lazarus, R.S. (1982). Thoughts on the relations between emotion and cognition. *American Psychologist*, **37**, 1019–1024.

Levenson, R.W., Ekman, P., & Friesen, W.V. (1990). Voluntary facial action generates emotion-specific autonomic nervous system activity. *Psychophysiology*, **27**, 363–384.

Martin, M. (1990). On the induction of mood. *Clinical Psychology Review*, **10**, 669–697.

Matsumoto, D., Kasri, F., & Kooken, K. (1999). American–Japanese cultural differences in judgments of expression intensity and subjective experience. *Cognition and Emotion*, **13**, 201–218.

Moyers, B. (1994). *Health and Mind*. BBC documentary produced and directed by David Grubin.

Nummenmaa, T. (1990). Sender repertoires of pure and blended facial expressions of emotion. *Scandinavian Journal of Psychology*, **31**, 161–180.

Pesochinsky, N.V. (1992). The actor in Vsevolod Meyerhold's theatre. In S.K. Bushueva (ed.), *Russian Acting Art in the Twentieth Century* (pp. 65–258). St Petersburg: The Russian Institute of History of the Arts.

Polti, G. (1990). *The thirty-six dramatic situations*. (transl. L. Ray). Boston: The Writer.

Ruch, W. (1997). Will the real relationship between facial expression and affective experience please stand up: the case of exhilaration. In P. Ekman & E.L. Rosenberg (eds), *What the face reveals: Basic and applied studies of spontaneous expression using the Facial Action Coding System (FACS)*. Series in affective science (pp. 89–111). New York: Oxford University Press.

Russell, J.A. (1991). The contempt expression and the relativity thesis. *Motivation and Emotion*, **15**, 149–168.

Shields, S.A. (1984). Distinguishing between emotion and non-emotion: judgements about experience. *Motivation and Emotion*, **8**, 355–369.

Snyder, M. (1974). The self-monitoring of expressive behaviour. *Journal of Personality and Social Psychology*, **30**, 526–537.

Stanislavsky, K. (1936). *An actor prepares*. New York: Hapgood.

Strasberg, L. (1988; ed. E. Morphos). *A dream of passion: the development of the method*. London: Bloomsbury, Davada Enterprises.

Wallbott, H.G. (1988). In and out of context: Influences of facial expression and context information on emotion attributions. *British Journal of Social Psychology*, **27**, 357–369.

Wang, K. (1984). Research on the feeling mind of actors during creative performances. *Information on Psychological Sciences*, **6**, 30–33.

Weisweiler, H. (1983). *Die Belastung des Schauspielers an seinem Arbeitsplatz [The stress of the actor in his working environment.]* Unpublished dissertation, Munich University, Munich.

Weisweiler, H. (1985). Die Belastung des Schauspielers auf der Bühne [The stress of the actor on the stage]. *Münchener Medizinische Wochenschrift*, **127**, 723–724.

White, R.W. (1959). Motivation reconsidered: the concept of competence. *Psychological Review*, **66**, 297–333.

Zajonc, R.B. & Sales, S.M. (1966). Social facilitation of dominant and subordinate responses. *Journal of Experimental Social Psychology*, **2**, 160–168.

Zuckerman, M. (1979). *Sensation seeking*. Hillsdale, NJ: Erlbaum.

Zuckerman, M., Buchsbaum, M.S., & Murphy, D.L. (1980). Sensation seeking and its biological correlates. *Psychological Bulletin*, **88**, 187–214.

Chapter 19

Non-expression of emotion and self among members of socially stigmatized groups

Implications for physical and mental health

Janel D. Sexton and James W. Pennebaker

Introduction

Being a member of a socially stigmatized group often plays a profound role in individuals' lives. By definition, such persons are conferred with an inferior status by society, and as a result they are often subject to multiple forms of discrimination such as social isolation, lack of access to employment and housing, and concerns about physical safety. Goffman, in his classic text on the subject, says, "We believe the person with a stigma is not quite human. On this assumption we exercise varieties of discrimination, through which we effectively, if often unthinkingly, reduce his [*sic*] life chances" (Goffman, 1963, p. 5). Not surprisingly, stigmatized persons do report experiencing discrimination on the basis of their group membership (Swim & Stangor, 1998), a factor that contributes to their overall levels of stress (Clark *et al.*, 1999; DiPlacido, 1998; Allison, 1998).[1] Factors that may buffer an individual from this stress are the creation of a personal narrative, or life story, which has been linked to social identity (McAdams, 1996b), and social support (DiPlacido, 1998; Williams *et al.*, 1999).

In this chapter we will review the literature on the association between stress, discrimination, and health among members of socially stigmatized groups. We will then explore the relationship between health and different forms of self-expression, such as group identification and personal disclosure. We will focus on two groups for which there is published research on the topic of group-related stress and health: African Americans and gay men, lesbians, and bisexuals; however, we suggest that the findings apply to members of all socially stigmatized groups.

---

1 On a theoretical level, we argue here that it is poor treatment resulting from group membership, rather than group membership itself, that is the stressor.

Defining stigma

A first step in studying health among socially stigmatized groups is defining what is meant by saying a group is socially stigmatized. Goffman states that stigma is "the situation of the individual who is disqualified from full social acceptance" (Goffman, 1963, p. i) and that a person who carries a stigma "is thus reduced in our minds from a whole and usual person to a tainted, discounted one" (Goffman, 1963, p. 3). The general definition used here is any group that is viewed negatively by society in general. Although some researchers have argued that stigma is relative and context-dependent, we argue that there are groups viewed relatively more negatively across context, and it is these groups which we will considered stigmatized in a permanent sense. Conceptualizing stigma as something more akin to an objective condition than a subjective and changing one gives credence to the importance of studying identity among members of these groups. This approach suggests that stigma is a relatively permanent condition that has a significant impact on a person's life.

In our own research, we have attempted to learn some of the rules by which groups of people define who is stigmatized. One of the first steps has been to provide validation for the categorization of specific groups into "stigmatized" and "non-stigmatized". Introductory psychology students ($N = 258$) were given a list of groups and were asked to "Please rate how you think students [at this university] regard certain groups by indicating your response using the scale below. Note: we are not interested in how you regard these groups but rather how you think students [at this university] regard these groups." Students were given a 1–10 Likert-format scale anchored by 1 = very positive to 10 = very negative. The groups listed were: gays/lesbians, Asian Americans, men, African Americans, Hispanics, Native Americans, Whites, Jewish persons, and poor/working-class people. We predicted that, in comparison to men and Whites, the other groups would be rated more negatively, because of their hypothesized stigma (see Table 19.1). We found that this was indeed the case. Collapsing across stigmatized and non-stigmatized group means reveals a significant difference, with the latter groups being rated more positively (paired sample t-test: $t(257) = 14.02, p = .0001$).

This study is important because it provides concrete validation for the categorization of groups as stigmatized or not stigmatized. Although participants were reluctant to use the higher end of the scale (i.e., to rate groups very negatively), a clear pattern does emerge which shows that the hypothesized non-stigmatized groups are seen more positively than the stigmatized groups. Other evidence corroborates this picture, suggesting that there are still widespread negative attitudes directed towards members of stigmatized groups in the United States (Clark *et al.*, 1999; Swim *et al.*, 1998; Herek, 1991). We turn now to a discussion about the implications of this lower status for health.

Table 19.1 Stigma ratings of various social groups

Group	N	Mean	Standard deviation
Non-stigmatized groups			
Men	258	2.02	1.89
Whites	258	1.81	1.82
Non-stigmatized groups mean	258	1.91	1.73
Stigmatized groups			
African Americans	258	3.19	1.87
Asian Americans	258	2.94	1.69
Hispanic/Latino Americans	258	3.50	1.84
Native Americans	257	3.21	1.70
Jewish	257	3.23	1.68
Gays	258	4.20	1.73
Poor	256	4.14	1.90
Stigmatized groups mean	258	3.42	1.30

Higher scores indicate a greater perception of stigma among the social groups. The response format used a 1–10 scale with 1 = very positive and 10 = very negative. A paired *t*-test indicates that the collapsed mean ratings for stigmatized groups differ significantly from the collapsed mean for non-stigmatized groups, $t(257) = 14.02, p = .0001$.

Social stigma and physical and mental health – general findings

A growing body of research focuses on health among members of socially stigmatized groups. Persons who are African American, Latino, Asian American, Jewish, and/or gay, lesbian, or bisexual, for example, are viewed more negatively by society in general and are more likely to experience discrimination (Swim *et al.*, 1998). What toll does this take on their physical and mental health?

The term "minority stress" was coined to describe the stress experienced by members of society who have inferior status. Such status may result from group memberships based on factors such as religion, race, or sexual orientation, and is described as a form of stress that comes from negative experiences as a result of living in a society that is racist, heterosexist, etc. (Brooks, 1981; Meyer, 1995). The notion that stress causes illness is not new; what this concept adds is the view that discrimination and the apprehension of being stereotyped are stressors which have implications for health.

African Americans

Some of the documented effects of experiences with racism include feelings of anger, rage, helplessness, and loss of self-esteem (Clark *et al.*, 1999). Physiological responses to prejudice have also been studied. These findings suggest that there is a measurable consequence of the fact that one is the target of discrimination. In one study, resting blood pressure was found to be positively associated with perceptions of racism among African Americans (Krieger & Sidney, 1996). Taking into account both the physiological and emotional sequelae of feeling like the target of discrimination, it is clear that such treatment serves as a stressor which can impair health.

It has long been known that there are marked differences by ethnic group in a wide range of physical health markers, but these have often been attributed to differences in lifestyle or socioeconomic disparities (Williams *et al.*, 1997, 1999). In the case of African Americans, health gaps are observed even when social class is taken into account (Williams *et al.*, 1997). Williams and colleagues have studied the relationship between experiences with discrimination and physical health among Blacks, and found that the more discrimination one experiences, the poorer is one's health. From this, Williams *et al.* put forward another possibility – that experiences with discrimination are at least in part to blame for the poorer health of African Americans.

In a biopsychosocial model for African Americans, Clark and colleagues conceptualize racism as a stressor which impacts health (Clark *et al.*, 1999). They cite widespread discrimination as a major factor that acts as a chronic stressor to African Americans. The response to a situation that is perceived as racist evokes a psychological and physiological stress response. The cumulative effect of these repeated responses results in problems for health. Although few studies have been done which demonstrate a direct and causal link between racism and health, an abundance of work shows that racism is a type of stressor and that stressors are a health risk. Racism can threaten self-esteem, cause a sense of helplessness and depression, and has been linked to higher blood pressure levels (Clark *et al.*, 1999; Krieger & Sidney, 1996).

Gay men, lesbians, and bisexuals (GLB)

Research on health in this community has found that lesbians have behavioral risk factors for cancer, heart disease, and sexually transmitted diseases. Lesbians are less likely to have routine health exams, and have concerns about disclosing their sexual orientation to health care providers (DiPlacido, 1998). A large-scale study on gay men found that both expectations about being discriminated against and personal experiences with discrimination were related to poor mental health (Meyer, 1995). Another study on GLB youth found that those who reported high levels of stress were also more likely to engage in high-risk sexual behaviors (Folkman *et al.*, 1992).

In the realm of health psychology there is a well-established link between stress and health, which finds that stress is related to poor physical health (Sapolsky, 1998). Chronic stress has been linked to lower natural-killer cell activity (Herbert & Cohen, 1993), memory problems, depression, ulcers, cardiovascular disease, and irritable bowel syndrome (Sapolsky, 1998). Although persons are susceptible to different forms of stress regardless of their group memberships, those who belong to socially stigmatized groups are disproportionately subject to a form of stress that is both outside their control and often unpredictable, factors which have been documented to exacerbate stress levels (Sapolsky, 1998).

Implications for coping

Discrimination and other forms of mistreatment based on group membership can be stressful and result in stigmatized persons feeling upset, confused, helpless, and angry (Clark *et al.*, 1999). Sometimes explicit instances of discrimination are not necessary to cause stress – simply the expectation that one will be evaluated or treated poorly by others as a result of a stigma can cause distress (Contrada *et al.*, 2001). However, not all members of socially stigmatized groups suffer from poor health. Many lead happy, healthy, and productive lives. How do such persons cope successfully with their lower status and with discrimination? There are many coping responses that have been addressed in the literature, both positive and negative. Some of the maladaptive coping responses are anger suppression, and drug and alcohol consumption (Clark *et al.*, 1999). Another way that members of socially stigmatized groups may cope with discrimination and the ensuing stress is through some form of self-expression, such as emotional disclosure or the formation of a self-narrative. These allow for emotional expression and validation, and bring clarity to upsetting events. We will focus on the known health outcomes for the adaptive modes of coping with stigmatization.

Expression and non-expression of emotion and stigmatization

A copious amount of research has found that inhibiting emotion can be harmful to one's health (Pennebaker, 1989; Vingerhoets *et al.*, 1997; Wegner & Pennebaker, 1993). It is thought that inhibition requires cognitive work that taxes the body over time, possibly impairing the functioning of the immune system. In a natural extension of this work, it has also been demonstrated that concealing an important aspect of oneself is associated with mental and physical health problems (Pennebaker, 1997), although few studies have explicitly studied this link among members of stigmatized groups. The work that has been done has centered around the stigmatized identity; for example, how keeping the stigmatized identity hidden from others or inhibiting feelings about mistreatment can have a negative impact on health.

A striking example of the deleterious effects of inhibition is the case of gay men, lesbians, and bisexuals (GLB) who keep their sexual orientation a secret from others. One might consider whether it is better for GLB persons to hide their sexual orientation from others. Although this may result in fewer instances of outward discrimination, the psychological costs associated with it are enormous (DiPlacido, 1998). In a study addressing this question on the lifestyle and health of GLB persons, it was found that persons who reported more instances of concealing their sexual orientation from others also tended to drink more alcohol and reported higher levels of internalized homophobia (DiPlacido, 1998). Inhibition about sexual orientation has also been linked to sexual risk behavior. Meyer and Dean (1998) examined the link between internalized homophobia (which they define as the extent to which a GLB individual is uncomfortable with his or her sexual orientation, and tries to inhibit homosexual feelings) and health. They found that internalized homophobia predicted poor mental health, intimacy problems, and AIDS-related risk-taking behaviors.

Additional support for the notion that being secretive about one's sexual orientation is harmful to one's health comes from the work of Cole and his colleagues (Cole *et al.*, 1996a, 1996b, 1997), who have investigated the link between being "out" versus "closeted" and physical health among gay men. They find that men who are more open about their sexual orientation have better physical health than their closeted counterparts. One study with HIV seronegative gay men (Cole *et al.*, 1996a) was part of the Natural History of AIDS Psychosocial Study and followed the men for five years. It was found that participants who reported that they kept their sexual orientation a secret from others were more likely to experience cancer, pneumonia, bronchitis, sinusitis, and tuberculosis. The researchers controlled for age, ethnicity, socioeconomic status, depression, and health behaviors such as exercise and drug use. In a second study (Cole *et al.*, 1996b), a similar design was applied with HIV seropositive men. At the start of the study participants were healthy other than being HIV positive; they were given a medical exam every six months for nine years. A significant dose–response relationship was found between keeping one's sexual orientation concealed from others and poor health outcomes, including having low CD4 T lymphocyte levels, being diagnosed with AIDS, and dying from AIDS (Cole *et al.*, 1996b).

Whether or not GLB persons decide to be open with others about their sexual orientation is strongly tied to their identity. This choice implicates the process of coming out and the role this plays in the lives of lesbians, gay men, and bisexuals. Unlike most other types of stigmatized groups, based on ethnicity or religion, for example, GLB persons face a unique situation: the coming-out process. In the vast majority of cases, they are not born in to a family of others who share their group membership. Because of this, young gay, lesbian, and bisexual persons are faced with a decision as to how, when, and to whom they should reveal their orientation. High rates of suicide in this population point to the risks associated with coming-out issues (Meyer, 1995). Even in adulthood, coming out and being out can still be a troublesome issue. In studies focusing on lesbians, it has been discovered that many conceal their sexual orientation and keep themselves distanced from others out of fear of losing their jobs (DiPlacido, 1998).

In contrast to GLB persons, African Americans are generally not able to conceal their group membership from others. However, it is still plausible to postulate that there are within-group differences in the degree to which African Americans associate themselves with domains that have been traditionally associated with their ethnic group, with the Black community, and/or with other Blacks. In a study on the effects of stereotype priming on African Americans it was found that persons who were reminded of a negative stereotype about Blacks (and hence might have been concerned about avoiding confirming that stereotype) were more likely to distance themselves from other domains that are stereotypically associated with African Americans, such as rap music and basketball (Steele & Aronson, 1995). To our knowledge, it is not known what effect such distancing might have on physical or mental health.

A few studies have measured different responses to racism to see how these relate to health among African Americans. These studies have found that reactions involving emotional inhibition are predictive of poor health. For example, anger suppression in response to racism has been linked to higher blood pressure; and passive reactions to racism, which may involve some form of inhibition, have also been connected to poor health (Clark *et al.*, 1999). In one study examining the health effects of racism and coping response among African American women, it was found that women who reacted to instances of discrimination passively were more likely to report having hypertension than their counterparts who were more active in their response (Krieger, 1990).

Stress and story-making

Many researchers have been intrigued by the idea that making sense of a chaotic experience may involve forming a coherent story or narrative (Manusco & Sarbin, 1998; Smyth *et al.*, 2001; Pennebaker & Sexton, 1999; Graybeal *et al.*, 2002). Indeed, the notion that the creation of coherence and/or meaning is therapeutic has a long tradition in psychology dating back to Freud (Bucci, 1995). More recently, constructivist psychologists propose that people try to organize confusing and upsetting events in their lives in meaningful ways (Mahoney, 1995) and narrative psychologists argue that finding a sense of meaning is critical for those who are coping with a major life tragedy (Neimeyer, 1999). Affleck and Tennen (1996) posit that bringing coherence to an upsetting experience can help individuals find positive outcomes in their adversity, improving mental health.

Story-making may also be important throughout the life span, not just in times of trouble. For example, McAdams (1996a, 1999) proposes that the creation of a "life story" helps one define and understand one's identity and promotes mental well-being. Similarly, Neimeyer (2000) argues that narratives help people maintain a sense of self because they allow individuals to feel continuity in their conceptions of themselves and incorporate validation and confirmation from others. They may also help people link self-relevant information and environmental demands or events in a coherent fashion (Gergen & Gergen, 1988). These processes may be even more critical for members of stigmatized groups because of the need to come to terms with being treated as a lower status member of society.

McAdams (1996b) has argued that personal narratives help people to create their identity, which is essential to functioning. He also states that gender, racial, and class structure in society come into play in the creation of these life stories. Having a strong level of group identification is one indication that a person has developed a coherent story about the self. We argue that stigmatized persons who have a stronger identification with their group tend to have better physical and mental health. Having a strong sense of identity can translate to having a coherent story about oneself as a member of one of these groups, which in turn promotes well-being.

Health and identity

Recent studies that have taken ethnic identification into account find that the link between discrimination and poor health is attenuated in the case of the person who has a strong racial identity. Williams *et al.* (1999) defined racial identity as a sense of closeness to one's race, as measured by two self-report items. Health was measured in two ways. First participants were asked to rate their overall health as excellent, very good, good, fair, or poor. Second, respondents were queried to indicate whether they had 14 chronic health problems such as high blood pressure, diabetes, heart problems, and high cholesterol. These two items were significantly negatively correlated. These researchers found a positive link between racial identity (reporting that one's race is a significant part of one's self-concept) and self-reported health. In this case, having a strong connection to one's Black identity can be seen as a coping mechanism that protects health (Williams *et al.*, 1999).

These findings have also been extended to mental health. Chambers *et al.* (1998) conducted a study at several historically Black universities and measured Africentric identity, along with several measures of mental well-being, including stress, depression, anger, and self-esteem. Using a cluster analysis, they found that the cluster with the highest Africentric identity had lower levels of perceived stress and depression and higher self-esteem and anger control. A similar study which measured racial identity development among Black men found that such development served as a buffer against racism. Racial identity development also helped them to feel less invisible and undermined in the face of racism (Franklin, 1999).

Interventions – writing and social stigma

How might writing about group membership impact attitudes and behavior? Studies by Pennebaker and others (see Smyth, 1998 for a review) have documented a link between expressive writing and improved physical health. We became interested in whether having members of stigmatized groups write about their group membership would affect their identity. More specifically, we hypothesized that having participants disclose their feelings about being a member of a stigmatized group would augment their group identification and improve their health. For 20 minutes over the course of three days student participants ($N = 52$) wrote about one of three different topics: their deepest thoughts and feelings about their membership in a stigmatized group, their deepest thoughts and feelings about being part of the campus community, or how they manage their time. People who wrote about their membership in a stigmatized group benefited more from writing than those who wrote about being a member of a general community or a control (time management) condition. Those in the stigma writing condition said they were ill fewer days of the semester and also reported higher levels of collective self-esteem (the sense of self-worth one derives from a group membership; Luhtanen & Crocker, 1992) one month after writing (Sexton & Pennebaker, 2000).

The implications of these findings are numerous. This gives support to the notion that doing "identity work" is important. It is also an indication that one's feelings about group membership merit time and space for expression, and that such expression is helpful. Instead of recommending that members of such groups try to assimilate, or blend with the larger community, it may be wise to provide the opportunity for such persons to develop, resolve, or otherwise deal with their feelings about being part of their group.

Potential mechanisms

There are a number of possible mechanisms underlying the link between social stigma, group identification, self-expression, and health. Based on the minority stress model, it has been established that membership in a socially stigmatizing group exposes one to a set of unique stressors that can threaten health. These stressors come in many forms, but one of the most studied is the experience of being a target of discrimination. Indeed, a growing body of research has found a link between discrimination and poor health. Group identification can serve as an important intermediary in providing a buffer to health (Williams et al., 1999). Although such identification cannot protect one from the deleterious effects of discrimination entirely, it may provide individuals with a racism or prejudice schema that helps them frame their experiences with prejudice in a more understandable and predictable manner. Furthermore, having a strong sense of belonging and pride with respect to one's group membership may provide a boost to self-esteem which acts as an additional fortification in protecting health. Finally, strong group identification can be thought of as a form of self-expression – a process that has well-established health benefits. In our work on identity and expressive writing, discussed above, we found that participants who wrote about their membership in a stigmatized group reported feeling more positively about this group and reported being sick less often. This writing exercise reduces inhibition and also provides members of such groups with an opportunity to relieve stress from being stigmatized.

Conclusions

Members of socially stigmatized groups are viewed relatively more negatively by society and are subject to discrimination. Being a member of a stigmatized group thus exposes one to a particular form of stress resulting from lower status in society, fear of being discriminated against, and actual experiences of mistreatment. All of these pose a health risk to these persons. In fact, health differences do exist between members of stigmatized groups and those who are not stigmatized.

One facet of dealing with stigmatized group membership is deciding how to manage one's identity and confront instances of prejudice. A growing body of research has found that the different ways in which people cope with their membership in a socially stigmatized group predict health outcomes. Inhibiting emotions in the face of discrimination is harmful, as is concealing one's identity from others. On the positive side, members of stigmatized groups employ many different coping mechanisms that may buffer their health, including the formation of a personal narrative and having a strong group identification. These strategies bolster the identity and in doing so may help individuals to deal better with instances of discrimination and to protect themselves when confronted with a threat.

It may also be possible to increase identification with the stigmatized identity by having persons complete an expressive writing task about their group membership. This allows for emotional disclosure about the experiences of being a group member and for an opportunity to develop the identity further.

The link between health and disclosure among members of socially stigmatized groups is a new area for research. Although the groundwork has been laid, much work remains to be done. We hope that future research will address questions such as the role of identity development in shaping physical and mental health, exploring the malleability of identity for the purpose of designing interventions designed to protect health, and exploring the ways in which members of these groups can protect themselves in the face of continuing threats.

Acknowledgments

We are grateful to Sean Massey, J. Bryan Sexton, and Anna Graybeal for comments on earlier versions of this chapter. The research reported was supported by a grant from the National Institute of Health (MH52391).

References

Affleck, G. & Tennen, H. (1996). Construing benefits from adversity: adaptational significance and dispositional underpinnings. *Journal of Personality*, **64**, 899–922.

Allison, K.W. (1998). Stress and oppressed social category membership. In J.K Swim & C. Stangor (eds), *Prejudice: the target's perspective* (pp. 145–170). San Diego, CA: Academic Press.

Brooks, V.R. (1981). *Minority stress and lesbian women*. Lexington, MA: Lexington Books.

Bucci, W. (1995). The power of the narrative: a multiple code account. In J.W. Pennebaker (ed.), *Emotion, disclosure, and health* (pp. 93–124). Washington, DC: American Psychological Association.

Chambers, J.W., Kambon, K., Birdsong, B.D., Brown, J., Dixon, P., & Robbins-Brinson, L. (1998). Africentric cultural identity and the stress experience of African American college students. *Journal of Black Psychology*, **24**, 368–396.

Clark, R., Anderson, N.B., Clark, V.R., & Williams, D.R. (1999). Racism as a stressor for African Americans. *American Psychologist*, **54**, 805–816.

Cole, S.W., Kemeny, M.E., & Taylor, S.E. (1997). Social identity and physical health: accelerated HIV progression in rejection-sensitive gay men. *Journal of Personality and Social Psychology*, **72**, 320–335.

Cole, S.W., Kemeny, M.E., Taylor, S.E., & Visscher, B.R. (1996a). Elevated physical health risk among gay men who conceal their homosexual identity. *Health Psychology*, **15**, 243–251.

Cole, S.W., Kemeny, M.E., Taylor, S.E., & Visscher, B.R. (1996b). Accelerated course of human immunodeficiency virus infection in gay men who conceal their homosexual identity. *Psychosomatic Medicine*, **58**, 219–231.

Contrada, R.J., Ashmore, R.D., Gary, M.L., Coups, E., Egeth, J.D., Sewell, A., Ewell, K., Goyal, T.M., & Chase, V. (2001). Measures of ethnicity-related stress: psychometric properties, ethnic group differences, and associations with well-being. *Journal of Applied Social Psychology*, **31**, 1775–1820.

DiPlacido, J. (1998). Minority stress among lesbians, gay men, and bisexuals: a consequence of heterosexism, homophobia, and stigmatization. In G.M. Herek (ed.), *Stigma and sexual orientation* (pp. 138–159). Thousand Oaks, CA: Sage.

Folkman, S., Chesney, M.A., Pollack, L., & Phillips, C. (1992). Stress, coping, and high-risk sexual behavior. *Health Psychology*, **11**, 218–222.

Franklin, A.J. (1999). Invisibility syndrome and racial identity development in psychotherapy and counseling African American men. *Counseling Psychologist*, **27**, 761–793.

Gergen, K.J. & Gergen, M.M. (1988). Narratives and the self as relationship. In L. Berkowitz (ed.), *Advances in experimental social psychology*, Vol. 21 (pp. 17–56). San Diego, CA: Academic Press.

Goffman, E. (1963). *Stigma: Notes on the management of a spoiled identity*. New York: Simon & Schuster.

Graybeal, A., Sexton, J.D., & Pennebaker, J.W. (2002). The role of story-making in benefiting from disclosure writing. *Psychology and Health*, **17**, 571–581.

Herbert, T.B. & Cohen, S. (1993). Stress and immunity in humans: a meta-analytic review. *Psychosomatic Medicine*, **55**, 364–379.

Herek, G.M. (1991). Stigma, prejudice, and violence against lesbians and gay men. In J.C. Gonsiorek & J.D. Weinrich (eds), *Homosexuality: Research implications for public policy* (pp. 60–80). Newbury Park, CA: Sage.

Krieger, N. (1990). Racial and gender discrimination: risk factors for high blood pressure? *Social Science & Medicine*, **12**, 1273–1281.

Krieger, N. & Sidney, S. (1996). Racial discrimination and blood pressure: the CARDIA Study of young Black and White adults. *American Journal of Public Health*, **86**, 1370–1378.

Luhtanen, R. & Crocker, J. (1992). A collective self-esteem scale: self-evaluation of one's social identity. *Personality & Social Psychology Bulletin*, **18**, 302–318.

McAdams, D.P. (1996a). Narrating the self in adulthood. In J.E. Birren & G.M. Kenton (eds), *Aging and biography: Explorations in adult development* (pp. 131–148). New York: Springer.

McAdams, D.P. (1996b). Personality, modernity, and the storied self: a contemporary framework for studying persons. *Psychological Inquiry*, **7**, 295–321.

McAdams, D.P. (1999). Personal narratives and the life story. In L.A. Pervin & O.P. John (eds), *Handbook of personality: Theory and research*, Vol. 2 (pp. 478–500). New York: Guilford Press.

Mahoney, M.J. (1995). Emotionality and health: lessons from and for psychotherapy. In J.W. Pennebaker (ed.), *Emotion, disclosure, and health* (pp. 241–253). Washington, DC: American Psychological Association.

Manusco, J.C. & Sarbin, T.R. (1998). The Narrative construction of emotional life. In M.F. Mascolo & S. Griffin (eds), *What develops in emotional development?* (pp. 297–316). New York: Plenum.

Meyer, I.H. (1995). Minority stress and mental health in gay men. *Journal of Health and Social Behavior*, **36**, 38–56.

Meyer, I.H. & Dean, L. (1998). Internalized homophobia, intimacy, and sexual behavior among gay and bisexual men. In G.M. Herek (ed.), *Stigma and sexual orientation* (pp. 160–186). Thousand Oaks, CA: Sage.

Neimeyer, R.A. (1999). Narrative strategies in grief therapy. *Journal of Constructivist Psychology*, **12**, 65–85.

Neimeyer, R.A. (2000). Narrative disruptions in the construction of the self. In R.A. Neimeyer, J.D. Raskin, *et al.* (eds), *Constructions of disorder: Meaning-making frameworks for psychotherapy* (pp. 207–242). Washington, DC: American Psychological Association.

Pennebaker, J.W. (1989). Confession, inhibition, and disease. In L. Berkowitz (ed.), *Advances in experimental social psychology*, Vol. 22 (pp. 211–244). New York: Academic Press.

Pennebaker, J.W. (1997). Writing about emotional experiences as a therapeutic process. *Psychological Science*, **8**, 162–166.

Pennebaker, J.W. & Seagal, J.D. (1999). Forming a story: the health benefits of narrative. *Journal of Clinical Psychology*, **55**, 1243–1254.

Sapolsky, R.M. (1998). *Why zebras don't get ulcers: an updated guide to stress, stress-related diseases, and coping*. New York: W.H. Freeman.

Sexton, J.D. & Pennebaker, J.W. (2000). *Expressive writing and social stigma: Benefits from writing about being a group member*. Unpublished manuscript.

Smyth, J.M. (1998). Written emotional expression: effect sizes, outcome types, and moderating variables. *Journal of Consulting and Clinical Psychology*, **66**, 174–184.

Smyth, J.M., True, N., & Souto, J. (2001). Effects of writing about traumatic experiences: the necessity for narrative structure. *Journal of Social and Clinical Psychology*, **20**, 161–172.

Steele, C.M. & Aronson, J. (1995). Stereotype threat and the intellectual test performance of African Americans. *Journal of Personality & Social Psychology*, **69**, 797–811.

Swim, J.K., Cohen, L.L., & Hyers, L.L. (1998). Experiencing everyday prejudice and discrimination. In J.K. Swim & C. Stangor (eds), *Prejudice: the target's perspective* (pp. 37–60). San Diego, CA: Academic Press.

Swim, J.K. & Stangor, C. (eds). (1998). *Prejudice: the target's perspective*. San Diego, CA: Academic Press.

Vingerhoets, A.J.J.M., Van Bussel, F.J., & Boelhouwer, A.J.W. (eds) (1997). *The (non)expression of emotions in health and disease*. Tilburg, The Netherlands: Tilburg University Press.

Wegner, D.M. & Pennebaker, J.W. (eds) (1993). *Handbook of mental control*. New York: Prentice Hall.

Williams, D.R., Spencer, M.S., & Jackson, J.S. (1999). Race, stress, and physical health: the role of group identity. In R.J. Contrada & R.D. Ashmore (eds), *Self, social identity, and physical health* (pp. 71–100). New York: Oxford University Press.

Williams, D., Yu, Y., Jackson, J., & Anderson, N. (1997). Racial differences in physical and mental health: socioeconomic status, stress, and discrimination. *Journal of Health Psychology*, **2**, 335–351.

Index

248–50, *250*; positive reappraisal 244, *244*, 245, 247, 248; stress and coping model 241; subjective interpretation of events 241, 242, 245, 247–8, 251; theorizing regarding anger 243–4, 245–6, 250, 251–2; theorizing regarding sadness 243–4, 245, 246, 248, 250, 251; theory of mind 241–3, 249; *see also* boys
clarity of feeling 156, 157, 158–9
cognition: and crying 277–8; regulation of self-image 55–6; relationship with emotion 257–8
cognitive bias 102–3
cognitive cueing 244, 247
cognitive emotion theory 303, 305; *see also* situational meaning-structure
cognitive reappraisal 50, 52–4
cognitive restructuring 73
coming-out issues 326
commissurotomy, functional 146–7
Community Clinical Oncology Program 207
concealment 126, 131, 325–6, 330
Confusing Experiment Scale 89–90
consciousness 119–20, 128; splitting of 83
consolidation 37
control: control precedence 262; emotional 52; perceived 106, 108; *see also* inhibition, emotional; non-expression of emotion; regulation, emotional; self-regulation, emotional; suppression, emotional
conversion symptoms 22, 92, 95
Cook-Medley Scale 109
Coping Resources Inventory (CRI) 175
coping strategies: active coping 164; crying as 281–2; definition 241; emotion-focused 241; non-expression of emotion as 119; primary control 241; problem-focused 241; psychological mindedness 4, 185–200; secondary control 241; somatization disorder as 23; for stigmatized groups 321, 325, 327–9, 330; stress and coping model 241; stress–coping–disease theory 103–5; Type C personality 123–4; *see also* repression
cortisol 107, 109, 157, 231
Courtauld Emotional Control Scale (CECS) 210, 213–14
creative imagination 83, 86–8, 90–1, 95
crying 5, 275–85; antecedents 291–4,

292; appraisal processes 290–4, *293*; catharsis of 275, 276, 279–81, 282–3, 285; cognitive theories 277–8; as coping strategy 281–2; cultural influences 284, 289–90, 299; display rules 295–6; duration 283; gender influences 5, 284, 289–99; and helplessness 5, 290–1, 293, 294, 299; hormonal explanation 290; intensity 283; memory bias regarding 283; prevalence 289; proneness 5, 278–9, 281, 290, 293, 299; quasi-experimental studies 278–83, 285; reductionist theories 277; regulation 290, 294–5; research 278–83; self-report studies of 279, 282–3, 284, 285; theories of 275–8; and well-being 5, 275, 281–2, 285, 296–8
daily stressors 103–4, 109, 161
Darwin, Charles 64, 277, 291
death 4, 206, 209–10, 211, *212*, *213*
deception 2, 11–25; adaptive function 2, 14, 17; altruistic lies 17; bending the truth 18; defensive lies 15; definition of lying 11–12; as driving force for evolution of the brain 14; euphemisms for 12; habitual (compulsive) 20–1; half truths 12; levels of 12–13; lies of loyalty 16; lies to establish autonomy 15–16; in medicine 17–20; non-verbal 12–13; as normal developmental skill 14–17; other-deception 16, 118, 120–2, 130, 304; pathological forms of 11, 20–4, 25; pseudologia fantastica 21; self-esteem promoting lies 17; sociobiology of 13–14; somatizing disorders 22–4; white lies 17; wish fulfillment lies 15; *see also* self-deception
defense mechanisms 93, 128–9, *128*; self-deception as 13, 19–20, 24–5
defensive deniers 177
defensiveness 186; measures 172–3; personal 3, 118, 122–3, 124, 130; in repressors 169, 172–3; social 3, 118, 122–3, 124, 130, 132
defining emotion 257
denial 171, 187; defensive deniers 177; pathological 21–2; of physical illness 19–20, 22, 117, 127, *128*, 131; psychodynamic interpretation 117, 128, *128*; of the seriousness of one's symptoms 117, 127, *128*, 131